CLASSICS
OF CHINESE
THOUGHT

Andrew H. Plaks and Michael Nylan, Series Editors

CLASSICS
OF CHINESE
THOUGHT

Exemplary Figures / Fayan
Yang Xiong, translated and introduced by Michael Nylan

Zuo Tradition / Zuozhuan
Commentary on the "Spring and Autumn Annals"
Translated and introduced by Stephen Durrant, Wai-yee Li, and David Schaberg

Garden of Eloquence / Shuoyuan
Liu Xiang, translated and introduced by Eric Henry

A Thorough Exploration in Historiography / Shitong
Liu Zhiji, translated and introduced by Victor Cunrui Xiong

The "Great Commentary" on the "Documents Classic" / Shangshu dazhuan
Translated and introduced by Fan Lin and Griet Vankeerberghen

The Great Commentary on the Documents Classic

Shangshu Dazhuan

尚書大傳

TRANSLATED AND INTRODUCED BY
Fan Lin and *Griet Vankeerberghen*

UNIVERSITY OF WASHINGTON PRESS
Seattle

The *"Great Commentary" on the "Documents Classic" / Shangshu dazhuan* was made possible in part by a grant from the Henry Luce Foundation.

Additional support was provided by generous gifts from Michael Burnap and Irene Tanabe.

Copyright © 2025 by the University of Washington Press

Design by Thomas Eykemans
Composed in Minion, typeface designed by Robert Slimbach

29 28 27 26 25   5 4 3 2 1

Printed and bound in the United States of America

All rights reserved. No part of this publication may be reproduced or transmitted in any form or by any means, electronic or mechanical, including photocopy, recording, or any information storage or retrieval system, without permission in writing from the publisher.

UNIVERSITY OF WASHINGTON PRESS
uwapress.uw.edu

LIBRARY OF CONGRESS CATALOGING-IN-PUBLICATION DATA
Names: Fu, Sheng, active 2nd century B.C., author. | Lin, Fan (Lecturer in Chinese art and material culture), translator. | Vankeerberghen, Griet, 1964– translator.
Title: The great commentary on the documents classic : Shangshu dazhuan = Shang shu da zhuan [Fu Sheng] ; translated and introduced by Fan Lin and Griet Vankeerberghen.
Other titles: Shang shu da zhuan. English
Description: Seattle : University of Washington Press, 2025. | Series: Classics of Chinese thought | Includes bibliographical references and index.
Identifiers: LCCN 2024003681 | ISBN 9780295753041 (hardcover)
Subjects: LCSH: Shu jing.
Classification: LCC PL2465.Z6 F813 2025 | DDC 931/.03—dc23/eng/20240627
LC record available at https://lccn.loc.gov/2024003681

♾ The paper used in this publication meets the requirements of ANSI Z39.48-1992 (Permanence of Paper).

Contents

Acknowledgments IX
Conventions XI
Chronology of Dynasties XIII
Introduction XV

The *Great Commentary* on the *Documents Classic* / *Shangshu dazhuan*

1. TRADITIONS ON TANG
    - **1.1** Canon of Yao 5

2. TRADITIONS ON YU / TRADITIONS ON YU AND XIA
    - **2.1** Nine Offers 33
    - **2.2** Gaoyao's Counsel 39

3. TRADITIONS ON YU AND XIA (CONTINUED)
    - **3.1** Tribute of Yu 57
    - **3.2** Oath at Gan 65

4. TRADITIONS ON YIN
    - **4.1** Proclamation of the Supreme Lord 75
    - **4.2** Tang's Oath 79
    - **4.3** Pangeng 85
    - **4.4** Charge to Yue 89
    - **4.5** Gaozong's Supplementary Sacrifice 97
    - **4.6** Admonitions to Gaozong 101
    - **4.7** The Prince of the West Attacks Qi 105

5. TRADITIONS ON ZHOU

- **5.1** Great Oath 115
- **5.2** Success through Battle 123
- **5.3** Great Plan 131
- **5.4** Great Proclamation 139
- **5.5** Metal Coffer 145
- **5.6** Charge to Prince Wei 153
- **5.7** Praising the Millet 159
- **5.8** Proclamation to Kang 167
- **5.9** Proclamation on Drink 173
- **5.10** Catalpa Wood 179
- **5.11** Proclamation of/to Shao 185
- **5.12** Proclamation on Luo 189
- **5.13** Many Officers 201
- **5.14** Do Not Slack 205
- **5.15** King Cheng's Government 209
- **5.16** Proclamation at Yan 213
- **5.17** Many Regions 215
- **5.18** Testamentary Charge / **5.19** King Kang's Proclamation 219
- **5.20** Charge to Jiong 227
- **5.21** Oath at Xian 229
- **5.22** Punishments of Fu 235

6. PRINCIPAL TEACHINGS

- **6.1** Principal Teachings, Part 1 251
- **6.2** Principal Teachings, Part 2 259

7. TRADITION ON THE GREAT PLAN'S FIVE PHASES

- **7.1** Tradition on the Great Plan's Five Phases, Part 1   281
- **7.2** Tradition on the Great Plan's Five Phases, Part 2   291
- **7.3** Tradition on the Great Plan's Five Phases, Part 3   303

Appendix: Chapter Titles in the *Great Commentary* and in the *Documents*   311
Bibliography   317
Place Name Index   337
Personal Name Index   341
General Index   347

Acknowledgments

We worked on the *Great Commentary* for a long time and in many places. Deciphering the text and its history was painstaking work. The pleasure lay in doing it together.

We owe thanks to many. Our series editor, Michael Nylan, tirelessly commented on consecutive versions of our manuscript. She and He Ruyue generously shared their work on the *Documents*. Three anonymous reviewers pointed out errors and provided valuable, insightful comments. Along the way, we received advice from Chen Xiaolan, Christoph Harbsmeier, Huang Yijun, Martin Kern, Li Geng, Sun Jinguo, and Yang Haizheng. Lorri Hagman, together with Joeth Zucco, at the University of Washington Press thoughtfully and expertly moved the manuscript along.

Librarians at McGill University and Leiden University, especially Marc Gilbert, Xiaoyan Sun, and Macy Zheng, helped us get the materials we needed. Itō Yumi shared with us his most recent work on the *Great Commentary*. Qinxin He, Mariko Hatta, Yijun Huang, Ma Nan, Doreen Mueller, and Mariko Murata kindly assisted us with the image credits. Jialong Liu's help with the bibliography and citations was made possible by a publication grant from the Leiden University Institute of Area Studies.

Finally, we would like to thank our families for their patience and unconditional support.

Conventions

SOURCE TEXT AND NUMBERING

We use the reconstituted text of the *Great Commentary* as provided in *Shangshu dazhuan zhuzi suoyin* 尚書大傳逐字索引. We adopt that edition's numbering system for parts and chapters. We further divide the chapters into numbered passages, sometimes deviating from the way *Shangshu dazhuan zhuzi suoyin* separates paragraphs from one another, and, when necessary, we alter the punctuation provided in *Shangshu dazhuan zhuzi suoyin*. For legibility, the English translation is, at times, divided into more paragraphs than the corresponding Chinese text. Also following *Shangshu dazhuan zhuzi suoyin*, we adopt parentheses to signify deletions, square brackets for additions, diamonds to mark empty spaces in the original, and squares for missing characters.

OVERLAP OF *DOCUMENTS* AND *GREAT COMMENTARY*

Bold terms and sentences in the Chinese text indicate where the *Great Commentary*'s text overlaps meaningfully with that of the *Documents*. Footnotes to the Chinese text refer the reader to the source in the transmitted *Documents* (*Shangshu zhuzi suoyin* edition).

FOOTNOTES TO THE ENGLISH TRANSLATION

In the footnotes, our choice of translation is explained by reference to an existing commentary (e.g., by Zheng Xuan or Pi Xirui) or on the basis of a parallel passage in another early Chinese text. Footnotes also provide background for the general reader.

TRANSLATORS' CHAPTER INTRODUCTIONS

The *Great Commentary*'s entries are contextualized in our chapter introductions vis-à-vis the corresponding *Documents* chapter. When necessary, we expand on the textual history of a *Great Commentary* chapter and indicate when Wang Kaiyun's edition shows major discrepancies with other critical editions.

TRANSLATIONS AND INTERPRETATIONS OF THE *DOCUMENTS*

In our chapter introductions and translations, especially in instances where the *Great Commentary* quotes the *Documents*, we draw freely on the forthcoming translation *The Documents* (Shangshu 尚書) by Michael Nylan and He Ruyue 何如月 and the Ph.D. dissertation of Ma Nan 馬楠, as well as earlier translations and interpretations by James Legge (1939), Bernhard Karlgren (1950), and Qu Wanli 屈萬里 (1983).

RHYME AND HOMOPHONY

In our translation of rhymed passages, we provide reconstructions of premodern pronunciations of Chinese characters to indicate rhyme or homophony. Such pronunciations are enclosed in parentheses and preceded by an asterisk, as in the line "The phoenixes join in (*kˤrəj)." These pronunciations are based on Axel Schuessler 2007 unless otherwise indicated.

Chronology of Dynasties

Xia (legendary)	ca 2100–ca 1600 BCE
Shang	ca. 1600–1046 BCE
Zhou	1045–256 BCE
Western Zhou	1045–771 BCE
Eastern Zhou	770–256 BCE
Spring and Autumn (Chunqiu)	770–476 BCE
Warring States (Zhanguo)	475–221 BCE
Qin	221–207 BCE
Han	206/202* BCE–220 CE
Western Han	206/202* BCE–8 CE
Xin	9–23 CE
Eastern Han	25–220 CE
Three Kingdoms	220–65
Jin	265–420
Western Jin	265–316
Eastern Jin	317–420
Southern and Northern Dynasties	420–589
Sui	581–618
Tang	618–907
Song	960–1279
Northern Song	960–1127
Southern Song	1127–279
Yuan	1279–1368
Ming	1368–1644
Qing	1644–1911

* The Han beginning date is often simplified to 206 BCE. In that year, Liu Bang was made King of Han by his rival Xiang Yu, with whom he entered into a civil war that lasted four years. He won and took the title of emperor in 202 BCE. The distinction matters here because the life of Fu Sheng, a pivotal figure in this volume, spanned the civil war and early Western Han period.

Introduction

Shangshu dazhuan 尚書大傳 is a commentary on the *Documents* classic (Shangshu 尚書) that is traditionally ascribed to Master Fu 伏生 (260?–161? BCE). Understanding the commentary required us to grapple with two episodes, far apart in time, in which learned men working under vastly different technological, cultural, and sociopolitical parameters, sought to restore a text to their community's collective memory.

The first episode took place in early imperial China. Transmitted histories describe how Master Fu, during the Qin (221–207 BCE) and Western Han (206/202 BCE–8 CE) dynasties, spearheaded efforts to rescue the *Documents*, a text ascribed to the ancient sages, from oblivion and promote it at the central court at Chang'an. They also document how Master Fu, his disciples, and their descendants—mostly of the Ouyang 歐陽, Zhang 張, and Xiahou 夏侯 families—provided interpretations of the *Documents* in order to make the text relevant to the budding empire. By 26 BCE, the year when Liu Xiang 劉向 (79/78–8 BCE) and his team started their work in the imperial archives, the glosses, commentaries, and interpretations of the *Documents* by Master Fu and his followers had already been condensed into a written text that was present in the imperial archives. As such, it was cataloged by Liu Xiang and his team as a "commentary" (*zhuan* 傳) in forty-one chapters (*pian* 篇).[1] The text, which later on was referred to as the *Great Commentary* (Dazhuan 大傳), circulated widely during Eastern Han (25–220) and beyond, remaining prominent into the Tang (618–907) dynasty.[2] That the *Great Commentary* received a commentary of its own by the great Eastern Han classicist Zheng Xuan 鄭玄 (127–200 CE), best known for his commentaries on the classics themselves, is testimony to the high regard in which the *Great Commentary* was held in the first centuries CE.

The second episode started in the eighteenth century, when scholars realized that the versions of the *Great Commentary* they had at their disposal were seriously defective, prompting them to engage in the painstaking process of restoring its text based on partial editions, quotations

xv

in other texts, and bibliographical notes found in transmitted texts. The collective efforts of scholars such as Hui Dong 惠棟 (1697–1758), Sun Zhilu 孫之騄 (fl. 1722–35), Lu Jianzeng 盧見曾 (1690–1768), Lu Wenchao 盧文弨 (1717–97), Chen Shouqi 陳壽祺 (1771–1834), Huang Shi 黃奭 (1809–53), Pi Xirui 皮錫瑞 (1850–1908), and Wang Kaiyun 王闓運 (1833–1916) resulted in the text offered here in translation, *The "Great Commentary" on the "Documents Classic"* (Shangshu dazhuan).[3] There is no single agreed upon reconstitution of the *Great Commentary*, as the reconstitution process was, inherently, messy and somewhat arbitrary. Different reconstitutions of the *Great Commentary* diverge on which passages they include or exclude, on their order, and on the chapter titles they place them under. The efforts of the Qing scholars ultimately led to two main editions of the *Great Commentary*, substantially different from one another: Wang Kaiyun's *The Great Commentary on the Documents Classic with Additional Annotations* (Shangshu dazhuan buzhu 尚書大傳補注), which we present here in translation, and Pi Xirui's *Notes and Corrections to The Great Commentary on the Documents Classic* (Shangshu dazhuan shuzheng 尚書大傳疏證), a text that we extensively consulted for both its organization and its textual notes.

The differences between the two episodes, one leading to the creation of the *Great Commentary*, the other to the reconstitution of a lost text, are apparent. First, the early episode was centered on the *Documents*, attempting to make the classic, through interpretation and explanation, relevant to the confused and insecure political situation of the newly established empire; the later imperial episode focused not on the classic but on restoring the *Great Commentary*. Second, the first episode took place during a time when the *Documents* itself was far from a stable text—even as the Western Han court used its authority to endorse its own version of the classic, individuals and groups repeatedly tried to bring newly discovered chapters and parts of the *Documents* to the attention of the court, exploiting the perception that the court-endorsed version of the classic constituted only a portion of a larger text.[4] The Qing scholars, in contrast, had what they considered to be a stable *Documents* text, even though a controversy on the authenticity of the so-called Old Script (Guwen 古文) chapters of the *Documents*—now generally regarded as forgeries from the fourth century CE—was brewing and threatened to, once more, destabilize the text.[5]

The most important difference, however, lay in the nature of the memorial cultures in the two periods.[6] The Qing scholars were interested in using newly discovered philological methods to reconstitute a lost written text as precisely and completely as possible—they were delighted when they were able to procure a copy that contained *Great Commentary*-related materials unattested before,[7] and they competed with one another to find more quotations to include and better ways of ordering them. Their memorial culture was, unequivocally, one of the written word. In the early imperial period, in contrast, although written texts played a distinct role, the memorial culture was overwhelmingly oral, geared toward textual recitation, orally delivered explanations, or court persuasions and debates.[8] Many of the textual passages contained in the *Great Commentary* read, to borrow the early Chinese manuscript specialist Dirk Meyer's terminology, like "context-based texts," in that they assume a shared knowledge of and appreciation for the *Documents* and can easily be imagined as parts of exchanges between a master and his disciples, between an advisor and his ruler, or between adherents of competing exegetical traditions.[9] Master Fu and his associates awarded their text the reverence due to a classic. They did so, however, not by painstaking efforts at restoring a lost written text but by reciting and explaining the portions they knew, by showing how the *Documents* offered a workable, time-tested blueprint for the societal order they were helping to create, often in competition with the proponents of other texts and traditions, classical or otherwise. Much of this rhetoric on behalf of the *Documents* comes through in the reconstituted text, as does a clear vision for the new society that was in the process of being created out of past traditions and current needs.

In this book, it is primarily the relevance of the *Great Commentary* to early imperial realities that we want to capture. Whereas both the early and the late imperial episodes are of intrinsic importance to understanding the *Great Commentary*, on balance, our interests are with the former. We have done our due diligence in examining the efforts of reconstitution by the Qing scholars—by reading their prefaces and by comparing their structures and texts—but ultimately it is the extraordinary contributions to the intellectual, ritual, and political life of the early imperial period made by Master Fu and his associates that we want to highlight. Rather than seeking to perfect the efforts of the Qing scholars—by adding yet another textual edition of the *Great Commentary* to the repertoire—we try to accept and work around the fact that, despite the Qing scholars' best efforts, the *Great Commentary* as it existed in Eastern Han is forever lost. The aim of our study, therefore, is not one of further textual reconstitution. Instead, in line with other scholars' efforts toward an "open philology," we acknowledge and accept the impossibility of such a task.[10] Instead, we wish to use the *Great Commentary*, as reconstituted by several Qing scholars, to gain glimpses of the heterogeneity of the Qin and Western Han exegetical traditions related to the *Documents* and to take stock of the intense struggles that took place in the period as men sought to promote their classic and their exegesis at the central court. Whereas other important Han exegetical traditions—in particular those related to *The Spring and Autumn Annals* (Chunqiu 春秋), commonly referred to as the *Annals*—have received ample attention in recent Western scholarship, the exegetical traditions surrounding the *Documents* have been largely left aside.[11]

If there is one message that the *Great Commentary* consistently conveys, it is that the *Documents* should not be neglected and that in its words, sentences, and stories all the necessary clues can be found to steer the search for a just, well-organized society. We want to take that claim seriously to examine, through the lens of the *Great Commentary*, the strategies that Western Han scholars and politicians associated with the *Documents* employed in the competitive social and ideological environment of the early empire and to take stock, wherever possible, of their successes and their failures.

As readers who follow us throughout this introduction will notice, almost everything about the *Great Commentary* is complicated. Not only is its own textual history complex; so is that of the *Documents* itself, and the two are inextricably linked to one another. Zheng Xuan, the great late Eastern Han classical scholar, readily acknowledged this complexity in remarks that he appended to his annotated edition of the *Commentary*:

> Master Fu was an academician under Qin. In Emperor Wen's (r. 180–57 BCE) time, he was close to one hundred years of age. Master Zhang and Master Ouyang followed his teachings and transmitted them. There were errors in pronunciation, and discrepancies regarding order. The differences between the seal and the clerical script compounded the problems.[12] It is hardly surprising that there were omissions. After the master's death, the various pupils each discussed what they had learned and patched up lacunae according to their own understanding. They wrote their separate "chapter and verse" commentaries and also wrote texts that focused on the general meaning. Basing themselves on the classic, they brought out its significance. They called it the *Commentary*.[13]

Zheng Xuan mentions issues with the text of the *Documents* itself (the order of its chapters/sections, uncertainty regarding pronunciation, omissions, different scripts). He acknowledges the important role of Fu Sheng and his early pupils while also indicating additions by later generations of disciples and the multiplicity of commentarial strategies they employed. Lastly, he posits that, ultimately, the goal of the pupils was not some kind of antiquarian reconstruction of the classic but to make the classic relevant by "bringing out its significance." In what follows we will take Zheng Xuan as our guide to introduce, as clearly as possible, a range of topics relevant to the genesis of both the *Great Commentary* and its Qing reconstitution. These topics will provide the background necessary for a fruitful reading of our translation; it will also highlight the multiple ways in which, during the early imperial period, scholars affiliated with the *Documents* interacted with their peers of other textual traditions as well as with the rapidly changing political environment at the central court.

MASTER FU'S LIFE

Master Fu is a pivotal figure both in the transmission of the *Documents* from Qin to Western Han and in the creation of the *Great Commentary*. He is also a somewhat shadowy figure about whom there is little solid information. As the *Documents* gained acceptance at court and as partisans of the classic, eager to translate their mastery of the text into political advantage, started to form scholarly lineages, they pointed to Master Fu as their scholarly ancestor. As they did so, Master Fu's star rose, and various assumptions about his life became firmly integrated into the biographical lore surrounding the figure. As noted by other scholars, even with the master's name we are not on solid ground. The *Scribe's Records* (Shiji 史記) (ca. 100 BCE) simply refers to him as Master Fu 伏生 (Fu sheng). Some centuries later, *The Book of Later Han* (Hou Hanshu 後漢書; 5th century CE) begins its biography of the prominent Eastern Han politician Fu Zhan 伏湛 (d. 37 CE) by claiming that he is a ninth-generation descendant of Master Fu: in substantiating that claim,[14] it provides the master with both a personal name (Sheng 勝) and a courtesy name (Zijian 子賤). It appears that over the course of the centuries Master Fu's name was fleshed out to remove the vagueness surrounding the figure and to make him into a proper ancestor for Fu Zhan and his lineage.[15]

The following examination of the little biographical information available concerning Master Fu shows that even *Scribe's Records*, the earliest source, infuses its narrative of Master Fu's life with a story of his heroic rescue of the *Documents* that can hardly be taken at face value.

AN ACADEMICIAN AT THE CENTRAL COURT

Master Fu's life was divided between his native area in what is now northern Shandong (included in what *Scribe's Records* discusses as the area of Qi 齊 and Lu 魯)[16] and the capital area of the Qin and Western Han dynasties, then known as the Area within the Passes (Guanzhong 關中—the location of both the Qin capital of Xianyang 咸陽 and the Western Han capital of Chang'an 長安) (see map 1).[17] Master Fu likely acquainted himself with the *Documents* in his home area when it was still part of the Warring States kingdom of Qi; the area of Qi and neighboring Lu was a well-known hotbed for the study and practice of the *Odes* and *Documents* classics.[18] According to the sources, Master Fu became an academician (*boshi* 博士) at the Qin court in Xianyang and must, therefore, have left his home region to move west to the capital.[19]

The Qin court employed many academicians, among them specialists in the classics.[20] The academicians were tasked with the texts of the past: they determined authoritative versions of texts, used texts and the historical precedents contained in them to formulate political advice, and drafted promotional texts for celebratory occasions.[21] The Stele Inscriptions, texts inscribed on stone stelae erected at the sacred sites visited by the First Emperor (Qin shi huangdi 秦始皇帝, r. 259/221–10 BCE) during his imperial tours, were most likely drafted by the academicians as well. It is striking how many of the sites the First Emperor traveled to were clustered in what, in preunification times, was the state of Qi.[22] Early China scholar Martin Kern's research has revealed how heavily the Stele Inscriptions were influenced by the classics (especially the *Odes*), in their form, content, and wording.[23] Perhaps the academicians—(including Master Fu?)—accompanied the emperor on his sacrificial tours: the Stele Inscriptions refer repeatedly, in general terms, to attending officials (*qunchen congzhe* 群臣從者, *congchen* 從臣, *qunchen* 群臣);[24] in some of the inscriptions, the attending officials are described as engaged in the recitation of the inscriptional texts.[25]

There was an interesting back and forth between the area of Qi (and Lu), known, among other things, for its classical scholarship, and the Qin central court that sought to harness that scholarship for its own purposes. Local scholars from Qi were given employment at the Qin court, and the First Emperor traveled to various places within former Qi to implant, possibly in the company of these same scholars, classically phrased inscriptional texts into the landscape.[26] But all this back and forth also points to tensions, as the Qin court's efforts at intellectual and religious colonization would surely have met with a measure of resistance, especially in Qi. At the time of the bibliocaust of 213 BCE, when, by imperial order, the Qin court proscribed all privately owned copies of the *Odes* and the *Documents* (and other texts), the area of Qi and Lu—the one place where classical traditions were strongly engrained and sustained throughout the turmoil of the wars of unification—was probably targeted and hit disproportionally hard. According to *Scribe's Records*, the bibliocaust explains why, when a rival regime to that of Qin arose (led by Chen She 陳涉), "all the classicists of Lu, grasping the Kong family's ritual vessels, flocked to it," despite this new regime's obvious weaknesses.[27] Chen She's rebellion, although short-lived, set in motion the chain of events that led to Qin's collapse.

BIBLIOCAUST AND RETURN TO QI/LU

Both the bibliocaust and the anti-Qin rebellions play a role in the account of the next event in Master Fu's life, his departure from the Qin capital area to return to his native region. "Biographies of Classical Scholars" (Rulin zhuan 儒林傳) in *Scribe's Records* states, first, that, "at the time of the burning of the books during Qin times, Master Fu hid the text [of the *Documents*] in a wall." It then asserts, "After this, when large-scale fighting broke out, he fled [the capital]."[28] The bibliocaust took place in 213 BCE, whereas major anti-Qin rebellions did not break out until 209 BCE. Most scholars assume that Master Fu hid a copy of the *Documents* in a wall at the time when he fled the capital. They are, however, divided on when this happened. Traditional historian Qian Mu 錢穆 (1895–1990), for one, postulates that, since the bibliocaust made it impossible for scholars of the *Odes* and *Documents* to maintain employment at the Qin court, Master Fu must have fled the court at the time of the bibliocaust, hiding his classic before departing. Others, including the *Documents Classic* specialist Liu Qiyu 劉起釪 (1917–2012), assume that Master Fu left the capital for Qi only when the anti-Qin revolts started and hid a copy of the *Documents* at that time.[29]

According to *Scribe's Records*, Master Fu would then have gone back to retrieve his copy of the *Documents* after Liu Bang 劉邦 (r. 206–195 BCE) had become emperor of Western Han (in 202 BCE), only to discover that many chapters of the text had gone missing: "When the Han was firmly established, Master Fu went to look for his text, but several tens of chapters had gone missing, and he retrieved a mere twenty-nine *pian*. Those he taught in the area of Qi and Lu."[30] That Master Fu went home after his employer's regime collapsed makes perfect sense. The problem seems to lie with the story of Master Fu first hiding and then retrieving the *Documents*. First, there would have been very little reason for Master Fu to hide a copy of the *Documents* during the bibliocaust of 213 BCE. As many previous scholars have pointed out, in the edict that launched the bibliocaust, only privately owned copies of the *Odes* and the *Documents* were targeted, not the versions that circulated at the court.[31] Master Fu was an academician, not a private person, and most certainly continued to have access to the classic in order to keep developing, as before, policy positions or draft texts for imperial consumption that drew on the classic. The bibliocaust, indeed, was not an all-out assault on texts and learning but an effort on the part of the Qin central court to monopolize the discourse about historical precedents and the interpretations of the classics.[32] Second, given the memorial culture of the time, a recognized expert in the *Documents* classic, on the payroll of the central court, would not have been dependent on a written version of the classic—even when such a version existed—but would have been able to recite the text from memory.[33] Why then would Master Fu need to hide a copy? Why would it have mattered that, after he retrieved the text, chapters appeared to be missing? Third, both Qian Mu and Liu Qiyu assume that Master Fu hid a copy of the *Documents* in or near the capital of Xianyang, but would he really have made the return trip from Qi to the Area within the Passes once the Western Han regime was firmly established? The Qin capital of Xianyang was partly burned and abandoned during the civil war that marked the

Qin–Han transition while its less central areas were being repurposed to form the new capital of Chang'an.[34]

Scribe's Records, in its short biographical account of Master Fu, was likely infusing the few known facts of Master Fu's life with elements of an alternative narrative. This alternative narrative was motivated by (1) a desire to cast Qin in a negative light by focusing on the bibliocaust of 213 BCE (and on the "burying alive of scholars" that allegedly took place a year after), a tendency that started early in Western Han but grew in vehemence so that by late Western Han these events came to define Qin, masking the Qin dynasty's considerable political achievements and cultural contributions;[35] (2) a concomitant desire to present Master Fu, who was promoted by classicists at the Western Han court as their teacher, in a positive light: not as a collaborator with the increasingly despised Qin regime but as one who actively resisted the evil sides of the regime; and (3) an attempt to explain, through a classic "rescue from a wall" story, not only why the version of the *Documents* known at the court in early Western Han had only twenty-eight chapters, but also why additional chapters associated with the classic ought to be accepted by the court as genuine chapters of the classic. Sima Qian's 司馬遷 (145?–86? BCE) account, in other words, is not to be taken as a string of facts to be made compatible but as a patchwork of competing (and not necessarily reconcilable) narratives. In the absence of new textual sources that can shed light on this episode, our best guess is that Master Fu, as the Qin regime was collapsing, left the capital area not necessarily with a written text but as someone wondering whether he would ever place his hard-earned skills with the *Documents* classic at the service of yet another court. It is also quite likely that in his home area of Qi not all copies of the *Documents* were burned at the time of the bibliocaust and that alternatives to the court version of the text continued to circulate (to resurface later, with or without intervention by the master himself).

A TEACHER IN QI/LU AND A VISIT BY AN ENVOY OF THE CENTRAL COURT

To follow *Scribe's Records* further, Master Fu stayed in his home area for the remainder of his life, making his living as a teacher of the *Documents* "in between Qi and Lu" 于齊魯之閒.[36] In 170 BCE, when Master Fu was already age ninety or over, he had one more opportunity to reconnect with the central court at Chang'an. Emperor Wen, who had heard of Master Fu's reputation as a former academician under Qin but was told that Master Fu, owing to his advanced age, would no longer be able to make the trip to the capital, ordered his Commissioner for Ceremonial (Taichang 太常)[37] to send an underling to pay a visit to Master Fu instead. The person who the Commissioner for Ceremonial chose for the mission, even though he was only a low official,[38] made the best of the chance

Fig. 1. Attributed to Wang Wei 王維 (699–759), *Fu Sheng Transmitting the Classic* (Fu Sheng shoujing tu 伏生授經圖). Tang dynasty, probably rendered from 9th–10th century. Handscroll, ink, and colors on silk, 25.4 × 44.7 cm. Osaka City Museum of Fine Arts, Japan.

he was offered. Indeed, when he returned from his visit to Master Fu's residence, he presented some policy recommendations to the emperor, sprucing them up with Master Fu's explanations of the *Documents*. This earned the official, Chao Cuo 鼂錯 (d. 154 BCE), promotion to the household of the heir apparent, the future Emperor Jing (r. 157–141 BCE), and marked the start of Chao Cuo's brilliant though ill-fated career.[39]

The story of the meeting between Chao Cuo and Master Fu received biographical embellishment soon after, as it came to involve not only Chao Cuo and Master Fu, but also the master's daughter. Wei Hong 衛宏 (1st c. CE) claims that Master Fu at the time of Chao Cuo's visit was not only old, but also barely able to speak and hence delegated his daughter to conduct the interview with Chao Cuo on his behalf. The problems with language apparently went beyond Master Fu's speech problems. Wei Hong adds, somewhat sarcastically, that, given that the daughter spoke in the local Qi dialect and Chao Cuo expressed himself in the dialect of his native Yingchuan, Chao Cuo missed 20 to 30 percent of what she said. As a result, he did not learn to recite the classic properly—apparently the goal of his mission—but was merely able to loosely paraphrase it 略以其意屬讀而已也.[40] Most later scholars of the *Documents* have ignored Wei Hong's statement on Chao Cuo's less than perfect mastery of the text and accepted, daughter and all, the idea that Chao Cuo during his visit to former Qi received, in written form, Master Fu's version of the *Documents* and brought the text back with him to Chang'an (figs. 1–2).

This is the extent of our knowledge about the life events of Master Fu. His life, like a drawing by Escher, appears very differently depending on the narrative angle one adopts. On the surface, he appears as a classicist who supported the Qin imperial project by accepting employment as an academician, only to find his career hampered first by military conflict

Fig. 2. Du Jin 杜堇 (ca. 1465–1509), *Fu Sheng Transmitting the Classic* (Fu Sheng shoujing tu 伏生授經圖). Ming dynasty. Hanging scroll, ink and colors on silk, 147 × 104.5 cm. The Metropolitan Museum of Art, New York.

and then by the early Western Han court's relative lack of interest in classical culture.[41] According to the standard narrative told by Sima Qian, Liu Xin, and countless later sources, however, Master Fu was a hero, a near-martyr who rescued a fuller version of the *Documents* classic from the claws of the Qin regime by burying it in a wall, only to retrieve some of its chapters, which he then transmitted to the Western

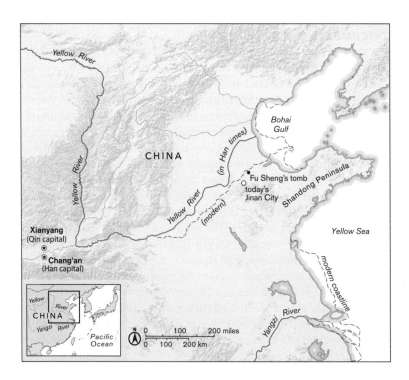

Map 1. The likely locations of Fu Sheng's tomb and the Qin/Han capital area. Map by Ben Pease.

Han court. This particular narrative ensured a rich afterlife for Master Fu. In 647 CE, he, together with twenty-one other famous classicists, received a spot in the temples and academies devoted to Confucius, receiving sacrifice as a "Former Teacher" (Xianshi 先師).[42] Despite occasional attempts to demote them, Fu Sheng and his fellow classicists were able to maintain their position in the Confucian temples until these places lost much of their meaning as sites of worship in the early twentieth century. Master Fu also inspired later scholars, particularly in the Qing, when his scholarship was regarded as the most direct route to understanding the intention of the sages, bypassing interpretations of Eastern Han and beyond.[43] Even in recent times, the master keeps making come-backs. In his presumed place of origin in Zouping 鄒平 County, Shandong, some people still trace their ancestry to the master, and there is an active shrine to his memory.[44] As part of a national revival movement, in 2014 the National Center for the Performing Arts (Guojia Da Juyuan 國家大劇院), in the political heart of Beijing, put on a play featuring Master Fu; the play pits him against Li Si 李斯 (280–208 BCE), the ill-reputed chancellor of the First Emperor, again setting the master up as someone who resisted the autocratic tendencies of Qin.[45]

DOCUMENTS

It is difficult to overstate the complexity of the textual history of the *Documents*. Given that *Documents* is the text that the *Great Commentary* sought to explain, it is especially important to gauge what *Documents* was like during the early imperial period. The early imperial *Documents* is substantially different from the transmitted *Documents*. The transmitted *Documents* in fifty-eight chapters is a product of only the third or fourth century CE, when new chapters were added to an existing core.[46] During the Qing dynasty, scholars separated within the transmitted *Documents* what they saw as an authentic core of twenty-eight chapters from the other chapters that they considered "forged";[47] the distinction between New Script chapters (the supposed authentic core) and Old Script chapters (the supposed forged chapters) is now widely followed in discussions of the transmitted *Documents*.[48] However, the *Documents* of the early imperial period cannot be equated with the New Script chapters of the *Documents* either: *Documents* quotations in early imperial sources show considerable variation when compared to the corresponding passages in the New Script chapters;[49] furthermore, early imperial sources like the *Great Commentary* and *Scribe's Records* quote from or refer to *Documents* chapters other than those included among the New Script chapters, indicating that there were still other materials in circulation.[50]

In what follows, we introduce the *Documents* of the early imperial period by distinguishing between a version in twenty-eight or twenty-nine chapters that was endorsed at the early imperial courts (a version close to but not identical with the twenty-eight New Script chapters) and *Documents* materials that circulated locally, outside of the court, but were occasionally brought to the central court's attention. We also trace how, by late Western Han, not only were the court-authorized versions of the *Documents* strongly perceived as incomplete, but blame for this sorry state of affairs was placed squarely on the court of Qin and its bibliocaust. Such a perception paved the way for the heightened antagonism between new-script and old-script scholars in Eastern Han,[51] and it created the proper imaginary space for the expansion of the *Documents* into the fifty-eight chapters of the transmitted version.

A COURT-AUTHORIZED VERSION OF THE *DOCUMENTS*

Before 221 BCE, the year in which Qin completed its conquest of the other states, "documents" (*shu* 書) referred to a category of texts that recorded the exemplary actions and speech of sages of the past, from legendary rulers of antiquity such as Yao 堯, Shun 舜, and Yu 禹 to the Zhou kings of the mid- to late seventh century BCE. Whereas there was a strong consensus that these were venerable texts with important implications for governance, there was disagreement as to which individual documents truly belonged to the collection, and there was no chapter count or list of chapters that everyone agreed on.[52] This point is illustrated well by the cache of bamboo strips acquired by Tsinghua University in Beijing in 2008: many of the 2,388 strips, carbon-dated to 305 BCE (plus or minus thirty years), have been understood by scholars to belong to this loosely defined category of *Documents*-related texts.[53] Whereas some textual units within the Tsinghua strips can be properly regarded as "versions" of chapters in the transmitted *Documents*,[54] other units remind one of known *Documents* chapters in terms of style or subject matter but have no obvious counterparts in the current collection. Yet others appear to be political lessons that, though formulated in the idiom of the Warring States, discuss earlier sage figures that play a prominent role in the *Documents* (e.g., Yi Yin, advisor to the founder of the Shang dynasty). The Tsinghua University strips bring out forcefully how, by the late fourth century BCE, there is a large corpus of *Documents*-related materials for which it is very difficult to distinguish canon from noncanon or classic from commentary.

The Qin court (after it completed its conquests in 221 BCE) most likely is where this vast and heterogeneous collection of texts was reviewed, revised, and ultimately redacted into an anthology that suited the First Emperor's imperial project.[55] From that perspective, the bibliocaust of 213 BCE that included a ban on privately owned copies of the *Documents* is best understood not as an anomalous event but as an almost inevitable corollary of the scholarly activities patronized by the Qin court. As Kern writes, "Such a proscription of heterogeneous writings among the population and the promotion of a defined textual corpus under imperial control is a typical case of the interplay of canon and censorship known to all textual cultures."[56] To make its texts authoritative and to prevent them from being turned into a weapon against itself the Qin court needed to bring its texts and their interpretation firmly under its control.[57] This view of the Qin court as the place where a classic was carefully and strategically created and nurtured is also compatible with a growing body of research that, building on archaeological discoveries of Qin period sites, texts, and artefacts, has demonstrated that Qin, rather than being an exception, was an integral part of the Zhou political and cultural realm.[58]

Primary sources such as *Scribe's Records*, in presenting the story of Master Fu's rescue of twenty-nine *Documents*' chapters and of the subsequent adoption of these chapters at the Western Han court, already assume a continuity between the Qin and Western Han versions of the *Documents*.[59] Even if this account of the manner of transmission is problematic, it implies that the *Documents* available at the early Western Han court might well have been the text redacted at the Qin court;[60] it is entirely possible that the court-authorized text simply remained at court

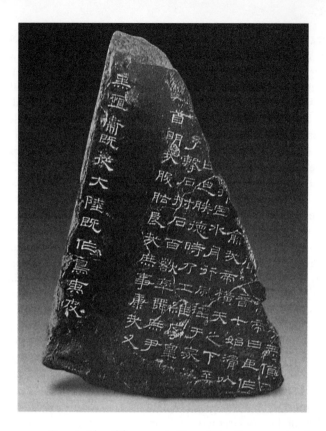

Fig. 3. Front side of fragment 6874 of the *Documents* of the Xiping Stone Classics of 175 CE, containing, from right to left, the lower parts of lines from "Gaoyao's Counsel," a blank space, and parts of the beginning of "Tribute of Yu." From Xu Jingyuan 1981, 188.

during the dynastic transition from Qin to Han. The Western Han rulers, like their predecessors, took measures to back up the authority of the *Documents* classic. Instead of using prohibitions—in 192 BCE the Han court rescinded Qin's 213 BCE ban on private ownership of certain texts[61]—the Western Han court preferred to appoint academicians (who were assumed to train disciples) to serve as guardians over its authoritative texts.[62] Early Western Han emperors had only mixed success in attracting specialists in the classics to court; in the case of the *Documents*, it was because Master Fu would or could not go to Chang'an that Emperor Wen had to send someone to visit Master Fu at his home.[63] But in 137 BCE, at the beginning of Emperor Wu's reign (141–87 BCE), academicians for the Five Classics (Wujing 五經), including the *Documents*, were established at the central court.[64] By the first century BCE, occasional court conferences were held in which the pros and cons of particular versions of the classics were debated, often in the presence of the emperor. The most important of these, held at the Shiqu 石渠 Pavilion of the Weiyang 未央 Palace in 51 BCE, resulted in the establishment of two additional academicians for the *Documents* classic.[65] Indeed, over the course of Western Han, the classics became increasingly important to the court's self-representation, prompting, by late Western Han, what has been called the "classical turn."[66]

It is strong testimony to the success of the Han central court's efforts that, until after the fall of Eastern Han in 220 CE, only one chapter was (possibly) added to the *Documents*, bringing the total chapter count from twenty-eight to twenty-nine.[67] The status quo was thus maintained despite occasional strong challenges. During Emperor Ai's 哀 reign (7–1 BCE) the court scholar Liu Xin 劉歆 (46 BCE–23 CE) sent an urgent plea to the Commissioner for Ceremonial, under whose ministry the academicians served, to have additional or alternative chapters of the *Documents* and other classics officially recognized (as well as variant versions of already included chapters). Liu Xin accused the academicians who resisted the inclusion of the texts he had discovered in the imperial archives of being uninspired traditionalists.[68] Still, the proposed changes were steadfastly refused. At the end of Eastern Han, in 175 CE, in order to ward off accusations that the texts of the classics were being tampered with for personal gain, Emperor Ling 靈 (r. 168–89) ordered that they be carved in stone, the most durable material available at the time.[69] These are the so-called Xiping 熹平 Stone Classics, of which only fragments survive (fig. 3). The surviving fragments of the *Documents* classic—particularly the remnants of its "Xu" 序, a list of titles of *Documents* chapters—demonstrate that the engraved text, in terms of titles and number of chapters, was still close to the version that was endorsed by the Western Han court.[70]

AN "UNDERGROUND" CLASSICAL CULTURE AND LOST OLD SCRIPT CHAPTERS

However hard the Qin and Han courts tried, they could hardly aspire to complete control over all *Documents*-related material. As one scholar suggests, efforts at censorship must have led to an "underground" classical culture in which materials not withheld in the classical texts of the central court were preserved and transmitted at local levels.[71] Some of these materials found their way to the central court in Chang'an, particularly when more and more professional avenues opened up at the capital for classically trained scholars. These include *Documents*-related materials from Lu 魯 brought to the attention of the central court by Kong Anguo 孔安國 (d. ca. 100 BCE), an academician and a descendant of Confucius, the same materials that Liu Xin later tried to promote to the academicians.[72] Given that these texts had not been transcribed into the clerical script (*lishu* 隸書) current at the courts of Qin and Han, the sources tend to refer to them as "old-script" (*guwen* 古文) texts. One Du Lin 杜林 (d. 47 CE), who found himself in the western provinces during the turmoil following the fall of Wang Mang's 王莽 regime (r. 9–23 CE), is said to have obtained there "one *juan* of an old-script *Documents* written on lacquer" 漆書古文尚書一卷 and brought it back to the capital.[73] The Song bibliophile Wang Yinglin 王應麟 (1223–96) indicates that some of these "lost old-script chapters" (*guwen yipian* 古文遺篇)—that is, chapters not included in the transmitted *Documents*—were still circulating as late as the Sui and Tang dynasties.[74] Scholars posit the existence, at one time or another, of up to five sets of old-script *Documents* materials.[75] These old-script materials play a role in the *Great Commentary* as well.

CONFUCIUS'S *DOCUMENTS*

In the case of the *Documents*, the appearance of additional or variant material was facilitated by something other than mere availability: over the course of the Western Han dynasty, a narrative appeared according to which the most perfect redaction of the *Documents* was not that of Qin but a longer one made centuries earlier by no lesser authority than Confucius (551–479 BCE). This narrative is most fully and powerfully told in Liu Xin's aforementioned accusatory letter to the academicians. Liu Xin—who worked with his father, Liu Xiang, on cataloging all items stored in the imperial archives—points to Confucius as the ultimate editor of a superior version of the *Documents*. Confucius, deeply distressed about the state of traditional knowledge in his own times, "edited the *Changes*, put the *Documents* in order, and compiled the *Annals*, so as to make a record of the ways chosen by the sovereigns and kings of old." Liu Xin then goes on to blame the Qin court for having suppressed Confucius's redactions of the classical texts. "The oppressive regime of Qin ... burned the texts that had been held in such high honor and put to death the specialists in traditional learning who were familiar with the old cultured way of life."[76]

The letter continues with a description of the gradual, but still incomplete, recovery of Confucius's texts in Western Han times. With regard to the *Documents* classic, Liu Xin mentions the following steps: (1) Chao Cuo's visit to Master Fu during Emperor Wen's reign to recover the text, which, as it was found in the wall of a residence, was "defective" and "in disarray"; (2) the coming to light of "Great Oath" (Taishi 泰誓)—the mysterious twenty-ninth chapter—during Emperor Wu's reign; (3) the recovery of sixteen *Documents* chapters written in old script from the wall of Confucius's old home also during Emperor Wu's reign; and (4) the rediscovery of these same chapters in the court archives at Chang'an in Liu Xin's own time.[77] In Liu Xin's narrative, the version of the *Documents* that the Han inherited was not a Qin redaction but what remained of

Confucius's authoritative redaction: Qin, rather than create a version of the *Documents*, had sought to destroy Confucius's version of the text. Liu Xin's narrative accomplishes two related but distinct goals: not only does it refuse Qin its rightful role as contributor to the transmission and enhancement of traditional culture; it also presents the version of the *Documents* in possession of the Western Han court as less than whole, as a butchered version of Confucius's redaction awaiting restoration.

Whereas at the time of the composition of *Scribe's Records*, ca. 100 BCE, certain elements of this narrative were available, it coalesced in this form only in late Western Han. *Scribe's Records* already points to Confucius as the person who "arranged (*xu* 序) the *Documents* and its traditions,"[78] and it indicates that Master Fu lost several chapters of the *Shangshu* as it was available at the Qin court,[79] but it is Liu Xin who in his letter couples the Qin bibliocaust with the demise of Confucius's redaction of the *Documents*.[80] *Book of Han* (Hanshu 漢書), written by members of the Ban 班 family in the first century of Eastern Han, adopts and amplifies Liu Xin's story, thus projecting it as a truism onto countless later generations not only of classical scholars but of the elite at large.[81]

Regarding the number of chapters supposedly contained in Confucius's version of the *Documents*, the story gradually thickens. At the time *Scribe's Records* was written, there was already a sense that tens of chapters (*shu shi pian* 數十篇) had been lost.[82] However, the first assertion that the original number of chapters in Confucius's version was one hundred comes in late Western Han. Liu Xiang, Liu Xin's father, deemed a collection of *Documents*-like material relating to the Zhou period (now known as *Yi Zhoushu* 逸周書) to be a "remnant of the one-hundred-chapter version that was appraised by Confucius" 蓋孔子所論百篇之餘也.[83] During the reign of Emperor Cheng 成 (33–7 BCE), a scholar from Donglai 東萊, Zhang Ba 張霸, was called to court because he possessed a copy of the *Documents* in 102 chapters; even though the copy was found to differ greatly from the *Documents* copies at the central court, the text was retained for a number of years, to be banned only in 14 CE, when one of Zhang Ba's father's pupils rebelled.[84] Yang Xiong 楊雄 (53 BCE–18 CE) states in his *Exemplary Figures* (Fayan 法言) that "those of long ago who explicated the *Documents* arranged it in one hundred chapters."[85] This belief in a *Documents* by Confucius in one hundred chapters that was destroyed by the aberrant Qin dynasty had become a certainty and instilled in the *Zeitgeist* a longing for a truly closed text beyond the chapters actually possessed.

This series of events set the stage not only for the particular intellectual atmosphere of Eastern Han, in which old-script scholars and new-script scholars were increasingly pitted against one another, but also for the supposed "forgeries" of *Documents* chapters of the third and fourth centuries CE and for their acceptance as a genuine part of the court-authorized canon. In 837 the extended version was carved in stone—the stelae carved at that time are still on view in Xi'an's "Forest of Stelae" museum.

The stelae version of the *Documents* served as a foundational pillar of the civil service examination system until the system's collapse in the early twentieth century and provided a political idiom to countless generations of statesmen in middle and late imperial China as well as in other areas of East Asia to which Chinese culture spread.[86]

MASTER FU'S DESCENDANTS AND DISCIPLES: A NONLINEAR GENEALOGICAL READING

Over time, two groups would claim to be heirs to Master Fu's legacy. The first group consists of his descendants. We have already mentioned Fu Zhan, who in early Eastern Han became chancellor and on that occasion was awarded a hereditary noble title.[87] The family passed this title on for seven generations, producing more distinguished officials and scholars along the way, but was decimated at the end of Eastern Han following the marriage of an heir to Fu Zhan's noble title to an imperial princess. A daughter born from that marriage became Emperor Xian's 獻 (r. 189–220) empress. She, with most members of the Fu clan, was killed in 214 CE for having opposed Cao Cao 曹操 (ca. 155–220 CE), whose son Cao Pi 曹丕 (r. 220–26) went on to found the Wei dynasty (220–66 CE).[88] The text in which the Eastern Han Fu family had most expertise and on which Fu Zhan as well as his father and brothers had built their reputations was, surprisingly, not the *Documents* but the Qi version of the *Odes* classic. Insofar as one can speak of one Fu family stretching from Master Fu to Fu Zhan and his descendants, the family's special connection with the *Documents* seems have ended early on: there is a record that a grandson of Master Fu was summoned to court to explain the classic but had proven totally unequal to the task.[89]

There are strong indications that Fu Zhan—as the first member of the family to acquire a noble title—was the hinge of the Fu family's genealogy. In other words, it is because Fu Zhan became such a prominent statesman and acquired a noble title that he (or members of his clan) found it necessary to look backward and claim Master Fu, by then famous for his role in the transmission of the *Documents*, as an ancestor. Rather than reading the family genealogy in the linear fashion in which it is presented in the sources, starting with Master Fu and branching out into later generations, one should focus on Fu Zhan as the central figure and read the genealogy as radiating backward and forward from the figure who brought the family political prominence. As figure 4 shows, the genealogy of the Fu family is fleshed out only starting with Fu Zhan's father, an eighth-generation descendant of Master Fu, and there are many blank spots in the intervening generations.[90]

This family model is useful in thinking about the other group that claimed Master Fu's legacy: his disciples and their intellectual heirs (fig. 5).

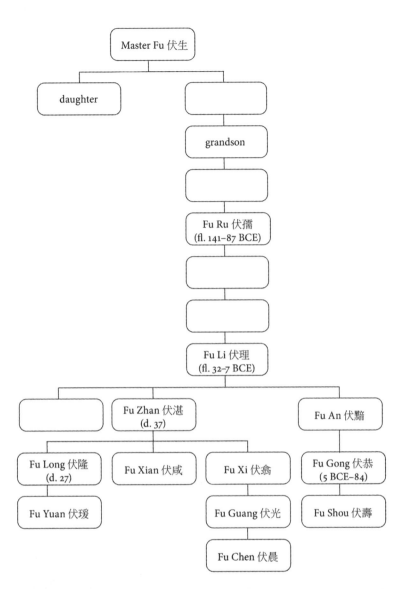

Fig. 4. Descendants of Master Fu, with Fu Zhan as pivot. *Sources:* Early sources such as *Scribe's Records* and *Book of Han* only carry information about Master Fu himself and a grandson who was called to the capital but proved unable to explain the classic (*Shiji* 121.3124–25; *Hanshu* 88.3603). Master Fu's daughter is mentioned by Wei Hong (1st c. CE); her name is given as Xi'e 羲娥 in later sources (the earliest we could find is *Xu wenxian tongkao* 續文獻通考, preface 1585). *Book of Later Han* is the source of information about Fu Ru (who moved the family to what was to be Fu Zhan's homestead) and about Fu Zhan's father, brothers, sons, and later descendants.

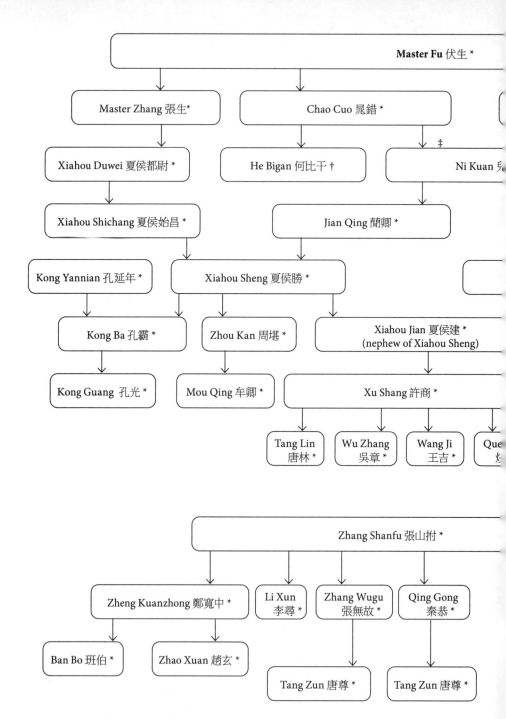

Fig. 5. Master Fu and his disciples, based on *Scribe's Records* and/or *Book of Han* (*), *Book of Later Han* (†), and *Weighed Discourses* (‡).

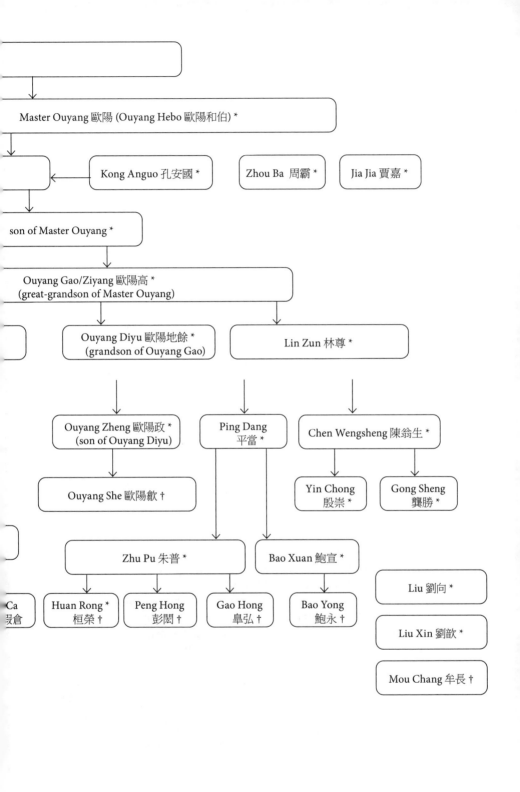

The "Biographies of the Classical Scholars" in *Scribe's Records* and, especially, in *Book of Han* present Master Fu as the prime mover of an increasingly proliferating nexus of scholars trained, generation upon generation, in Master Fu's version of the *Documents*.[91] Here too it is striking how bare and tentative the early chains in the transmission are: Masters Zhang and Ouyang, who supposedly studied with Master Fu in Qi, lack personal names and have unclear career paths, as if they are mentioned only because they enabled later men to establish a connection with Master Fu.[92] Among these later men, Ni Kuan 兒寬 (d. 103 BCE) stands out as a key figure, as he seems to have been one of the first to have really bridged the world of "Qi and Lu" and the imperial court at Chang'an (aside from the aforementioned visit to Master Fu of Chao Cuo).

Ni Kuan had come to Chang'an from Qiancheng 千乘 Commandery, located just north of Master Fu's home area, as a promising student of the *Documents* and was assigned as a student to the academician Kong Anguo, also a specialist in the *Documents*.[93] Ni Kuan fulfilled various low-level clerical positions, including one in the office of the superintendent of trials (*tingwei* 廷尉). In that position, he gained notoriety because he had drafted a successful verdict in a difficult case—one in which the emperor had already repeatedly refused to endorse the advice of his officials. After that, he was gradually promoted until he became imperial counselor (*yushi dafu* 御史大夫), the second highest position in the imperial bureaucracy, a post that he occupied from 110 BCE until his death in 103 BCE. Together with Gongsun Hong 公孫弘 (d. 121 BCE), a specialist in the *Annals* classic who became chancellor in 124 BCE, Ni Kuan was one of only a handful of classically trained scholars—and the only one with expertise in the *Documents*—to attain high political office during Emperor Wu's reign.[94] Surely, his remarkable political success was instrumental in enhancing the reputation of the *Documents* at court and in highlighting the importance in the transmission of the *Documents* of the masters from former Qi (i.e., Master Fu and Master Ouyang, the latter being Ni Kuan's teacher.) His expertise in the *Documents* would be sought by Emperor Wu (and partially applied) in the time leading up to the calendar reform of 105–4 BCE.[95]

Ni Kuan is connected with all three major scholarly lineages associated with the *Documents* in Western Han. He reportedly transmitted his own knowledge of the classic to the son of his teacher, Master Ouyang, but it is only a few generations further, with the academician Ouyang Gao 歐陽高, probably appointed during the reign of Xuandi 宣帝 (74–48 BCE), that there is evidence that a member of the Ouyang family obtained an official appointment at the Chang'an court.[96] Since the so-called Ouyang version of the *Documents* was already current at court before Ouyang Gao's appointment, the classic should, perhaps, be more appropriately viewed as Ni Kuan's *Documents*.[97] Ni Kuan also, either directly or via his disciple Jian Qing 蕑卿, transmitted his knowledge to Xiahou Sheng 夏侯勝 (fl. 70 BCE), who passed it on to his nephew Xiahou Jian 夏侯建; the latter also received instruction from Ouyang Gao. Xiahou Sheng and Xiahou Jian each produced his own version and interpretation of the *Documents* in twenty-eight or twenty-nine chapters that was endorsed by the Western Han court. Their versions together with the Ouyang version received official recognition during Xuandi's reign.[98]

Xiahou Sheng is also connected with a crucial moment in the history of *Documents* scholarship in Western Han. Even though his career never rose to the same heights as that of Ni Kuan, his use of the *Documents* in the ultimately successful indictment of a reigning emperor in 74 BCE (see below) projected a *Documents*-related omenological tradition to the very heart of political discourse.[99] Xiahou Sheng, as the "Biographies of the Classical Scholars" in *Book of Han* indicates, spawned not only an important network of further disciples; his disciples were also able to use, to an extent not seen before, their classical training as political capital.[100]

After Emperor Wu, being a classical scholar increasingly opened up avenues to political office even though classical training was by no means yet a prerequisite for office.[101] The teacher-disciple networks of the first century BCE are described in *Book of Han* in much greater detail than those of the previous century, indicating their enhanced societal importance.[102] It is also striking how the classicists of the first century BCE are often no longer exclusively associated with only one of the classics—as was the case in the previous century—but often sought and received training in several of them.[103] This development likely reflects the greater political currency that could be gained from classical training as well as the realization that common ground existed between the hitherto relatively separate classical traditions. There seems to have been, over the course of the first century BCE, some joining of ranks among classicists around a common cause, perhaps out of opposition to other groups such as the *fangshi* 方士, who were specialists in the mantic arts sometimes employed at the court.[104]

The landscape of *Documents* scholarship in Western Han over which Master Fu came to tower as a founding father was varied and complex, with, starting in Emperor Wu's reign, an important back and forth between the area of Qi and Lu and the capital. We follow Zheng Xuan in thinking that the *Great Commentary* contains *Documents*-related teachings that cannot be ascribed to Master Fu alone, but also to several of the Western Han *Documents* specialists who came after him.[105] All these experts in the *Documents*, whether they were attached to the central court or working at the local level, were not only concerned with establishing the correct version of the classic, but also offered their interpretation of words, sentences, passages, and chapters of the *Documents* or even of the classic as a whole. It appears that at least some of their work became integrated into the *Great Commentary*.[106] The name of Master Fu can, perhaps, best be seen as a quality label that became attached to the collective efforts of this group of experts in the *Documents*.

FORMAL FEATURES OF THE *GREAT COMMENTARY*: COMMENTARIAL MODES AND INTERTEXTUALITY

In contrast to other early Chinese exegetical texts that usually employ a uniform exegetical mode, the *Great Commentary* presents a mixture of commentarial forms.[107] It contains, as one would expect from a commentary, explanations of words or sentences from the *Documents*; but, besides that, it also features anecdotes, historical narratives, and theoretical expositions (frequently on matters of ritual), some of which may be only loosely associated with the classic. The *Great Commentary*'s lack of uniformity in format is in line with our hypothesis that it is not the text of one master or of one period but an amalgam of different efforts at mastering the *Documents* during the first two centuries BCE. As Zheng Xuan indicates in his "Xu" to the *Commentary* (see his remarks above), Han students of the *Documents* ("the various pupils") engaged with the classic in multiple ways, and the resulting textual practices (*lun* 論, "discourses"; *mifeng qi que* 彌縫其闕, "patching up lacunae"; *zhangju* 章句, "chapter and verse commentaries"; *da yi* 大義, "general meaning") are all reflected in the *Great Commentary*.

TEXTUAL LAYERS

Internal evidence shows that several sections in the *Great Commentary* contain multiple textual layers, in the sense that different commentarial modes build on one another. Thus, there are several references to a *Commentary* (Zhuan 傳) and one to an *Explanation* (Xun 訓) that form part of a wider discussion of a *Documents* fragment. Since both the *Commentary* and the *Explanation* are invoked as sources of authority in the *Great Commentary* and are always followed by specific quotations, these terms likely refer to known texts (whether in oral or in written form). This raises the possibility that Fu Sheng, as he worked with the *Documents*, had at his disposal preexisting commentarial traditions, traditions that might well have come to him from preimperial times; alternatively, those quoting the *Commentary* and the *Explanation* would have been *Documents* exegetes from later generations.

In addition to quotations from texts called *Commentary* or *Explanation*, the *Great Commentary* contains a fragment of an arrangement document ("Xu"; see below); it also contains several clusters of passages in which the person who engages with the *Documents* as a whole or with particular concepts or passages in the *Documents* is none but Confucius 孔子 himself (with or without his disciples), constituting a noteworthy textual layer of its own.

A *COMMENTARY* (*ZHUAN*) WITHIN THE *GREAT COMMENTARY*

In nine of its passages, the *Great Commentary* explicitly quotes a *Commentary* to explain either a sentence or a term from the *Documents*.[108] In the following example from the chapter "Charge to Yue" (Yue ming 說命), the term to be explained is "beamed shack" (*liangyin* 梁闇), a place where the powerful Shang king Wuding 武丁 (r. ?–1189 BCE), here named Gaozong 高宗, is supposed to have stayed.

> The *Documents* says, "Gaozong stayed in the beamed shack. He did not speak for three years." What is "beamed shack"? The *Commentary* says, "Gaozong stayed in the mourning hut and did not speak for three years." The mourning hut is what "beamed shack" is about. ("Charge to Yue" 4.4.1)

In this example, it is as if one is witnessing an active teaching scene: someone raises a question about the meaning of an obscure term within the classic ("beamed shack"), and that question is answered by reference to a certain *Commentary* ("it is the mourning hut"). That the phrase from the *Commentary* carries the authority to fix the meaning of the obscure term is emphatically confirmed in the sentence that concludes the fragment.

To understand how this fragment from a *Commentary* is embedded in further commentarial layers within the *Great Commentary*, it is instructive to consider the remainder of the "Charge to Yue" as well. The chapter goes on to discuss the implications of the fact that the *Documents*, if indeed one abides by the reading of "beamed shack" as mourning hut, seems to be demanding that a newly acceded ruler start his reign by absenting himself for three years. It first provides confirmation that this, indeed, is what the *Documents* demands by citing a reply Confucius made to his disciple Zizhang when the latter questioned him about the meaning of the mourning hut passage:

> In antiquity, after the ruler passed away, it was the heir apparent who received the prime minister's reports. For three years, he did so without daring to wear his father's robes or occupy his father's seat. From the perspective of his ministers and his people, the ruler cannot be absent for even one day. That the ruler cannot be absent for even one day is just like the sky that is always there. That the filial son should observe a period of retreat means that for three years he should not assume his father's position. That is

> why it is said, "So, on the one hand, there is the perspective of ministers and people, and, on the other, there is the observation of a period of retreat. Although the former is important, the latter is absolutely essential for completing the way of the filial son." ("Charge to Yue" 4.4.2)

Confucius readily acknowledges that the three-year mourning hut requirement may be difficult to observe, given that propriety demands that a ruler ought to be available to his ministers and subjects every single day. Still, he continues, the new ruler should retire in order to fulfill his duties as a filial son. The imperative to be filial simply outweighs any other concerns, including the continued presence of the ruler at the center of power.

Following this dialogue with Confucius is a passage that seems meant to assuage those who might be disturbed by this interpretation of "beamed shack" in the *Documents*. The passage takes on the objection (unstated) that prolonged absence of the ruler will surely lead to rebellion and counters the objection by suggesting that, given proper preparation before the death of his father, a new ruler can comfortably retire for three years once his father passes away.

> After his father passed away, Gaozong spent three years in the mourning hut without speaking of matters of state. Still, no one in the realm harbored rebellious intentions. Why is this? It is because, during his time as heir apparent, he already fully understood the likes and dislikes of the people in the realm. Hence, even though he did not discuss matters of state, he knew that no one in the realm harbored rebellious intentions. ("Charge to Yue" 4.4.3)

It is as if the active teaching scene continues as teachers and pupils think through the potentially dire political consequences of understanding "beamed shack," as the *Commentary* tells them to, as mourning hut; they address objections that will surely be raised once the *Documents* is truly adopted as a guide to rulership.

Our reading of "Charge to Yue" as one extended scene that offers an exchange on the appropriate interpretation of the term "beamed shack" in the *Documents* is strengthened by the fact that a late-twelfth-, early-thirteenth-century source also presents the three fragments (4.4.1, 4.4.2, and 4.4.3) as belonging together.[109] This sequence is rather unusual for the *Great Commentary*, which, as a reconstituted text, often appears as a loose collection of fragments. It allows one to imagine the text as the written condensation of an actual teaching scene with a setting that might have been like the one depicted on an Eastern Han stone from Chengdu (fig. 6).

Fig. 6. Anonymous, *Teaching the Classics* (Jiangjing tu 講經圖). Han dynasty. Rubbing, 52 × 57.5 cm. National Museum of History, Taipei.

AN *EXPLANATION* (XUN) WITHIN THE *GREAT COMMENTARY*

One section of the "Canon of Yao" (Yao dian 堯典) chapter of the *Great Commentary* (1.1.29) refers to an *Explanation*, the only time that a text by that title (or, alternatively, a commentarial practice by that name) is quoted in the *Great Commentary*.[110] As with the embedded *Commentary* fragments, the quoted text (layer 2) is sandwiched between a quotation from the *Documents* itself (layer 1) and further elaborations (layer 3).

> The *Documents* says, "Every three years he reviewed their achievements and after three reviews demoted the undeserving and advanced the deserving." (layer 1)

> The *Explanation* of this phrase says: "The purpose of the minor review every three years is to evaluate performance and make sure that affairs are taken care of; the purpose of the major review every nine years is to demote nonperformers and reward those with merit." (layer 2)

INTRODUCTION XLI

Those with merit are rewarded as follows: those regional lords who are given bow and arrow have the authority to initiate a military expedition; those who are given the execution axe have the authority to kill; and those who are given ladle-shaped wine cups have the authority to make sacrificial wine. Those who do not have the authority to initiate a military expedition have to subordinate their armies to those domains that have this authority; those who do not have the authority to kill have to submit their legal cases to domains who do have this authority; those who are not given ladle-shaped wine cups have to obtain their sacrificial wine from the Son of Heaven's domain, only then can they make sacrifice. ("Canon of Yao" 1.1.29, layer 3)

The last commentarial layer spells out three privileges that deserving regional lords can receive (the power to go to war, to speak justice, and to conduct rituals) and clarifies the procedures that lords who are not given one or more of these privileges should follow: they have to submit to the authority of more deserving lords and need to obtain their sacrificial wine directly from the Son of Heaven. The concreteness of the recommendations is striking: whereas the relationship with the lines of the classic is still apparent, the classic's message is here translated, for the benefit of the ruler, into concrete policies on how to review and reward the regional lords.

AN ARRANGEMENT DOCUMENT (*XU*)

Some texts in early China come with a "Xu," a part of the paratext (in the sense of Gérard Genette) that appeared after the main text and contents, and, as a minimum, specified titles of subunits of the text and the order in which they appeared but were sometimes accompanied by short summaries of each subunit.[111] Well-known examples of such arrangement documents are found in the three major inclusive texts of the early imperial period, *Mr. Lü's Annals* (Lüshi chunqiu 呂氏春秋), *The Master of Huainan* (Huainanzi 淮南子), and *Scribe's Records*.[112]

Such arrangement documents existed for the *Documents* as well, in various versions that reflect the complexities of the classic itself.[113] As indicated above, enough fragments of a "Xu" that followed the *Documents* on the Xiping Stone Classics of 175 CE have survived to enable modern scholars to reconstruct how the various *Documents* chapters were arranged on the stones. Scholars assume that such a "Xu" to the court-approved version of the *Documents* already existed in Western Han.[114] *Scribe's Records*, written around 100 BCE, incorporates what appears to be fragments of a "Xu" into a version of the *Documents* other than the court-authorized version. It offers some fifty-two segments of texts that explain how and why *Documents* chapters—or units that very much look like *Documents* chapters—came to be composed.[115] Sources attest that in Eastern Han several old-script scholars had access to an arrangement document that accompanied their version of the *Documents*. Then there is the "Xu" that was integrated into the transmitted *Documents* in fifty-eight chapters that became authoritative in Eastern Jin; often referred to as the "Minor Xu" 小序, this document has been split, its various parts added to the corresponding *Documents* chapters, so that most chapters now start with a formulaic account of how specific historical circumstances prompted a sage person of the past to compose (*zuo* 作) the chapter.

One passage in the *Great Commentary* reads as a "Xu."[116] The fragment introduces the circumstances that led Boqin 伯禽, the son of the Duke of Zhou, to compose "Oath at Xian" (Xian shi 鮮誓). It contains all the elements typically seen in these formulaic phrases: an indication of time and place, an event, and a sagely agent who in reaction to the event composes a text.

> Early in the Zhou, in both Huaipu and Xuzhou, riots occurred. Boqin attacked them at Xian and composed "Oath at Xian."
> ("Oath at Xian" 5.21.2)

Scribe's Records contains a similar passage. In comparison to the *Great Commentary* passage, *Scribe's Records* uses a more precise indication of time and also names the non-Zhou groups that rebelled (rather than just giving place names). There is also significant variation in the wording:

> After Boqin had assumed his position, the rebellion of Guan and Cai occurred. Moreover, the Yi of the Huai area and the Rong of Xu also both rose up in revolt. Thereupon, Boqin led his forces to attack them at Bi and composed "Oath at Bi."[117]

The "Minor Xu" includes yet another version of what prompted the composition of this particular *Documents* chapter:

> When Lord of Lu Boqin first resided in Qufu, the Xu and the Yi both rebelled. The Eastern suburb remained closed. He composed "Oath at Bi."[118]

If it were not for the addition of the sentence "the eastern suburb remained closed," the version in the "Minor Xu" would read as a pared down version of that in *Scribe's Records*. The *Great Commentary*'s version, in contrast, seems to stand apart from the other two: (1) it names the place of the attack and the oath "Xian" rather than "Bi"; (2) it uses *wei gou* 為寇 as a term for the rebellion rather than *xingfan* 興反 or *xing* 興; and (3) it refers to the rebels by place names ("Huaipu and Xuzhou") rather than group names ("the Yi of the Huai/the Rong of Xu" or simply "the Xu and the Yi.")

Does all this indicate the existence of a full "Xu" with different origins from the one used in *Scribe's Records* or the "Minor Xu" with 5.21.1 as its only trace?

ENUNCIATIONS BY CONFUCIUS

Lastly, the many passages in the text that feature Confucius and/or his disciples too can be regarded as constituting a textual layer within the *Great Commentary*: one finds comments of the master on how particular *Documents* chapters affected him;[119] dialogues between Confucius and his disciples on *Documents* phrases or sections, or on the *Documents* as a whole;[120] as well as dialogues or pronouncements of Confucius or his disciples on specific topics, often involving law and punishment.[121]

Confined as these passages are to just a handful of chapters, they can be interpreted as attempts to ally the reputation of the master with *Documents*-related traditions. Particularly noteworthy in this regard is 6.2.22 of "Principal Teachings" (Lüe shuo 略說), a dialogue between Confucius and Zixia 子夏 with an intervention by another disciple, Yan Hui 顏回. In the dialogue, Zixia uses lofty words to indicate what he has learned from the *Documents*, and Confucius praises him as "almost ready" to discuss the *Documents*. When Yan Hui calls his master out on this judgment, Confucius indicates that Zixia's view of the *Documents* is only superficial, as if he is only "peeping in from the outside," whereas Confucius himself has unimpeded visual access to the room in which all the treasures of the *Documents* are stored:

> If you peeped through the door without going inside, would you be able to see where deep-stored treasures are? Nonetheless, that they are stored should not be a difficulty. Once I, Qiu, wholeheartedly and purposefully entered the room. Before me, a high cliff arose; behind me, a great stream. Steadfast I stood there. That is how I came to see beauty through "Canon of Yao," affairs through "Tribute of Yu," good governance through "Gaoyao," measure through "Great Plan," duty through the Six Oaths, benevolence through the Five Proclamations, and admonishment through "Punishments of Fu." Having mastered those seven vistas, the ultimate meaning of the *Documents* issued forth. ("Principal Teachings" 6.2.22)

Mr. Han's Outer Commentary on the Odes (Hanshi waizhuan 韓詩外傳) recounts a nearly identical episode, with much overlap in wording.[122] Interestingly, in *Mr. Han's Outer Commentary on the Odes* the text the master and his disciples are discussing is the *Odes*, rather than the

Documents. This borrowing of Confucius's authority (and words) by proponents of different traditions hints at a mentality in which classical traditions coexisted as separate entities rather than a unified tradition.[123] Passages such as this, in which Confucius expresses his admiration for one classic, stand in contrast to other parts of the corpus in which Confucius does not advocate for one or the other classic but has mastered them all and understands the strengths and weaknesses of each.[124] Perhaps this contrast can be related to changes in the nature of classical learning over the course of Western Han: as becomes clear from the biographies of scholars in *Scribe's Records* and *Book of Han*, in the early decades of the dynasty most classicists specialized in only one canonical text, but later on many sought instruction in and were recognized for their mastery of more than one of the classics.

COMMENTARIAL TECHNIQUES

There is great variety in the manner in which the *Great Commentary* explains words or sentences from the *Documents*. Commentarial techniques go from a very direct relationship between explanation and the word or sentence to be explained to only a very loose association.

Explaining Words of the *Documents*

Various chapters of the *Great Commentary* contain glosses of words occurring in the *Documents*. For example, "Canon of Yao" glosses "incipient" (*shuo* 朔) as "to begin" (*shi* 始) (1.1.4); "Oath at Gan" (Gan shi 甘誓) explains "to battle" (*zhan* 戰) as "to strike fear into" (*danjing* 憚驚) (3.2.2.); whereas "Catalpa Wood" (Zi cai 梓材) defines an "orphan" (*gu* 孤) as a person "young in age but fatherless" (*you er wufu* 幼而無父) (5.10.1).

In some passages sequences of such glosses (sometimes in combination with a catechismus-style question/answer format) yield meaning, as in the following examples: in "Canon of Yao" a concatenation of glosses is used to explain a sentence of the classic; in "Principal Teachings" the technique is used to explain sacrificial performance as a positioning of oneself on the Way (Dao 道).

> What is the northern region? It is the region of hiding. It is where the myriad things are in the phase of hiding. Being in the phase of hiding, why is it called "winter"? "Winter" means center. "Center" means that the myriad things are stored at the center of it. That is why it is said: "The northern region stands for winter." ("Canon of Yao" 1.1.2)
>
> The meaning of the word "to sacrifice" is to scrutinize. "To scrutinize" is to reach. "To reach" applies to human affairs.

> After human affairs have been fully pursued, one sacrifices. "To sacrifice" is to offer. The meaning of the word "to offer" is to be present. "To be present" is to be in the same place as the Way. ("Principal Teachings" 6.1.10)

Sometimes, rather than serving as the basis for direct glosses, the words of the *Documents* are but a pretext for the *Commentary*'s own theorizing. One noteworthy passage in the *Commentary*'s "Canon of Yao" describes a supposedly ancient ritual according to which regional lords (*zhuhou* 諸侯) were assigned *gui* 圭 jades that they had to join during each court visit with the *mao* 冒 jade of the Son of Heaven. The Son of Heaven, if a regional lord had behaved poorly, could withhold the latter's *gui* jade until his behavior had improved. If, after nine years, no amends were made, the regional lord lost his territory.

> In ancient times, a *gui* jade needed a cover jade. This means that subordinates must have received a cover jade; they would not dare to communicate with the ruler on their own initiative. The Son of Heaven held the cover jade when he received the regional lords at court, and, when he interviewed them, he put the cover over their *gui* jades. Therefore, the cover jade and the *gui* jades are what sealed the pact between the Son of Heaven and the regional lords. The regional lords held the *gui* they had received when they visited the court of the Son of Heaven. A "pact" establishes relations. Those who had no erroneous conduct were allowed to have their *gui* back and to return to their domains. The *gui* of those with erroneous conduct were retained and given back to them when they were able to rectify their behavior. If they had not received them back after three years, their noble rank was slightly reduced. After six years, their territory was also slightly reduced. After nine years, their territory was completely taken away. This describes court visits between the regional lords and the Son of Heaven. If they behaved properly then relations were maintained; if not, they were terminated. ("Canon of Yao" 1.1.15)

As will be discussed below, the proper management of the relations between the emperor and the regional lords is an important theme in *The "Great Commentary" on the "Documents Classic,"* especially in the sections dealing with "Canon of Yao." The ritual of the jades that is discussed in this passage symbolizes the importance of the regional lords to the realm but also serves as a means for the emperor to discipline the regional lords if necessary.

One passage in the "Canon of Yao" chapter of the *Documents* describes how the legendary Shun first gathers in jade insignia (*rui*) of subordinate rulers (Si Yue, Pastors) and, after holding a meeting with them, distributes them again.

> He gathered in the five [kinds of] insignia (*rui*); and, when he had determined a month, he determined the day and saw the Si Yue and all the Pastors, and [again] distributed the insignia (*rui*) to all the princes.[125]

The relationship between the two passages is complex. In the *Documents* neither *gui* 圭 nor *mao* "cover" 冒 is mentioned: the concrete objects that were first collected and then distributed to the many princes (*qunhou* 群后) are called *rui* 瑞. The word *rui* also occurs in the *Commentary*'s passage but has acquired a more abstract meaning; in 1.1.15 it refers to two types of jade that belong to one another like parts of a tally, in other words, to a "pact." There is a clear mimetic relationship between what happens in both passages: a ritual of collecting and returning jades marks political time and steers a political relationship. However, the *Commentary* explains the *Documents* passage not by glossing its obscure language but by transferring the scene to the early imperial context. Moreover, the goal is not explanation but the creation of a new ritual the performance of which would define the relationship between emperor and regional lords. Still, the word *rui*, shared by the two passages, grounds the newly invented ritual in the *Documents* and hence legitimizes it.

Explaining Lines of the *Documents*

The *Great Commentary* also displays much variety when it comes to explaining lines of the *Documents*, going from direct explanations of the meaning of particular lines to loose associations of lines of the classic with either elements of political theory or historical accounts or anecdotes.

The *Great Commentary*'s "Punishments of Fu" contains the following example of a direct explanation of a sentence from the *Documents*:

> As the *Documents* says, "Bo Yi sent down the rites; for regulating the people, he used punishments." That means that rites preceded punishments. ("Punishments of Fu" 5.22.5)

The *Great Commentary* here reads one of its prominent law-related themes (how the administration of justice presupposes ritual) into a sentence of the classic. However, there is a twist to this too. The *Great Commentary* reproduces the line of the *Documents* as "Bo Yi sent down the rites (*li*)," whereas the transmitted version of this line reads "Bo Yi sent down the rules (*dian* 典)."[126] The *Great Commentary*'s reading would make no sense if it was applied to the version of the sentence found in the transmitted *Documents*. Such variants give a sense of the fluid nature of the text of the *Documents* itself in early imperial times, even where it concerns chapters such as "Punishments of Fu" (Fu xing 甫刑) that securely belonged to the court-endorsed portion of the text.

In the following example from "Proclamation on Drink" (Jiu gao 酒誥), the *Commentary* employs yet another technique. Rather than explaining a single sentence or passage, it seeks to reconcile two passages of the chapter on alcohol, one of which approves the social use of alcohol, whereas the other cautions against its overuse. The *Commentary* does so by pointing out that the two lines each had a different audience in mind: to promote clan cohesion, it is important that the clan appears generous to its members and, hence, serves them liquor; however, individual members of the family have to be careful lest they squander their personal reputations within the clan by becoming drunk.

> Therefore, "drinking to the point of drunkenness" refers to the intention of the clan, whereas "Be disciplined in virtue; do not get drunk" refers to the will of individual clan members. ("Proclamation on Drink" 5.9.2.)

A passage such as this, once more, conjures up the image of a teaching setting in which the teacher answers questions raised by disciples unsure how to handle apparent contradictions within the classic.

There are also many passages in the *Great Commentary* that quote a line of the classic only at the end, using a formula such as "as the *Documents* says" (*Shu yue* 《書》曰), or simply "as it says" (*yue* 曰); sometimes the connection between the explanation and the quoted fragment is clinched by the phrase "that is what it is about" 此之謂也. Often the linkage between the explanation—which can be a historical anecdote, a description of a ritual, or an element of political theory—is loose. The goal in these cases is not direct exegesis but to borrow the authority of the classic to endorse a particular position. The archaic language of the classic is thus connected to contemporary issues. This is a technique often adopted in other texts of the late preimperial period, such as *Master Xun* (Xunzi 荀子) or *Master Han Fei* (Han Fei zi 韓非子), or in texts firmly associated with the early empire (*Mr. Han's Outer Commentary on the Odes*, *The Master of Huainan*).

Examples abound in the *Great Commentary* and are easy to spot. We will analyze only one such passage here to illustrate the complex intertextuality between the *Great Commentary* and other contemporary texts. The *Great Commentary*'s "Canon of Yao" starts out in the following way:

> Spread presides over spring; when it culminates at dusk, one can plant grain. The Fire Star presides over summer; when it

culminates at dusk, one can plant millet and beans. Ruins presides over autumn; when it culminates at dusk, one can plant wheat. Topknot presides over winter; when it culminates at dusk, one can harvest and store. The yield from hunting and woodcutting should be reported to the Son of Heaven, and it is the Son of Heaven who will distribute it to the people. Therefore, the Son of Heaven faces south and observes the culmination of these four stars to understand whether people are relaxed or busy. If they are busy, he does not burden them with public tasks or raise a labor force. Therefore, when the text says, "Carefully transmit to humankind the rhythms of the seasons," that is what it is about. ("Canon of Yao" 1.1.1)

The passage links certain agricultural activities with seasons and the asterisms that define them. It closely adheres to the terminology of the *Documents*' "Canon of Yao" in which Yao regulates or creates time and space by assigning Xi 羲 and He 和 to take charge of various directions and their associated seasons and asterisms. However, it weaves "Canon of Yao's" terminology into a message that is not about calendrical creation but about the need for the ruler to restrain himself in the tax burdens he places on the people (*min* 民). The passage acknowledges, as was indeed the case in early imperial times, that products yielded by the forests (hunting, wood-cutting) were destined for the emperor's private purse.[127] But it warns the ruler that he can only requisition people's labor in the proper season, when they are not busily engaged with agricultural tasks on their own properties. For that, he needs to carefully observe the appearance of asterisms in the sky, as they alert him to the agricultural task at hand. The *Documents* phrase at the end of the passage, "carefully transmit to humankind the rhythms of the seasons" 敬授民時, is thus explained in terms of early imperial concerns about the need for humane taxation.[128]

A passage in the chapter "The Ruler's Techniques" (Zhushu 主術) of *The Master of Huainan* shows clear similarities with the *Great Commentary* passage. The passage in *The Master of Huainan* too stresses that the ruler should take heed of the needs of his people, but as part of a more general exhortation that the ruler should cultivate his heart so that it follows the Way (the methods for doing so are not specified).

Thus, according to the administrative policies of the former kings, When the clouds from the Four Seas gathered, the field boundaries were repaired. When frogs and toads called and the swallows descended and arrived, the roads were opened and byways cleared. When yin [*qi*] descended to the hundred springs, the bridges were repaired. **When Spread culminated at dusk, grain was industriously planted. When the Great Fire Star culminated**

at dusk, millet and beans were sown. When Ruins culminated at dusk, winter wheat was planted. When Topknot culminated at dusk, reserves of grain were stored, and firewood was cut. The ruler reported upward to Heaven, and he made pronouncements downward to the people.

The reason the former kings in those ways responded to the seasons and put all in order, strengthened the state and benefited the people, and populated the wilds and attracted [settlers] from distant lands was because their Way was complete. It was not that they were able to see with their own eyes and personally went on foot [to investigate]. They wanted to benefit the people. Their wanting to benefit the people was never neglected in their [own] hearts, so the officials naturally were conscientious. The heart is incapable of accomplishing even one of the tasks of the nine apertures and the four limbs [of the body], but in moving, resting, hearing, and seeing, all take the heart as their master because it never forgets to benefit them.[129]

The core of this passage (printed in bold) is very clearly related to the initial lines of *Great Commentary* passage; like its counterpart, it takes up language from the *Documents* "Canon of Yao" (varying from it in the same way as the *Great Commentary* does) and refers to nearly the same activities to be performed during each season. However, whereas the *Great Commentary* insists that its message of being reasonable in the burdens one places on the populace derives from the *Documents* itself, *The Master of Huainan* uses this tradition without explicitly referring to the *Documents*. Moreover, it wants to make a point not so much about the need to adjust the burdens a ruler places on the population to the seasons (which is taken as something everyone would agree to) but about how the ruler should go about implementing such policies: not by going out himself on inspection tours but by cultivating his heart in such a manner that he inspires all of his officials to work toward benefiting the people. *The Master of Huainan* thus bends the message of the *Great Commentary* passage (or one ancestral to it) into one about the need for rulers to engage in self-cultivation, one of the major themes of *The Master of Huainan*.

Elaborating on Themes in the *Documents*

The *Great Commentary* also contains many passages without clear links to the *Documents* apart from the fact that they feature the same historical figures, use the same vocabulary, or draw on the same general themes. These passages can be separated into theoretical passages (e.g., on the relations with the regional lords, on sumptuary laws, on rituals, on law, on the need to protect the weaker members of society), anecdotes (featuring either protagonists of the *Documents* or Confucius and his disciples),[130] or historical lore about Yao and Shun, and the Xia, Shang, and Zhou dynasties, thus contributing to the making of a unified, linear story about the past.[131]

In all three of these groups there is much overlap with passages in other texts, and, indeed, we often used parallels in other pre-Han or Han texts as a reference when we were translating. These texts include *The Bamboo Annals* (Zhushu jinian 竹書紀年) and *Scribe's Records* for historical passages,[132] the ritual classics for ritual theory, and Liu Xiang's *Garden of Eloquence* (Shuoyuan 說苑) as well as *The Kong Family Masters* (Kong congzi 孔叢子) for anecdotes. Even when parallels exist with other texts, the *Great Commentary* is worth consulting, as it often preserves stories, songs, points of view, or historical perspectives that are either unique to the text or appear to be earlier versions of stories that also occur elsewhere.

Indeed, within the vast intertextual universe of early imperial China, the *Great Commentary* occupies a place of its own, though one that is often not recognized as such. Here are just a few examples of the treasures that can be found in the *Great Commentary*. In "Gaoyao's Counsel" (Gaoyao mo 咎繇謨), the text of the hymn "Auspicious Clouds," is provided, including its famous closing phrase "As morning turns into morning" (*dan fu dan xi* 旦復旦兮); this phrase, not found elsewhere in the textual corpus, not only became part of the national anthem during the Republican period, but was also used to name Shanghai's most famous university (Fudan) (2.2.6). "Punishments of Fu" relates that, according to *Documents*' legal theory, improper sexual relations (*jian* 姦) should be punished with castration: this is a notable nugget of classical legal theory that too is not found elsewhere (5.22.1).[133] The story in "Catalpa Wood" in which the father is compared to a tree named "Upturning" and the son to the catalpa tree (with its fruit that hangs downward) is unique to the *Great Commentary* (5.10.2). More on the importance of "Tradition on the Great Plan's Five Phases" (Hongfan Wuxing zhuan 洪范五行傳) (7) will follow: its first part (7.1) shows the importance of the *Documents* "Great Plan" (Hongfan 洪範) chapter in Western Han omenological traditions; its second part (7.2) is closely related to the Monthly Ordinances (Yueling 月令) found in *Mr. Lü's Annals*, *Master of Huainan*, and *Records of Ritual* (Liji 禮記) but is rarely mentioned or studied in connection with this subject.[134] Our hope is that this translation and study will help to make the *Great Commentary*'s voice stronger as one in a diverse chorus of voices worth hearing on a wide variety of subjects related to early China.

THE *GREAT COMMENTARY* ON QUESTIONS OF POLITICAL AND SOCIAL ORDER

The prime concerns of *Documents* scholars in the early imperial period were to make their classic relevant to the burning social and political questions of their day. *Documents* exegetes had a strong conviction that their text, as the repository of the words and deeds of the early sages, had something truly valuable to offer in the rapidly evolving political, social, and military environment of early imperial China. Moreover, those who managed to translate their mastery of the *Documents* into concrete policy proposals that were accepted at court could experience significant boosts to their careers. Success at court did not come easy: not only did specialists in the *Documents* face stiff competition from others who formulated proposals based on a wide range of other texts; there also needed to be a synergy between the needs of potential patrons and the policy positions they could responsibly develop on the basis of *Documents* lore.

The following case studies introduce some of the *Great Commentary*'s major themes, while linking these to periods, or even moments, in the political history of the early imperial period. Even if these linkages remain tentative, they make the point that the *Documents* exegesis in the *Great Commentary* is far from a scholastic exercise but was meant to be applied concretely in the organization of society.[135] As is well known, that society, following Qin unification, was far from static and underwent dramatic changes before reaching its classical form toward the end of Western Han.[136]

CASE 1. NO MONOPOLY ON POWER: REGIONAL LORDS IN QIN AND EARLY WESTERN HAN

It is commonly thought that the early empire, with its centralizing tendencies, was inimical to the idea of delegating power to secondary rulers established in the regions. Invoked as proof of that point of view are (1) the decision the First Emperor made in 221 BCE not to promote his own sons as kings and award them with hereditary domains and (2) the steep decline in power the kings (*zhuhouwang* 諸侯王) of Western Han experienced after the suppression of the Seven Kingdoms Rebellion of 154 BCE. Classical theory, however, did not regard delegation of power to regions as contrary to the project of unification and, indeed, proposed a political model in which regional lords, in return for a share of power, contributed toward the integration of outlying areas into the realm. The *Great Commentary* contains many passages on the regional lords that can be taken as representative of this classical theory; they may well have been developed at the Qin court itself.

The *Great Commentary*, most prominently in its "Canon of Yao," provides a detailed account of the relations between the regional lords and the ruler in the center. It not only outlines the practical contributions regional lords make to the realm (as they delegate men of talent to the central court, execute military tasks, or participate in court rituals), but also stresses their ideological importance as participants in a system of corulership (*gongzhi* 共治). One of the most stunning sentences in the *Great Commentary* states that having such corulership is important as it allows the ruler to show that he is not bent on monopolizing power (*duzhuan* 獨專):

> Hence, through the exchange of worthy men, they became corulers, and demonstrated the excellence of a system in which power was not monopolized and in which the people were valued. ("Canon of Yao" 1.1.25)

Conversely, the *Great Commentary* also shows great awareness of the dangers of delegating power to regional lords: it details various mechanisms that are designed to prevent individual regional lords from overplaying their hands lest they endanger the unity of the realm.[137]

That the *Great Commentary*'s views on the regional lords were developed at the Qin court cannot be definitively proven. However, the regional lords were an important topic of debate at the outset of the imperial period. Contrary to what is often assumed, the question of whether or not to install members of the Qin dynastic house of Ying 嬴 (especially the First Emperor's sons) as regional lords (or kings) was repeatedly brought up for debate at the Qin court, even after 221 BCE. Furthermore, Liu Bang's words and deeds after he became emperor of Han indicate that he drew inspiration from the classical position in these debates. Despite Liu Bang's own assertions to the contrary, it is now well established that there was much continuity between Qin and early Western Han.

It is true that the First Emperor of Qin never installed his own sons as kings. Moreover, *Scribe's Records* asserts that the First Emperor made a formal decision to that effect in the year 221 BCE (the year of unification), as he chose to follow Li Si's procentralist arguments, an assertion that has led most scholars to conclude that 221 BCE was the year in which the debate on whether or not to install the Qin princes as regional lords was formally closed.[138] However, other passages in *Scribe's Records* present evidence that this debate occasionally surged to the fore again at the Qin court even after 221 BCE. One of these is the famous scene that led to the bibliocaust of 213 BCE: at a symposium in the Xianyang Palace 咸陽宮, Chunyu Yue 淳于越, an academician from Qi, presented a toast in which he insinuated that the First Emperor's failure to install his brothers and sons as regional lords had made him vulnerable to overzealous ministers who were eager to usurp their ruler's position.[139] Apparently, the question of whether or not to appoint the emperor's sons had remained a polarizing issue, and academicians such as Chunyu Yue might well have been using their positions at the Qin court to develop a model for the unified realm that included the regional lords who are so often mentioned in the classics. Given Master Fu's position as an academician at the Qin court, we speculate that he might have contributed, there and then, to theories on how to integrate regional lords in a unified empire, theories that then found their way into the *Great Commentary*.[140]

Shortly after he had become emperor of Han in 202 BCE, Liu Bang issued an emotionally phrased instruction in which he demanded respect for the men he had previously, during the civil war, endowed with a title and a domain (*shiyi* 食邑). He argued that they, like him, are to be considered "rulers of men" (*renjun* 人君).[141] This expression, here applied to men awarded rank 7 and above, resonates well with the idea of corulership featured in the above-quoted sentence from the *Great Commentary* "Canon of Yao." Landed titles delivered more than economic and social benefit, also endowing their recipients with hereditary membership in the ruling class. During his years as emperor (202–195 BCE), Liu Bang actively pursued a policy of installing his male relatives as regional lords (now called "regional kings," *zhuhouwang*), thus awarding them a place in the social/political hierarchy below himself but above the system of ranks (*jue* 爵).[142] Whereas there were important pragmatic reasons for these appointments, it is possible that Liu Bang drew on an already well formed political theory that justified their presence in the political hierarchy. It is significant that, even though the power of these kings was drastically curtailed during the reigns of subsequent Western Han emperors, the legitimacy of the institution *in se* was rarely, if ever, questioned.[143] Indeed, with the classical revival of late Western Han, the kings, by then politically as good as powerless, saw their symbolic power once more confirmed.[144]

In 128 BCE Emperor Wu asked his officials to deliberate instituting a legal obligation for commandery officials to more regularly recommend men of talent to the throne. The court officials begin their affirmative response by citing a passage that corresponds verbatim with 1.1.25 of "Canon of Yao."

> In antiquity, the regional lords presented to the Son of Heaven men of service. The first time a lord succeeded in advancing a man of service he was called a "lover of virtue"; if he succeeded a second time, he was called "one who recognizes worth"; the third time, he was called "the achieved one." If they did not recommend men of service, the first time their ranks were reduced, the second time their lands were diminished, and the third time they lost both noble rank and their lands.[145]

The passage does not say who these court officials were, and we do not claim that they were citing the *Great Commentary* as now known. Still, there is an important synergy between both texts, and it is conceivable that the person who introduced this nugget of classical lore into the officials' reply was connected with *Documents* traditions from the eastern regions of the realm where Master Fu had been active after the fall of Qin. In any case, in the *Book of Han* example, the process of translation has progressed further, as the regional lords of "antiquity" are now made to stand in for commandery governors, who, despite their elevated status, were not given their own territory to rule.

CASE 2. EMPEROR WU'S CALENDAR REFORM OF 105–4 BCE AND THE *GREAT COMMENTARY*'S THREE GOVERNORS THEORY

The year 105–4 BCE is the year in which Emperor Wu adopted a new calendrical system, known as the Grand Inception (Taichu 太初).[146] The change in calendar was accompanied by various symbolic measures, including a change to yellow as the official color and the adoption of official seals inscribed with five instead of six characters. All this was to signal the long-awaited beginning of a new era in which the phase Earth had succeeded Water and in which the human world, led by the emperor, was in full alignment with Heaven.[147] The reform package also included a change in the start of the year; henceforth the month chosen as the first month of the calendar would be the one that started sixty days after the winter solstice.[148] Not often mentioned is the involvement of *Documents* scholar Ni Kuan in the process of the Grand Inception calendar reform. Relying on *Documents*-related scholarship, Ni Kuan is the one who successfully advocated to move the start of the year three months later. As a comparison of *Book of Han* and *Great Commentary* passages on the calendar reform will show, not all aspects of the reforms implemented in 105/104 BCE followed Ni Kuan's agenda, indicating an environment of intense competition among advisors of different persuasions.

In 110 BCE, in a congratulatory speech to Emperor Wu at the completion of the Feng and Shan sacrifices, Ni Kuan had already alluded to the calendrical significance of the solstice that was calculated to arrive at the end of 105 BCE.[149] When the year 105 BCE had come, some court officials, including the director of astronomy Sima Qian, urged Emperor Wu to reform the calendar. Ni Kuan was among the first courtiers Emperor Wu consulted with. The emperor ordered Ni Kuan to chair a formal court debate (*yi* 議) on the appropriateness of the proposed calendrical change with the participation of the academicians at court.[150] After the debate, Ni Kuan presented the following concluding statement on behalf of his group.

> It behooves a true king or emperor to adjust the timing of the first month [of the year] and to change the color of [the official] garments. This, indeed, is how he publicizes his receipt of the Heavenly Mandate. After the changes associated with a new

founding have been carried through, the regulatory system should not duplicate that [of the previous dynasty]. If we use the *Commentary* to order the patterns, we are now in a Xia period. We are only shallow scholars, and have, so far, failed to elucidate this. You, Your Majesty, in your sagely wisdom, have energetically promoted the idea of change, thus having shown yourself to be a match to Heaven and Earth. We respectfully maintain that according to the system of the Three Governors (Santong 三統), when later sages duplicate former sages, they should go back two eras.[151] However, recently the succession from one era to another has been cut off, and the eras are out of order. It is only because Your Majesty, with your sagely charisma, has broadly examined the extremes of Heaven and Earth and of the Four Seasons that yin and yang will be followed to establish the regulatory system of the great brightness and be taken as a model for myriad generations to come.[152]

Ni Kuan's statement on behalf of the academicians does not address the technical inefficacy of the current calendrical system—the reason Sima Qian had gone to the emperor in the first place. Instead, taking the need for calendar reform as a given,[153] it urges the emperor to use the moment as an occasion to mark his receipt of the Heavenly Mandate by making changes to the start of the year and to the color of official vestments.

A cyclical understanding of history underlies the passage: history is understood as a concatenation of an ever-repeating sequence of three phases, the Three Governors, that succeed each other cyclically and in fixed order. That order is determined by the three historical periods from which the phases take their name: Xia (mentioned here), followed by Yin (or Shang), and then Zhou.[154] Ni Kuan's argument is that, with the end of the previous era (Zhou), they now find themselves in a Xia era; this he determined by going back two eras (i.e., from Zhou to Xia, skipping Shang). The underlying message is that this new era of Xia be marked by changes both in the start of the year and in the color of official garments. In Ni Kuan's statement as reproduced in *Book of Han*, there is no specification as to when the year should now start and what color should be adopted.

The "Oath at Gan" chapter of the *Great Commentary* contains a passage on the succession of the three eras (Xia, Yin/Shang, and Zhou) that closely matches the statement Ni Kuan made on behalf of the academicians. That passage, moreover, is much more generous with specifics:

> A king has to abide by [the traditions] of the era following the previous two eras, thus completing a triad that includes his own era. That is how he connects with the Three Governors (*tong*), and establishes the Three Regulators (*zheng*).[155] Therefore, the

people of Zhou made the winter solstice their regulator; the people of Yin, the thirtieth day after the solstice; and the people of Xia, the sixtieth day after the solstice. Thus, Zhou used the moment of stirring at the time of the solstice; Yin, the moment of sprouting; and Xia, the moment of forming shoots.[156] Because Heaven has the Three Governors, and things have the three moments of transformation, each of the Three Regulators has its own color. Because Heaven has three separate cycles of life and death, earth needs three types of king, one to preside over each cycle of life and death. Therefore, for Xia the regulator was the first month of spring, for Yin the last month of winter, and for Zhou the middle month of winter. Xia made the thirteenth month its regulator, privileged the color black, and started the new month at dawn; Yin made the twelfth month its regulator, privileged the color white, and started the new month at cock's crow; Zhou made the eleventh month its regulator, privileged the color red, and started the new month at midnight. That they did not make a later month the regulator is because the myriad things do not grow evenly and hence would not fit their governor. Therefore, it is necessary to designate only the three months of incipient growth as the year's regulators.[157] Through the Three Governors, the rhythms of life are ordered; through the Three Regulators, all-under-Heaven is governed. This is why the Three Regulators and the Three Governors are like continuous cycles, starting again when completed and returning to the root when exhausted. That Xia chose the first month of spring as its regulator is because it valued things that have already acquired form. ("Oath at Gan" 3.2.1)

While laying out the same theory of history as a triadic cycle of change, the *Great Commentary* passage is mainly concerned with linking the Three Governors (also featuring in Ni Kuan's statement) with the Three Regulators (Sanzheng 三正), a term that also occurs in the "Oath at Gan" chapter of the *Documents*. However, whereas in the classic "Three Regulators" refers to three principles of government, in the *Great Commentary* it is understood in a more technical meaning as the first month of the year. According to the passage, the first day of the year was supposed to fall at differing intervals from the date of winter solstice depending on which era/governor of the cycle one was in. The passage, furthermore, connects each era/governor with a color. The information it provides is summarized in table 1.

The passage from the "Oath at Gan" chapter of the *Great Commentary* clearly resonates with Ni Kuan's statement in *Book of Han* in that both refer to Three Governors theory and envision an orderly transition between the eras of Xia, Shang, and Zhou and their associated

TABLE 1. The Three Governors according to the *Great Commentary*'s "Oath at Gan"

Era/Governor (*dai* 代/*tong* 統)	Xia	Yin	Zhou
Regulator (*zheng* 正)	month that starts 60 days after winter solstice = first month of spring = thirteenth month	month that starts 30 days after solstice = last month of winter	month that starts at solstice = middle month of winter
Color	black	white	red
Time of new moon	at dawn	at cock's crow	at midnight

symbols.[158] But there is more. Ni Kuan's statement, as *Book of Han* reproduces it, makes a reference to a *Commentary* (Zhuan 傳) that had allowed his team to infer that "we are now in a Xia period." The *Commentary* Ni Kuan refers to might well have been the "Oath at Gan" passage now in the *Great Commentary* or a text closely related to it.[159] If this assumption is correct, one can use the *Great Commentary* passage to flesh out Ni Kuan's statement in *Book of Han*: Ni Kuan, on behalf of the academicians he consulted with, should then have proposed to Emperor Wu (1) to start the year sixty days after the winter solstice (i.e., late January or early February) and (2) to adopt black as the color for the official garments. Is this what happened? Sources indicate that, starting with the Grand Inception calendar reform, the year indeed began sixty days after the winter solstice.[160] However, they also indicate that the color Emperor Wu adopted along with calendar reform was not black but yellow. Two conclusions are possible: either Ni Kuan and his team won only a partial victory, and other advisors put forward more successful arguments as to which color should be adopted,[161] or our assumption that Ni Kuan used a passage akin to the one now in the *Great Commentary* is unfounded.

The setting and the content of Ni Kuan's statement to Emperor Wu in 105 BCE on Three Governors theory are highly relevant for two reasons. First, they demonstrate that, contrary to what is assumed in most of the secondary literature on this topic, Three Governors theory is more reliably associated with the *Documents* scholar Ni Kuan than with Dong Zhongshu 董仲舒 (ca. 179–104 BCE), a scholar of the *Annals*.[162] Second, Ni Kuan's statement is one of the early instances in which a policy proposal, explicitly based on an interpretation of the *Documents* put forward by the academicians, was adopted at court, even if only partially. This modest first success had much to do with Ni Kuan's double position as a member of the Executive Council (he had been imperial counselor since 110 BCE) and as someone with a reputation for "understanding the classical arts" (*ming jingshu* 明經術). Whereas alone the academicians might not have been able to gain Emperor Wu's ear, their association with Ni Kuan, a former disciple of the academicians who at the time held high political office, made it possible to contribute some of their scholarship to an ambitious calendar reform project that was the target of extensive lobbying at court by many interest groups other than classical scholars. Their 105 BCE piece of advice on the changes to the start of the year and official vestments, partially put into practice, represents an isolated instance in which classical scholars during Emperor Wu's reign were able to contribute to policy decisions.[163] It was also the moment at which the cyclical Three Governors theory, developed as part of *Documents*-related traditions circulating in classical circles, made its formal entry at court.

CASE 3. EMULATING FORMER SAGES

After Emperor Wu's death in 87 BCE, classicists were more frequently promoted to important political or advisory positions,[164] while the discourse at court became increasingly permeated with references to the classics. An early sign of this development came just a few years before Emperor Wu's death, when the elderly ruler presented Huo Guang 霍光 (d. 68 BCE), one of his officials at court, with a painting of the Duke of Zhou (Zhougong 周公). In the painting the Duke of Zhou carried on his back the infant King Cheng (Chengwang 成王, r. 1042/35–1006 BCE), and together they received the feudal lords in audience. The emperor clarified the meaning of the painting five years later on his deathbed: by gifting the painting to Huo Guang, he had intended to appoint the latter as guardian over his young son, whom he wanted as his successor.[165] As such the story should not be taken at face value and might well represent a conscious attempt to fabricate historical memories. The parallel between Huo Guang and the Duke of Zhou was central to Huo Guang's claim to power and provided legitimacy to the all-controlling power over the court Huo Guang acquired during the two decades after Emperor Wu's death. The Duke of Zhou was used because, certainly by Western Han times, he was regarded as a shining example of virtue: having served as regent for King Cheng, he voluntarily gave up power when the latter reached his majority.[166] The Duke of Zhou is an important figure in the *Documents* and, by extension in the *Great Commentary* too.

In the *Great Commentary*, the Duke of Zhou's relationship with King Cheng is invariably portrayed as one of propriety. For example, the *Great Commentary*'s "Praising the Millet" (Jia he 嘉禾) relates how the Duke of Zhou's reputation for virtue prompted people living in the southern borderlands to travel to court and offer a pheasant in tribute:

> South of Jiaozhi is the territory of Yuechang. The Duke of Zhou had been regent for six years, had arranged the rites and composed music, and the realm was in a state of harmony and peace. The Yuechang came with three southern and nine northern translators, and offered a white pheasant. They explained: "The journey

is long and far, with steep mountains and deep valleys. Since we were afraid that our envoys would not be able to understand one another, we came with multiple translators to pay respect." King Cheng gave the pheasant to the Duke of Zhou. The duke said: "A noble person cannot enjoy the gifts from a place where his virtue and influence do not reach; he cannot subjugate the people of a territory where his policies and ordinances are not implemented. How can I accept this gift?" Their envoy pleaded and said: "I received an order from my country's elders, and it says, 'For a long time there have been no windstorms or torrential rains. This must mean that there is a sage in the central domains. Given that that is the case, we should go there and pay a court visit.'" The Duke of Zhou then returned the pheasant to the king. He called up the spirits of the former kings and made King Cheng present it as a sacrificial offering at the ancestral temple. After the waning of the Zhou, such visits petered out. ("Praising the Millet" 5.7.2)

Note how clear it is in the story that the "sage in the central domains" who prompted the visit of the delegation from Yuechang 越裳 was the Duke of Zhou, not King Cheng, and how King Cheng immediately delegated the handling of the visit to the Duke of Zhou. At the same time, the Duke of Zhou remained entirely proper in his handling of ritual: aware that only the king can offer the pheasant to the ancestral spirits, he returned the animal to the king and assisted him in the performance of the ritual offering of the bird at the ancestral temple.

The story of the Duke of Zhou's deft handling of the visit of the delegation from Yuechang was exploited by Wang Mang while he was governing on behalf of the infant Emperor Ping (r. 1 BCE–6 CE). Like Huo Guang, Wang Mang was eager to boost his legitimacy by presenting himself as a latter-day Duke of Zhou. "Annals of Emperor Ping" in *Book of Han* contains an entry stating how a delegation from Yuechang, in the deep south, came to court offering one white and two black pheasants and then mentions that the birds were sacrificed at the ancestral temple.[167] The short entry in the imperial "Annals" can only describe a staged event that evoked the story of the Yuechang to demonstrate how Wang Mang, like the Duke of Zhou, was an exemplary regent. Stories linked with the *Documents* were also exploited for political use.

CASE 4. PRAISING AND NOURISHING THE ELDERS

Respect and care for the elderly was part and parcel of the sociopolitical culture in early China and affected the population at large; it cannot easily be tied to a specific period or to a specific doctrine. The "Statutes on Enrollment" (Fu lü 傅律) from Zhangjiashan 張家山 specify the ages at which elderly men are entitled to receive a staff, which entitled them to special privileges. Examples of such staffs have been found in tombs, including the one at Zhangjiashan (dated to 186 BCE).[168]

Classical doctrine, as found in the *Great Commentary*, agrees with this seemingly general societal tendency but seeks to ground it in the behavior of the sages of the past as attested in the classical texts.[169] In a conversation about the exemplary way King Wen ruled his community before he went on to conquer Shang, it is explained that King Wen already allotted staffs to the elderly, making differentiations between those who reached the ages of fifty, sixty, seventy, eighty, and ninety. The passage then continues with a description of how the emperor feasted the very oldest:

> The audience completed, they were escorted by carriage to their lodgings. The Son of Heaven considered feasting the village elders important. Diviners and healers attended to them in front, chanting charms so that they would not choke. They mounted small-wheeled carriages as the musicians who performed throughout the meal escorted them home. If the ruler wished to consult them, he would go to their residence the next day, accompanied by precious gifts. ("Principal Teachings" 6.2.23)

According to records, a ceremony at the central court to nourish the elders took place at least twice during the Han, once in 6 CE and once in 59 CE, in a ritual building called the "Circular Moat" (Biyong).[170] The description of the ceremony of 59 CE, part of an address by Emperor Ming 明 to his deceased father,[171] matches the passage from the *Great Commentary* in some of its details:[172] special carriages that were to guarantee a maximum of comfort to their elderly riders, the charms intended to prevent the elderly from choking on their food, the personal interventions of the ruler, musical performances.

> And in this auspicious month, on a favorable day, [I] have again set foot in the Circular Moat, where [I] served the Threefold Elder (Sanlao) as [my] father and the Fivefold Experienced (Wugeng) as [my] elder brother. They rode in **comfortable carriages with soft wheels**. I handed them the ascent cords [for climbing into their carriages.] Nobles and kings set forth dishes, and the [three] excellencies and [nine] ministers offered them delicacies to eat. I bared and cut up the meat and handed them their wine cups so they could rinse their mouths. **Charms** [against] **choking** and suffocating were chanted before and behind [them]. Above they sang "The Call of the Deer," and below the flutes played "The New Palace." **Dancers** performed in eight rows, and the dance "The Myriad" was executed in the courtyard.[173]

There is no doubt that this ceremony—and most likely its predecessor in 6 CE as well—was a kind of enactment of a passage like the one in the *Great Commentary*.[174] Emperor Ming, in his ritual in honor of the Threefold Elder and the Fivefold Experienced, is doing more than simply honoring the elderly (something that was already part of the political culture); he is restaging a performance at the Circular Moat, a ritual site that is attested in the classics, and according to a script that is detailed in commentarial texts to the classics. The mediation of politico-ritual practices through the textual universe of the classics was in full swing by the first century CE. The *Great Commentary*, widely available during the Eastern Han, likely played an important role in this process, even if it is difficult to pin down with any precision. Like other commentarial texts, the *Great Commentary* offered the court concrete hints regarding how to translate the obscure language of the classics into something that could be implemented in practice, enabling the ruler to emulate the sages of the past.[175]

CASE 5. LAW AND THE *ZOUYANSHU* FROM ZHANGJIASHAN

Law is the dominant topic in the *Great Commentary*'s "Punishments of Fu."[176] The chapter starts out with what looks like a simple body of law in five rubrics.

> Those who trespass passes or bridges, transgress the city walls, or seize and steal: their punishment is to have their legs cut off at the knee.
>
> Those men and women who have improper sexual relations: their punishment is castration.
>
> Those who offend against or alter their lord's decrees, who fail to abide by the regulations concerning carriages or clothing, who engage in seditious acts, thievery, and robbery, or who injure others: their punishment is to have their nose cut off.
>
> Those who serve those they should not serve, who enter and leave without authorization, or who utter inauspicious words: their punishment is tattooing.
>
> Those who surrender to rebels and bandits, who plunder, rob, and embezzle: their punishment is death. ("Punishments of Fu" 5.22.1)

The same Five Punishments are enumerated in the corresponding chapter in the *Documents* ("Punishments of Fu/Lü") with the sums required to redeem them. The *Great Commentary* does not mention redemption but specifies the crimes that lead to each of the Five Punishments.[177]

Charles Sanft has noted how some *Documents* chapters accept penal law as a permanent feature of human society, whereas others only condone it as a necessary evil to be abolished once a more sagely society was realized.[178] The *Great Commentary*'s "Punishments of Fu" comes down on the former side of the debate: as it links the Five Punishments with five types of crime, the text affirms the use of penal law as an important aspect of *Documents*-inspired governance. One passage (5.22.2) even explicitly evokes this debate: a disciple challenged Confucius by deeming the Five Punishments "not worthy of inclusion in the *Documents*"; but Confucius's response was firm, "The Five Punishments are an intrinsic part of the teaching."[179]

Having endorsed the Five Punishments, the "Punishments of Fu" chapter in the *Great Commentary* carefully defines the parameters within which penal law can be used. It insists that punishments ought to be harmonized with ritual and that law and ritual should jointly serve societal goals. Many passages stress the importance of applying the law fairly, leniently, with compassion for the criminal. It condemns practices—no doubt prevalent in the administration of law in early imperial China—such as bribery, sloppy investigations that lead to wrongful convictions, or a failure to allow all parties involved to make statements. The administration of justice, according to the *Great Commentary*'s "Punishments of Fu," is not a mechanical process in which a determination of the nature of the crime inescapably entails specific punishments. Instead, again and again, a case is made that justice requires the full participation of the judge/administrator not as an expert in the text of the law, but as a sensible (*qing* 情) human being, capable of allowing for extenuating circumstances and, when called for, showing lenience toward vulnerable criminals. Law is an intrinsic part of society, but all depends on its implementation.

Anthony Barbieri-Low and Robin Yates, in their translation of *Book of Submitted Doubtful Cases* (Zouyanshu 奏讞書; 186 BCE), have proposed that the text, although based on genuine cases, was compiled with the purpose of entertaining legal scribes. They discern an underlying narrative in which petty criminals have Confucius's last name (Kong 孔, case 4.22) and in which magistrates who invoke attenuating circumstances (as in case 4.4 but most clearly in case 4.18) are ridiculed in favor of magistrates who strictly follow the letter of the law. They go as far as to call Tui 雁, the magistrate in case 4.18 who wrote to the emperor in person to plead for mercy, a "closet Confucian."[180] At the least, the fact that a local judiciary scribe recalled gossip about the newly arrived magistrate to the effect that he "was unusual and was not of the same type as other Magistrates"[181] indicates that there were ideological fissures among magistrates. In *Book of Submitted Doubtful Cases*, Magistrate Tui ends up with a criminal conviction. The *Great Commentary*'s "Punishments of Fu," instead, would have provided fairly concrete arguments to back up Magistrate Tui in his wish to "let guilty persons go." Whether *Documents*-related traditions on law inspired Magistrate Tui and likeminded individuals in early Western Han is, unfortunately, untraceable; however, such traditions were part of a chorus of alternative voices on the issue of law in the early imperial period.

CASE 6. READING SIGNS: "TRADITION ON
THE GREAT PLAN'S FIVE PHASES"

To interpret signs that warned, with different degrees of urgency, of impending harm was an important technical art in early China.[182] Throughout Western Han but increasingly by the first century BCE, many classicists occupied themselves with sign interpretation, be it signs observed by contemporaries or signs recorded in texts of the past.[183] Thus Dong Zhongshu used the *Annals*, and Jing Fang 京房 (d. 37 BCE) availed himself of traditions associated with the *Changes* (Yi 易). It is less well known that the *Documents* too, particularly its "Great Plan" chapter, was an important source of sign interpretation in Western Han. "Tradition on the Great Plan's Five Phases"(Hongfan Wuxing zhuan 鴻范五行傳), a three-part text integrated into Qing editions of the *Great Commentary*, reveals that a flourishing mantic tradition based on the *Documents*' "Great Plan" indeed existed. Passages in *Book of Han* reveal the use of the text (or a text like it) at the Han court after Emperor Wu's demise.

"Tradition on the Great Plan's Five Phases" is built around key terms from the *Documents*' "Great Plan," such as Five Material Resources/Phases (Wuxing), Five Tasks (Wushi 五事), and the Royal Standard (Wangji 王機).[184] It interprets natural disasters and prodigies (*zaiyi* 災異) as an imbalance of the Five Phases that is caused by the failure of agents to heed the Five Tasks and the Royal Standard, each failure resulting in a particular type of harm (*li* 沴). The first part of "Tradition on the Great Plan's Five Phases" (7.1) explains these processes and prescribes apotropaic rituals to ward off such harms. Its second part integrates the Five Phases, the Five Tasks, and the Royal Standard within a set of monthly ordinances and seasonal sacrifices that, if executed properly, could avert the occurrence of the harms altogether (7.2).

The first part of "Tradition on the Great Plan's Five Phases" contains all the information a sign interpreter would have needed to interpret a sign of harm. As table 2 shows, the text organizes undesirable events (signs that something is awry) under six categories drawn from the "Great Plan's" Five Tasks—demeanor (*mao*), speech (*yan*), vision (*shi*), hearing (*ting*), mindfulness (*xin*)—supplemented by the Royal Standard, another central concept of the "Great Plan." There are various types of negative occurrences (scourge, punishment, extreme, deviance, anomaly, disaster, malady) that, depending on which of the six categories they are correlated with, manifest themselves in different meteorological phenomena, animals, body parts, and elsewhere. The categories are also associated with a color and a harm. Thus, when someone notices creatures whose lower limbs appear on their upper bodies or unusually long spells of rain, an interpreter could categorize these signs as a result of failing to observe properly the first of the "Great Plan's" Five Tasks (namely, "demeanor") and explain them in cosmological terms as a case of "metal harming wood." The Western Han exegetes engaged with signs on a practical level too, as they claimed the ability to dispel the underlying harms: "Tradition on the Great Plan's Five Phases" ventures deeply into ritual practice as it describes—complete with liturgical texts—the rituals needed to dispel the Six Harms (7.1.1 and 7.1.11).

Whereas part 1 of "Tradition on the Great Plan's Five Phases" occupies itself with negative signs of the apotropaic rituals needed to dispel the harm, its second part carries a more positive message. As already announced in some transitional passages in the first part (7.1.8 and 7.1.10), it is also possible to avoid such harm, provided one strictly abides by monthly ordinances and prohibitions and observes seasonal sacrifices correlated with the four directions. Part 2 of "Tradition on the Great Plan's Five Phases" infuses the monthly ordinances and seasonal instructions—attested in several other texts as well—with language of the "Great Plan." The language of part 1 of "Tradition on the Great Plan's Five Phases" is embedded in part 2 within the list of ordinances of the first month of each season (in the case of summer, both the first and the last month): thus, to resume the earlier example of demeanor, whereas in part 1 it is indicated that disrespectful demeanor (*mao zhi bu gong* 兒之不恭) will result in "prolonged rain" (*heng yu* 恆雨), under the first month of spring, one is urged on by the following words: "Your demeanor must be respectful, and the corresponding blessing will be timely rain (*shi yu* 時雨)." Clearly, a ruler should not anxiously await the appearance of inauspicious bouts of rain but has some control over the weather provided he correctly follows ritual prescriptions.[185] Thus, part 1 and part 2 of "Tradition on the Great Plan's Five Phases" appear as each other's complements. Together they provide a complete guide that allows a ruler to prevent inauspicious signs from occurring and, if they do anyway, to attack and remove the underlying causes.

The eminent position of "Tradition on the Great Plan's Five Phases" among sign interpreters addressing the Western Han court might be linked to Xiahou Sheng's much noticed use of the text in 74 BCE. In that year, Xiahou Sheng tried to prevent Liu He 劉賀 (ca. 92–59 BCE), who had been appointed successor to Emperor Zhao 昭 (r. 87–74) less than a month earlier, from going on an excursion, arguing that the prevailing signs (prolonged cloudiness combined with an absence of rain 天久陰而不雨) indicated an active political plot against him: "If the sovereign does not abide by the Standard, the punishment is prolonged cloudiness. Sometimes those below will attack those above" 皇之不極，厥罰常陰，時則有下人伐上。[186] Here Xiahou Sheng is quoting from two different sections

TABLE 2. Inauspicious signs, correlated with the Great Plan's Five Tasks and Royal Standard, and the Six Harms

	Scourge 咎	Punishment 罰	Extreme 極	Deviance 孽
Demeanor 兒	insolence 狂	prolonged rain 恆雨	wickedness 惡	garments 服
Speech 言	usurpation 僭	prolonged dry spells 恆陽	anxiety 憂	songs 詩
Vision 視	sluggishness 荼	prolonged heat 恆燠	disease 疾	grasses 艸
Hearing 聽	crisis 急	prolonged cold 恆寒	poverty 貧	drums 鼓
Mindfulness 思心	confusion 霿	prolonged winds 恆風	early death 凶短折	fatty liver, too much sweating 脂夜
Royal Standard 王極	chaos 瞀	prolonged clouds 恆陰	weakness 弱	archery 射

of "Tradition on the Great Plan's Five Phases" as featured in the *Great Commentary*. He is invoking "its punishment is prolonged rain" (indicative of a problem with demeanor) from 7.1.2 and "sometimes there will be maladies such as those below attacking those above" from 7.1.7 (indicative of a problem with the Royal Standard).

It so happened that, when Xiahou Sheng admonished the emperor, an active plot to depose Liu He was indeed being concocted by Huo Guang and Zhang Anshi 張安世 (d. 62 BCE) at the very highest levels of government.[187] As *Book of Han* tells the story, Huo Guang was genuinely baffled that Xiahou Sheng, based on his interpretation of the signs he observed, had known about the still secret plot, and he summoned Xiahou Sheng. The scholar came and offered Huo Guang and Zhang Anshi a copy of a text called *The Tradition on the Great Plan's Five Phases* (Hongfan Wuxing zhuan 洪範五行傳) so that Huo Guang and Zhang Anshi were able to read (*du* 讀) it themselves and see how he had come to his prediction.[188] Ten days later, Huo Guang and others ("those below who attack those above") indeed succeeded in removing Liu He from the throne, installing Emperor Xuan 宣 (r. 74–48 BCE) as the successor of

Anomaly 孽	Disaster 禍	Malady 痾	Ill Omen / Inauspicious Omen 眚/祥	Harm 沴
turtles 龜	chickens 雞	lower limbs on upper body 下體生于上	blue 青	metal harms wood 金沴木
beetles 介蟲	dogs 犬	mouth 口舌	white 白	wood harms metal 木沴金
insects 倮蟲	sheep 羊	eye 目	red 赤	water harms fire 水沴火
fish 鼓	pigs 豕	ear 耳	black 黑	fire harms water 火沴水
earthworms 夸	oxen 牛	heart and liver 心腹	yellow 黃	wood, metal, water, and fire harm earth 木金水火沴土
dragons and snakes 龍蛇	horses 馬	those below attack those above 下人伐上		sun and moon move erratically; stars and planets go backward 日月亂行;星辰逆行

Emperor Zhao.[189] *Book of Han* further notes how, as a result of Xiahou Sheng's powerful prediction, "practitioners of arts associated with the Five Classics were treated with increased deference" 益重經術士.[190]

That Xiahou Sheng had used *The Tradition on the Great Plan's Five Phases* to correctly predict the downfall of Liu He—no doubt a very significant event in the history of Western Han—explains the continued popularity of the text. "Tradition on the Great Plan's Five Phases" in the *Great Commentary* must be akin to the text that Xiahou Sheng had used so effectively.[191]

MASTER FU, THE *GREAT COMMENTARY*, AND THE NEW SCRIPT/OLD SCRIPT CONTROVERSY

In much *Documents* scholarship, Master Fu's name is associated with the New Script version of the *Documents*. This is because Master Fu is the central figure in Sima Qian's story of how twenty-nine chapters of the *Documents* (thought to correspond to the *Documents*' New Script version) were retrieved from a wall after the fall of the Qin dynasty to subsequently arrive at the court of Emperor Wen. Given that the *Great Commentary* too is strongly associated with Master Fu, one would assume that the New Script chapters of the *Documents* form the sole target of the *Great Commentary*'s exegesis. This is not the case. Instead, the *Great Commentary*, while displaying certain features commonly associated with the New Script *Documents*, takes into account a wider panoply of *Documents* chapters than the twenty-eight New Script ones. This inclusiveness toward chapters that are not New Script is another indication that the *Great Commentary* is a Western Han text. It also lacks the bellicose attitude that generally characterized the new script/old script controversies of the Eastern Han period.

Among its features that are commonly associated with the New Script *Documents*, first, the *Great Commentary* provides its exegesis on "Canon of Yao" and "Canon of Shun" under one title, whereas one finds the two canons separated in the Old Script version of the *Documents*. The same goes for the *Documents* chapters "Gaoyao's Counsel" and "Supplementary Sacrifices" (Yi ji 益稷): the *Great Commentary* discusses fragments of both Old Script chapters under the title "Gaoyao's Counsel."[192] Second, the *Great Commentary* preserves New Script readings or variants for chapter titles: most prominently, like *Scribe's Records*, the *Great Commentary* uses "Punishments of Fu" instead of "Punishments of Lü."[193] Third, scholars have used a line from a fragment of the *Documents* that was retrieved from the Xiping Stone Classics of 175 CE, firmly associated with the new script traditions of early China, to demonstrate that the corresponding line in the transmitted (Old Script) *Documents* is corrupt. The *Great Commentary*, however, conforms in its reading of the line with the Xiping Stone Classics (the term at issue here is *qishi* 七始: the characters can be seen in the third column from the right on the stone depicted in figure 3).[194] These three features suggest a New Script affiliation for the *Great Commentary*.

However, the *Great Commentary* does not limit itself to the twenty-eight New Script chapters of the *Documents*. As can be seen from the table in the Appendix, some chapters of the *Great Commentary* (for both Wang Kaiyun's and Pi Xirui's editions) do not have an equivalent in the twenty-eight New Script chapters. Moreover, several of these chapters also have no equivalent in the transmitted Old Script chapters. In Wang Kaiyun's and Pi Xirui's editions, seven chapters of the *Great Commentary* do not correspond to New Script chapters (2.1 "Nine Offers" 九共; 4.1 "Proclamation of the Supreme Lord" 帝告; 5.1 "Great Oath" 大誓; 5.2 "Success through Battle" 武成/ "Great War" 大戰; 5.7 "Praising the Millet" 嘉禾; 5.16 "Proclamation at Yan" 揜誥; 5.20 "Charge to Jiong" 冏命); moreover, four of these seven have no correspondence with Old Script chapters ("The Nine Offers," "Proclamation of the Supreme Lord," "Praising the Millet," and "Proclamation at Yan").[195]

In many of these cases, these titles are not additions by Qing scholars. The most important witness here is the Southern Song bibliophile Wang Yinglin, who examined versions of the *Great Commentary* in circulation in his time. He provides three chapter titles that lacked content in his copy. Of these, "Charge to Jiong" has an equivalent in the Old Script *Documents*,[196] whereas "Praising the Millet" and "Proclamation at Yan" have no Old Script alternative. Wang also drew attention to two quotations from lost *Documents* chapters—"Nine Offers" (2.1) and "Proclamation of the Supreme Lord" (4.1)—contained in his version of the *Great Commentary*. Wang Yinglin concludes from his examination that Master Fu, to whom he assigns authorship of the *Great Commentary*, was familiar with the "lost old script chapters" (*yi guwen pian* 逸古文篇).

> *The Great Commentary on the Documents*, in the part titled "Traditions on Yu," has a chapter titled "Nine Offers." It quotes the following sentence from the *Documents*: "In managing my land, I strive to treat the people fairly so that they may be without presumption." The part titled "Traditions on Yin" has a chapter titled "Proclamation of the Supreme Lord" with the following quotation from the *Documents*: "Apply patterns to clothing, and high and low will be clear." It must be that Master Fu had also seen the lost old script chapters![197]

Recent work on a copy of the *Ceremonials* (Yili 儀禮) that was archaeologically retrieved in the northwest in 1959 from a late Western Han tomb and is therefore more firmly dated than the *Great Commentary* has shown within that text a similar mixture of what, with hindsight, would come to be called Old Script and New Script elements. Whereas most chapters of the Wuwei *Ceremonials* correspond, with only minor variations, with the court-authorized version, one chapter, "Mourning Clothes" (Sangfu 喪服), is deemed to have derived from a pre-Qin text that did not form part of the court-authorized ritual classic.[198] Our working hypothesis is that this inadvertent mixing of old-script and new-script elements indicates that the *Great Commentary*, like the more securely dated Wuwei *Yili Ceremonials*, indicates a Western Han date for the text (with the possibility of later alterations and interpolations). Indeed, the open antagonism between new script and old script flared up only in Eastern Han.[199]

THE QING SEARCH FOR THE *GREAT COMMENTARY*

During the Qing dynasty, several scholars embarked on a quest to recover the text of the *Great Commentary*. These scholars belonged to a movement known for its innovative philological methods (*kaozheng* 考證) that, over time, came to embrace New Script texts as more authentic than and therefore superior to their Old Script counterparts. The movement, both in its inception in the late Ming and during its revival in the late eighteenth and nineteenth centuries, had clear political overtones, seeking to use texts to reform a sociopolitical system that was perceived as ossified and easily corruptible. The Gongyang commentary to the *Annals*, with all its potential for political critique, had a particularly central role in this movement.[200]

Documents, too, was important. The new philological movement of the Qing dynasty was jolted into existence after Yan Ruoqu 閻若璩 (1636–1704) provided philological proof that the Old Script chapters of the fifty-eight-chapter transmitted *Documents* were forgeries of the fourth century CE. However, it was not until the early nineteenth century that scholars started to treat the New Script version of the *Documents* as the most trustworthy part of the classic and to raise doubts about the ability of Western Han scholars (particularly Liu Xin) to transcribe the Old Seal characters in which the old script texts were written into the script current at their time.[201] Simultaneously, Han learning (Hanxue 漢學) scholars of the Qing dynasty, who collectively preferred the textual approaches of Han exegetes over those of the Song exegetes, started to differentiate between Eastern Han and Western Han textual traditions and, increasingly, embraced the latter over the former.[202]

It is in this environment that Master Fu received renewed attention. Not only was his name firmly associated with the New Script *Documents* (in fact, the New Script *Documents* was often referred to as Master Fu's *Documents*) but as the reputed author of the *Great Commentary* he was also touted as an important Western Han classicist whose exegesis could bring the Qing scholars into close proximity to the intent and aspirations of the sages who composed the chapters of the classic. It is no coincidence, therefore, that several of the scholars who played an important role in the Qing efforts to reconstitute the *Great Commentary* were associated with the Han Learning and New Script movements of the Qing dynasty. Hui Dong had followed in Yan Ruoqu's path and, independently, came to the conclusion that the Old Script chapters of the *Documents* were inauthentic;[203] Hui Dong would be the first Qing scholar to reconstitute the *Great Commentary*. Lu Wenchao was not only "a major figure in the transmission of Han Learning to Changzhou,"[204] but also crucial in promoting the version of the *Great Commentary* that became ancestral to all major reconstitutions of the late nineteenth century. Chen Shouqi, who completed a major edition of the *Great Commentary* in 1830, was also one of first to promote the value of the New Script chapters of the *Documents* not only over the forged old script chapters, but also over the lost old script chapters that circulated during the Han dynasties.[205]

By the time Pi Xirui, the late-nineteenth-century scholar and author of the *Notes and Corrections to the Great Commentary on the Documents*

Classic (Shangshu dazhuan shuzheng 尚書大傳疏證), was active, these trends in favor of the New Script texts and the Western Han exegetes had been firmly established. It is no coincidence that Pi Xirui called his studio the "Hall in Honor of Master Fu" (Shi Fu Tang 師伏堂)[206] and that the first book he ever wrote was *Annotations to the Great Commentary* (Shangshu dazhuan jian 尚書大傳箋, completed in 1887),[207] the precursor of his *Notes and Corrections*, published nearly a decade later, in 1896.[208] In what follows, we will draw on Pi's *History of Classical Thought* (Jingxue lishi 經學歷史, completed in 1905) and on Xia Jingzhuang's 夏敬莊 1896 preface to Pi's *Notes and Corrections* to characterize Pi Xirui's approach to the *Documents* and the *Great Commentary*. Xia Jingzhuang, the son of a powerful Hunanese official and both student and patron of Pi Xirui,[209] formulates the major issues in his preface more bluntly and succinctly than Pi does in his. Pi and Xia both made differentiations among Han *Documents* scholars: sharply critical of Liu Xin, whose pernicious influence they trace all the way to Zheng Xuan, they situate the authentic heart of *Documents* scholarship in the first century and a half of the Western Han dynasty, when the new script version of the *Documents* was, as yet, unadulterated by the old script texts and when Master Fu's exegesis of the text reigned supreme.

PACE LIU XIN

Although Pi Xirui in late Qing concurred with Liu Xin's assessment of late Western Han classicism in two respects, he sharply disagreed with the main thrust of Liu Xin's letter to the academicians.

Pi agreed with Liu Xin regarding Confucius's role in the composition of the *Documents* and the transmission of the text into early Han. Like Liu Xin, he believed that Confucius edited an authoritative version of the classic in one hundred chapters out of a more abundant supply of texts and that this version of the classic was destroyed under Qin and transmitted to the Western Han court through the agency of Master Fu and Chao Cuo.[210] Pi Xirui, however, had absolutely no use for the old script texts that were so dear to Liu Xin and for which Liu Xin had wished to establish academic chairs, and he blamed Liu Xin for having overstated his case in his letter to the academicians. According to Pi, in his desire to "elevate and promote the old script texts," Liu Xin had become "extreme in his condemnation of the new script texts" 極詆今學.[211] Pi, therefore, calls the academicians' refusal to establish academic chairs for the old script texts "appropriate" 宜. He writes: "As [Liu Xin] already knew of their faults, why was it again necessary to preserve them? Rather than preserving them in spite of their shortcomings, would it not be better to abandon them because of their shortcomings?" 既知其過，又何必存；與其過存，無寧過廢.[212]

Xia Jingzhuang's preface echoes this judgment, when he accuses Liu Xin of having been the first one "to use the old script texts to confuse the new script [*Documents*]." Xia does not deny that some old script texts circulated in Western Han (he cites in particular the texts found in Confucius's residence in Lu) but thinks that this did not arouse a lot of controversy in Western Han. "The old and new script texts of the Han dynasty were in fact one school, without different aims." It is Liu Xin, through his bitter advocacy to establish academic chairs for the old script texts, who disturbed this peaceful coexistence of new and old script texts and pitted the two against one another.[213]

Pi Xirui and his disciple Xia Jingzhuang concluded that the best way to regain touch with the most authentic heart of the *Documents* and other classical traditions was to consult the Western Han masters who were active before Liu Xin. In the case of the *Documents*, that brings them to Master Fu and his *Great Commentary* as well as to the Simas and their *Scribe's Records*. Hence their adamant insistence that the author of the *Great Commentary* was indeed Master Fu even though they were well aware that much of what was in the text was not by his hand. According to Xia, "It is said that the *Great Commentary* was composed and collected, after Master Fu's death, by masters Ouyang and Zhang. This is no different from the *Analects* 論語, which was written down by Confucius's disciples. There is absolutely no reason to say that it would not be Jinan's 濟南 [Master Fu's] book."[214] In this manner, they make the *Great Commentary* into the repository of as yet unadulterated new script readings, interpretations, and ideas dating to early Western Han.

Thus, the evidential scholars of the Qing dynasty refused to accord to Liu Xin the role that he assumed for himself: that of a reformer eager to advance the old script versions of the *Documents* at the central court so as to clear away the pernicious legacy of Qin and get closer to the message of Confucius, the sage responsible for the constitution of the *Documents* and other classics in their most ideal form. The Qing scholars' efforts to redeem the spirit of the classical scholarship of early Western Han too was not unconnected from a political agenda, most clearly so by the late nineteenth century. As China was under the assault of a modernized Japan and the Western powers, nearly everyone realized the importance of engaging in political reform and shedding past traditions that hampered such reform efforts. The Qing New Script scholars believed that, by bypassing Liu Xin and the scholarly trends that he had set in motion, they would uncover a more vibrant part of the classical tradition, one with the capacity to change society and ward off the foreign threats. Liu Xin became the villain in a story in which portions of the classics were forged, and commentaries became ossified in order to serve immediate political goals.[215]

AMBIVALENT ATTITUDES TOWARD ZHENG XUAN

Undoubtedly, Zheng Xuan played a significant role in the transmission of the *Great Commentary*. He not only edited the text but, by composing a commentary to it (the only of the commentarial traditions to a classic to which he awarded that honor), he ensured that the *Great Commentary* would be read and appreciated for many centuries. At the same time, Zheng Xuan was regarded with suspicion by many of the Qing New Script scholars, including Pi Xirui. They respected his scholarship but feared that it was somehow contaminated by Old Script readings and interpretations. Once more, Xia Jingzhuang is the one who formulates this most forcefully. Xia argues that, even though Liu Xin's old script texts were not given official recognition during Eastern Han, the brief tenure of Wang Mang, who officially supported Liu Xin and his texts, was sufficient to get the word out and create a community of believers among Eastern Han scholars. These scholars are faulted not only for mixing old and new script *Documents* traditions, but for adulterating the text of the new script *Documents* with old script texts of other classical traditions, particularly the *Rituals of Zhou* (*Zhouli* 周禮).

> The first one to use the old script text to confuse the new script text was Liu Xin. Liu Xin came across an opportunity when Wang Mang was on the throne, and the old script *Documents* was given recognition at the court academy. Liu Xin added his own comments in chapter and verse (*zhangju*) and his own explanations (*xunjie*). Even though the chair for the old script text was abolished during the Jianwu era (25–55), Liu Xin's teachings had already spread, and Wei Hong, Jia Kui 賈逵 (30–101), Ma Rong 馬融 (79–166), and Xu Shen 許慎 (ca. 55–ca. 149) staunchly believed them. That Xu Shen, in his *Divergent Interpretations of the Five Classics* (*Wujing yiyi* 五經異義), when he explains passages in the old *Documents*, often replaced new script meanings with readings based on the *Rituals of Zhou* is a methodology that originates with Liu Xin. The popularity of Liu Xin's ideas was such that these scholars were all under the yoke of just two words: "old script."[216]

Xia draws a direct line from Eastern Han scholars such as Wei Hong, Jia Kui, Ma Rong, and Xu Shen to Zheng Xuan, all of them unable to escape the influence of Liu Xin.

> Despite Zheng Xuan's sophisticated understanding, in his comments on the *Great Commentary*, he still made many changes to its characters, changing its meaning, thus failing to preserve

the original teachings of Master Fu. Would this not have to be attributed to the erroneous ways of the old script learning? [217]

In other words, the *Great Commentary*, as a text that predates Liu Xin, is more pristine as long as it is cleansed of possible old script intrusions and readings that might have entered the text by way of Zheng Xuan.

Even though Pi Xirui's own attitude toward Zheng Xuan was more complex and evolved over the course of his long career as a classical scholar,[218] wariness about possible old script intrusions into the *Great Commentary* by way of Zheng Xuan pervades Pi Xirui's writings. In his *History of the Classics*, Pi, while acknowledging Zheng Xuan as a pivotal figure in reshaping the direction of Han scholars, criticizes him for blurring the boundary between new script and old script learning.[219] In the preface to his much earlier *Notes and Corrections*, Pi had already voiced his suspicions about deep problems with Zheng Xuan's approach:

> Since Zheng Xuan annotated this book, he should have faithfully followed the text. He slandered Ouyang for being sloppy and untrustworthy, instead putting his trust in the talents of Wei Hong and Jia Kui. He randomly inserts his own ideas, just as he did in annotating the Mao *Odes*, or changes the text as in his annotations to the *Rites* classic. He replaces *yuerong* 曰容 with *yuerui* 曰睿 and *dajiao* 大交 with *nanjiao* 南交 and uses the institutions of the Zhou dynasty to explain the Six Ministers mentioned in "Oath at Gan." The "Eight Earls" in "Canon of Yao" he wrongly claims to be Shun's officials. Zheng believed that the clothes of the supreme lord have five patterns and the perimeter of the town of the Son of Heaven is nine *li* because he was mired in ancient ways. This will inevitably raise issues. Recently scholars mixed the words of Master Fu and Zheng Xuan, thus masking the differences between old script and new script. Xizhuang (Wang Mingsheng 王鳴盛, 1722–97) flatters Zheng Xuan excessively in his *Latest Opinions on the Documents* (*Shangshu hou an*); Puyuan (Chen Qiaozong 陳喬樅, 1809–69) in his examination of the New Script chapters wrongly blames Master Fu.[220] I intend to isolate Zheng Xuan's annotations to safeguard the legacy of the academician of Qin.[221]

Putting this into practice, in his annotations (*an* 案) to passages of the *Great Commentary*, Pi Xirui frequently points to strings of characters as possible intrusions of Zheng Xuan's commentary into the text (e.g., "I suspect this is Zheng's comment and not the text of the *Commentary*" 疑是鄭注，非傳文). Moreover, in several of his annotations, Pi also directly challenges Zheng Xuan's interpretations, calling them "incorrect" (*fei* 非). For example, in understanding Shun's use of the "jade crossbeam of the revolving mechanism" to level the Seven Stars in the "Canon of Yao" chapter of the *Great Commentary* (1.1.13), Pi quotes extensively from the Han texts to prove that Shun manipulated the stars directly and deems Zheng Xuan's reading of the *xuanji* 旋機 as an actual measuring instrument (*huntianyi* 渾天儀) intellectually destructive. Zheng Xuan's interpretation, Pi protests, is not only anachronistic, but also sets off the erratic explanations of the old script traditions (*guwen yishuo* 古文異說).[222]

After the First Sino-Japanese War (1894–95), Pi became increasingly concerned about the deteriorating situation of the Qing and became an even stronger advocate of social reform. In 1897, he struck up a friendship with Liang Qichao 梁啓超 (1873–1929) and became deeply involved in the Hundred Days' Reform (1898).[223] However, there is no direct evidence from his *Notes and Corrections* that he mobilized his work on the *Great Commentary* in the cause of the reformers.

PI XIRUI AND WANG KAIYUN

The position of Pi Xirui in the Old Script/New Script debate as it played out in late-nineteenth-century China is important not only because his views on this issue are easy to establish, but also because his *Notes and Corrections* shaped the present reading of the *Great Commentary*. But what about Wang Kaiyun, the author of the edition of the *Great Commentary* that we are translating here? Despite the textual differences between Pi's and Wang's editions, ideologically, Pi and Wang are very much in agreement.

Even though Wang Kaiyun outlived Pi Xirui, he was the senior of the two, and Wang, who like Pi Xirui was from Hunan, served as a mentor of sorts to Pi. Wang wrote a poem when Pi Xirui had his first successes in the examination system in 1873;[224] and, in 1894, Pi recalled an earlier period in his life when Wang Kaiyun encouraged him to focus on the study of a single classic (advice Pi Xirui did not heed).[225] Wang's work on the *Great Commentary* also predates that of Pi Xirui. Wang Kaiyun, who claims to have started his work on the *Documents* at age twenty-five (in 1857), states in his preface that he finished two versions of his edition of the *Great Commentary* (the *Shangshu dazhuan buzhu*), in 1871 and in 1885. Pi Xirui, in contrast, completed his first book on the *Great Commentary* in 1887 and continued altering and correcting it until the publication of his *Notes and Corrections* in 1896. Pi Xirui does not seem to have had a complete copy of Wang's work available; Wang, from his side, seems to have eagerly awaited the publication of Pi Xirui's *Notes and Corrections*. Pi Xirui's chronological biography for 1896 notes how "Wang Kaiyun had strong words of praise for Pi Xirui's *Shangshu dazhuan shuzheng*, for its accurate and precise use of evidence. Given that his grandson still had not received instruction in the *Documents*,

Wang Kaiyun said that he would wait until Pi Xirui's *shuzheng* came out so that he could use it to teach his grandson."[226]

Wang Kaiyun's preface does not dwell much on the rationale behind his approach to the *Great Commentary*, choosing, instead, to point out the good and bad points of previous efforts at reconstitution. That he was on the same ideological ground as Pi Xirui is revealed in his statement that his goal was "to expound Master Fu's ideas in order to replace those of Zheng Xuan" 多申伏以易鄭.[227]

In their zeal to promote the New Script texts over the Old Script texts, which they regarded as possible or outright forgeries, late Qing scholars seem to have glossed over the fact that scholars in Western and Eastern Han (including perhaps Master Fu himself) had at their disposal old script texts that they regarded as genuine. Unlike the Song scholar Wang Yinglin, who called attention to the importance of the "lost old script chapters" to Master Fu and his *Great Commentary*, Wang Kaiyun and Pi Xirui do not dwell on the reasons for the presence of Old Script chapters in the *Great Commentary* as they try to associate the master and his commentary entirely with New Script traditions. Moreover, wishing to get as close as possible to the sages whose traces are captured in the *Documents*, they sometimes fail to see how embedded the *Great Commentary*, despite all of its classicizing tendencies, is in the particular political culture of Western Han.

TEXTUAL TRANSMISSION OF THE *GREAT COMMENTARY*

Compilers' prefaces, biographical comments by scholars, and the appearance of the *Great Commentary* in the various editions inform our understanding of the transmission of text as well as its reconstitution during the Qing dynasty.

To briefly summarize its early history, the *Great Commentary* came into being in the Western Han period owing to the collective efforts of *Documents* scholars who regarded Master Fu as their teacher. Liu Xiang obtained a *Commentary* in forty-one *pian* and reported it to the emperor.[228] Almost two centuries later, Zheng Xuan reorganized this text into eighty-three *pian* and added a "Xu";[229] he also wrote a commentary (*zhu* 注) to the text, something he did not do for a commentarial tradition to any of the other classics. The *Great Commentary* is often quoted in a broad range of texts from Eastern Han through to the Song. The bibliographical treatises of *Book of Sui* (Suishu 隋書) and *New Book of Tang* (Xin Tangshu 新唐書) list a *Great Commentary to the Documents* in three *juan*.[230]

Although the book was collected in the Song imperial library and was recorded by a few erudite scholars and bibliophiles, it had become difficult to find a complete edition during the Song dynasty. Several editions are reported, sometimes with brief descriptions. The *Catalog of Chongwen Imperial Library* (Chongwen zongmu 崇文總目) and Chao Gongwu's 晁公武 (1105–80) *Record of Reading Books at the Commandery Study* (*Junzhai dushu zhi* 郡齋讀書志) both have a record of an edition in three *juan*.[231] Chen Zhensun 陳振孫 (ca. 1183–after 1249) claims to have seen Zheng Xuan's edition but states that, because of defective printing blocks (*yinban wanque* 印板刓缺), a more complete version was needed.[232] Wang Yinglin saw an edition in four *juan* and calls it disordered (*shouwei bulun* 首尾不倫).[233] Throughout several of his writings, Wang comments on structural features of the *Great Commentary*, notes the intrusion of passages that can only have come from lost old script chapters, or engages critically with interpretations that the text provides.

In the early Yuan, while composing his epic *Comprehensive Study of Government Institutions Based on Authoritative Sources and Later Interpretations* (Wenxian tongkao 文獻通攷), Ma Duanlin 馬端臨 (1254–1323) listed a *Great Commentary* in three *juan* and accompanied his entry with the notes he had found in the Chongwen Imperial Library catalog and in the works of Chao Gongwu and Chen Zhensun.[234] Ma makes many references to the *Great Commentary* throughout his book, even though it is not certain that he had a complete edition at his disposal. During the Ming dynasty, the text was not actively transmitted. Two meager passages appear in the encyclopedia *Florilegium of Minor Literature* (Shuofu 說郛), which dates to the Yuan–Ming transition period. The passages are listed under the rubric "Excerpts from Ancient Classics" (Gudian lulüe 古典錄略), and, as the word "excerpts" in the title suggests, the compiler of *Florilegium* never intended to provide a complete version of the text.[235]

In the early Qing, with the rise of new philological methods, the *Great Commentary* starts garnering interest again, and many scholars commit themselves to reconstituting the text. It is worth considering whether, in their reconstitution efforts, they started from scratch or had versions of the text to work with. Many scholars comment on the sorry state in which they find the *Great Commentary*, often calling the text "lost" (*wang* 亡 or *yi* 佚).[236] But what precisely did they mean by this? Should one follow the conventional reading of "lost" and assume there was no surviving text at all? Evidence suggests that, although there was no complete transmitted edition by the early Qing, there were a few defective editions in circulation on the basis of which Qing scholars' reconstitution of the *Great Commentary* was made. In the first half of the eighteenth century, Hui Dong and Sun Zhilu were the first to try their hand at creating new editions. These fed into the crucial edition under the auspices of Lu Jianzeng and Lu Wenchao. The Lu edition marked a new point of departure, ultimately leading to the late Qing editions of Wang Kaiyun and Pi Xirui.

The *Catalog of the Imperially Authorized Complete Library of the Four Branches* (Qinding Siku quanshu zongmu 欽定四庫全書總目) indicates that there were no printed editions from the Song dynasty, but there were still fragmentary manuscripts in circulation.

> The *Great Commentary* by Master Fu has not been printed for a long time. Outside of the imperial library, fragmented versions of the text circulated and were transcribed, but these contained errors, lacunae, and were so disordered that they were nearly illegible.[237]

In fact, one of these incomplete editions was also stored in the library of Ji Yun's 紀昀 (1724–1805) family.[238] Hui Dong, the first Qing scholar to reconstitute the *Great Commentary,* might also have possessed such a text. He turned it into an edition that includes, besides four *juan* of material arranged chapter by chapter, one *juan* of "Supplementary Material" (Buyi 補遺). Only in the supplementary chapter does he indicate the derivation of the quotations that he lists. This suggests that the first four *juan* are derived from a base edition in his possession. Hui's edition only existed as a manuscript and thus was not widely circulated.[239]

In comparison to Hui Dong who had four *juan* to start with, Sun Zhilu relied mostly on reconstitution, not on a transmitted text. Sun recounts in his preface:

> Now since the text in my possession has missing portions and has decayed significantly, and it is out of order, I had no basic structure under which to order the fragments. I browsed through many books, collecting the fragments and indicating their sources. I divided them into three *juan* and kept the old title. The titles of forty-one chapters by Fu Sheng and eighty-three chapters rearranged by Zheng Xuan have been lost. Whom are we to follow and whom to make inquiries of?[240]

It is clear that Sun had an edition of *Great Commentary* at his disposal, but its condition was too defective to be used as a base text. Most entries in Sun's edition were retrieved from other sources; he indicates these sources at the end of each entry. The Siku editors' *Catalog* confirms that the entries without source came from Sun's original but incomplete text.[241] Sun's edition circulated more widely than the manuscript copy of Hui Dong. It was printed and was collected in the *Siku quanshu*.[242] As Sun was a native of Hangzhou, his edition was called the Hangzhou edition in the *Catalog*.[243] Dong Fengyuan 董豐垣 (fl. 1738–44) supplemented Sun's work with more passages attributed to the *Great Commentary* in an encyclopedia, anthologies, commentaries to the classics, and other works.[244]

Hui Dong's and Sun Zhilu's works found their way into the edition compiled by Lu Jianzeng, collated and supplemented by Lu Wenchao. In his 1756 preface, Lu Jianzeng claimed to have discovered another extant edition of the *Great Commentary*:

> This book was still extant during Yuan times, but no bibliographical entries were made during the Ming.... It has long been on my mind to look for a copy, but not until now did I obtain one from a book collector in Wuzhong [present-day Suzhou]. Although the copy still has missing parts, "Tradition on the Five Phases" is complete from beginning to end.[245]

Lu Jianzeng then invited the more established philologist Lu Wenchao, also of the Lu clan, to collate the text. Lu Wenchao was also excited about this discovery but cautioned that the text in question might have been a later reconstruction, "not the original text passed down from the Sui and Tang dynasties" 而非復隋唐以來之完書.[246] The Siku editors' *Catalog* refers to this text as a Song edition by stating that "recently a Song edition reappeared" 近時宋本複出.[247] Lu Wenchao admitted to the limitation of what philologists could do, claiming that "it would be impossible to retrieve what has been lost."[248]

In the meantime, the identity of the "book collector in Wuzhong" mentioned in Lu Jianzeng's preface provoked heated debates and suspicion. Wang Kaiyun, even though he used the Lu edition as his base text, voiced some concerns about the text's provenance. "Lu Jianzeng claimed that he had acquired an edition in Wuzhong, but he refused to disclose its origin. We do not even know whether it was printed or copied by hand."[249] Yan Yuanzhao 嚴元照 (1773–1817) suspected that the book collector of Wuzhong was in fact Hui Dong.[250] Between 1754 and 1758, Hui Dong had assisted Lu Jianzeng, who was then the salt distribution commissioner, in compiling his multivolume *Collection from Elegant Rain Studio* (Yayutang congshu 雅雨堂叢書), which includes the *Great Commentary*.[251] Hui Dong's edition does share a significant portion of text with Lu's, especially a three-part version of "Tradition on the Great Plan's Five Phases" that does not exist in any other edition of the time.[252]

In 1757, Lu Wenchao compared the text found by Lu Jianzeng with Sun Zhilu's edition and concluded that Lu Jianzeng's text was more substantive and complete.[253] Lu Wenchao, after having collated the two texts, further added two *juan* of supplementary materials (*buyi* 補遺) and one *juan* of textual variants (*kaoyi* 考異).[254] The endorsement of a scholar of Lu Wenchao's stature helped to establish the authority of the edition in possession of the Lu family. It was repeatedly printed and circulated either as a stand-alone monograph or as part of a series. For the remainder of the Qing dynasty, this edition became the base text for all future reconstitution efforts.

At least eleven reconstitutions were attempted based on the Lu edition; they used a variety of methods and strategies. Wang Mo 王謨 (fl. 1778) concentrated on collecting missing or variant quotations from the Han and early medieval periods specifically. The texts of Yao Dongsheng 姚東昇 (1782–1835) and Wang Renjun 王仁俊 (1866–1913) consist only of supplementary materials. Ren Zhaolin 任兆麟 (fl. 1780s) collected excerpts from the *Great Commentary* in his *Compiled Records from the Forest of Arts* (Yilin shuji 藝林述記), which was originally prepared as a textbook for his family school.

Chen Shouqi, Pi Xirui, and Wang Kaiyun used the editions of Lu Jianzeng and Sun Zhilu to compile the most comprehensive editions, which also include supplementary passages and extensive comments. Chen Shouqi, confidently titling his text the *Great Commentary*'s "definitive edition" (*dingben* 定本), completed his work in 1796. Chen included in this edition one chapter that contains his preface and a record (*lu* 錄) providing an annotated list of written records, paintings, and steles pertaining to Master Fu. The contents show that Chen especially valued Zheng Xuan's commentary for its interpretation of rituals and the Five Phases: "Zheng Xuan, the master classicist of a hundred generations, annotated the *Great Commentary* alone. In his explanations of the three classics on *Ritual* and in his annotations of the old script *Documents* . . . he always uses the *Great Commentary* to clarify the issue."[255]

Not satisfied with the work of Sun and Chen, Wang Kaiyun reverted to the Lu edition, which he supplemented as he saw fit. However, Wang is not always clear about the editorial choices that he made.[256] Shortly before completing his edition in 1885, Wang accepted an offer from Ding Baozhen 丁寶楨 (1820–86), the governor-general of Sichuan who was a well-known advocate of the Self-Strengthening Movement, to become director at the Academy of Revering the Classics (Zunjing Shuyuan 尊經書院).[257] Consequently, he transformed the reconstitution he had been working on into a textbook for the academy.[258]

Pi Xirui built on the editions of Lu Jianzeng and Chen Shouqi but was much more partisan in his emphasis on New Script interpretations and in his preference for Master Fu over Zheng Xuan.[259] Pi's edition in seven *juan* was the last in this long trajectory of reconstructing the *Great Commentary* and is definitely the most comprehensive. Not only is it the most exhaustive reconstitution; it is also equiped with a formidable exegetical apparatus.

We have chosen to translate Wang Kaiyun's text. Included in the Ancient Chinese Texts Concordance Series and its e-version, the Chinese Ancient Texts Database (CHANT), it is today the most readily accessible of all the editions.[260] Moreover, perhaps because Wang had adapted his edition for teaching purposes, it is devoid of the cumbersome repetition of passages that characterizes Pi Xirui's work. We also like the fact that Wang has appended "Tradition on the Great Plan's Five Phases" as a separate chapter at the end rather than, as Pi Xirui does, incorporating it with the commentary on the *Documents*' "Great Plan" chapter.

TEXTUAL TRANSMISSION OF "TRADITION ON THE GREAT PLAN'S FIVE PHASES"

The textual history of "Tradition on the Great Plan's Five Phases" is inextricably related to that of the *Great Commentary*, and it played a distinctive role in the rediscovery of the *Great Commentary* during the Qing dynasty, when Lu Jianzeng identified it as an integral part of the latter text. However, during Western Han *The Tradition on the Great Plan's Five Phases* (Hongfan wuxing zhuan 洪範五行傳) circulated as an independent text, known under that title or simply as *The Tradition on the Five Phases* (Wuxing zhuan 五行傳).[261] "Tradition on the Great Plan's Five Phases" does not abide by the hermeneutical techniques of the other *Great Commentary* chapters but is a stand-alone composition that uses the language of the *Documents*' "Great Plan" chapter for its own purposes. Regular commentary to the *Documents*' "Great Plan" is present within the *Great Commentary*'s section 5.3.

AN INDEPENDENT TEXT IN WESTERN HAN

The text's early textual history can be pieced together from various passages in *Book of Han*. One such passage explains how the text surfaced at court. Case 6 of the section "The *Great Commentary* on Questions of Political and Social Order" above shows how Xiahou Sheng had used a *Tradition on the Great Plan's Five Phases* to warn Liu He, the successor of Emperor Zhao, of a pending plot against him. Caught off guard, Huo Guang demanded that Xiahou Sheng reveal to him the basis of his foreknowledge. At that point, Xiahou Sheng offered (*shang* 上) him *The Tradition on the Great Plan's Five Phases*.[262]

In another passage, *Book of Han* provides a lineage of scholars who availed themselves of *Tradition on the Great Plan's Five Phases*. The lineage starts with Master Fu's direct disciple Master Zhang, who passed it along to his student Xiahou Shichang 夏侯始昌 (fl. 90–80 BCE). (Xiahou Shichang was also the tutor of the King of Changyi 昌邑, the favorite son of Emperor Wu and the father of Liu He.)[263] Xiahou Shichang, in turn, passed it along to his clansman Xiahou Sheng, an academician at the court, who applied the text, with great effect, to the case of Liu He.[264] *Tradition on the Five Phases*, according to this same *Book of Han* passage, was also transmitted to Xu Shang 許商 (fl. 27–8 BCE); he and Xiahou Sheng are said to have taught the text to their finest students. Liu Xiang also made use of this text, as it had been transmitted through the Xiahou lineage. Liu Xiang's son, Liu Xin, instead used a different text.[265] *Book of Han* thus provides an impressive intellectual pedigree for *Tradition on the Great Plan's Five Phases*, one that covers the two centuries of Western Han.

Lastly, the "Bibliographical Treatise" of *Book of Han* asserts that *The*

Tradition on the Great Plan's Five Phases became itself the basis for further textual elaboration. The treatise lists a *Notes on the Tradition on the Five Phases* (Wuxing zhuan ji 五行傳記) in eleven *juan* by the hand of Liu Xiang and a text of the same title in one *pian* by Xu Shang.[266] Liu Xiang's work as listed in the "Biographical Treatise" is likely the same as his *On the Tradition on the Great Plan's Five Phases* (*Hongfan wuxing zhuan lun* 洪範五行傳論), a work that receives more ample description in Liu Xiang's biography:

> Liu Xiang collected records of auspicious and inauspicious events starting in antiquity throughout the Spring and Autumn period, the period of the Six Kingdoms, until Qin and Han. He analyzed these events, systematically commented on their auspiciousness or inauspiciousness, indicated the kind of prognostication that was used, and organized them into categories depending on their kind, each with its own label. There were eleven chapters in total and, having titled his work *On the Tradition on the Great Plan's Five Phases*, he presented it to the emperor.[267]

In other words, Liu Xiang's work was a catalog of events and associated omens from the past as he found them in historical records, organized within an eleven-part structure. (Liu Xiang, at this point, was already assigned to do cataloging work in the imperial archives, so he had privileged access to texts stored at court.)[268] *Book of Han* clarifies Liu Xiang's intent in compiling this catalog: he wanted to provide Emperor Cheng with means to control the Wang consort family, something that, *Book of Han* adds, Emperor Cheng was never able to do effectively.[269] Given the assertion of *Book of Han* that Liu Xiang, unlike his son, used the Xiahou tradition on "Great Plan," it seems as if Liu Xiang organized his catalog of omens within an eleven-part structure provided by *Tradition on the Great Plan's Five Phases*. This assumption gains force once we take into consideration *Book of Han*'s own "Treatise on the Five Phases."

RELATION WITH "TREATISE ON THE FIVE PHASES" OF *BOOK OF HAN*

Liu Xiang's *On the Tradition on the Great Plan's Five Phases* is no longer extant. Still, if one maps the actual structure of "Treatise on the Five Phases" onto a description of Liu Xiang's work (both in *Book of Han*), the similarities are striking. First, both texts are structured in eleven sections. It can be seen from *Book of Han*'s "Treatise" that these eleven sections derive from adding the Great Plan's Five Phases together with the Five Tasks and the Royal Standard.[270] That there is a relation with "Tradition on the Great Plan's Five Phases" is shown by the quotations

TABLE 3. Passages of "Tradition on the Great Plan's Five Phases" of the *Great Commentary* found in "Treatise on the Five Phases" of *Book of Han*

Structure of "Treatise on the Five Phases" of *Book of Han*	Passages of "Tradition on the Great Plan's Five Phases" found in "Treatise on the Five Phases" of *Book of Han*
Part 1 Five Material Resources/Phases *Hanshu* 27A.1318	
1 Wood/East *Hanshu* 27A.1318	7.2.3 + 7.2.18
2 Fire/South *Hanshu* 27A.1320	7.2.7 + 7.2.18
3 Earth/Center *Hanshu* 27A.1338	7.2.9 + 7.2.18
4 Metal/West *Hanshu* 27A.1339	7.2.12 + 7.2.18
5 Water/North *Hanshu* 27A.1342	7.2.16 + 7.2.18
Part 2 Five Tasks + Royal Standard *Hanshu* 27B(A).1351	
6 Demeanor *Hanshu* 27B(A).1352	7.1.2
7 Speech *Hanshu* 27B(A).1376	7.1.3
8 Vision *Hanshu* 27B(B).1405	7.1.4
9 Hearing *Hanshu* 27B(B).1421	7.1.5
10 Mindfulness *Hanshu* 27C(A).1441	7.1.6
11 Royal Standard *Hanshu* 27C(A).1458	7.1.7

from a "Tradition" the *Book of Han* "Treatise" provides at the outset of each section. The quotations can be found within "Tradition on the Great Plan's Five Phases"—the first five in part 2 (7.2), the latter six in part 1 (7.1)—as shown in table 3.[271]

Second, Liu Xiang used these eleven categories to organize a list of omen-inducing events that he culled from historical records; this is exactly what *Book of Han*'s "Treatise" does as well. *Book of Han* organizes events chronologically within each of the eleven sections; but in sections 6 through 11 the organization is even more intricate. For example, if, as is the case with section 6 in table 3, the overall organizational category is "demeanor" (*mao*), the section is further subdivided in subsections based on the various disasters associated with problems with demeanor (as listed in 7.1.2). These subsections are not marked by new quotations but stand out because each section starts with a new chronology. Very likely, *Book of Han*'s "Treatise" took over the organizational scheme of Liu Xiang's text but amplified its contents with more omen-induced events (stretching into Wang Mang's period) and with interpretations of these events by experts other than Liu Xiang.[272]

It does, therefore, appear that *Book of Han*'s "Treatise on the Five Phases" owes a great debt to the *Documents*' "Great Plan" tradition—mediated via *Tradition on the Great Plan's Five Phases* and Liu Xiang's work on that latter text. This, however, is not exactly what the "Treatise," in its introduction, invites its readers to understand. That introduction, consciously or not, muddies the waters. It mentions its debt to the *Documents*' "Great Plan" but makes every effort to demonstrate that "Great Plan" and the *Changes*' eight trigrams are but the inside and the outside, the warp and the weft of the same divine truth, a truth the historical instantiation of which is also revealed in Confucius's *Annals*; it also equates the *Documents*' "Great Plan" with *Writing of the Luo River* (Luo shu 雒書; transmitted via Yu of Xia), a divinely sent text that the sages can use to decipher the will of Heaven as it manifests itself via omens in actual historical events.[273] Hence the *Book of Han* treatise abides by a trend in Eastern Han (not yet as clear in Western Han works, including the *Great Commentary*) according to which the various classics were taken together as a set of divine texts with a unified message.[274] Furthermore, while crediting Liu Xiang as the person who organized the auspicious and inauspicious events found in the *Annals* tradition according to "Great Plan's" categories, "Treatise on the Five Phases" stresses that it wants to complement Liu Xiang's interpretations with those of others. It is particularly striking how, in the text of the "Treatise," the interpretations of *Chunqiu* master Dong Zhongshu are consistently placed before those of Liu Xiang.[275]

INTEGRATION OF "TRADITION ON THE GREAT PLAN'S FIVE PHASES" INTO THE *GREAT COMMENTARY*

In the Song encyclopedia *Imperial Readings Compiled in the Taiping Era* (Taiping yulan 太平御覽), "Tradition on the Great Plan's Five Phases" is cited as a chapter of the *Great Commentary*.[276] A Ming reconstitution of the lost *Six Arts in Genres and Subgenres* (Liuyi liubie 六藝流別) contains the complete part 1 and part 2 (except for 7.2.18) of "Tradition on the Great Plan's Five Phases"; *Old Books on Subtle Matters* (Gu wei shu 古微書) contains part 1 with minor variations and 7.2.18.[277]

By Qing times "Tradition on the Great Plan's Five Phases," with Zheng Xuan's commentary, was integrated into the *Great Commentary* as a chapter. All the Qing editions of the *Great Commentary* that we have consulted contain one or more of the three parts of "Tradition on the Great Plan's Five Phases." Indeed, the history of the reconstitution of "Tradition on the Great Plan's Five Phases" confirms that the division of the text into three parts (part 1 dealing with the Six Harms as caused by failures in the Five Tasks or the Royal Standard, part 2 correlating the twelve months and five directions with the Five Phases; and part 3 consisting of miscellaneous passages) can be made not only based on content but also by textual history. As cited in the "Textual Transmission of the *Great Commentary*" section of this introduction, in a preface from 1756, Lu Jianzeng made it known that he had obtained a copy of the *Great Commentary* in which "Tradition on the Five Phases" was "complete from beginning to end."[278] What Lu Jianzeng must have meant by the "complete" "Tradition on the Five Phases" corresponds only to what we designate as part 1 (7.1) and part 2 (7.2) of the text. Indeed, part 1 appears in all of the earliest Qing editions (Sun Zhilu, Dong Fengyuan, Hui Dong),[279] so Lu Jianzeng must have been familiar with it earlier, but part 2 only appears in the editions of Hui Dong and Lu Jianzeng/Lu Wenchao; therefore, it must have been the presence of part 2 in Lu's copy that caused his excited reaction. Part 3 (7.3) has its basis in Sun Zhilu's edition and consists of fragments Sun excerpted from other texts. Therefore, it was not part of what Lu Jianzeng designated as the "complete" "Tradition on the Five Phases." The editions from later in the Qing, including Pi Xirui's and Wang Kaiyun's, contain all three parts. Wang Kaiyun stands apart in that he does not merge "Tradition on the Great Plan's Five Phases" (7.1, 7.2, 7.3) with the *Great Commentary*'s commentary on the "Great Plan" chapter (5.3) but includes it as a separate seventh *juan*.

CLASSIFICATION OF "TRADITION ON THE GREAT PLAN'S FIVE PHASES"

Wang Kaiyun's decision was a sound one for several reasons. First, there is good evidence (see above) that "Tradition on the Great Plan's Five Phases" originally circulated as an independent text. Second, "Tradition on the Great Plan's Five Phases" displays an essaylike coherence that is lacking in the other *Great Commentary* chapters, including 5.3. Third, "Tradition on the Great Plan's Five Phases" uses the term *wuxing* in a meaning quite distinct from the way it is used in "Great Plan" itself and in the other fragments associated with the *Documents*' "Great Plan" in the *Great Commentary* (especially 5.3.2 but with the exception of 5.3.5).[280] Whereas in the *Documents* and in 5.3.2, *wuxing* refers to material resources, these have, in "Tradition on the Great Plan's Five Phases," become abstract categories that, when locked in relations of mutual harm, produce all kinds of undesirable phenomena.

Given that usage of *wuxing*, the question has sometimes been raised of whether "Tradition on the Great Plan's Five Phases" (and by extension the *Great Commentary*) should be regarded as part of the *chenwei* 讖緯 corpus, texts—usually rendered as "apocrypha" in Euro-American scholarship—that draw on terminology and passages from the court-authorized classics but are in fact predictions of a political nature.[281] *Book of Sui* classifies a text titled "Commentary on the Five Phases" 五行傳 under the apocrypha (*chenwei zhi shu* 讖緯之書), although it is unclear if the title refers to "Tradition on the Great Plan's Five Phases" or to Liu Xiang's treatise.[282] The late Ming scholar Sun Jue 孫瑴 (1585–1643), in his collection of apocrypha, quoted two sections (7.1 and 7.2.18) from "Tradition on the Great Plan's Five Phases" and ascribed them as the beginning of apocryphal traditions.[283] In the Ming and Qing periods, some shared this opinion. In the light of the discovery of a "complete" "Tradition on the Great Plan's Five Phases" by Lu Jianzeng, the Siku editors' *Catalog* considers this chapter the beginning of the apocryphal tradition of the Han. They also extended this view to regard the *Great Commentary* as a whole as an apocryphal text.[284] Such an opinion, however, was not popular among the scholars who collated the *Great Commentary* in the Qing.[285] Although excerpts from the *Great Commentary* frequently appear in *Documents: Accurate Observations* (Shangshu zhonghou 尚書中候), which clearly is a *chenwei* text, modern scholars have refrained from including "Tradition on the Great Plan's Five Phases" or the *Great Commentary* as part of their reconstitution of the *chenwei* corpus.[286] In our view, "Tradition on the Great Plan's Five Phases" is first and foremost an omenological guide that was both used in historical settings (e.g., Xiahou Sheng's reprimand of Liu He) and retroactively applied to historical omenological records (e.g., Liu Xiang's enterprise). We situate it firmly in Western Han.

NOTES

1. *Hanshu* 30.1705. On archives and libraries in late Western Han, see Nylan 2011 and Fölster 2018.
2. According to Yang Jie 2014, the title *Great Commentary* surfaced in early Eastern Han, that is, before Zheng Xuan's time; see also Hou Jinman 2000, 42–44. Li Huiling 2008 studies the twelve different names under which the *Great Commentary* is referred to in Kong Yingda's 孔穎達 (574–648) *Correct Meanings of the Mao Odes* (Maoshi zhengyi 毛詩正義).
3. For the possible meanings of *Shangshu*, see note 60.
4. See the section "*Documents*" of this introduction.
5. Elman 1983.
6. Assmann 2011.
7. See Lu Jianzeng's 1756 preface, quoted in the section "Textual Transmission of the *Great Commentary*" of this introduction.
8. Brashier 2014; Nylan 2000; Kern 2000a.
9. Meyer 2012. The obvious exception is the "Tradition on the Great Plan's Five Phases" (*juan* 7), which reads much more as an "argumentative" text.

10. The concept of "open philology" was developed by Jonathan Silk to grapple with the many parallel versions of Buddhist sutras; see Silk 2013–14.
11. For scholarship regarding the *Annals*, see Queen 1996, Gentz 2001, W. Li 2007, Csikszentmihalyi 2015, and Van Auken 2016; on the state of *Shangshu* scholarship in the West, see the introduction to Kern and Meyer 2017.
12. Clerical script developed during the late Warring States period and was the most commonly used script throughout Western Han. Seal script had developed earlier, out of Zhou script, and was standardized in Qin during the Warring States period; it was used in Western Han for decorative purposes only (for example, on seals). See Qiu 2000, 78–112. The assumption here is that Master Fu (and his disciples) converted what he had salvaged of the *Documents* (written in seal script) into the clerical script current in Western Han.
13. Zheng Xuan's "Xu," preserved in *Yuhai* 37.25b (708).
14. He was chancellor (*da situ* 大司徒). For his biography, see de Crespigny 2007.
15. *Hou Hanshu* 26.893; L. Cai 2014, 81–82. The *Book of Later Han* biography, itself a text of the fifth century, most likely is basing this information on a genealogy of the Fu family. Zhang Yan 張晏 (fl. 3rd century CE), in a commentary to the account of Master Fu in *Book of Han*, claims to have seen the personal name Sheng on a stele honoring the master; see *Hanshu* 88.3603.
16. Master Fu, in sources such as *Scribe's Records* and *Book of Han*, is said to have come from Jinan 濟南. In 221 BCE, Jinan was incorporated within the Qin commandery of Qi, which became the Western Han Kingdom of Qi in 201 BCE. From 187 to 181 BCE, it was incorporated into Lü 呂 Kingdom. Jinan became a kingdom in 164 BCE and in 155 BCE, a commandery under direct control of the central court in Chang'an. See Loewe 2000, 784 and 794; Zhou Zhenhe 2017, chap. 9. According to the *Zouping County Gazetteer* (*Zouping xianzhi* 鄒平縣志), Master Fu's hometown was within the noble domain of Liang Zou 梁鄒, which was in the hands of Wu Hu 武虎 and his descendants from 201 to 112 BCE. Chen Yang 2009, 8–9; see also Guojia Wenwu Ju 2007, 346–47 and 882.
17. Master Fu's biography is included in the "Biographies of the Classical Scholars" (Rulin liezhuan 儒林列傳) chapter of *Scribe's Records*; *Shiji* 121.3125–26; For a translation into English, see Watson 1993, 2:365–67.
18. *Scribe's Records* relates how, during the wars that led to the Qin unification, classical scholarship disappeared everywhere except in the area of Qi and Lu, casting it essentially as a local tradition (儒術既絀焉，然齊魯之閒，學者獨不廢也); *Shiji* 121.3116. Chen Feisheng 陳棐聲 (1864–1945), on the basis of a passage in the Eastern Han text *Obscure Records from the Cavern* (*Dong ming ji* 洞冥記), speculates heavily that in 251 BCE Master Fu, as a ten-year-old boy traveled all the way to a grotto in the western part of the kingdom of Wei 魏 (near present-day Hancheng 韓城) to receive the *Shangshu* from Li Ke 李克 (fl. 4th century), who himself had received instruction in the text from Confucius's disciple Zixia 子夏 (b. 507 BCE). Besides being improbable in terms of chronology, this speculation also leans heavily on the idea of transmission exclusively via written texts; see *Fu cheng*, 10–13.
19. It is unknown whether he came of his own volition or whether he was summoned by Qin as a useful expert. The possibility that he was already employed at the Qin court before unification cannot be excluded either.
20. Qian Mu 2012, 25–27. *Scribe's Records* mentions a gathering of seventy academicians; *Shiji* 6.254.
21. *Scribe's Records* quotes one such text offered to wish the emperor long life at the occasion of a reception; *Shiji* 6.254.
22. Kern 2000b, 186–87; Tian Tian 2015 provides a map and discusses the political ramifications of the First Emperor's travels.

23 Kern 2000b, esp.180–81 (focusing on the role of the Qin academician Shusun Tong 叔孫通 in the transition from Qin to Western Han); 106–18 examines the mimetic relation between Shun's 舜 travels as documented in the "Canon of Yao" chapter of *Documents* and the First Emperor's imperial tours.

24 Kern 2000b, 13 ("Inscription on Mt. I"), 19 ("Inscription on Mt. T'ai"), 35 ("Inscription on Mt. Chih-fu"), 38 ("Inscription on the Eastern Vista of Mt. Chih-fu"), 43 ("Inscription at the Gate of Chieh-shi"), 45 and 49 ("Inscription on Mt. K'uai-chi").

25 Kern 2000b, 19 ("Inscription on Mt. T'ai"), 35 ("Inscription on Mt. Chih-fu"), 45 and 49 ("Inscription on Mt. K'uai-chi").

26 Seventy scholars from Qi and Lu were summoned to organize sacrifices at Mount Tai 泰山 and then dismissed; *Shiji* 28.1366.

27 *Shiji* 121.3116.

28 *Shiji* 121.3124.

29 Chen Yang 2009, 19–22, citing Qian Mu 2001 and Liu Qiyu 1989, 67.

30 *Shiji* 121.3124–25. Some assume this was only possible after Emperor Hui rescinded the ban on books in 192 BCE; for this event, see *Hanshu* 2.90.

31 *Shiji* 6.255, 87.2546.

32 Kern 2000b, 183–96. In Martin Kern's assessment, "it can easily be seen that neither academicians nor canonical texts were seriously affected by the events of 213 and 212 BCE" (184).

33 Song scholars such as Xue Jixuan 薛季宣 (1134–73) account for fragments of the *Documents* classic precisely by assuming Fu Sheng had committed the text to memory. *Shu guwen xun* 16.1b–2a.

34 Chen Yang 2009, 19–22. Robert Eno suggests that Master Fu took a copy of the *Documents* home with him in a private capacity after the fall of Qin; since private ownership of the text was forbidden until Emperor Hui lifted the ban in 192 BCE, he would have needed to hide the text; Eno 2018, 62.

35 Nylan 2018.

36 *Shiji* 121.3124–25.

37 The Commissioner for Ceremonial was one of the nine ministers (*jiu qing* 九卿); one of his many functions was the supervision of academicians at court.

38 The official was a recorder of precedent (*zhanggu* 掌故) in the office of the Commissioner for Ceremonial; how low his status was is not quite certain. The commentaries to both *Scribe's Records* and *Book of Han* cite Ying Shao 應劭 (140–206 CE): in the commentary to *Scribe's Records*, the office is said to stand at 100 *shi* 石 (the lowest official status); in that *Book of Han*, it stands at 600 *shi*. Given that, according to *Book of Han*, academicians were at 600 *shi*, the lower figure is probably correct; *Hanshu* 19A.1726.

39 *Shiji* 101.2745; *Hanshu* 49.2276–77. Chao Cuo, who became an imperial counselor under Jingdi's reign, sought to limit the influence of the Liu kings (*zhuhouwang*) and, when they threatened to rebel, was executed to appease them. A major rebellion occurred anyway in 154 BCE. It is perhaps significant that *Scribe's Records*, unlike *Book of Han*, recounts the encounter between Chao Cuo and Master Fu in Chao Cuo's and not Master Fu's biography.

40 Wei Hong, "Guwen qizi xu" 古文奇字序, cited in *Shiji* 121.2746 n. 2. *Shangshu zhushu* 1.9b.

41 Eno 2018, 61–64.

42 Wilson 1995, 55–56; *Xin Tangshu* 15.374–76 and 123.5636.

43 See the section "The Qing Search for the *Great Commentary*" of this introduction.

44 Qu Yanqing 2000.

45 Bao Jiashu 2014.

46 *Shangshu zhuzi suoyin* reproduces the transmitted version of the *Documents*; for a list of titles, see Appendix.

47 Kern and Meyer 2017, 1–11. Sun Xingyan's 孫星衍 (1753–1818) *Shangshu jinguwen zhushu* 尚書今古文注疏 (1815) is the most important attempt at reconstructing the New Script *Documents* 尚書集釋 in twenty-nine chapters. Qu Wanli 屈萬里 (1907–79) bases his *Shangshu jishi* on Sun Xingyan's text with the exception of the "Great Oath" (Taishi 泰誓) chapter, which he does not include; see Qu Wanli 1983. It is Qu's twenty-eight chapters that we refer to in this volume as the New Script chapters; for a list of titles, see Appendix. When we refer to "Old Script" and "New Script" (with capitalization), we refer to the chapters that are excluded or included in Qu Wanli 1983; when the words "old script" and "new script" are not capitalized, they refer to usages before the 3rd–4th century CE, when the referents of the terms are less clear.

48 Martin Kern and Dirk Meyer distance themselves from the characterization of the Old Script chapters as forgeries; Kern and Meyer 2017, 4–6. On forgeries in East Asian history, see also Breuker 2008.

49 Michael Nylan and He Ruyue attempt to reconstruct early imperial readings for the New Script chapters (including the "Great Oath" chapter); see the volume on *Shangshu* in this series, *The Documents* / Shangshu 尚書.

50 For the *Great Commentary*, see the section "Master Fu, the *Great Commentary*, and the New Script/Old Script Controversy" of this introduction; for *Scribe's Records*, see table 5 in Vankeerberghen 2010.

51 Tjan 1949, vol. 1, 137–45.

52 Chen Mengjia 2005, 3–30; Lewis 1999, 99–146, Nylan 2011, 127–28, Allan 2012, Kern and Meyer 2017, 1–11; Meyer 2021.

53 Guozhong Liu 2016, esp. 111–19. For a discussion of the problems associated with authenticating "purchased manuscripts," see Foster 2017 and Goldin 2013.

54 Liu Guangsheng 2012; Meyer 2014.

55 Kern 2000b, 110–11 and 191–92; Chen Mengjia 2005, 132–42; Chen views "Canon of Yao" as one of the latest texts in the *Documents*, adapted to the needs of Qin. See also Yang Jiagang 2013. Liu Qiyu argues that the core text of "Canon of Yao" was written down in the Spring and Autumn period but was adapted in the Qin and Han dynasties (2007, 156–73). Nylan suggests that a state-sponsored edition of the *Documents* in twenty-nine chapters came together at the court of Emperor Wen (r. 179–56 BCE), not at the Qin court (2001, 128).

56 Kern 2000b, 191.

57 Petersen 1995.

58 Pines, von Falkenhausen, and Yates 2014.

59 See the section "Master Fu's Life" of this introduction.

60 Different explanations exist for the title *Shangshu*, which is already attested in a version of the *Changes* found at Mawangdui (before 168 BCE); Shaughnessy 1997, 238. *Scribe's Records* interprets *shang* as "remote in time," but another possibility is "best of," as in the kind of anthology that was presumably made at the Qin court; *Shiji* 1.46. See also Nylan 2001, 125–26.

61 *Hanshu* 2.90.

62 *Hanshu* 19A.726, 88.3596; Nylan 2009, 765–73.

63 *Shiji* 121.3124.

64 *Hanshu* 8.159.

65 This would have increased the number of academicians to three. Each specialized in slightly different versions of the classic. The version established during Emperor Wu's reign was presumed to be the Ouyang version, whereas the new academicians established during Emperor Xuan's 宣 reign (74–48 BCE) were for the versions of Xiahou the elder 大夏侯 and Xiahou the younger 小夏侯. The academician for the Ouyang version had been appointed during Emperor Wu's reign. *Hanshu* 8.272, 88.3620–21. For the various members of the Ouyang and Xiahou families

active in *Documents* scholarship, see the "Master Fu's Descendants and Disciples" section of this introduction.
66. Nylan 2009 and 2018.
67. See the introduction to the "Great Oath" chapter in this translation.
68. *Hanshu* 36.1968–71; trans. Loewe 2015, 380–84.
69. *Hou Hanshu* 8.336.
70. Chen Mengjia 2005, 89–93 and 248–57. There were twenty-nine chapters, followed by the "Xu" and a chapter outlining the differences between the Xiahou and Ouyang versions ("Notes on Collation" [Jiaoji 校記]). Chen, basing himself on Ma Heng's 馬衡 (1881–1955) *The Collection of Fragmented Texts from Han Steles* (Han shijing jicun 漢石經集存), does not reconstruct the entire preface but is able to reconstruct the chapter order and to determine, for example, that the "Pangeng" chapter is said to be in "three chapters" but is codicologically treated as one. Based on fragments discovered later, Xu Jingyuan deduces that the "Xu" follows the last lines of the "Oath at Qin" chapter and introduces the content of twenty-seven (rather than Chen's twenty-nine) *Documents* chapters (as "Proclamation to Kang," "Proclamation on Drink," and "Catalpa Wood" are introduced together). Xu Jingyuan 2007, 62–67; see also Xu 1981, 185–97.
71. Eno 2018, 61–64; Eno uses the term "Ru underground."
72. *Hanshu* 88.3607.
73. *Hou Hanshu* 27.937.
74. *Kunxue jiwen* 1:142–43.
75. Chen Mengjia 2005, chap. 2.
76. *Hanshu* 36.1968–71; trans. Loewe 2015, 380–84.
77. *Hanshu* 36.1968–71; trans. Loewe 2015, 380–84.
78. *Shiji* 13.487, 47.1935–36.
79. *Shiji* 121.3124.
80. *Hanshu* 36.1968.
81. *Hanshu* 88.3589, 130.1706.
82. *Shiji* 121.3124.
83. *Hanshu* 30.1705, n. 3. On the *Yi Zhoushu*, see Shaughnessy 1993b and Grebnev 2016 and 2017.
84. *Hanshu* 88.3607. According to a lost fragment from *Weighed Discourses* (Lunheng 論衡), Zhang Ba had come to his version by filling in an "Arrangement" document that listed 102 chapters with content from other sources, especially *Zuo Tradition* (Zuozhuan 左傳); *Hanshu buzhu* 88.15a–b.
85. *Fayan*, trans. Nylan, 5.8.
86. Nylan 2001, chap. 3; Shaughnessy 1993c.
87. He became Noble of Yangdu 陽都侯 in 27 CE; his title was changed to Noble of Buqi 不其侯 in 29 CE. It was the custom in Western and Eastern Han that a chancellor, on taking office, would receive a noble title.
88. *Hou Hanshu* 10B.452–54, 26.893–98; Chen Yang 2009, 5–16; *Fu cheng*, j. 2–3; Han Yude 1999.
89. *Shiji* 121.3125; *Hanshu* 88.3603.
90. See Assmann 2011, 34–41, for how this may be a sign of the active construction of memory. The names of descendants of Fu Zhan's younger son, Fu Xi 翕, who inherited his father's noble title, are available for several more generations.
91. *Shiji* 121.3124–26; *Hanshu* 88.3603–7. We also consulted Liu 1989, 74, and Tjan 1949, vol. 1, table 2.
92. As noted in L. Cai 2014, 109–10. See also Csikszentmihalyi and Nylan 2003.
93. Kong Anguo was the scholar who allegedly discovered an old-script version of the *Documents* in a wall in Lu.
94. L. Cai 2014, 22–23.

95 See case 2 of the section "The *Great Commentary* on Questions of Political and Social Order" of this introduction.
96 *Hanshu* 88.3603; Chen Mengjia 2005, 68–69.
97 *Hanshu* 88.3620–21 ("Rulin zhuan," appraisal) does not give a precise date for when the Ouyang version became the accepted court version. It merely says, "Originally, there was only the Ouyang version, and it was only at the time of Xuandi that the versions of Xiahou senior and Xiahou junior were added." The bibliographical treatise of *Book of Han* mentions the three schools under its listing of the classic in twenty-nine *juan*; *Hanshu* 30.1705–6. Chen Mengjia posits that Ouyang Gao was a contemporary of Xiahou Sheng, as both are mentioned as teachers of Xiahou Jian (2005, 68–69).
98 *Hanshu* 8.272
99 See case 6 of the section "The *Great Commentary* on Questions of Political and Social Order" of this introduction.
100 *Hanshu* 75.3155, 27.1459; L. Cai 2014, 156–57.
101 L. Cai 2014, chap. 1.
102 *Hanshu* 88.
103 As opposed to the situation reported by *Scribe's Records* for the second century BCE; see Vankeerberghen 2010.
104 Tian Tian 2015.
105 See Zheng Xuan's "Xu," the brief remarks appended to his annotated edition of the *Commentary*, which are quoted in full at the end of the opening section of this introduction.
106 See *Book of Han* for a list of titles related to the *Documents* classic and its interpretation; some of these texts might well have fed into the *Great Commentary*; *Hanshu* 30.1705.
107 For example, the Gongyang 公羊 and Guliang 穀梁 commentaries to the *Annals* employ a catechismus style throughout, whereas the main mode of *Zuo Tradition* is that of historical anecdotes. *Mr. Han's Outer Commentary on the Odes* (Han Shi waizhuan 韓氏外傳) is a collection of didactic stories each rounded off with a quotation from the *Odes* classic, as are the "Responses of the Way" (Daoying 道應) chapter of the *Master of Huainan* (Huainanzi 淮南子) and the "Applying the Old Master" (Yu Lao 喻老) chapter of *Master Han Fei* (Han Fei zi 韓非子); the "Explaining the Old Master" (Jie Lao 解老) chapter of *Master Han Fei* provides philosophical explanations of individual lines in its mother text, *The Old Master* (Laozi 老子), also known as *Classic of the Way and the Power* (Daodejing 道德經).
108 These are "Canon of Yao" (1.1.3, 1.1.4, 1.1.13), "Gaoyao's Counsel" (2.2.12), "Charge to Yue" (4.4.1), "Great Oath" (5.1.2), "Great Plan" (5.3.3), "Proclamation on Luo" (5.12.1), and "Principal Teachings" (6.1.3); in 6.1.3 the term or sentence to be explained is missing.
109 *Wenxian tongkao* 120.1079 a–b.
110 *Xun* 訓 appears in the title of the text *Thorough Explanations of the Documents* (Shangshu changxun 尚書暢訓). According to the bibliographical treatise in *Old Book of Tang* (Jiu Tangshu 舊唐書), this text has three *juan* and is annotated by Fu Sheng; *Jiu Tangshu* 46.1969.
111 Grebnev translates "Xu" as "sequential outline" (2022, 43).
112 Vankeerberghen 2010, 477–79; in *Mr. Lü's Annals* this document was titled "Xu yi" 序意 and follows the "Annals" (Ji 紀) section of the text; the *Master of Huainan*'s twenty-first chapter, titled "Overview of the Essentials" (Yao lüe 要略), surveys the preceding twenty chapters after offering some thoughts on the rationale for composing the text. Kern 2014 identifies the "Yao lüe" as a *fu* 賦-poem and underlines how the text was likely performed orally before the emperor.

The last chapter in *Scribe's Records*, "Author's Postface" (Zixu 自序), contains a history of the Sima family, titles and brief summaries of each chapter, and some concluding remarks pertinent to *Scribe's Records* as a whole. Such arrangement documents started to precede texts only in the early medieval period; the customary translation of *xu* as "preface" hence does not work for the early imperial context.

113 For an extensive discussion, see He and Nylan 2015.
114 Chen Mengjia 2005, 281. Ma Nan 2013.
115 *Scribe's Records* does not attribute its source, but all the quotations follow a fairly regular pattern, indicating the historical circumstances under which a sage person of antiquity had "authored" (*zuo* 作) a particular document. Hence, it is quite possible that *Scribe's Records* used a "Xu" as a source and distributed its contents over various *Scribe's Records* chapters; for a table listing these passages, see Vankeerberghen 2010, 471–73 (table 5); Chen Mengjia 2005, 78–83 (table 7), 253–80.
116 Possibly 5.11.1 stems from such an arrangement document as well.
117 *Shiji* 33.1524; for an explanation of the differences in title (Bi vs. Xian), see the introduction to "Oath at Xian" (5.21).
118 *Shangshu zhengyi* 31.311b. As the commentary explains, "The eastern suburb remained closed" to prevent the Xu and Yi rebels from entering the Lu capital.
119 "Gaozong's Supplementary Sacrifice" (4.5.2); "Proclamation on Luo" (5.12.3).
120 "Charge to Yue" (4.4.2); "Principal Teachings" (6.2.22).
121 "Punishments of Fu" (5.22.2, 5.22.3, 5.22.5, 5.22.7–9); "Principal Teachings" (6.1.9, 6.2.24, 6.2.25–26, 6.2.28–29).
122 *Hanshi waizhuan zhuzi suoyin* 2.29/14/11–18; the passage is also related to two passages in the *Analects* (1.15 and 3.8). On the relation between *Hanshi waizhuan* 2.29 and *Analects* 3.8, see Hunter 2017, 173–74.
123 In a Mawangdui manuscript dated no later than 168 BCE, Confucius is featured as an ardent supporter and interpreter of the *Changes*; Shaughnessy 1997.
124 Hunter 2017, 135–36.
125 *Shangshu zhuzi suoyin* 2/2/16–17; trans. Karlgren 1950, 4 (no. 18). Sima Qian rephrased this sentence as 揖五瑞，擇吉月日，見四嶽諸牧，班瑞; *Shiji* 1.24. Both Sun Xingyan's and Qu Wanli's understanding of the passage is heavily influenced by the *Great Commentary*; see Qu Wanli 1983, 19–20; *Shangshu jinguwen zhushu*, 41–42.
126 *Shangshu zhuzi suoyin* 55/50/15.
127 During Western Han, the emperor was entitled to the "income from the mountains, seas, ponds, and marshes . . . as well as to the taxes collected from traders in the market place." The superintendent of the lesser treasury (*shaofu* 少府, one of the nine ministers) used this income to manage the imperial household and imperial possessions; see Bielenstein 1980, 54–55.
128 There is a strong resonance between this passage and the text "Monthly Ordinances of the Four Seasons" (Sishi yueling 四時月令) from 5 CE found carved on a wall in Xuanquan (in the far west), which can be seen as an attempt to put this policy in practice. "Monthly Ordinances of the Four Seasons" quotes a version of the same fragment from the *Documents*, "carefully transmit to the people the rhythms of the seasons" (Sanft 2008–9, 153–58). As Sanft notes, attempts to bring policies in line with the seasons can be documented as far back as the pre-Qin period; alignment with the seasons is also the main theme of other texts in the Monthly Ordinances genre. The *Great Commentary* itself (7.2.1–7.2.17) contains an example of a Monthly Ordinances text.
129 *Huainanzi zhuzi suoyin* 9/79/18–22; translation modified from Major et al. 2010, 331–32.

130 Krijgsman 2016 explores the distinctions between anecdotes and the historical narrative (also commemorative) one finds in the *Documents*. For more on anecdotes, see van Els and Queen 2017.
131 Modern historical scholarship and archaeological discoveries have challenged that view of the past. For example, Yao and Shun are now generally regarded as legendary figures; it is still unclear how the traditional narrative on Xia and pre-Anyang Shang maps onto the realities that archaeology continues to reveal. On the historicity of the Xia, see Liu and Xu 2007, 886–901; Allan, 1991.
132 *Bamboo Annals* are the annals of the preimperial polity of Wei, buried in the tomb of King Xiang 襄 of Wei 魏 (r. 318–296 BCE) and discovered and transcribed some centuries later in 281 CE. On *Bamboo Annals*' complicated and contested history, see Knechtges and Chang 2010–14, vol. 4 (2014), 2342–48.
133 As such, the *Great Commentary* was quoted in Matthew Sommer's book *Sex, Law, and Society in the Late Imperial Period* (2000, 33).
134 For an example of a study of this genre that does not mention the *Great Commentary*, see Major 1993. Feng Haofei 1997 pleads for the importance of the "Tradition on the Great Plan's Five Phases" for understanding Han dynasty correlative thinking; see also the work of his student Zhang Bing 張兵. For Li Ling's 李零 views, see Harper and Kalinowski 2017, 266–67.
135 Few articles have been written on the contents of the *Commentary* so far. Wu Zhixiong 2008 analyzes the *Great Commentary*'s political theory, its ideas on harmony between humans and Heaven, its cyclical view on history, its ideal of a hierarchical, ritually ordered society, and its contributions in the domain of Four Seasons or Five Phases correlative thinking; see also Itō Yumi 2020 for additional citations.
136 Nylan and Vankeerberghen 2015.
137 "Canon of Yao" 1.1.15, 1.1.19, 1.1.20, 1.1.21, 1.1.25, 1.1.29; "Gaoyao's Counsel" 2.2.1; "Tribute of Yu" 3.1.2; "Pangeng" 4.3.2; "Proclamation on Drink" 5.9.1, 5.9.5; "Proclamation on Luo" 5.12.1, 5.12.2; "Testamentary Charge" 5.18.1, 5.19.1; "Punishments of Fu" 5.22.5; "Principal Teachings" 6.1.2, 6.1.5, 6.1.7; "Tradition on the Great Plan's Five Phases" 7.3.7; see also Vankeerberghen 2007.
138 *Shiji* 6.238–39.
139 *Shiji* 6.254–55. It comes up once more in 207 BCE, as the Second Emperor, about to be deposed, begs to be made a king over a territory the size of a commandery (得一郡為王); *Shiji* 6.274.
140 Some scholars have argued that the sections on Shun in the *Documents*' "Canon of Yao" might have been redacted or edited during late Warring States or Qin times. Particularly the resonance between the First Emperor's famous tours of inspection and the account in "Canon of Yao" of similar tours by Shun has fueled such speculation; Kern 2000b, 111–12; Kern 2017, 23–24 n. 3. "Canon of Shun," as Martin Kern has demonstrated, presents a unique vision of rulership in which the ruler is not a charismatic and activist figure à la Yao—which would make him potentially unpredictable and autocratic—but someone who remains a largely invisible part of a well-organized society; Kern 2017, 23–61. The *Great Commentary*'s sections on the regional lords, which justify the establishment of regional rulers while seeking to curtail possible abuses, fit well into such a view of rulership. Also note the extensive sections of the *Great Commentary* devoted to Shun's tours of inspection (1.1.16–18 and 2.2.6–9).
141 *Hanshu* 1B.54–56.
142 Loewe 1986, 123–27.
143 Not even by figures such as Jia Yi 賈誼 and Dong Zongshu 董仲舒, known advocates for the curtailment of the power of the regional kings. For this theme in *Master of Huainan*, see Vankeerberghen 2014.

144 Vankeerberghen 2015.
145 *Hanshu* 6.166–67.
146 The 105/104 calendrical reforms are further discussed in Cullen 1993; Morgan 2017, 26–28; and Robinson 2021.
147 *Shiji* 28.1401–02; trans. Watson 1993, 48–49.
148 *Shiji* 122.1141; Chavannes 1967, 3:123; Morgan 2017.
149 *Hanshu* 58.2632. Ni Kuan, apparently, was using the calendrical predictions the *fangshi* Gongsun Qing 公孫卿 had presented to the emperor in 113 BCE; see Cullen 1993, 201 (Cullen mistakenly writes Ni Xuan for Ni Kuan).
150 Only the first name (Ci 賜) of one of these academicians is known; *Hanshu* 21A.975. The academicians reported to the office of the Commissioner for Ceremonial, not that of the imperial counselor. For a discussion of other formal court debates on calendrics, see Cullen 2007 (on Eastern Han) and Morgan 2013, chap. 4 (on a court debate of 226 CE).
151 I.e., number 4 should be modeled after number 1, number 5 after 2, and so forth.
152 *Hanshu* 21A.975.
153 Earlier in the Han, once during Emperor Wen's reign and at the outset of Emperor Wu's reign, there had been unsuccessful attempts to implement changes to the calendar; see the summary of these events in Cullen 1993, 193–95.
154 In contrast, the order of the Five Phases was subject to significant change and contention; see A. Wang 2000.
155 Given that the context here is the establishment of the calendar, "regulator" (*zheng*) refers to the first calendrical month, which is still called *zhengyue* 正月 in modern Chinese.
156 The text intends to link the calendar not only to astronomical phenomena, but also to processes of growth and decay of life on earth. Therefore, the beginning of the year is linked to the start of the life cycle. The stirring of plant seed, sprouting, and shooting represent three stages all at the beginning at the life cycle.
157 After the third regulator, which falls sixty days after the winter solstice, growth becomes uneven in the sense that some plants grow faster than the others. That makes it difficult to regulate or categorize them.
158 In the passage from *Book of Han*, the idea of having to go back two eras is expressed as "systems of ritual regulations cannot alternate between them" 制不相復, as compared to the *Great Commentary*'s "the era following the previous two eras, thus completing a triad that includes his own era" 存二代之後，與己為三. The language of an edict issued on Emperor Cheng's behalf in 8 BCE closely matches the language of the *Great Commentary*: "It is common knowledge that a true king has to abide by [the traditions] of the era following those of the two previous kings; that is how one abides by the Three Governors 蓋聞王者必存二王之後，所以通三統也; *Hanshu* 10. 328.
159 This reading is not the only one possible. In a discussion of calendrical reforms during Emperor Wen's time, a similar expression is used, 推終始傳. Using our explanation, this could mean "extrapolating from the *Commentary* regarding the cyclical time," but Yan Shigu proposes reading 傳 as 轉, which would yield the translation "extrapolating from the succession of the cycles of time"; *Hanshu* 25A.1212. This reading is possible for our passage too. However, in a similarly constructed passage in *Hanshu*'s "Treatise on the Five Phases" (*shan tui wuxing zhuan* 善推五行傳), the editors indicate typographically that they see it as a reference to a text; *Hanshu* 27B(A).1353.
160 Wang Mang briefly interrupted this, reverting back to the Yin system, but, by Eastern Han, the Xia system had been taken up again.
161 Perhaps by following the arguments of theoreticians who advocated for the Five Phase cycle: in that cycle yellow followed black, the color adopted by Qin.

162 Gopal Sukhu 2005 and Morgan 2013, 286–87, are examples of secondary scholarship attributing Three Governors theory to Dong Zhongshu. Michael Loewe 2011 has convincingly shown that the attribution of the theory to Dong Zhongshu is entirely based on chapter 23 of *Luxuriant Gems of the Spring and Autumn* (Chunqiu fanlu 春秋繁露) and, given the likely Eastern Han date of the chapter, a later construction.

163 Classical scholars, during Emperor Wu's reign, were hired mostly for their rhetorical skills in phrasing imperial texts in classical language; see *Shiji* 122.3139.

164 L. Cai 2014.

165 *Hanshu* 68.2932.

166 For the view that the Duke of Zhou, instead of being the exemplary figure of the later tradition, was in fact forced to resign, see Shaughnessy 1993a.

167 *Hanshu* 12.348; note that the versions in *Garden of Eloquence* and *Mr. Han's Outer Commentary on the Odes* lack the coda about the sacrifice of the pheasant in the ancestral temple; *Hanshi waizhuan zhuzi suoyin* 5.12/37/5–10 and *Shuoyuan zhuzi suoyin* 18.15/155/10–16.

168 M. Kim 2014, 105; Barbieri-Low and Yates 2015, 833–50, esp. n. 10.

169 For a discussion of the Ceremony to Nourish the Elders in the *Great Commentary*, see Gu Ying 2005, chap. 5.

170 In the case of Western Han, the Circular Moat was erected south of the capital of Chang'an and was probably one and the same building as the Bright Hall; in the case of Eastern Han, the Circular Moat was south of the capital Luoyang and had its own building. See Tseng 2011, 51–54, 59–69. The ceremonies are described in Bodde 1975, chap. 16, but he wrongly gives the dates of 1 CE and 56 CE.

171 Emperor Ming, significantly, refers to himself in the language of the *Documents* classic, "眇眇小子"; see *Hou Hanshu* 2.102 and n. 2.

172 Terms that occur in both texts or are nearly identical are printed in bold.

173 *Hou Hanshu* 2.102–04; translation adapted from Bodde 1975, 366–67.

174 Among the elders present, two were especially singled out in the ceremony: Huan Rong 桓榮, who taught the emperor the *Documents*, as Fivefold Experienced and Li Gong 李躬 as Threefold Elder. See de Crespigny 2007, 336–37 and 412.

175 Zito 1997 and Sanderovitch 2017.

176 Law is also touched on in "Canon of Yao," "Tang's Oath," and "Principal Teachings."

177 This bears some resemblance to Liu Bang's intention to simplify "Qin's cruel laws." Liu Bang sought to win the hearts of the people of the area within the passes—an area dominated for centuries by Qin—by announcing that he would simplify the laws to a basic three items ("one who kills another will die, and one who harms another or steals will pay recompense for the crime"); even though this simplification likely never took effect, it communicated a powerful message about the new regime; *Hanshu* 1A.23; Sanft 2014, 135–36. For the punishments actually used in early Western Han, see Barbieri-Low and Yates 2015.

178 Sanft 2017.

179 This is consistent with Sanft's (2017) reading of the *Documents'* "Punishments of Lü" as excluding the idealistic vision, present in other *Documents* chapters, of a future in which punishment would no longer be necessary, even though here the debate is phrased not in terms of a distant future but as one about the authenticity of canonical passages.

180 Barbieri-Low and Yates 2015, 89–110, 1207–15, and 1332–58.

181 Barbieri-Low and Yates 2015, 1343.

182 For an interpretation of *Zuo Tradition* from the perspective of signs, see W. Li 2007; on the mantic arts in early China, see Kalinowski 2010.

183 For more on the "Treatise on the Five Phases" of *Book of Han*, see Wang 2000, Su 2013, Espesset 2016, and Nylan, 2021.

184 Named Huangji 皇機 in the transmitted version of the *Documents*.
185 See also 7.2.18, the concluding passage of part 2, where a failure to abide by the ritual regulations is associated with problems with the Five Resources/Five Phases. There the text recaptures language not of part 1 but of the *Documents'* "Great Plan" itself.
186 *Hanshu* 27C(A) 1459–60; see also *Hanshu* 27B(A).3155 and *Hanshu* 75.3156–57.
187 Liu He's tomb in Jiangxi, where he was eventually installed as Noble of Haihun 海昏侯, was recently excavated, drawing much attention to its opulent contents; for an overview, see Xin Deyong 2016.
188 *Hanshu* 27C(A) 1459–60.
189 *Hanshu* 75.3155. One modern scholar has offered the more cynical reading that Huo Guang had the interpretation fabricated (and endorsed by Xiahou Sheng) only after the successful removal of Liu He from the throne. See L. Cai 2014, 155–57.
190 *Hanshu* 75.3155.
191 See also the section "Textual Transmission of 'Tradition on the Great Plan's Five Phases'" of this introduction.
192 Qu Wanli's *Shangshu jishi* (1983), an often-used edition of the *Documents* in its New Script version, does not provide "Canon of Shun" or "Supplementary Sacrifices" as separate chapters. This structure agrees with how scholars have reconstructed the New Script *Documents* after their rejection of the Old Script chapters as forgeries (see below).
193 *Great Commentary* 5.22; *Shiji* 13.502; *Qu Wanli 1983*, 250. In the Xiping stone inscriptions, firmly linked to the new script edition, Fu is used; see Chen Mengjia 2005, 89–92; Xu Jingyuan 2007, 62; Ma Nan 2013, 18.
194 Xu Jingyuan 2007, 61; Ma Nan 2013, 9. the term *qishi* 七始 is placed under "Canon of Yao" (1.1.16) in Wang's edition of the *Great Commentary*; the line from the *Documents* is from "Supplementary Sacrifices."
195 We leave "Principal Teachings" (6) and "Tradition on the Great Plan's Five Phases" (7) out of consideration here, as these *Great Commentary* chapters are not intended as commentary on specific *Documents* chapters.
196 Note the new script reading, in line with the character Jiong in *Scribe's Records*: 䌛 vs. 冏.
197 *Kunxue jiwen*, 1:142–43; Wang follows up by saying that these chapters were not entirely lost by Sui and Tang times.
198 Zhang and Diao 2009, 1–12. Zhang and Diao reject methods such as those employed by Chen Mengjia, who used Zheng Xuan's characterization in his *Sanlizhu* of certain terms as *jinwen* or *guwen* to try to determine the allegiance of the Wuwei *Ceremonials*; instead, they see such variants as the natural outcome when a text that originally circulated orally is written down.
199 Tjan writes that "the New Text and Old Text controversy did not arise until the end of the Former Han period" (1949, Introduction, part 2, section 36). For a thorough discussion of the New Script/Old Script controversy, see Nylan 1994 and 1995, and van Ess 1994 and 1999. Van Ess 1994 interprets one example from late Western Han (the debate about the abolishment of the Bureau of Music) in terms of different readings of the word "Zheng/*zheng*" as provided by new vs. old script positions but acknowledges (n. 61) that "these terms were not yet used at the time."
200 Elman 1990.
201 Elman 1990, esp. 103–6 and 191–98.
202 Elman 1990, esp. 222–26.
203 Elman 1990, 103–4.
204 Elman 1990, 190 (Ch'ang-chou in Elman's quotation converted to pinyin). Elman's book singles out Zhuang Cunyu 莊存與 (1719–88) and Liu Fenglu 劉逢祿

(1776–1829), both from Changzhou, as the two most important figures in the late-eighteenth- to early-nineteenth-century emergence of New Script studies.
205 Elman 1990, 1992–93. On the revival of the *Great Commentary* in the Qing and on the text's textual history, see the next section as well as Hou Jinman 2000.
206 Gu Qian 2014; *Qing Pi Lumen xiansheng Xirui nianpu* 1, trans. Aque 2004, 232.
207 Pi Xirui's literary productions before this date consisted mostly of poems; he had turned to studying the classics only in 1879, when he was already thirty *sui*. See *Qing Pi Lumen xiansheng Xirui nianpu*, 16, trans. Aque 2004, 263.
208 He changed the title to *shuzheng* in 1895, while including additions and corrections. See *Qing Pi Lumen xiansheng Xirui nianpu*, 31, 38, trans. Aque 2004, 299 and 304.
209 As the preface makes clear, he sponsored the publication of the book. In 1902, Xia's daughter married Pi Xirui's son; *Qing Pi Lumen xiansheng Xirui nianpu*, 78, trans. Aque 2004, 341.
210 *Jingxue lishi*, 19–20, trans. Aque 2004, 373–74.
211 *Jingxue lishi*, 65, trans. Aque 2004, 520–21.
212 *Jingxue lishi*, 81–82, trans. Aque 2004, 568.
213 *Shangshu dazhuan shuzheng* (hereafter *SSDZSZ*), "Xu," 1a (697).
214 *SSDZSZ*, "Xu," 1a (697).
215 This ultimately led to Kang Youwei's 康有為 (1858–1927) politicized and overblown accusations against Liu Xin. According to Kang, Liu Xin had single-handedly forged Old Script texts such as *Rituals of Zhou* and *Zuo Tradition*. See van Ess 1994, 148–50.
216 *SSDZSZ*, "Xu," 1a–b (697).
217 *SSDZSZ*, "Xu," 1b (697).
218 Cai Changlin 2014.
219 *Jingxue lishi*, 141–49.
220 Chen Qiaozong is the son of Chen Shouqi.
221 For Pi's detailed refutation against Zheng Xuan, see *SSDZSZ* 4.11b (745).
222 *SSDZSZ* 1.8b–10b (703–4).
223 *Qing Pi Lumen xiansheng Xirui nianpu*, 45–67; trans. Aque 2004, 313–33.
224 *Qing Pi Lumen xiansheng Xirui nianpu*, 10; trans. Aque 2004, 247.
225 *Qing Pi Lumen xiansheng Xirui nianpu*, 28; trans. Aque 2004, 295; for Pi's praise of Wang Kaiyun's approach to the classics, see pp. 26–27; trans. Aque 2004, 290–91.
226 *Qing Pi Lumen xiansheng Xirui nianpu*, 43; trans. Aque 2004, 307.
227 *Shangshu dazhuan buzhu* (hereafter *SSDZBZ*) 1b (797).
228 *Hanshu* 30.1705.
229 *Yuhai* 37.25b (708).
230 *Suishu* 32.913; *Xin Tangshu* 57.1427.
231 *Chongwen zongmu*, 7b (j.1); *Junzhai dushu zhi jiaozheng* 53 (j. 1).
232 *Zhizhai shulu jieti* 28.
233 *Junzhai dushu zhi jiaozheng* 53 (j. 1).
234 *Wenxian tongkao* 177.11.
235 *Shuofu sanzhong* 2.2a–b (26); *Qinding Siku quanshu zongmu* (*zhengliben*) 1644 (j. 123).
236 *Jingyi kao* 76.1a–4b.
237 *Qinding Siku quanshu zongmu* (*zhengli ben*) 185 (j. 14).
238 *Qinding Siku quanshu zongmu* (*zhengli ben*) 163 (j. 12).
239 Hui Dong's reconstitution of the *Great Commentary* has two editions: one preserved at the National Library in Beijing and the other at the National Library in Taiwan. It is possible that the Taipei edition is a working draft, and the Beijing edition came out later as a more mature edition. See Zheng Yuji 2009, 288.
240 *Shangshu dazhuan* (Sun Zhilu edition), 1.2b–3a.

241 *Qinding Siku quanshu zongmu (zhengli ben)* 185 (j. 14).
242 *Siku quanshu*, vol. 68.
243 *Qinding Siku quanshu zongmu (zhengli ben)*, 163–64 (j. 12).
244 Dong Cong's 董熜 (1680–1747) preface (1738) to Dong Fengyuan's *Shangshu dazhuan* 1b; *Siku tiyao bianzheng* 1.28–31.
245 Lu Jianzeng's and Lu Wenchao's *Shangshu dazhuan* 1b.
246 Lu Jianzeng's and Lu Wenchao's *Shangshu dazhuan* 1b.
247 *Qinding Siku quanshu zongmu (zhengli ben)*, 185 (j. 14). Lu Jianzeng's edition is usually referred to as the Yangzhou edition, as he had been appointed to the important position of salt distribution commissioner in Yangzhou since 1736.
248 Lu Jianzeng's and Lu Wenchao's *Shangshu dazhuan* 1b.
249 *SSDZBZ* 1a–b (797).
250 Yu Jiaxi endorses Yan Yuanzhao's opinion. *Siku tiyao bianzheng* 1.27–30.
251 *Yangzhou huafanglu*, 230. For the relationship between Hui Dong and Lu Jianzeng, see Cao Jianghong 2012.
252 The editions of Lu Jianzeng and Hui Dong contain 7.1 and 7.2 but not 7.3; Sun Zhilu's edition contains 7.1 and 7.3 but not 7.2. For a careful comparison between Lu Jianzeng's and Hui Dong's editions, see Hou Jinman 2019.
253 *Shangshu dazhuan* (Lu Jianzeng's edition), "Kaoyixu," 1a–b.
254 See Lu Wenchao's preface to the "Kaoyi" 考異, *Shangshu dazhuan* (Lu Jianzeng's edition), 2a–b.
255 Chen Shouqi's *Shangshu dazhuan* (Sibu congkan chubian edition), 1.2a.
256 Zheng Yuji 2009; Jiang Qiuhua 2013; Hou Jinman 2000.
257 Li Xiaoyu 2008; Jiang Qiuhua 2013.
258 Li Xiaoyu 2008; Jiang Qiuhua 2013.
259 Gu Qian 2014.
260 *Shangshu dazhuan zhuzi suoyin* (*SSDZZZSY*); CHANT (Chinese Ancient Texts Database): http://www.chant.org/.
261 Starting from the Northern and Southern Dynasties, the titles *Hongfan wuxing zhuan* 洪範五行傳 and *Hongfan wuxing zhuan lun* 洪範五行傳論 were used interchangeably. For example, Liu Zhao 劉昭 (6th c.), in his annotation to *Book of Later Han*, attributes *Hongfan wuxing zhuan* to Liu Xiang. *Hou Hanshu* 64.2117 n. 2. The foundational bibliographical treatise in *Book of Sui* states that Liu Xiang and Liu Xin composed *Wuxing zhuan*; *Suishu* 32.913–15. For a more detailed study of the relationship of Liu Xiang and Liu Xin to *Tradition on the Great Plan's Five Phases*, see Huang Chi-shu 2007.
262 *Hanshu* 27C(A).1459. The title of Xiahou Sheng's text is given as *The Tradition on the Great Plan's Five Phases* (Hongfan wuxing zhuan). Elsewhere in the chapter the title is simply *Tradition on the Five Phases* (Wuxing zhuan); *Hanshu* 27B(A).1353.
263 *Hanshu* 75.3154.
264 Since Xiahou Shichang was the first to transmit *The Tradition on the Great Plan's Five Phases*, some scholars also argue that he was the first author of the work. For a detailed discussion on Xiahou Shichang's relationship with the text, see Xu Xingwu 2012, 30–41, and Ma Nan 2012a.
265 *Hanshu* 27B(A).1353.
266 *Hanshu* 30.1705. For a more detailed discussion of the transmission of *The Tradition on the Great Plan's Five Phases*, see Cheng Sudong 2016.
267 *Hanshu* 36.1950.
268 Nylan 2011; Cheng Sudong 2022.
269 *Hanshu* 36.1950. On the use of omen interpretation during Emperor Cheng's reign by and against the Wang family, see Shao-yun Yang 2015.

270 Espesset 2016.
271 In "Treatise on the Five Phases" in *Book of Han*, the quotations from "Tradition on the Great Plan's Five Phases" are followed by further explanations (*shuo* 說) for sections 1–5.
272 *Hanshu* 27A.1317. Liu Xiang, Dong Zhongshu, and Liu Xin are frequently cited in "Treatise on the Five Phases." Among them, Liu Xiang's interpretations are cited in more than 150 places; the other two are cited about 80 times each.
273 *Hanshu* 27A.1315–16.
274 Zhao 2019, chap. 2.
275 This is congruent with the increasing stature awarded to Dong Zhongshu; compare the length of his biography in *Scribe's Records* with that in *Book of Han*.
276 E.g., *Taiping yulan* 377.1871a.
277 *Liuyi liubie*, 17.9b–13b; *Gu wei shu* 5.1a–3b.
278 Lu Jianzeng's and Lu Wenchao's *Shangshu dazhuan* 1b; for the full quotation, see above.
279 As well as in Wang Yinglin's *Ocean of Jade* (Yuhai 玉海); *Yuhai* 5.30b–32a (108–9).
280 Hence our translation in 7.1 of *wuxing* as Five Phases; see also case 6 above.
281 Espesset 2014; Di Giacinto 2012; Zhao 2019, 63.
282 *Suishu* 32.941.
283 *Gu wei shu* 5.1a–3b.
284 *Qinding Siku quanshu zongmu (zhengli ben)*, 164 (j. 12). In addition to "Tradition on the Great Plan's Five Phases," other often-quoted chapters of the *Great Commentary* include "Canon of Yao," "Gaoyao's Counsel," "Tribute of Yu," and "Great Oath"; see Yasui and Nakamura 1975.
285 See the section "The Qing Search for the *Great Commentary*" of this introduction.
286 Neither the *Great Commentary* nor the chapter "Tradition on the Great Plan's Five Phases" is considered an apocryphal text in the seminal research by Yasui and Nakamura (1975) and Hans van Ess (1999).

The *Great Commentary*
on the *Documents Classic* /
Shangshu dazhuan

卷一
唐傳

1
Traditions on Tang

1.1
Canon of Yao

"*Canon of Yao*," the New Script chapter that opens the Documents, deals with the sage-rulers Yao and Shun, and with the forms of rulership that they established.[1] *The first part of the chapter gives an account of Yao, containing an important early cosmogony as well as the story of how Yao preferred Shun as his successor over his own progeny;*[2] *the latter part deals with the ritual aspects of Shun's kingship. It tells of Shun's travels throughout his realms, the sacrifices he made, the relations of trust he cultivated with the various constituents in his realm and with his ministers, and the penal system he established.*[3] *Many scholars have concluded that "Canon of Yao," especially the part dealing with Shun, was redacted either late in the Warring States period or in postunification Qin and therefore was one of the most recent additions to the* Documents.[4] *In the Old Script* Documents, *the part dealing with Shun is a chapter of its own, called "Canon of Shun"* 舜典.[5]

Canon of Yao" in the Great Commentary *translates many of the issues broached in the* Documents *in the idiom of the early imperial period, creating a true blueprint for various government institutions based on the classic. It provides concrete detail on what a ruler should look for in order*

---

1   See Kern 2017 for the view that Yao and Shun stand for two different models of rulership: a charismatic, activist ruler who chooses the most capable person as his successor versus one who plays a largely ritual role as the head of a well-organized state machinery.
2   Kalinowski 2004.
3   For a summary of the contents of "Canon of Yao," see Nylan 2001, 142–45.
4   For references, see Kern 2017, 24 n. 3 and 38.
5   Kern 2017 argues that "Canon of Yao" and "Canon of Shun" should be considered two separate texts.

to align human and cosmological time, always with an eye to lessening the burdens he puts on the people (1.1.1–4). It contains numerous passages that outline an ideal for the relations between the ruler and the regional lords (1.1.19, 20, 21, 24, 25). It also specifies that the penal system Yao and Shun fostered is one that privileged symbolic punishments over real punishments and sought to instill shame rather than inflict pain or death (1.1.26–27). Further, it defines the titles and functions of the three excellencies (San Gong 三公) and a system of promotion based on merit (1.1.30–31). It also contains numerous narrative passages (with normative intent) that involve Shun, including a lengthy description of Shun's tours of inspection and the sacrifices and music he performed while traveling (1.1.16–18).

The Wang and Chen/Pi editions of the reconstituted Great Commentary follow the New Script arrangement in that they arrange under the title "Canon of Yao" sections that deal with what in the Old Script Documents is "Canon of Shun." Sections 1.1.1 to 1.1.4 deal with Yao's rulership; the remainder, with Shun.

1.1
堯典

1.1.1 主**春**者張,**昏中**,可以穜穀。主**夏**者**火**,**昏中**,可以穜黍朮。主**秋**者**虛**,**昏中**,可以穜麥。主**冬**者**昴**,**昏中**,可以收斂蓋藏。田獵斷伐,當告乎天子,而天子賦之民。故天子南面而視四**星**之中,知**民**之緩急,急則不賦籍,則不舉力役。故曰「**敬授人時**」,此之謂也。[1]

1.1.2 東方者何也?動方也,物之動也。何以謂之**春**?春、出也,萬物之出也,故曰「東方春也」。

---

[1] Cf. *Shangshu zhuzi suoyin* 1/1/3–12 (堯典). *Shangshu zhuzi suoyin* has 日中 for 昏中.

1.1

Canon of Yao

Spread presides over spring; when it culminates at dusk, one can plant grain. The Fire Star presides over summer; when it culminates at dusk, one can plant millet and beans. Ruins presides over autumn; when it culminates at dusk, one can plant wheat. Topknot presides over winter; when it culminates at dusk, one can harvest and store.[1] The yield from hunting and woodcutting should be reported to the Son of Heaven, and it is the Son of Heaven who will distribute it to the people. Therefore, the Son of Heaven faces south and observes the culmination of these four stars to understand whether people are relaxed or busy. If they are busy, he does not burden them with public tasks or raise a labor force. Therefore, when the text says, "Carefully transmit to humankind the rhythms of the seasons," that is what it is about.[2]

1.1.1

What is the eastern (*tôŋ) region? It is the region of movement (*dôŋ). It is things that move. Why is it called "spring"? "Spring" (*thun) means to come out (*k-hlut). The myriad things come out. That is why it is said: "The eastern region stands for spring."

1.1.2

---

1   This passage interprets a cosmogonic passage from "Canon of Yao" in the *Documents* in which Yao orders Xi and He to use certain stars to fix the seasons from certain areas. The *Documents* passage mentions Bird instead of Spread (Bird is the larger constellation of which Spread forms a part); apart from that, the lodges and stars named in the *Documents* and the *Great Commentary* are the same. Spread is lunar lodge 26; Ruins, lodge 11; and Topknot, lodge 18. The Fire Star (Antares) is the central star of Heart (lodge 5). The translations of lunar lodges and stars are after Pankenier 2013.

2   The same *Documents* passage is also quoted in the preamble to a 5 CE edict containing Monthly Ordinances (Yue Ling 月令) found at Xuanquanzhi 懸泉置; see Sanft 2008–9, 178 and 189 n. 13.

南方者何也?任方也。任方者,物之方任。何以謂之**夏**?夏者、假也,吁荼萬物而養之外也,故曰「南方夏也」。

西方者何也?鮮方也。鮮、訊也,訊者、始入之皃。始入者,何以謂之秋?秋者、愁也。愁者、萬物愁而入也,故曰「西方者**秋**也」。

北方者何也?伏方也。萬物之方伏。物之方伏,則何以謂之**冬**[1]?冬者、中也。中也者、萬物方藏于中也,故曰「北方冬也」。

陽盛則吁荼萬物而養之外也;陰盛則呼吸萬物而藏之內也。故曰「吁吸也者,陰陽之交接,萬物之終始」。

1.1.3 「**寅餞入日,辯秩西成**」[2]。《傳》曰:天子以秋命三公將帥選士厲兵以征不義,決獄訟,斷刑罰,趨收斂,以順天道,以佐秋殺。

1　Cf. *Shangshu zhuzi suoyin* 1/1/8–12 (堯典).
2　Cf. *Shangshu zhuzi suoyin* 1/1/10–11 (堯典). *Shangshu zhuzi suoyin* has 寅餞納日,平秩西成 for 寅餞入日,辯秩西成; *Shiji* 1.16 has 敬道日入,便程西成.

What is the southern (*nêm) region? It is the region of reliance (*nəm). The "region of reliance" is where the things are in the phase of relying. Why is it called "summer"? "Summer" (*krâʔ) means to lend (*grâʔ). It gives breath to the myriad things and nourishes them from outside. That is why it is said: "The southern region stands for summer."

What is the western (*səi) region? It is the region of diminution (*san). "Diminution" means interrogation (*sin!)."Interrogation" coincides with the start of withdrawal. The start of withdrawal: why is it called "autumn" (*tshiu)? "Autumn" means sadness (*dzruʔriw). "Sadness" means that the myriad things are saddened and withdraw. That is why it is said: "The western region stands for autumn."

What is the northern (*pêk) region? It is the region of hiding (*bək). It is where the myriad things are in the phase of hiding. Being in the phase of hiding, why is it called "winter"? "Winter" (*tûŋ) means center (*truŋ). "Center" means that the myriad things are stored at the center of it. That is why it is said: "The northern region stands for winter."[1]

When yang is at its peak, it lends its breath to the myriad things, thus nourishing them and bringing them out. When yin is at its peak, then it withdraws its breath from the myriad things, thus storing them and taking them in. That is why it is said: "Lending and withdrawing breath is that by which yin and yang take over from one another, thus determining the cycle of the myriad things."[2]

"Reverently, he bade farewell to the setting sun and brought order to the harvest associated with the west."[3] The *Commentary* says, "In autumn, the Son of Heaven commands the three excellencies and the military commanders to select soldiers and sharpen their weapons to campaign against the unrighteous, to settle legal disputes, to decide on punishments and fines, and to hasten to take in the harvest. Thus, he follows the Way of Heaven and assists the autumn killing."[4]

1.1.3

---

1   We have added phonetic reconstructions because of the significant patterns of homophony in this passage, as if directions and seasons come with their own sound.
2   In 1.1.2, there are five instances of *guyue* 故曰 ("That is why the text says"). None of them appears in the transmitted *Documents*. Therefore, it is unclear which text the *Great Commentary* is quoting here.
3   For the ritual for receiving the sun performed in spring, see 6.1.1.
4   The military, legal, and agricultural activities prescribed here must be part of an autumn ritual that also included a sacrifice. In 6.1.1, such a sacrifice is detailed for spring and associated with a parallel phrase from the same *Documents* passage. It is possible that 1.1.3, 1.1.4, and 6.1.1 have to be read together, detailing ritual activities and sacrifices to be performed in each of the four seasons (with the summer section entirely missing).

CANON OF YAO

1.1.4 「**辯在朔易。日短**」[1]。朔、始也。《傳》曰：天子以冬命三公謹蓋藏，閉門閭，固封竟，入山澤田獵，以順天道，以佐冬固藏也。

1.1.5 孔子對子張曰：男子三十而娶，女子二十而嫁。女二十而通織紝績紡之事、黼黻文章之美，不若是，則上無以孝于舅姑，下無以事夫養子也。舜、父頑母嚚，不見室家之端。故謂之鰥。《書》曰：「**有鰥在下，曰虞舜**[2]。」

1.1.6 否[3]、不也。

1.1.7 **堯**為天子，**丹朱**為太子，**舜**為左右。堯知丹朱之**不肖**[4]，必將壞其宗廟、滅其社稷，而天下同賊之。故堯推尊舜而尚之，屬諸侯焉，**納之大麓之野，烈風雷雨不迷**[5]，致之以昭華之玉。

---

1   Cf. *Shangshu zhuzi suoyin* 1/1/12 (堯典). *Shangshu zhuzi suoyin* has 平 for 辯.
2   Cf. *Shangshu zhuzi suoyin* 1/2/3–4 (堯典).
3   Cf. *Shangshu zhuzi suoyin* 1/2/3 (堯典).
4   Cf. *Shangshu zhuzi suoyin* 59.22/59/9 (逸文). *Shangshu zhuzi suoyin* has 堯子不肖，舜使居丹淵為諸侯，故號曰丹朱 for 堯知丹朱之不肖.
5   Cf. *Shangshu zhuzi suoyin* 2/2/13–14 (舜典). *Shangshu zhuzi suoyin* has 納于大麓，烈風雷雨弗迷 for 納之大麓之野，烈風雷雨不迷.

"Follow and examine the incipient changes. The days are short."[5] "Incipient" means to begin. The *Commentary* says, "In winter, the Son of Heaven commands the three excellencies to carefully cover and hoard, to close the village gates, to reinforce the borders, and to enter the mountains and marshes for the hunt. Thus, he follows the Way of Heaven and assists the winter to solidify and hoard."[6]

1.1.4

Confucius told Zizhang, "A man marries at age thirty; a woman, at age twenty. At age twenty, a woman should be versed in spinning and weaving and be able to create beautiful patterns. If not, how can she demonstrate filial piety to her parents-in-law above or, below, serve her husband and raise her children? Shun's father was stupid, his mother blunt, so his family was not considered a proper one. Therefore, he is called a 'bachelor.'" The *Documents* says, "There is a bachelor among the lowly, named Shun of Yu."[7]

1.1.5

"Nay" means "No."[8]

1.1.6

When Yao was Son of Heaven, Danzhu was his heir apparent, and Shun was his aide. Yao knew that Danzhu was unfit and would surely bring ruin to the ancestral temple and destroy the altars of soil and grain so that all-under-Heaven would unite and kill him. Therefore, Yao propelled Shun into a position of power and honor, with regional lords subordinated to him. He sent [Shun] to the great foothills,[9] and, despite violent wind, thunder, and rain, he did not get lost. Yao gave him a luminous jade.

1.1.7

---

5   A similar phrase occurs in the "Canon of Yao" chapter of the *Documents*, *Shangshu zhuzi suoyin* 1/1/12.
6   See note 6 to 1.1.3.
7   Since Shun was not from a good family, he was not able to marry a suitable woman, versed in tasks associated with an ideal wife.
8   This sentence was first cited in Li Shan's 李善 (630–89) commentary to a *fu* in *Selections of Refined Literature* (Wenxuan 文選). Chen Shouqi assumed it came from Zheng Xuan's commentary to the *Great Commentary* and assigned it to the phrase *fou de* 否德 in "Canon of Yao." Wang Kaiyun, unlike Chen Shouqi, thinks the sentence was a part of the *Great Commentary* (which, indeed, is what Li Shan's commentary states), but, like Chen Shouqi, he makes it part of "Canon of Yao." See *Shangshu zhuzi suoyin* 1/2/3; *Wenxuan* 8/389; *SSDZJJ* 1.3a; *SSDZBZ* 1.3b (800).
9   Yao is putting Shun to the test by sending him to the wilds. The term *lu* 麓, as it occurs in the *Documents*, has been explained in two different ways in the tradition: as indicating an inhospitable land (a forest, foothills), or as referring to administrative acts (when *lu* is read as *lu* 錄, "record"). The first reading is embraced by *Scribe's Records* and the *Great Commentary*, whereas *Book of Han*, Zheng Xuan, and others adopt the second reading (Ma Nan 2012b, 61–62). Pi Xirui, in his *Jingxue lishi*, forcefully rejected the second reading, which he understood as the Xiahous subverting the reading of Master Fu himself and the Ouyangs. *Jingxue lishi*, 77–78; trans. Aque 2004, 554–56.

1.1.8　舜漁于靁澤[6]之中。

1.1.9　陶于河濱，販于頓丘，就時負夏。

1.1.10　舜耕**于歷山**[7]，夢眉與髮等。

1.1.11　舜**修五禮五玉三帛**[8]。

1.1.12　舜以天德嗣堯，西王母來獻白玉琯。

1.1.13　**正月上日，受終于文祖，在旋機玉衡，以齊七政**[9]。旋機者何也？《傳》曰：旋者、還也，機者、幾也，微也。其變幾微，而所動者大，謂之旋機。是故旋機謂之北極。受、謂舜也。上日、元日。

1.1.14　萬物非天不生，非地不載；非春不動，非夏不長，非秋不收，非冬不藏。故《書》[10]「**煙于六宗**[11]」，此之謂也。

6　靁 = 雷: *Shiji* 1.32.]
7　Cf. *Shangshu zhuzi suoyin* 3/6/3 (大禹謨)。
8　Cf. *Shangshu zhuzi suoyin* 2/2/18 (舜典)。
9　Cf. *Shangshu zhuzi suoyin* 2/2/15 (舜典)。*Shangshu zhuzi suoyin* has 璿璣 for 旋機。
10　Read 故《書》as 故《書》曰: cf. SSDZSZ 1.10b (704)。
11　Cf. *Shangshu zhuzi suoyin* 2/2/16 (舜典)。*Shangshu zhuzi suoyin* has 禋 for 煙。

Shun fished in Lei Marsh. 1.1.8

He made pottery on the banks of the Yellow River, sold goods at Dunqiu,[10] and engaged in seasonal trade at Fuxia. 1.1.9

Shun farmed at Mount Li and dreamed that his eyebrows had grown to the same length as his hair.[11] 1.1.10

Shun arranged the five rites, the five jades, and the three kinds of silk.[12] 1.1.11

When Shun succeeded Yao owing to Heaven's favor, the Queen Mother of the West came to offer him a white jade flute. 1.1.12

"On the upper day of the first month, he received the abdication before the cultured ancestors.[13] Observing *xuanji* and jade transverse, he equilibrated the seven regulators."[14] What is "*xuanji*"? According to the *Commentary*, "*xuan*" (*s-wen) means "to revolve" (*s-wen), and "*ji*" (*kəi) means incipient (*kəi) or subtle. Its change is incipient and subtle, but the thing it moves is big. This is what it meant by *xuanji*. Therefore, *xuanji* refers to the North Star.[15] The one who receives the abdication is Shun. "Upper day" means the first day. 1.1.13

Without Heaven, the myriad things cannot be born; without earth they cannot be sustained. They cannot be set in motion without spring, grow without summer, be harvested without autumn, or be hoarded without winter. Hence, when the *Documents* says, "He performed the smoke sacrifice to the six honored ones,"[16] that is what it is about. 1.1.14

---

10   Alternatively, *Shiji* 1.32 writes Shouqiu 壽丘, located to the north of the eastern gate of the Lu capital.
11   For passages 1.1.8–1.1.10, see *Shiji* 1.32–34 for a more detailed narrative.
12   In the *Documents*, this sentence is included as part of the ritual that Shun initiated at Mount Tai during his inspection tour.
13   It is Shun who received the abdication of Yao before Yao's cultured ancestors. *Shiji* 1.22.
14   For the translation of *yuheng* as jade transverse, see Pankenier 2013, 460. *Yuheng* is not further explained in the *Great Commentary*.
15   Most Western Han texts claimed that both *xuanji* and *yuheng* are names of the stars of the Great Dipper. However, in Eastern Han, Ma Rong and Zheng Xuan associated the two terms with the armillary sphere (*huntian yi* 渾天儀). We follow Cullen and Farrer in interpreting the *Great Commentary*'s explanation of *xuanji* as pertaining to real life observation of the sky, more particularly the movement of the Great Dipper that appears to be steered by the North Star, which they refer to as T. S. Eliot's "still point of the turning world." Cullen and Farrer 1983, 57–58. This matches well with the identification of *xuanji* as the North Star. For other early views on *xuanji* and *yuheng*, see SSDZSZ 1.8b–1.10b (703–4); Ma Nan 2012b, 64–65. For Pi Xirui's understanding of *xuanji*, see the introduction to this volume.
16   Although the term *liuzong* 六宗, "six honored ones," of the *Documents* has been explained in many different ways, the *Great Commentary* is here committing to an interpretation as Heaven, Earth, and the four seasons.

1.1.15 古者、圭必有冒,言下之必有冒,不敢專達也。天子執冒以朝,諸侯見則覆之,故冒圭者,天子所以與諸侯為**瑞**[12]也,諸侯執所受圭以朝于天子。瑞也者、屬也。無過行者,得復其圭以歸其國;有過行者,留其圭,能正行者,復之。三年圭不復,少黜以爵;六年圭不復,少黜以地;九年圭不復,而地畢削。此謂諸侯之朝於天子也。義則見屬,不義則不見屬。

1.1.16 維元祀,**巡狩四嶽**八伯[13],壇四奧,沈四海,**封十有二山**,兆十有二州[14]。樂正定樂名。

元祀**代**[15]泰山,貢兩伯之樂焉:陽伯之樂舞侏離,其歌聲比余謠,名曰晢陽;儀伯之樂舞鼚哉,其歌聲比大謠,名曰南陽。

---

12 Cf. *Shangshu zhuzi suoyin* 2/2/16 (舜典).
13 Cf. *Shangshu zhuzi suoyin* 2/3/1–5 (舜典). *Shangshu zhuzi suoyin* has 守 for 狩 and 岳 for 嶽.
14 Cf. *Shangshu zhuzi suoyin* 2/3/1 (舜典).
15 Cf. *Shangshu zhuzi suoyin* 2/2/17 (舜典). *Shangshu zhuzi suoyin* has 岱 for 代.

In ancient times, a *gui* jade needed a cover jade. This means that subordinates must have received a cover jade; they would not dare to communicate with the ruler on their own initiative. The Son of Heaven held the cover jade when he received the regional lords at court, and, when he interviewed them, he put the cover over their *gui* jades. Therefore, the cover jade and the *gui* jades are what sealed the pact between the Son of Heaven and the regional lords. The regional lords held the *gui* they had received when they visited the court of the Son of Heaven. A "pact" establishes relations. Those who had no erroneous conduct were allowed to have their *gui* back and to return to their domains. The *gui* of those with erroneous conduct were retained and given back to them when they were able to rectify their behavior. If they had not received them back after three years, their noble rank was slightly reduced. After six years, their territory was also slightly reduced. After nine years, their territory was completely taken away. This describes court visits between the regional lords and the Son of Heaven. If they behaved properly, then relations were maintained; if not, they were terminated.

1.1.15

In the first year of his reign, Shun went on an inspection tour to the Four Marchmounts and their Eight Earls,[17] set up shrines to the Four Regions, made offerings to the Four Seas, erected altars to the Twelve Mountains, and sacrificed to the Twelve Provinces. The director of music decided on the musical pieces.

1.1.16

He offered the spring sacrifice to Mount Tai at Dai and presented the music of the two earls: to the music of Earl Sunlight the dance "Nurturing" was performed; the song was matched to the extremely wide-ranging melody and was named "Bright Sunlight";[18] to the music of Earl Yi the dance "Initiating Movement" was performed; the song was matched to the wide-ranging melody and was named "Southern Light."

---

17 We use marchmounts in Schafer's sense, as referring to the Four Sacred Peaks that present "the extremities of the habitable world"; in 1.1.17 the four are combined with a fifth central peak in the center. Schafer 1977, 6. For an overview of the Five Marchmounts, see Kleeman 1994. Each of the Four Marchmounts is associated with two earls; they are named throughout 1.1.16. In the *Documents*, the Four Marchmounts also stand for the caretakers of the mountains who are directly addressed by Shun, whereas, in this *Great Commentary* passage, they only refer to the sacred peaks themselves.

18 The translations of the dances' names are based on Zheng Xuan's glosses. According to Zheng Xuan, *yao* 謠 (melody) is a song unaccompanied by instruments; there are four types of *yao* defined by the range of high (*qing* 清) and low (*zhuo* 濁) notes they contain. *SZDZSZ* 2.6a–2.8b (711–12).

中祀大交霍山，貢兩伯之樂焉：夏伯之樂舞謾或，其歌聲比中謠，名曰初慮；**羲**[16]伯之樂舞將陽，其歌聲比大謠，名曰朱于。

秋祀**柳穀**[17]華山，貢兩伯之樂焉：秋伯之樂舞蔡俶，其歌聲比小謠，名曰芩落；**和**[18]伯之樂舞玄鶴，其歌聲比中謠，名曰歸來。

幽都[19]宏[20]山祀，貢兩伯之樂焉：冬伯之樂舞齊落，歌曰縵縵。

并論**八音**[21]四會，歸假于禰祖，用特。

1.1.17 五載一巡守，群后[22]德讓，貢正聲而九族[23]具成。雖禽獸之聲，猶悉關于律。樂者、人性之所自有也。故聖王巡**十有二州**[24]，觀其風俗，習其性情，因論十有二俗，定以**六律**、**五聲**、**八音**、**七始**[25]。著其素，蔟以為八，

16　Cf. *Shangshu zhuzi suoyin* 1/1/7–13 (堯典).
17　Cf. *Shangshu zhuzi suoyin* 1/1/10 (堯典). *Shangshuzhuzi suoyin* has 昧谷 for 柳穀.
18　Cf. *Shangshu zhuzi suoyin* 1/1/7–13 (堯典).
19　Cf. *Shangshu zhuzi suoyin* 1/1/12 (堯典).
20　宏 = 弘: SSDZSZ, 2.8a (712).
21　Cf. *Shangshu zhuzi suoyin* 5/7/14 (益稷).
22　Cf. *Shangshu zhuzi suoyin* 2/3/1 (舜典).
23　族 = 奏: Zheng Xuan's commentary, SSDZSZ 2.9a (713).
24　Cf. *Shangshu zhuzi suoyin* 2/3/1 (舜典).
25　Cf. *Shangshu zhuzi suoyin* 5/7/14 (益稷). *Shangshu zhuzi suoyin* has 在治 for 七始.

He offered the summer sacrifice to Mount Huo at Dajiao and presented the music of the two earls: to the music of Earl Summer the dance "Growth" was performed; the song was matched to the middle-ranging melody and was named "Initial Thoughts"; to the music of Earl Xi the dance "Maturity" was performed;[19] the song was matched to the wide-ranging melody and was named "Red Glow."

He offered the autumn sacrifice to Mount Hua at Liugu and presented the music of the two earls: to the music of Earl Autumn the dance "Starting Decay" was performed; the song was matched to the small-ranging melody and was named "Leaves Falling"; to the music of Earl He the dance "Crane's Migration to the South" was performed; the song was matched to the middle-ranging melody and was named "Return."

He presented the winter sacrifice to Mount Hong at the Dark City and presented the music of the two earls: to the music of Earl Winter the dance "Finishing" was performed; the song was called "Folding Back."

All together he arranged the Eight Timbres for the four sacrificial gatherings. Having returned, he sacrificed an ox at the ancestral temple.

Shun made an inspection tour once every five years. All the lords were virtuous and yielding. As tribute, he presented the proper music, and, after nine times, the musical performance was complete. Even the sounds of birds and beasts were completely in accordance with the pitch pipes. Music is what human nature spontaneously possesses. Therefore, a sage king makes an inspection tour to the twelve provinces, observes their airs and customs, and learns about their inclinations and sensibilities. Based on this, he arranges the Twelve Customs and fixes the Six Pitch Pipes, the Five Tones, the Eight Timbres, and the Seven Beginnings.[20] Showing their origins and organizing them into eight groups

1.1.17

19　The "Canon of Yao" in the *Documents* mentions Xi and He as a pair. The commentators to 1.1.16 of the *Great Commentary* dispute whether Earl Xi and Earl He can be identified with Xi and He of the *Documents* or with their descendants. See *Shangshu zhuzi suoyin* 1/1/7–12; *SSDZSZ* 2.6b–2.7b (711–12); Ma Nan 2012b, 40–41.

20　We follow Zheng Xuan's commentary in interpreting *wusheng* 五聲 as the Five Tones Gong 宮, Shang 商, Jue 角, Zhi 徵, and Yu 羽, and *bayin* 八音 as the timbres produced by eight different musical instruments. Zheng Xuan interprets *qishi* 七始 as the Seven Pitches, including Huangzhong 黃鐘, Taicou 太簇, Dalü 大呂, Nanlü 南呂, Guxian 姑洗, Yingzhong 應鐘, and Ruibin 蕤賓; Kong Yingda extrapolates that these Seven Pitches correlate with seven tones, including the Five Tones mentioned above and two altered tones (*biansheng* 變聲), namely, Biangong 變宮 and Bianzhi 變徵. See *SSDZSZ* 2.10a–b (713); *Liji zhushu* 22.433. Other texts explain the Seven Beginnings as the four seasons plus the triad of Heaven, Earth, and Humankind; *Hanshu* 21A.972 and *SSDZSZ* 2.10a–b (713).

此八伯之事也。分定於五，此五嶽之事也。五聲、天音也，八音、天化也，七始、天統也。

1.1.18　古者巡守以遷廟之主行，出以幣帛皮圭告于祖，遂奉以載于齊[26]車。每舍奠焉，然後就舍，反必告，奠卒，斂幣玉藏之兩階之閒，蓋貴命也。

1.1.19　五年一朝，王者亦貴得天下之歡心，以事其先王。因助祭以述其職，故分四方諸侯為四輩，輩主一時。

1.1.20　古者諸侯于天子，五年一朝。見其身，述其職。述其職者、述其所職也。

1.1.21　見諸侯，問百年，[27]大師陳詩以觀民風俗，命市納賈以觀民好惡。山川神祇有不舉者為不敬。不敬者、削以地；宗廟有不順者為不孝。不孝者、

26　齊 = 齋.
27　百年 = 百年者: *Liji zhuzi suoyin* 5.22/32/27, 25.44/129/4; *Kong congzi zhuzi suoyin* 3.1/16/9; and *Shuoyuan zhuzi suoyin* 19.17/164/20.

is the task of the Eight Earls. Assigning them to the five categories is the task of the Five Marchmounts.[21] The Five Tones are the heavenly sounds, the Eight Timbres are the heavenly transformations, and the Seven Beginnings are the heavenly governors.[22]

1.1.18 In ancient times, during inspections tours, he took along the spirit tablets as he traveled. Before he left, he announced his departure to the ancestors with gifts of silks, skins, and a *gui* jade. Then, having paid his obeisance, he loaded them into the wagon of purification.[23] After a day's travel, he made offerings to them before going to his lodgings. Upon coming back, he had to announce his return. Having finished the offerings, he collected the silks and jades, and stored them between the two stairs. If this is not valuing one's mandate!

1.1.19 The lords paid a court visit once every five years. Truly, the king valued gaining the endorsement of the realm so as to serve the ancestral kings. As the lords came to assist in the sacrifice and report on their duties, the king, accordingly, divided the regional lords from the four quarters into four groups and made each responsible for one season.

1.1.20 In ancient times, the regional lords visited the Son of Heaven's court once every five years. They appeared in person and reported on their duties. "To report on their duties" means to report on the way they carried out their duties.

1.1.21 He received the regional lords in audience and inquired about the centenarians. The music masters displayed the songs to show the customs of the people. He ordered the market supervisors to report on prices to show the likes and dislikes of the people.

Failing to sacrifice to the gods of the mountains and rivers was considered irreverent. Those found guilty of irreverence had their land reduced.

Failing to observe the proper order at the ancestral temple was considered unfilial. Those found guilty of unfilial behavior had their rank reduced.

Changing the rites and altering music was considered disobedient. Those lords found guilty of disobedience were exiled.

---

21 The *Documents* mentions only the Four Marchmounts. That the *Great Commentary* mentions five here can perhaps be explained by the thinking in fives (the four directions plus the center) that became fashionable in the early imperial period.
22 For more on governors (*tong* 統), see 3.2.1.
23 In a conversation between Zengzi and Confucius, two scenarios are laid out: the ruler, when he travels, takes either the ancestral tablets or the offerings with him. *Liji zhuzi suoyin* 7.17/53/9. Here in 1.1.18, it is not entirely clear whether he took only the tablets, the offerings, or both.

黜以爵。變禮易樂者為不從。不從者、君流；改制度衣服為畔。畔者、君討。有功者賞之。《書》曰：「**明試以功，車服以庸**[28]。」

1.1.22　以賢制爵，以庸制祿，故人慎德興功，輕利而重義。

1.1.23　古之帝王，必有命民。民能敬長憐孤，取舍好讓，舉事力者，命于其君。得命，然後得乘飾車駢馬，衣文駢錦。未有命者，不得衣，不得乘。乘、衣有罰，庶人木車單馬，衣布帛。

1.1.24　未命為**士**[29]者，車不得有飛軨，不得朱軒。

1.1.25　古者諸侯之於天子也，三年一貢**士**[30]，天子命與諸侯輔助為政，所以通賢共治，示不獨專，重民之至。大國舉三人，次國舉二人，小國舉一人。一適，謂之攸好德；再適，謂之賢賢；三適，謂之有功。有功者，天子一賜以車服弓矢，再賜以秬鬯，三賜以虎賁百人，號曰命諸侯。命諸侯得專征。

28　Cf. *Shangshu zhuzi suoyin* 2/3/1 (舜典); *Shangshu zhuzi suoyin* 5/7/17–18 (益稷) has 庶 for 試.
29　Cf. *Shangshu zhuzi suoyin* 2/3/11 (舜典), 3/5/3 (大禹謨), 3/6/1 (大禹謨).
30　Cf. *Shangshu zhuzi suoyin* 2/3/11 (舜典), 3/5/3 (大禹謨), 3/6/1 (大禹謨).

Violating the regulations concerning clothing was considered rebellious. Those lords found guilty of rebellion were subjected to a punitive expedition.

Those with achievements were rewarded.

The *Documents* says: "They were assessed in light of their achievements. They were awarded chariots and robes according to their merits."

Establish ranks according to worth, and distribute stipends according to merit. In this manner, people will cautiously guard their virtue and attain achievements, disregard profit, and value duty. 1.1.22

Sovereigns of ancient times always had people who received special recognition. People who demonstrated respect for their elders and compassion for orphans, who were predisposed to yield while receiving and giving, and who carried out their tasks with dedication were recognized by their ruler. On receiving such recognition, they were allowed to drive an ornamental cart with a pair of horses and to wear patterned and brocaded clothes. Those without such recognition were not allowed to dress and drive in such a manner. If they did so anyway, they were punished. Commoners rode in a wooden cart with a single horse and wore cotton or silk. 1.1.23

Those who had not yet received recognition as men of service were not allowed to have flying banners on their carts or to have carts with vermilion curtains.[24] 1.1.24

In antiquity, once every three years, the regional lords presented to the Son of Heaven men of service. The Son of Heaven ordered them to assist him in the administration together with the regional lords. Hence, through the exchange of worthy men, they became corulers and demonstrated the excellence of a system in which power was not monopolized and in which the people were valued. 1.1.25

Large domains recommended three people, medium-sized ones two, and small domains one. The first time a lord succeeded in advancing a man of service, he was called a "lover of virtue"; if he succeeded a second time, he was called "one who recognizes worth"; the third time, he was called an "achieved one."

As to the "achieved ones," at first the Son of Heaven rewarded them with carts, clothes, bows, and arrows; next he gave them sacrificial wine; and the third time he bequeathed them one hundred warriors and

---

24 The term *shi* 士, which we render as "man of service," occurs repeatedly in the *Great Commentary*. In preimperial times it referred to a group of low-level aristocrats who were forced to rely on means other than rank to find their position in society; it gradually evolved to refer to a service class that supported the courts with a variety of skills and know-how. K. Kim 2013. Regarding the cart with vermilion curtains, see Sun Ji 2008, 90 (23-3). See also 4.1.2.

得專征者，鄰國有臣弒其君，孼代其宗者，弗請于天子，征之而歸其地于天子可也。有不貢士，謂之不率正。不率正者，天子絀之。一不適，謂之過；再不適，謂之敖；三不適，謂之誣。誣者，天子絀之。一絀、少絀以爵，再絀、少絀以地，三絀、而爵地畢。

1.1.26 唐虞**象刑**[31]而民不敢犯，**苗民用**刑而**民興犯漸**[32]；唐虞之象刑，上刑赭衣不純，中刑雜屨，下刑墨幪，以居州里而民恥之。

1.1.27 唐虞**象刑**[33]：犯墨者蒙皁巾，犯劓者赭其衣，犯臏者以墨幪臏處而畫之，犯大辟者布衣無領。

---

31 Cf. *Shangshu zhuzi suoyin* 2/3/2 (舜典): 象以典刑 for 象刑; *Shangshu zhuzi suoyin* 5/8/3 (益稷).
32 Cf. *Shangshu zhuzi suoyin* 55/50/10–12 (呂刑). *Shangshu zhuzi suoyin* has 苗民弗用靈 for 苗民用刑 and 民興胥漸 for 民興犯漸.
33 Cf. *Shangshu zhuzi suoyin* 2/3/2 (舜典): 象以典刑 for 象刑; *Shangshu zhuzi suoyin* 5/8/3 (益稷).

awarded them the title of "recognized regional lord." A recognized regional lord had the authority to initiate a military expedition.

As to those who had the authority to initiate a military expedition: when in a neighboring domain a minister assassinated his ruler or a branch lineage usurped the main lineage, they were, without petitioning the Son of Heaven, allowed to organize a military expedition against their neighbors and return their lands to the Son of Heaven.

Those who did not present men of service were called "those who refuse to follow the lead."[25] The Son of Heaven reduced the ranks and domains of those who refuse to follow the lead. The first time a lord did not advance men of service, he was called "at fault"; if it happened again, he was called "overbearing"; if it happened a third time, he was called an "impostor." The Son of Heaven reduced the ranks and domains of impostors. Upon the first infraction, their noble rank was slightly reduced; the second time, their lands were slightly reduced; the third time, they lost both their noble rank and their lands.[26]

Yao and Shun used symbolic punishments, and the people did not dare to commit crimes. When the Miao people used real punishments, people were aroused, and crimes gradually increased.[27] With Yao and Shun's symbolic punishments, the most severe punishment was to wear reddish brown clothes of mixed color; the medium punishment was to wear two different shoes; the lightest punishment was to use a black scarf. With these the offenders were made to reside in villages and hamlets where the people would shame them.[28]

1.1.26

With Yao and Shun's symbolic punishments, those whose crimes merited tattooing had to wear black coifs; those whose crimes merited cutting off the nose had to stain their clothes a reddish brown; those whose crimes merited cutting the kneecap had to wear a marked black scarf around the knee; those whose crimes merited death had to wear collarless clothes.[29]

1.1.27

25　Our translation follows Zheng Xuan's gloss of *shuai* 率 as *xun* 循 and *zheng* 正 as *you* 由; *SSDZJJ* 1.17a (4121).

26　In the "Annals" (*benji* 本紀) of the reign of Emperor Wu, this passage is integrated into the preamble of a proposal made by officials in 128 BCE. The proposal called for all two-thousand-bushel officials to recommend candidates known for their filial behavior and integrity (*xiaolian* 孝廉) for office. *Hanshu* 6.166–67. See also case 1 of the section "The *Great Commentary* on Questions of Political and Social Order" of the introduction to this volume.

27　A similar phrase occurs in the "Punishments of Fu (Lü)" chapter of the *Documents*; *Shangshu zhuzi suoyin* 55/50/11–12.

28　The symbolic punishments are also mentioned in *Master Xun*; *Xunzi zhuzi suoyin* 18/85/5–10.

29　Whereas 1.1.26 divides symbolic punishments into three levels (severe, medium, and light), 1.1.27 provides the symbolic punishments that correspond to four out of the five corporeal punishments (excluding castration). These are detailed in 5.22.1.

1.1.28　帝猶反側晨興，**闢四門**[34]，來仁賢。

1.1.29　《書》曰：「**三歲考績，三考黜陟幽明**[35]。」其訓曰：三歲而小考者，正職而行事也。九歲而大考者，黜無職而賞有功也。其賞有功也：諸侯賜弓矢者，得專征；賜鈇鉞者，得專殺；賜圭瓚者，得為鬯以祭。不得專征者，以兵屬於得專征之國；不得專殺者，以獄屬於得專殺之國；不得賜圭瓚者，資鬯於天子之國，然後祭。

1.1.30　三年一使三公**黜陟**[36]。

1.1.31　天子三公：一曰**司徒公**，二曰司馬公，三曰**司空公**。**百姓不親，五品不訓**，則責之司徒。**蠻夷猾夏，寇賊奸宄**[37]，則責之司馬。溝瀆雍遏，**水**為民害，則責之司空。

34　Cf. *Shangshu zhuzi suoyin* 2/3/5 (舜典).
35　Cf. *Shangshu zhuzi suoyin* 2/4/4 (舜典). *Shangshu zhuzi suoyin* has 載 for 歲.
36　Cf. *Shangshu zhuzi suoyin* 2/4/4 (舜典).
37　Cf. *Shangshu zhuzi suoyin* 2/4/4 (舜典), 2/3/8–11 (舜典). *Shangshu zhuzi suoyin* has 遜 for 訓, 猾 for 滑, and 姦 for 奸.

The supreme lord kept tossing from one side to another in his sleep and arose early. He opened the four gates to invite the benevolent and the worthy. 1.1.28

The *Documents* says, "Every three years he reviewed their achievements and after three reviews demoted the undeserving and advanced the deserving." The *Explanation* of this phrase says:[30] "The purpose of the minor review every three years is to evaluate performance and make sure that affairs are taken care of; the purpose of the major review every nine years is to demote nonperformers and reward those with merit." 1.1.29

Those with merit are rewarded as follows: those regional lords who are given bow and arrow have the authority to initiate a military expedition; those who are given the execution axe have the authority to kill; and those who are given ladle-shaped wine cups have the authority to make sacrificial wine.[31]

Those who do not have the authority to initiate a military expedition have to subordinate their armies to those domains that have this authority; those who do not have the authority to kill have to submit their legal cases to domains who do have this authority; those who are not given ladle-shaped wine cups have to obtain their sacrificial wine from the Son of Heaven's domain; only then can they make sacrifice.

Once every three years the three excellencies receive their promotions or demotions. 1.1.30

As to the Son of Heaven's three excellencies: The first excellency is called minister over the masses; the second, minister of military affairs; the third, minister of works.[32] When the Hundred Families are alienated or the five classes not well managed,[33] then the minister over the masses bears responsibility. When the Man and Yi trouble our Xia lands, and bandits and robbers commit treacherous acts, the minister of military affairs bears responsibility. When drainage channels are blocked and subsequent floods harm the people, then the minister of works bears responsibility. 1.1.31

---

30   The bibliographical treatise of *Old Book of Tang* lists a *Thorough Explanations of the Documents* in three *juan*, annotated by Fu Sheng; *Jiu Tangshu* 46.1969.
31   The ideas and vocabulary in this passage overlap with 1.1.25.
32   For alternative names of the three excellencies, see 6.1.6. See also 5.1.2.
33   Given that *baixing* 百姓 here is quoted from the *Documents*, we translate it as "Hundred Families," meaning the prominent families. However, by Warring States times, the term had come to refer to people generally. We translate it as "people" in 5.3.2, 6.2.25, 7.2.12, and 7.2.18.

1.1.32 **舜讓于德不怡**[38]。

1.1.33 **惟刑之謐哉**[39]。

1.1.34 堯南撫交阯。

1.1.35 堯時麒麟在郊藪。

11.36 堯使**契**[40]為田。

38　Cf. *Shangshu zhuzi suoyin* 2/2/15 (舜典). *Shangshu zhuzi suoyin* has 弗嗣 for 不怡.
39　Cf. *Shangshu zhuzi suoyin* 2/3/3 (舜典). *Shangshu zhuzi suoyin* has 恤 for 謐.
40　Cf. *Shangshu zhuzi suoyin* 2/3/8, 2/3/10 (舜典).

When Shun had to yield on account of his virtue, he was not joyful.	1.1.32
As to punishments, be careful with them.³⁴	1.1.33
In the south, Yao pacified Jiaozhi.³⁵	1.1.34
In Yao's time there was a *qilin* in the wetlands.³⁶	1.1.35
Yao ordered Xie to manage the fields.³⁷	1.1.36

---

34 The variants of *mi* 謐 (translated as careful) include *jing* 靜 and *xu* 恤. According to Wang Niansun, they are all variants meaning *shen* 慎, "careful." *Jingyi shuwen* 3.17b–18a (321–22).
35 In texts such as *Master Mo* and *Master Han Fei*, *jiao* 交, as it occurs in the "Canon of Yao" of the *Documents*, is interpreted as Jiaozhi in the south and paired with Youdu 幽都 in the north to indicate the scope of the realm of Yao. *Mozi zhuzi suoyin* 6.2/37/13, *Hanfeizi zhuzi suoyin* 10/17/7. In 111 BCE, Jiaozhi was established as a commandery; see *Hanshu* 28A.1543. It comprised what is now northern Vietnam and the southern parts of Guangdong and Guangxi. The region is also featured in 5.7.2 of the *Great Commentary*.
36 The word *qilin* is often translated as unicorn.
37 Shun had appointed Xie as his minister over the masses; see *Shiji* 3.91.

卷二
虞傳
虞夏傳

2
Traditions on Yu
Traditions on Yu and Xia

2.1

Nine Offers

The transmitted Documents has no chapter called "Nine Offers" even though, according to some, remnants of such a chapter still existed in Eastern Han times.¹ The "Minor Xu," as preserved in the received Documents, mentions the "Nine Offers" and has it occupy nine chapters of the presumed one-hundred-chapter version (chaps. 4-12).

Wang Yinglin notes that the Great Commentary had a "Nine Offers" chapter and that it contained a sentence not present in his Documents text.² Xue Jixuan 薛季宣 (1134-73) also reproduced this sentence, claiming it was a sentence Master Fu "roughly remembered" 略能記其語 from the lost text.³

Wang Kaiyun reproduces this "lost" sentence at the beginning of his "Nine Offers" chapter (2.1.1) and adds five more passages. In the Chen and Pi versions, it is the only passage.

The other five passages in our translation contain historical lore regarding Shun, and two of these are set as part of a dialogue. All five fragments highlight Shun's uninvolved, but yet effective, style of government and remind one of the passages on Shun in the Analects (especially 15.5, where he is associated with nonpurposeful rulership, wuwei 無為).⁴

---

1   Pi Xirui thought that Ma Rong and Zheng Xuan might have seen the chapter, if only in an already fragmented (yi 逸) state; SSDZSZ 2.1a.
2   Yuhai 37.25a (749); Kunxue jiwen 1:142.
3   Shu guwen xun 16.2a (373).
4   Leys 1997, 74.

2.1
九共

2.1.1 「予辯下土,使民平平,使民無敖。」

2.1.2 舜彈五弦之琴,歌《南風》之詩,而天下治。

2.1.3 舜攝時,三公九卿百執事。此堯之官也,故使百官事舜。

2.1.4 成王問周公曰:「舜之冠何如焉?」周公曰:「古之人有冒皮而句領者,然鳳皇巢其樹,麒麟聚其域也。」

2.1

Nine Offers

"In managing my land, I strive to treat the people fairly so that they may be without presumption."[1]	2.1.1
Shun played the five-stringed zither and chanted the ode "Southern Wind." Subsequently the realm was ordered.[2]	2.1.2
When Shun took over, there were the three excellencies, the nine ministers, and the one hundred managers. Since they were Yao's officials, he transferred them all to serve Shun.	2.1.3
King Cheng asked the Duke of Zhou, "What was Shun's cap like?" The Duke of Zhou answered, "Among the ancients some wore a leather hat with a hooked-on collar. Even so, phoenixes chose their trees to nest, and *qilin* gathered on their domains."[3]	2.1.4

---

1   According to Wang Yinglin, this sentence is originally from the currently lost "Nine Offers" (Jiu gong) chapter of the *Documents*. *Kunxue jiwen* 1:142–43.
2   Shun's playing "Southern Wind" is also seen in *Records of Ritual* and *Scribe's Records*. *Scribe's Records* tells the story of Shun playing "Southern Wind" in the context of his filial behavior: just as the southern wind nourishes the crops, parents nourish their children and are owed a debt of gratitude. Performing "Southern Wind" thus contributes to a well-ordered society. *Shiji* 24.1197, 24.1235; *Liji zhuzi suoyin* 19.7/100/11.
3   The word *qilin* is often translated as unicorn. A leather hat with a hooked-on collar was the modest headgear supposedly worn by ancient kings like Shun. *SSDZJJ* 3.2b (4147). A more elaborate parallel dialogue in *Master Xun*, with Lord Ai of Lu and Confucius as interlocutors, also conveys the message that sagely rule lies not in outside appearances but in caring government. Phoenixes and *qilin* were Heaven's signs of the presence of a true king. *Xunzi zhuzi suoyin* 31/146/13–15.

2.1.5　舜不登而高，不行而遠，拱揖於天下，而天下稱仁。

2.1.6　子曰：「參，女[1]以為明主為勞乎？昔者舜左禹而右皋陶，不下席而天下治。」

1　女＝汝.

Without climbing, Shun reached high places; without traveling, he reached great distances. He saluted the realm, and the realm praised his humaneness.   2.1.5

The master spoke: "Shen, do you really think that being an enlightened ruler is hard work? Shun, in ancient times, was assisted by Yu on the left, and by Gaoyao on the right. He did not leave his mat, but the realm was in order."[4]   2.1.6

---

[4] This passage also appears in *Da Dai liji zhuzi suoyin* 1.1/1/24.

2.2

Gaoyao's Counsel

"Gaoyao's Counsel" occurs in both the New and Old Script versions of the Documents. The New Script version combines in one chapter what in the Old Script version are two separate chapters, "Gaoyao's Counsel," and "Supplementary Sacrifices" (Yi ji 益稷). The text consists of dialogues in which Gaoyao and Yu provide extensive advice on government to Shun.

The Great Commentary *explains words, sentences, or passages now in the chapters "Gaoyao's Counsel" and "Supplementary Sacrifices" of the Old Script* Documents *under the title "Gaoyao's Counsel." In doing so, it deals with various topics important to the organization of the empire as ruled by the Son of Heaven: sumptuary laws regulating the clothing of the members of the ruling group (2.2.1), which bells to strike in the ceremonies to announce the departure and arrival of the Son of Heaven (2.2.2), an explanation of the* Documents' *"four associates" in terms of four types of advisor who helped sustain the Son of Heaven's regime (2.2.3), vocabulary for the administrative divisions in which to organize the population (2.2.4), and details on the performance of "Pure, the Ancestral Temple" (2.2.5).*

After these sections, the focus shifts to the supreme lord (di 帝*), here a reference to Shun. What is at stake here is not, as in the "Nine Offers," Shun's personality and governing style but the ritual and musical performances he engaged in during different years of his reign; these served to show Shun's qualities and facilitated the nonhereditary dynastic transitions from Yao to Shun and from Shun to Yu (2.2.6–9). The texts of various hymns that were performed are given and are not found in any other early sources.*

The last sections (2.2.10–14) are isolated explanations of sentences or glosses. In one case the Commentary *is explicitly quoted.*[1]

---

1   As explained in the section "A *Commentary* (Zhuan) within the *Great Commentary*" of the introduction to this volume.

2.2
咎繇謨

2.2.1 天子衣服,其文**華蟲**,**作會**,**宗彝**,**璪火**,**山龍**。
諸侯作會,**宗彝**,**璪火**,**山龍**。
子男,**宗彝**,**璪火**,**山龍**。
大夫,**璪火**,**山龍**。
士,**山龍**。[1]
故《書》曰:「**天命有德,五服五章哉**。」[2] 山龍、青也,華蟲、黃也,作會、黑也,宗彝、白也,璪火、赤也。天子服五,諸侯服四,次國服三,大夫服二,士服一。

1　Cf. *Shangshu zhuzi suoyin* 5/7/12–13 (益稷). *Shangshu zhuzi suoyin* has 予欲觀古人之象,日、月、星辰、山、龍、華蟲作會;宗彝、藻、火、粉米、黼、黻、絺繡,以五采彰施于五色,作服。
2　Cf. *Shangshu zhuzi suoyin* 4/6/19–20 (皋陶謨).

2.2
Gaoyao's Counsel

As to the Son of Heaven, his robe is decorated with pheasants (*hua-chong*), emblems (*zuohui*), ancestral vessels (*zongyi*), an assemblage of water plants and flames (*zaohuo*), and an assemblage of mountains and dragons (*shanlong*). 2.2.1

As to the regional lords, their robes have emblems, ancestral vessels, an assemblage of water plants and flames, and an assemblage of mountains and dragons.

As to the princes,[1] their robes have ancestral vessels, an assemblage of water plants and flames, and an assemblage of mountains and dragons.

As to the ministers, their robes have an assemblage of water plants and flames, and an assemblage of mountains and dragons.

As to the men of service, their robes have an assemblage of mountains and dragons.

Hence, the *Documents* says, "Heaven gives charge to those with virtue and awards them the Five Robes with the five insignia!" The assemblage of mountains and dragons is associated with the color green, pheasants with the color yellow, emblems with the color black, ancestral vessels with the color white, and the assemblage of water plants and flames with the color red. The robes of the Son of Heaven have the five insignia, whereas the robes of the regional lords have four, those of the rulers of secondary kingdoms three, those of the ministers two, and those of men of service one.[2]

---

1   *Zi* 子 and *nan* 男 are steps four and five of the five-rank noble system: *gong* 公, *hou* 侯, *bo* 伯, *zi*, and *nan*.
2   Scholars disagree on the meanings of the five items. We base ourselves on *SSDZSZ* 2.20a–22b (718–20) and Qu Wanli 1983, 40–41 n. 54. The opening sentence of 2.2.1 is closely related to a sentence in the "Supplementary Sacrifices" chapter of the *Documents*; moreover, even though "Supplementary Sacrifices" is an Old Script chapter,

2.2.2 **六律**[1]者何？黃鐘、蕤賓、無射、大蔟、夷則、姑洗是也。
　　　故天子左五鐘，右五鐘。天子將出，則撞黃鐘之鐘，右五鐘皆應〔之〕。馬鳴中律，步者皆有容，駕者皆有文，御者皆有數。步者中規，折還中矩，立則磬折，拱則抱鼓。然後大師奏樂登車，告出也。
　　　入則撞蕤賓，左五鐘皆應〔之〕，以治容皃。容皃得，則氣得；氣得，則肌膚安；肌膚安，則色齊矣。蕤賓聲，狗吠鵽鳴，及倮介之蟲，皆莫不延頸以聽蕤賓。在內者皆玉色，在外者皆金聲。然後少師奏〔樂〕登堂就席，告入也。
　　　此言至樂相和，物動相生，同聲相應之義也。

2.2.3 古者天子必有四鄰：前曰疑[2]，後曰承，左曰輔，右曰弼。天子有問，無以對，責之疑；可志而不志，責之承；可正而不正，責之輔；可揚而不

1　Cf. *Shangshu zhuzi suoyin* 5/7/14 (益稷).
2　疑=儀。SSDZSZ 2/26a–b (721).

What are the six pitch pipes? They are Huangzhong, Ruibin, Wuyi, Taicou, Yize, and Guxian.[3] Hence, the Son of Heaven has five bells at his left and five bells at his right.

2.2.2

When he is about to depart, he strikes the Huangzhong bell, and the five bells at the right all resonate. The neighing of the horses follows the pitch, the footmen all adopt the proper posture, the horsemen all take their positions, and the charioteers all arrange themselves. The footmen form a square; then, reversing position, they arrange themselves in a circle. Standing still they bend like a chime stone; saluting, they are as if holding a drum. Then, the great music master performs the music and mounts the chariot to announce the Son of Heaven's departure.

When he enters, Ruibin is struck, and the five bells at the left all resonate. This is to adjust everyone's posture and facial expression. With the proper postures and facial expressions, the breath is wholesome, the flesh and skin at ease, and the appearance peaceful. At the sound of Ruibin, dogs bark and hogs grunt; all insects, with or without a shell, stretch their necks in order to hear Ruibin. Those inside all have the appearance of jade; those outside, voices of gold. After this the lesser music master performs, ascends the hall, and goes to his mat to announce the Son of Heaven's entry.

This explains how with good music all is in harmony, how things stir and generate one another, and how compatible sounds resonate with one another.

In ancient times, the Son of Heaven had to have four associates: the one in front is called problem solver, the one at the rear the deputy, the one to the left the assistant, and the one to the right the aide. When the Son of Heaven has questions that no one is able to answer, he assigns them to the problem solver; when there are goals that have yet to be pursued, he assigns them to the deputy; when there are things that have yet to be rectified, he assigns them to the assistant; when there are issues that have yet to be raised, he assigns them to the aide. Their ranks are like

2.2.3

---

there is evidence for the sentence circulating well before the fourth century CE (for Zheng Xuan's citation of the sentence, see *Zhouli zhushu*). If we had understood the opening sentence of 2.2.1 based on the sentence now in "Supplementary Sacrifices," our view would have been substantially different. For example, *zuohui* in "Supplementary Sacrifices" is clearly a verb, and *shan, long, zao,* and *huo* are often taken as separate items. However, the last sentence of 2.2.1 prompted us to consider the option we have chosen here: five *binomina*, each associated with one of the five colors.

3   The names of six pitch pipes as provided in 2.2.2 correspond well with those given in the "Treatise on Pitch Pipes" (Lü shu 律書) chapter in *Scribe's Records* and the "Treatise on Pitch Pipes and Calendars" (Lü li zhi 律曆志) chapter in *Book of Han*. *Shiji* 25.1244-48; *Hanshu* 21A.958-59. "Imperial Readings Compiled in the Taiping Era" (Shixu bu yi 時序部一) provides explanations for the names of the pitch pipes in terms of the changes of yin and yang throughout the year; *Taiping yulan* 16.210b.

揚,責之弼。其爵視上卿,其祿視次國之君。天子中立而聽朝,則四聖維之。是以慮無失計,舉無過事。故《書》曰「欽四鄰」[3],此之謂也。

2.2.4 古之處師:八家而為鄰,三鄰而為朋,三朋而為里,五里而為邑,十邑而為都,十都而為師,**州有十二師**[4]焉。家不盈三口者,不朋。由命士以上,不朋。

2.2.5 古者帝王升歌《清廟》之樂,大琴練弦達越,大瑟朱弦達越,以韋為**鼓**,謂之**搏拊**[5]。何以也?君子〔有〕大人聲,不以鐘鼓竽瑟之聲亂人聲。《清廟》升歌者,歌先人之功烈德澤也,故欲其清也。其歌之呼也,曰「於穆清廟」。於者,歎之也,穆者、敬之也,清者、欲其**在位**[6]者

---

3   Cf. *Shangshu zhuzi suoyin* 5/7/15 (益稷).
4   Cf. *Shangshu zhuzi suoyin* 5/8/2 (益稷). *Shangshu zhuzi suoyin* has 十有二 for 有十二.
5   Cf. *Shangshu zhuzi suoyin*, 5/8/4 (益稷).
6   Cf. *Shangshu zhuzi suoyin* 5/7/9 (益稷).

that of the highest ministers, their salaries like that of a lord of a secondary kingdom. When the Son of Heaven takes the central position to hold court, the four sages support him. That is why in planning nothing is overlooked, and, in executing, nothing goes awry. Therefore, when the *Documents* says "Respect the four associates," that is what it is about.[4]

In antiquity the population was organized in districts: eight households formed a neighborhood, three neighborhoods a hamlet, three hamlets a village, five villages a town, ten towns a city, ten cities a district. A province has a total of twelve districts.[5] When a household has three or fewer members, they are not grouped into a hamlet; nor are those of the rank of recognized men of service on up.[6]

2.2.4

In ancient times, when the sovereign ascended to perform the melody "Pure, the Ancestral Temple,"[7] the great *qin*-zither had white silk strings and a hole at the bottom, the great *se*-zither had red silk strings and a hole at the bottom,[8] and with leather they made a drum and called it "the leather drum" (*bofu*). Why is this? A noble man has the voice of an accomplished person; the sounds of bells, drums, flutes, and zithers should not overwhelm the human voice. Those performing "Pure, the Ancestral Temple" sing of the splendid merit and penetrating power of the ancestors; that is why they wanted it to be pure. The invocation of the song is as follows: "Oh, how solemn the Pure Temple!"[9] "Oh" is an exclamation; "solemn" is to show respect; "pure" means that they wanted participants in the ritual to be able to hear it all around.[10] Therefore, when the Duke of Zhou ascended to sing of the splendid merit and penetrating power of King Wen, if the audience had seen King Wen perform

2.2.5

---

4   "Gaoyao's Counsel" ("Yi ji" chapter in the Old Script *Documents*); Karlgren 1950 translates: "Be reverent, you four (neighbors=) associates!" ("Book of Documents", 11 [no. 13]).

5   "Gaoyao's Counsel" ("Yi ji" chapter in the Old Script *Documents*); Karlgren 1950 translates: "In a province there are 12 districts." (12 [no. 17]).

6   The units are reminiscent of the administrative units into which the population was organized during the early imperial period, but the terminology that the *Great Commentary* offers is different from what was actually adopted; see Loewe 2006, 46–47. It is noteworthy that the *Great Commentary* wants to show that the *Documents* has contributions to make in this area too.

7   "Pure, the Ancestral Temple" (Qingmiao 清廟) is the first of the "Sacrificial Odes of Zhou" (Zhou song 周頌) of the *Odes*, Mao no. 266.

8   According to Zheng Xuan's commentary, *yue* 越 refers to the hole made at the bottom of the instrument; *Shiji* 23.1158 n. 6.

9   This is the first line of "Pure, the Ancestral Temple."

10 The expression *zaiwei* 在位 (participants in the ritual) also occurs in various *Documents* chapters including "Canon of Yao" and "Great Yu's Counsel," where it means the ruler or office holders; *Shangshu zhuzi suoyin* 1/2/2, 2/4/4.

徧聞之也。故周公升歌文王之功烈德澤，苟在廟中嘗見文王者，愀然如復見文王。故《書》曰：「**搏拊琴瑟以詠，祖考來格。**」[7]此之謂也。

2.2.6 維五祀，奏鐘石，論人聲乃及鳥獸，咸變於前。故更箸四時，推六律六呂，詢十有二變，而道宏廣。五作十道，孝力為右。秋養耆老，而春食孤子，乃浡然**招**[8]樂，興于**大鹿**[9]之野。

---

7 Cf. *Shangshu zhuzi suoyin* 5/8/4 (益稷).
8 Cf. *Shangshu zhuzi suoyin* 5/8/5 (益稷). *Shangshu zhuzi suoyin* has 韶 for 招. 招 = 韶: *Lu shi houji* 路史後紀, quoted in *SSDZJJ* 1.12b (4118); *SSDZSZ* 2.11b (714).
9 Cf. *Shangshu zhuzi suoyin* 2/2/14 ("Canon of Shun"). *Shangshu zhuzi suoyin* has 大麓 for 大鹿.

in the temple before, they would be transfixed because they seemed to see him again. Hence, the *Documents* says: "The leather drum (*bofu*) and the zithers are used to chant; the ancestors come."[11] That is what it is about.

In the fifth year of his reign, there was a performance with bells and chime stones. How human voices and the sounds of beasts and birds were rendered completely differed from the previous reign.[12] They recalibrated themselves with the four seasons, expanded the pitch pipes to six upper ones and six lower ones,[13] and applied this to the twelve changes. Hence, the Way was encompassing and broad. Among the five teachings and the ten methods,[14] diligent pursuit of filial piety took pride of place.[15] In autumn he cared for the elderly; in spring he fed the orphans. Then, with great excitement, the "Shao" melody was performed to celebrate the moment he was established in the great foothills.[16]

2.2.6

---

11 "Gaoyao's Counsel" ("Yi ji" chapter in the Old Script *Documents*); Karlgren 1950 translates "The small leather drum, the guitar and the lute, when with them one sings, the (Spirits of the) ancestors come" (12 [no. 18]).

12 The "fifth year" refers to Shun's reign, and hence the "previous" (*qian* 前) reign is Yao's.

13 The twelve pitch pipes were ordered according to a scheme that correlates the six *lü* 律 (yang) and six *lü* 呂 (yin) to the twelve months; see *Hanshu* 21A.958-9. For the six *yang* pitch pipes, i.e., Huangzhong, Ruibin, Wuyi, Taicou, Yize, and Guxian, see 2.2.2.

14 Zheng Xuan's commentary lists the ten methods: "the lord is in charge, the minister serves, the father is kind, the son is filial, the older brother is loving, the younger brother is respectful, the husband is even-tempered, the wife is soft, the mother-in-law kind is, the daughter-in-law is obedient." See *SSDZSZ* 2.11a (714).

15 Shun was renowned for his filial service to his father, stepmother, and half-brother. See *Shiji* 1.33–34.

16 The chronology in this part of 2.2.6 conflicts with that in other passages in the *Documents*, the *Great Commentary*, and *Scribe's Records*. The *Great Commentary*'s "Canon of Yao" (1.1.7) refers to the foothills as the place where Shun was sent by Yao to be tested and confirmed. The *Documents*' "Gaoyao's Counsel" ("Yi ji" in the Old Script version) mentions how the "Shao music with flute" ("Xiao Shao" 簫韶) was performed after Shun heard the counsels of Gaoyao and Yu at the end of Shun's reign; see *Shangshu zhuzi suoyin* 5/8/5. *Scribe's Records* paraphrases "Gaoyao's Counsel" and makes it clear that the "Shao music with flute" was played after Shun appointed Yu rather than Gaoyao as his successor; *Shiji* 2.81. Subsequently, the melody has been associated with the celebration of abdication; *SSDZSZ* 2.11a–b (714).

報事還歸二年，謥然乃作大唐之歌。其樂曰：「舟張辟雝，**鶬鶬**[10]相從；八風回回，**鳳皇**[11]喈喈。」歌者三年，昭然乃知乎王世，明有不世之義。

　　《招》為賓客而《雝》為主人，始奏《肆夏》，納以《孝成》。舜為賓客而禹為主人。樂正進贊曰：「尚攷大室之義，唐為**虞賓**[12]，至今衍于**四海**[13]，成禹之變，垂於萬世之後。」

　　于時卿雲聚，**俊乂**[14]集，**百工**[15]相和而歌卿雲。帝乃倡之曰：「卿雲爛兮，禮縵縵兮。日月光華，旦復旦兮。」

10　Cf. *Shangshu zhuzi suoyin* 5/8/5 (益稷). *Shangshu zhuzi suoyin* has 蹌蹌 for 鶬鶬.
11　Cf. *Shangshu zhuzi suoyin* 5/8/5 (益稷).
12　Cf. *Shangshu zhuzi suoyin* 5/8/4 (益稷).
13　Cf. *Shangshu zhuzi suoyin*, 5/7/7 (益稷).
14　Cf. *Shangshu zhuzi suoyin*, 4/6/17 (皋陶謨).
15　Cf. *Shangshu zhuzi suoyin* 5/8/7 (益稷).

Two years after the return of the reporters of affairs, the "Great Tang" melody was performed with great aplomb.[17] Its lyrics are as follows:

> Around and around the Circular Moat (*ʔoŋ),[18]
> They pursue each other (*dzoŋ);[19]
> The eight winds whirl about (*[ɢ]ʷˤəj),
> The phoenixes join in (*kˤrəj).[20]

After performing the piece for three years, everyone clearly understood the royal transmission and the significance of nonhereditary succession.

The "Shao" melody was performed for the guest, the "Yong" melody for the host. When the ceremony started, the "Great Xia" melody was played; during the offerings there was a performance of "Piety Achieved."[21] Shun was the guest and Yu the host.[22]

The director of music entered and praised this: "In ancient times, according to the norms of the Great Hall, Yao was the guest of Shun. This practice has been continued till today within the Four Seas. It caps Yu's transformation and is thus extended to the myriad later generations."

At that moment auspicious clouds gathered, and the outstanding men assembled. The one hundred artisans joined in harmony and sang the tune "Auspicious Clouds." The supreme lord then led them in song:

> The auspicious clouds are lustrous (*[r]ˤan-s)
> the rites are without interruption (*mans)
> Sun and moon are brilliant (*(g)wrâʔ)
> As morning turns into morning (*tâns).[23]

---

17 Tang is another name for Yao. According to Zheng Xuan, the melody celebrates Yao's abdication to Shun; *SSDZSZ* 2.11a (714).

18 Circular Moat (Biyong) is the name of a ritual building. Note the significant rhyme in the song lyrics.

19 Based on the corresponding line in the *Documents*, this must refer to birds and beasts (*qinshou* 禽獸).

20 Reconstructions of "whirl about" 回 and "join in" 喈 are from Baxter and Sagart 2014, 343, 346.

21 "Shao," "Yong," and "Great Xia" are commonly mentioned as musical pieces in other early Chinese texts; "Piety Achieved" is unique to the *Great Commentary*.

22 According to Zheng Xuan, this was after Shun had charged Yu with taking care of government matters. The versions of Chen Shouqi and Pi Xirui indicate that the performances that follow took place in the fifteenth year of Shun's reign. *SSDZSZ* 2.13a (715); *SSDZJJ* 1.13b (4119).

23 This song became part of the national anthem in vogue in the early Republican period, from 1913 to 1926; Fudan University derives its name from "As morning turns into morning" (*dan fu dan* 旦復旦). Reconstructions of "lustrous" 爛 and "without interruption" 縵 from Guo Xiliang 郭錫良 2010, 311, 313.

八伯咸進稽首而和曰:「明明上天,爛然星陳。日月光華,宏予一人。」
　　　　帝乃載歌曰:「日月有常,星辰有行。四時從經,萬姓允誠。於予論樂,配天之靈,還于賢聖,莫不咸聽。鼚乎鼓之,軒乎(憮)〔舞〕之,菁華已竭,褰裳去之。」
　　　　于時乃八風修通,卿雲蓬蓬,蟠龍賁信于其藏,蛟魚踴躍于其淵,龜魚咸出于其穴,遷虞而事夏也。

2.2.7　維十有三祀,帝乃稱王而入唐郊,猶以丹朱為尸。於是百執事咸昭然乃知王世不絕,爛然必自有繼祖守宗廟之君。

The Eight Earls[24] jointly came forward and, prostrating themselves, responded:

> Bright, the high Heaven (*thîn)
> lustrous the arranged stars (*drən)
> Sun and moon are brilliant (*(g)wrâ?)
> To the glory of the One Man (*nin).

The supreme lord then continued the chanting:

> The sun and moon are eternal (*daŋ),
> the stars and planets stay their course (*gaŋ).
> The four seasons follow the norm (*kêŋ),
> the myriad surnames are indeed loyal (*geŋ?).
> You communicate with My Person via music (*kêŋ)
> to match numinous Heaven (*reŋ),
> and return to the worthies and sages (*hjeŋh?),
> everybody will have heard of it (*lheŋ).
> Rom rom go the drums (*ka?),
> Whirl whirl go the dancers (*ma?).
> My essence is spent (*grat),
> I lift my robes and leave (*khak).

At this moment the eight breezes blew, the auspicious clouds gathered, the coiled-up dragons leapt up in their caves, the giant fish sprang from the deep water, and the turtles all left their caverns. This is how they moved away from the one from Yu in order to serve the Xia.[25]

In the thirteenth year, the supreme lord assumed the title of king and entered Yao's suburb, while continuing to use Danzhu as impersonator. Thus all the one hundred officials clearly understood that the royal transmission would not be interrupted and that, splendidly, there now was, with certainty, a lord who would continue the lineage and preserve the ancestral temples.[26]

2.2.7

---

24 The Eight Earls are named in the *Great Commentary*'s "Canon of Yao," in connection with music.
25 "The one from Yu" refers to Shun. *Bamboo Annals* mentions the appearance of auspicious clouds for year 14 of Shun's reign, coinciding with the transfer of power to his successor Yu. See *Zhushu jinian zhuzi suoyin* 1.6.4/4/4.
26 Danzhu was Yao's son, but Yao preferred Shun as a successor. The "Supplementary Sacrifices" in the *Documents* has a passage in which Yu speaks of Danzhu's arrogance as something to avoid. See *Shangshu zhuzi suoyin* 3/7/18.

還歸二年，而廟中苟有歌《大化》、《大訓》、《六府》、《九原》，而夏道興。[16]

2.2.8 維十有四祀，鍾石笙[17]管變聲，樂未罷，疾風發屋，天大雷雨。帝乃雍而歌者重篇，沈首而笑曰：「明哉！非一人之天下也，乃見于鍾石笙筦乎？」

2.2.9 維十有五祀，祀者貳尸。

2.2.10 「元首明哉，股肱良哉。」[18]元首，君也；股肱，臣也。

2.2.11 翊[19]，輔也。

2.2.12 「天功人其代之。」[20]傳曰：「夫成天地之功者，未嘗不蕃昌也。」

2.2.13 有德[21]者，尊其位而重其祿。

2.2.14 予辛壬娶塗山，癸甲生啟。[22]

---

16 Following Zheng Xuan's commentary, the event described in this paragraph took place two years after the fifteenth year of Shun's reign; see SSDZSZ 2.15a (716).
17 Cf. *Shangshu zhuzi suoyin* 5/8/4 (益稷).
18 Cf. *Shangshu zhuzi suoyin* 5/8/8 (益稷).
19 Cf. *Shangshu zhuzi suoyin* 5/7/12 (益稷). *Shangshu zhuzi suoyin* has 翼 for 翊.
20 Cf. *Shangshu zhuzi suoyin* 4/6/18 (皋陶謨). *Shangshu zhuzi suoyin* has 工 for 功.
21 Cf. *Shangshu zhuzi suoyin* 4/6/14, 4/6/19 (皋陶謨).
22 Cf. *Shangshu zhuzi suoyin* 5/7/19–5/8/1 (益稷). *Shangshu zhuzi suoyin* has 予創若時，娶于塗山，辛壬癸甲。啓呱呱而泣。

When he returned after two years, pieces such as "The Great Transformation," "The Great Exhortation," "The Six Bureaus," and "The Nine Fields" were still performed at the ancestral temple. Thus the way of Xia flourished.[27]

2.2.8 In the fourteenth year, the bells and stones, and the pipes of the mouth organ emitted odd sounds; then, before the music had finished, a hurricane shook up houses, and there was a big thunderstorm. The supreme lord retained his composure and chanted a melody twice. He lowered his head and said laughingly: "Right! All-under-Heaven is not just mine. Is this not shown clearly in the bells, stones, and musical pipes?"

2.2.9 In the fifteenth year, the person who offered the sacrifice was assisted by two impersonators.

2.2.10 "When the head of all shines brightly, the legs and arms are fine." "The head of all" refers to the ruler. "Legs and arms" refers to the ministers.

2.2.11 "Wings" refers to the assistants.

2.2.12 "Heaven's work is taken over by humans." The *Commentary* says: "Those who complete the work of Heaven and Earth will always prosper."

2.2.13 The one with charismatic virtue will attain a higher position and double his salary.

2.2.14 On the days *xing/ren*, I obtained a wife from Tushan; on the days *gui/jia*, Qi was born.[28]

---

27 According to Zheng Xuan, the musical pieces named here are in praise of Yu; SSDZSZ 2.15a (716).
28 The transmitted *Documents* places the dates in different positions in this sentence. Hence, it can mean that Yu, after marrying his wife, only stayed home for four days. The *Great Commentary* clearly associates the first two days with his marriage and the last two with the birth of his son. These four days (*xing, ren, gui*, and *jia*) are four consecutive days in the system of the ten heavenly branches.

卷三
虞夏傳

3
Traditions on Yu and Xia (Continued)

3.1
Tribute of Yu

"Tribute of Yu" is one of the New Script chapters of the Documents. In this chapter, Yu busied himself traveling through the realm, creating and assessing some of its basic features, especially rivers and mountains. The chapter presents two systems to organize geographical space, namely, the Nine Provinces and the Five Dependencies. For each of the Nine Provinces (zhou 州), it lists the main mountains and rivers, grades the quality of the soil from the perspective of agricultural production and possible tax revenue, and lists items that the provinces have to offer the center in tribute. The Five Dependencies (fu 服)[1] consist of areas extending concentrically out from the center, each with a lesser level of civilization and hence progressively more in need of civilizing interventions and military preparedness. The chapter as a whole is the locus classicus for geographical and cartographic thinking in imperial China.[2]

Only fragmented entries of the Great Commentary's "Tribute of Yu" survive, and most of them focus on places, creatures, and terms that relate to water. The first entry echoes a sentence in the "Supplementary Sacrifices" in the Documents and links the Four Seas with the Five Dependencies. This is followed by a list of tribute goods to be obtained from the seas, the rivers, and the marshes (3.1.1). Further entries discuss the sacrificial administration of sacred rivers and mountains, provide the names of the Five Marchmounts and Four Rivers, and include a theory about the rain-making capacities of high mountain peaks (3.1.2–3). The chapter also contains definitions and interpretations of various geographical terms (3.1.4–13).

---

1   "Tribute to Yu" describes each of the Five Dependencies, but the collective term "Five Dependencies" only appears in the "Supplementary Sacrifices" chapter of the Documents; see Shangshu zhuzi suoyin 5/8/1.
2   Lewis 2006, 249.

3.1
禹貢

3.1.1 **夏成五服,外薄四海。**
東海:魚須魚目;南海:魚革珠璣大貝;西海:魚骨魚幹魚翯;北海:魚劍魚石,出瑱擊闔。

河魿,江鱏**大龜**,[1]五湖(元)〔玄〕唐,鉅野菱,鉅定嬴,濟中詹諸,

---

1 Cf. *Shangshu zhuzi suoyin* 5/8/1-2 (益稷). *Shangshu zhuzi suoyin* has 弼 for 夏. Cf. *Shangshu zhuzi suoyin* 6/9/10 (禹貢).

3.1
Tribute of Yu

The Xia brought about the Five Dependencies, surrounded at the outside   3.1.1
by the Four Seas.
The Eastern Sea provided baleen plates and whale eyes;[1]
the Southern Sea fish skins, pearls, and large cowries;[2]
the Western Sea fish bones, fish keels, and fish flanks;[3]
the Northern Sea fish swords, fish stones, jellyfish, and mackerel.[4]

Turtles from the Yellow River,
alligators and giant tortoises from the Yangzi,
yuantang from the Five Lakes,[5]
water chestnuts from Juye,
cowry shells from Juding,
toads from amidst the Ji River,

---

1   Zheng Xuan explains that baleen plates of whales were used as hairpins and their eyes as pearls. We translate *yu* 魚 (fish) as whale on the basis of a parallel passage in *Shuyi ji* 1.19a; *SSDZSZ* 3.1a–b (724).
2   According to Zheng Xuan, fish skin was used to decorate small chariots and was wrapped around swords. *SSDZSZ* 3.1b (724).
3   Zheng Xuan claims that he has never heard the terms. *SSDZSZ* 3.1b (724).
4   We follow Zheng Xuan and Pi Xirui in interpreting *chuzhen* 出瑱 as jellyfish and *jilü* 擊閭 as a mackerellike fish. *SSDZSZ* 3.2a (725).
5   According to Zheng Xuan, the Five Lakes refers to the Taihu area around present-day Yangzhou. The names of the Five Lakes are provided in *Shuijing zhu*: Changdang 長蕩, Tai 太, She 射, Gui 貴, and Ge 滆. *Shuijing zhushi* 28.26b. As to *yuantang* 元唐, Zheng Xuan admits that he has no idea what it is; it must be some kind of aquatic creature. *SSDZSZ* 3.2a (725).

孟諸靈龜，降谷玄玉，大都鰹魚魚刀，咸會於中國。

3.1.2　五嶽視三公，四瀆視諸侯，其餘山川視伯，小者視子男。

3.1.3　**高山大川**五嶽四瀆之屬：五嶽，謂**岱**山、霍山、**華**山、**恆**山、嵩山也，**江**、**河**、**淮**、**濟**為四瀆。
　　　禹敷[2]南方霍山，五嶽皆觸石而出雲，扶寸而合，不崇朝而雨天下。

3.1.4　大川相閒，小川相屬，東歸於海。

3.1.5　非水無以準萬里之平，非水無以通遠道任重也。

3.1.6　「**東原底平**」[3]，大而高平者，謂之大原。

2　Cf. *Shangshu zhuzi suoyin* 6/8/15; *Shangshu zhuzi suoyin* has 禹敷土，隨山刊木，奠高山大川 (禹貢). *Shangshu zhuzi suoyin* frequently mentions the other highlighted texts in the this chapter; *Shangshu zhuzi suoyin* 6/8–10 (禹貢).
3　Cf. *Shangshu zhuzi suoyin* 6/9/1 (禹貢).

divination carapaces from Meng reservoir,
dark jade from Xianggu,
breams and knifed fish from Dadu,
all of these goods converged upon the central domains.⁶

[Sacrifices to] the Five Marchmounts are overseen by the three excellencies, those to the Four Rivers by the regional lords, those to other mountains and rivers by the earls, and those to small mountains and rivers by the princes.⁷ 3.1.2

As to "the high mountains and great rivers," this refers to the Five Marchmounts and the Four Rivers. 3.1.3
The Five Marchmounts are Mount Dai, Mount Huo, Mount Hua, Mount Heng, and Mount Song.
The Four Rivers are the Yangzi, the Yellow River, the Huai, and the Ji.
Yu fixed Huoshan in the southern region. At the Five Marchmounts, clouds are formed through contact with the rocks. Bit by bit they condense so that before the end of the morning all-under-Heaven receives rain.⁸

The great rivers are far apart; small rivers form a network. Eastward they flow into the sea. 3.1.4

If it were not for water, one could not assess where over tens of thousands of *li* the ground is level; if it were not for water, one could not forge routes to faraway places or transport heavy loads. 3.1.5

"The eastern plains are low and level;"⁹ a plateau is called a "great plain." 3.1.6

---

6   Zheng Xuan identifies the location of Juding, Ji River, Mengzhu, Xianggu, and Dadu: they are situated in present-day Henan, Shandong, and Jiangxi. *SSDZSZ* 3.2a–3b (725). The "central domains" is a collective name for various Zhou allied polities, especially those situated around the lower reaches of the Yellow River.

7   According to Zheng Xuan, the inspection applied to ritual vessels and implements. The "Royal Regulations" chapter in *Records of Ritual* and the "Treatise on the Feng and Shan Sacrifices" (Fengshan shu 封禪書) chapter in *Scribe's Records* contain parallel passages; the translations by Legge and Watson yield a very different interpretation: according to them, the Five Marchmounts "are regarded as" (*shi* 視) the three ministers, and so forth. *Shiji* 28.1357; Watson 1993, 6; *Liji zhushu* 242-2; Legge 1879–1885, 27:225. The five ranks listed in this passage follow the traditional five-rank noble system: *gong, hou, bo, zi*, and *nan*, with the first two adapted to Han institutions.

8   The Gongyang commentary has a very similar passage applied not to the Five Marchmounts but only to Mount Tai 泰. *Gongyang zhuan zhuzi suoyin* 5.31.3/56/26.

9   In *Documents* "Tribute of Yu," the eastern plains, located in the east of Xuzhou, are leveled after the taming of the flood. *Shangshu zhuzi suoyin* 6/9/1.

3.1.7 下而平者謂之隟，[4]隟之言溼也。
　　　　下溼曰隟。

3.1.8 澤障曰陂。[5]

3.1.9 順流而下曰沿。[6]

3.1.10 文皮千合。

3.1.11 禹鐵。[7]

3.1.12 「滎播既都」。[8]

3.1.13 被明都。[9]

4　Cf. *Shangshu zhuzi suoyin* 6/9/17 (禹貢).
5　Cf. *Shangshu zhuzi suoyin* 6/10/12 (禹貢).
6　Cf. *Shangshu zhuzi suoyin* 6/9/6 (禹貢).
7　Cf. *Shangshu zhuzi suoyin* 6/8/20 (禹貢); *Shangshu zhuzi suoyin* has 嵎夷 for 禹鐵..
8　Cf. *Shangshu zhuzi suoyin* 6/9/11 (禹貢); *Shangshu zhuzi suoyin* has 滎波既豬 for 滎播既都.
9　Cf. *Shangshu zhuzi suoyin* 6/9/11 (禹貢); *Shangshu zhuzi suoyin* has 孟豬 for 明都. Also see *Shiji* 2.62.

Lands that are low and level are called "lowlands." "Lowlands" refer to swamps. Low-lying swamps are called "lowlands." 3.1.7

Dikes erected in marshes are called "banks." 3.1.8

To follow the river downstream is called "to float." 3.1.9

Patterned hides, one thousand units. 3.1.10

"Yuyi." 3.1.11

"Yingbo was made into a reservoir."[10] 3.1.12

"it covered Meng reservoir." 3.1.13

---

10 For variants of this sentence, see Ma Nan 2016, 101.

3.2
Oath at Gan

The "Oath at Gan" chapter in the Documents *is a short New Script chapter. In it the king, who is either Yu or Yu's son Qi, addresses a group just before the battle at Gan against the lord of Hu* 扈, *inciting them with threats and incentives to do their utmost to settle the upcoming battle in the king's favor.*[1] *The lord of Hu stands accused of violating the Five Material Resources (Wuxing)*[2] *and of "neglectfully discarding the Three Regulators (Sanzheng)." What the Three Regulators were is unclear: Zheng Xuan explains the terms as the triad of Heaven, Earth, and Humans, whereas Ma Rong opts for three different months that can start the calendar year.*[3]

In the Great Commentary, the "Oath at Gan" consists of a long core passage (3.2.1) and some shorter passages: a gloss on the word "battle" (3.2.2) and two passages that echo the core passage in theme in that they try to understand the need for the alternation, historically, of different styles of governing (and, therefore, the need for dynastic change) (3.2.3–4). The Three Regulators (and the Three Governors linked to them) are explained at length in the core passage (3.2.1). The Three Regulators are the winter solstice, the thirtieth, and the sixtieth day after the winter solstice, moments in time that for Zhou, Yin (Shang), and Xia respectively marked the start of the new calendar year. Ma Rong's interpretation of the term as

---

1 *Shiji* 2.84. However, other early texts, such as *Zhuangzi* and *Mr. Lü's Annals*, point to Yu as the speaker. *Zhuangzi zhuzi suoyin* 4/9/10; *Lüshi chunqiu zhuzi suoyin* 3.3/14/12–14.
2 On Wuxing, see the section "Textual Transmission of 'Tradition on the Great Plan's Five Phases'" in this book's introduction as well as the introduction to section 5.3 and the introductions and notes to *juan* 7.
3 *Shangshu zhushu* 98.2; *Shiji* 2.84.

it occurs in "Oath at Gan" in the Documents *might be drawn from the Great Commentary. For more on how these calendrical theories were applied at the Western Han court, see case 2 of the section "The* Great Commentary *on Questions of Political and Social Order" of the introduction to this book, including table I.1, which presents 3.2.1 in tabular form.*

In Pi Xirui's edition, the long passage that makes up the bulk of this chapter (3.2.1) is placed under "Principal Teachings" (Lüeshuo). The reason Wang Kaiyun placed this passage under "Oath at Gan" must be that he thinks that it explains the term "Three Regulators" in "Oath at Gan" in the Documents.

3.2
甘誓

3.2.1 王者存二代之後，與己為三，所以通三統，立**三正**[1]。是故周人以日至為正，殷人以日至三十日為正，夏以日至六十日為正；周以至動，殷以萌，夏以牙[2]。天有三統，物有三變，故正色有三。天有三生三死，故土有三王，王持一生死。是故夏以孟春為正，殷以季冬為正，周以仲冬為正，夏以十三月為正，色尚黑，以平旦為朔；殷以十二月為正，色尚白，以鷄鳴為朔；

1　Cf. *Shangshu zhuzi suoyin* 7/11/1 (甘誓).
2　牙 = 芽.

3.2
Oath at Gan

A king has to abide by [the traditions] of the era following the previous two eras, thus completing a triad that includes his own era. That is how he connects with the Three Governors and establishes the Three Regulators.[1] Therefore, the people of Zhou made the winter solstice their regulator; the people of Yin, the thirtieth day after the solstice; and the people of Xia, the sixtieth day after the solstice. Thus, Zhou used the moment of stirring at the time of the solstice; Yin, the moment of sprouting; and Xia, the moment of forming shoots.[2] Because Heaven has the Three Governors, and things have the three moments of transformation, each of the Three Regulators has its own color. Because Heaven has three separate cycles of life and death, Earth needs three types of king, one to preside over each cycle of life and death. Therefore, for Xia the regulator was the first month of spring, for Yin the last month of winter, and for Zhou the middle month of winter. Xia made the thirteenth month its regulator,[3] privileged the color black, and started the new month at dawn; Yin made the twelfth month its regulator, privileged the color white, and started the new month at cock's crow; Zhou made the eleventh month its regulator, privileged the color red, and

3.2.1

---

1. Given that the context here is the establishment of the calendar, "regulator" (*zheng*) refers to the first calendrical month, which is still called *zhengyue* 正月 in modern Chinese.
2. The text intends to link the calendar not only to astronomical phenomena, but also to processes of growth and decay of life on earth. Therefore, the beginning of the year is linked to the start of the life cycle. The stirring of plant seed, sprouting, and forming shoots represent three stages all at the beginning at the life cycle.
3. Regarding the adoption of the Xia calendar in the Western Han, see case 2 of the section "The *Great Commentary* on Questions of Political and Social Order" of the introduction to this book.

周以十一月為正，色尚赤，以夜半為朔。不以三月後為正者，萬物不齊，莫適所統，故必以三微之月為歲之三正也。三統者、所以序生也，三正者、所以統天下也。是故三統、三正若循連環，周則又始，窮則反本也。夏以孟春為正者，貴形也。

3.2.2　戰[3]者、憚驚之也。

3.2.3　王者一質一文，據天地之道。

3.2.4　三王之治，若循環之無端，如水之勝火。

3　Cf. *Shangshu zhuzi suoyin* 7/10/24 (甘誓).

started the new month at midnight. That they did not make a later month the regulator is because the myriad things do not grow evenly and hence would not fit their governor. Therefore, it is necessary to designate only the three months of incipient growth as the year's regulators.[4] Through the Three Governors, the rhythms of life are ordered; through the Three Regulators, all-under-Heaven is governed. This is why the Three Regulators and the Three Governors are like continuous cycles, starting again when completed and returning to the root when exhausted. That Xia chose the first month of spring as its regulator is because it valued things that have already acquired form.

"To battle" means to strike fear into them.[5] 3.2.2

That kings alternate between simplicity and refinement is because they rely on the Way of Heaven and Earth.[6] 3.2.3

The succession of the rule of the three kings is like an unending cycle, just as water conquers fire.[7] 3.2.4

---

4   After the third regulator, which falls sixty days after the winter solstice, growth becomes uneven in the sense that some plants grow faster than the others. That makes it difficult to regulate or categorize them.
5   The word for "battle" (*zhan* or *dan*) is semantically related to the word for "fear" (*dan*). On the relationship, see Schuessler 2007, 605; Schuessler points out that the same semantics hold for the ancient Greek word for battle (*pólemos*).
6   The *Great Commentary* is claiming that eras of simplicity and refinement alternate. The cycle of these two is not necessarily linked to that of the Three Regulators outlined in 3.2.1. In several passages in *Analects*, Confucius was recorded discussing simplicity and refinement: *Analects* 3.14, 6.18, and 12.8.
7   Early imperial texts are replete with references to the fivefold system in which the phases succeed each other through conquest (*sheng* 勝: wood, earth, metal, fire, water) or generation (*sheng* 生: metal, water, wood, fire, earth).

卷四
殷傳

4
Traditions on Yin

4.1
Proclamation of the Supreme Lord

"Proclamation of the Supreme Lord" is the opening chapter of a new part of the Great Commentary that deals with Shang (or Yin). The textual history of "Proclamation of the Supreme Lord" is very similar to that of "Nine Offers." The chapter has no corresponding chapter in the transmitted Documents, but its presence in the Great Commentary is known through the work of the Song scholar Wang Yinglin. Wang identifies one quote from the Documents (not in the transmitted version of the Documents) as belonging to the Great Commentary's "Proclamation of the Supreme Lord" (4.1.1).[1]

An entry in Scribe's Records details the circumstances of the composition of the Documents' "Proclamation of the Supreme Lord" (there is no such entry for "Nine Offers" in Scribe's Records). According to Scribe's Records, Tang, who would defeat Jie of Xia to become the first dynastic Shang ruler, returned to the ancestral site of Bo 亳 and composed "Proclamation of the Supreme Lord."[2]

The Great Commentary chapter, in Wang's edition, quotes the Documents on the importance of sumptuary rules regarding clothing (4.1.1). It then provides one additional fragment that spells out the type of clothing and chariots available for men of service (4.1.2). This latter fragment is similar to 1.1.24 of "Canon of Yao."

---

1   *Kunxue jiwen*, 1:142–43.
2   *Shiji* 3.93.

4.1
帝告

4.1.1　《書》曰:「施章乃服,明上下。」

4.1.2　未命為士者,車不得朱軒及有飛軨,不得乘飾車駢馬,衣文繡,命然後得以旌有德。

4.1
Proclamation of the Supreme Lord

The *Documents* says: "Apply patterns to clothing, and high and low will be clear." 4.1.1

Those who had not yet received recognition as men of service were not allowed to have carts with vermilion curtains or flying banners.[1] They also were not allowed to ride in an ornamental cart with two horses or to wear clothes with patterns woven into them. Once they had received recognition, they were allowed to use the above markers to display their status.[2] 4.1.2

---

1   See 1.1.24.
2   The Chinese term used here is *de* 德, which is often translated as "virtue." Here the assumption is that the ones with status and power are the ones with virtue.

4.2
Tang's Oath

"*Tang's Oath*" *is a New Script chapter of the* Documents *consisting of a harangue by Tang meant to incite support for his campaign against Jie of Xia.*

The Great Commentary's "*Tang's Oath" provides snippets of historical narrative that explain the dynastic transition from the Xia (under Jie) to the Shang (under Tang). The chapter downplays the violence that must have accompanied this transition, instead emphasizing the voluntary submission of people (including former subjects of Xia) and lords to the new regime. Fragment 4.2.1 explains how Yi Yin, Tang's great advisor, was persuaded to abandon Xia and join Shang; 4.2.2 describes the consistent defections of Xia subjects after Tang's victory over their ruler; 4.2.3 (see also 4.2.8) describes the ritual whereby Tang was installed as ruler during a great gathering of regional lords—Tang not only ritually declined the throne three times; he promised that he would put the Way (Dao 道) before the interests of his family (jia 家)—4.2.4 and 4.2.6 serve as explanations of what was wrong with the rule of Jie of Xia, whereas 4.2.5 and 4.2.7 articulate actions Tang undertook once installed as ruler to atone for the evils of his predecessor.*

4.2
湯誓

4.2.1 湯誓云:夏人飲酒,醉者持不醉者,不醉者持醉者,相和而歌曰:「盍歸于薄[1]?盍歸于薄?薄亦大矣!」故伊尹退而閒居,深聽歌聲。更曰:「覺兮較兮,吾大命假[2]兮;去不善而就善,何不樂兮?」伊尹入告于王曰:「大命之亡有日矣。」王憪然歎,啞然笑,曰:「天之有日,猶吾之有民也。日有亡哉!日亡,吾乃亡矣。」[3]是以伊尹遂去夏適湯。

4.2.2 湯放桀,居中野。士民皆奔湯,桀與其屬五百人南徙千里,止于不齊,不齊士民往奔湯,桀與屬五百人徙于魯,魯士民復奔湯。桀曰:「國、君之有也。吾聞海外有人。」與五百人俱去。

---

1   薄 = 亳.
2   假 = 格: SSDZSZ 3.13a (730).
3   Cf. *Shangshu zhuzi suoyin* 10/12/24 (湯誓); *Shangshu zhuzi suoyin* has 時日曷喪?予及汝皆亡 for this passage.

4.2
Tang's Oath

As "Tang's Oath" tells it,[1] "When the people of Xia consume alcohol, those who are drunk and those who remain sober support each other and, in harmony with one another, burst out in song: 'Why don't we go to Bo?[2] Why don't we go to Bo? Bo indeed is a great place.'"[3] Therefore, Yi Yin, who had withdrawn to live a life of leisure, was deeply affected by the songs he heard. Time after time they sang: "Finally we've woken up! Finally we see things clearly! Our great mandate has ended. Leaving a bad place, we will go to a good one. Why not rejoice?" Yi Yin came forward to report to the king:[4] "The day at which your great mandate will perish is near." Snorting and sneering, the king let out, "Heaven has a sun just as surely as I have my people. What's this talk about the sun perishing? When the sun perishes, only then will I perish!" Because of this, Yi Yin left Xia and went to Tang.[5]

4.2.1

Tang deposed Jie and settled in the central plain. The officials and the people all flocked to Tang. Jie, with five hundred of his followers, migrated a thousand *li* southward, halting in Buqi. However, the men of service and the people of Buqi all left and flocked to Tang. Thus, Jie, with five hundred of his followers, migrated to Lu. However, the men of service and the people of Lu also flocked to Tang. Jie said: "The state is all yours. I have heard that there are humans beyond the seas." He and his five hundred followers all left.

4.2.2

---

1   What follows does not occur in the transmitted *Documents*.
2   Bo was Tang's stronghold; see *Zhushu jinian zhuzi suoyin* 1.24.1/12/3.
3   Thus the people of Xia expressed their longing to subject themselves to Tang, who had established himself in Bo, and abandon the Xia dynasty.
4   I.e., Jie 桀, the last ruler of the Xia.
5   Yi Yin became Tang's most important advisor. Yi Yin was viewed in various ways depending on the period and the text; see Xia and Huang 2014; Shaughnessy 2006, 190.

4.2.3 湯放桀而歸于薄,三千諸侯大會,湯取天子之璽,置之于天子之坐左,復而再拜,從諸侯之位。湯曰:「此天子之位,有道者可以處之矣。夫天下、非一家之有也,唯有道者之有也,唯有道者宜處之。」湯以此三讓,三千諸侯莫敢即位,然後湯即天子之位。

4.2.4 桀殺刑彌厚而民彌暴,故爾梁[4]遠,遂以是亡。

4.2.5 獄省。[5]

4.2.6 桀無道,囚湯,後釋之。諸侯八譯來朝者六國。

4.2.7 湯代桀之後,大旱七年。史卜曰:「當以人為禱。」湯乃翦髮斷爪,自以為牲而禱于桑林之社,而雨大至,方數千里。

4.2.8 景亳之命,費昌為御。

4　故 = 窮; 爾 = 邇; 梁 = 掠: SSDZSZ 3.15a (731), Zheng Xuan's commentary.
5　亳 = 薄.

After Tang had deposed Jie and returned to Bo, there was a grand gathering of three thousand regional lords. Tang took the imperial seal and placed it to the left of the Son of Heaven's seat. He stepped back and bowed repeatedly before taking his place among the regional lords. Tang said: "This is the seat of the Son of Heaven; the one who has the Way can occupy it. Now, all-under-Heaven is not one family's possession. Only the one who has the Way can have it; only the one who has the Way can properly take possession of it." Tang, in this way, yielded three times.[6] Only when none of the three thousand regional lords dared to go take the seat did Tang occupy the Son of Heaven's position. 4.2.3

Under Jie, capital punishments became increasingly severe and the people increasingly violent. Having exhausted resources close by,[7] he had to go plunder afar. This, in consequence, led to his demise. 4.2.4

The number of prisons was reduced. 4.2.5

Jie had lost the Way. He imprisoned Tang, later to release him. The regional lords who came to court with multiple translators were from the six states.[8] 4.2.6

After Tang succeeded Jie, there were seven years of drought. The scribe divined and said, "We have to make a supplication involving human sacrifice." Hence, Tang cut his hair and nails, thus turning himself into an offering, and made a supplication at the altar in Mulberry Forest.[9] Thereafter, abundant rain arrived over thousands of *li*. 4.2.7

The mandate was conferred at the majestic city of Bo.[10] Fei Chang became his charioteer.[11] 4.2.8

---

6   For some preliminary references to this custom that new dynastic rulers refused three times to accept the mandate, see Yakobson 2021.
7   Based on Zheng Xuan's gloss of *gu* 故 as *qiong* 窮. "故爾, 窮其近也." *SSDZSZ* 3.15a (731).
8   Literally "eight translators." The term 八譯 indicates that the lords came from afar and had to bridge linguistic differences.
9   Wang Chong doubts this story; *Lunheng zhuzi suoyin* 19/69/6. *Bamboo Annals* registers several years of drought that ended with a sacrifice at Mulberry Forest in year twenty-four of Tang's reign; *Zhushu jinian zhuzi suoyin* 1.24.7/12/15.
10 According to *Bamboo Annals*, the place of the meeting of the lords. *Zhushu jinian zhuzi suoyin* 1.23.15/11/23.
11 Fei Chang was a subject of Xia who became Tang's charioteer when Tang defeated Jie; *Shiji* 5.174.

4.3
Pangeng

The Documents *chapter "Pangeng" consists of three speeches by the Shang king Pangeng* 盤庚 *after he decided to move his capital to a new settlement called Yin* 殷 *but found that his men were unwilling to follow him there.*[1] *The chapter contains three addresses through which Pangeng sought to drum up support for the move of the capital. In the New Script* Documents, *the three addresses are combined into one chapter, whereas in the Old Script* Documents *they are divided into three separate "Pangeng" chapters. According to* Scribe's Records, *the "Pangeng" chapter was committed to writing by Pangeng's successor.*[2]

The "Pangeng" in the Great Commentary *provides two quotations from the* Documents. *The first one (4.3.1) does not occur in the transmitted* Documents *but is there on the authority of Wang Yinglin.*[3] *The second passage (4.3.2), which derives from the received "Pangeng," is preceded by an explanatory passage that postulates that every enfeoffed lord should also receive an estate. In this manner, even if the fief was abolished, sacrifices to the founding father of the lineage could continue. This was also an important concern in the Western Han regarding the noble or royal lines.*

---

1 Pangeng's new capital is now identified as Huanbei 洹北, a fortified Shang city to the north of the Huan River. After Pangeng, the capital was moved to the south of the river, now known as Yinxu 殷墟. See Tang Jigen et al. 2016, 324; F. Li 2013, 66–83.
2 *Scribe's Records* also mentions the composition of a "Pangeng" in three chapters; *Shiji* 3.102.
3 *Kunxue jiwen* 1:208.

4.3
般庚

4.3.1 《書》曰：「若德明哉，湯任¹父²言，卑應言。」

4.3.2 古者諸侯始受封，則有采地。百里諸侯以三十里，七十里諸侯以二十里，五十里諸侯以十五里，其後子孫雖有罪黜，其采地不黜。使其子孫賢者守之，世世以祠其始受封之人。此之謂興滅國、繼絕世。《書》曰：「**茲予大享于先王，爾祖其從與享之。**」³此之謂也。

1　Cf. *Shangshu zhuzi suoyin* 18/18/14 (般庚上)
2　Cf. *Shangshu zhuzi suoyin* 18/18/23 (般庚上).
3　Cf. *Shangshu zhuzi suoyin* 18/18/24 (般庚上).

4.3
Pangeng

As the *Documents* says, "How bright his virtue is! Tang relied on the advice of the elders, humbly echoing their words."[1] 4.3.1

In ancient times, when a regional lord first received his fief, he also received an estate.[2] For a regional lord of 100 *li*, the size of the estate amounted to 30 *li*; for a regional lord of 70 *li*, to 20 *li*; for a regional lord of 50 *li*, to 15 *li*. Even if among his descendants there were sons or grandsons who were deposed because of a crime, his estate was not abolished. In this manner, worthy sons and grandsons could preserve it and, for generation upon generation, perform sacrifices to the person who originally received the fief. This is what is meant by "reviving abolished domains" or by "continuing family lines that have been interrupted." When the *Documents* says, "Now when I offer the great sacrifices to the former kings, your ancestors in attendance savor the sacrifices together with them," that is what it is about.[3] 4.3.2

---

1 According to Pi Xirui, this sentence explains another sentence in "Pangeng" in the *Documents*: "In times past, our former kings endeavored to rely on their elders, sharing rule with them" 古我先王，亦惟圖任舊人共政. *SSDZSZ* 3.17a (732).
2 In the Western Zhou, the fief and the estate could be in two different zones: the fiefs were almost certainly in the eastern regions where the regional lords were the delegated rulers; the latter might have been located in the west, in areas over which the Zhou government exercised direct control. See F. Li 2008, 45–46.
3 In Western Han times as well, there was a persistent concern that sacrifices to the founders of royal or noble lines should not be allowed to stop, causing the phenomenon of reinstallments of descendants even after a royal or noble domain had been abolished. The *Great Commentary* thus provides canonical support for such practices. For some examples of reinstallments during Emperor Cheng's (33–7 BCE) reign, see Vankeerberghen 2015.

4.4
Charge to Yue

This chapter falls in the reign of the twenty-first Shang king Wuding 武丁 *(d. ca. 1189 BCE), who brought the Shang dynasty to the heights of its power and who is known from the numerous divination records inscribed on oracle bones.*[1] *In later sources he is also known as Gaozong* 高宗.[2] Scribe's Records *carries the story of how Wuding dreamed of meeting a sage named Yue. After a search, he found him not among his officials, but engaged in dangerous construction work near a cliff. He made him his prime minister.*[3] *The "Minor Xu" to the transmitted* Documents *adds that at this occasion Wuding composed the "Charge to Yue."*[4] *The New Script* Documents *does not have such a chapter, but three versions of "Charge to Yue" are attested in the Old Script* Documents. *The Tsinghua bamboo slips carry a "Charge to Yue" in three chapters.*[5]

Central to the "Charge to Yue" in the Great Commentary *is the explanation of the term liangyin* 梁闇 *as mourning hut (4.4.1). This explanation is arrived at by reference to a* Commentary *and is then elaborated on through a dialogue between Confucius and his disciple Zizhang about the* Documents *passage (4.4.2) and by a passage that points out that Gaozong prepared for state affairs well before the death of his father so*

---

1   Keightley 2014, 207–27.
2   Zu Ji 祖己, one of Wuding's sons, established a temple in his father's honor, which he named Gaozong; see *Shiji* 3.104. Note how the name Wuding itself is already a temple name, i.e., a name given to the king after his death as part of the process that made him into an ancestor. See Keightley 2014, 162–66.
3   *Shiji* 3.102.
4   Qu Wanli 1983, 297.
5   *Qinghua daxue cang Zhanguo zhujian*, vol. 3.

that he could observe the full mourning period without repercussions for the realm (4.4.3).⁶

The entire sequence is preserved as one unit in Ma Duanlin's (1254–1323) Comprehensive Study of Government Institutions Based on Authoritative Sources and Later Interpretations *(Wenxian tongkao)*, where it is attributed to the Great Commentary.⁷ *In the* Documents, *the term* liangyin, *also written as* liangyin 亮陰, *appeared in both the New Script chapter "Do Not Slack" and the Old Script chapter "Charge to Yue."*⁸ Pi Xirui followed Chen Shouqi and placed the sequence in the chapter "Do Not Slack."⁹ Wang Kaiyun, however, saw the sequence as a commentary to the "Charge to Yue," a chapter that he believes was lost early on until another version of it was included in the Old Script Documents.¹⁰

---

6   For a fuller discussion, see the section "A *Commentary* within the *Great Commentary*" in the introduction to this book.
7   *Wenxian tongkao* 120.1079 a–b.
8   *Shangshu zhuzi suoyin* 21/20/16, 43/39/12.
9   SSDZSZ 6.6b–6.9a (773–74).
10 SSDZBZ 4.3b–4.4b.

4.4
說命

4.4.1 《書》曰:「**高宗梁闇,三年不言**。」[1]「何為梁闇也?」《傳》曰:「高宗居凶廬,三年不言。此之謂梁闇。」

4.4.2 子張曰:「何謂也?」孔子曰:「古者君薨,世子聽于冢宰,三年,不敢服先王之服,履先王之位而聽焉;以臣民之義,則不可一日無君矣。不可一日無君,猶不可一日無天也;以孝子之隱乎,則孝子三年弗居矣。故曰:義者、彼也,隱者、此也,遠彼而近此,則孝子之道備矣。」

---

[1] Cf. *Shangshu zhuzi suoyin* 21/20/16 (說命上), 43/39/12 (無逸). *Shangshu zhuzi suoyin* has 亮陰 for 梁闇, 祀 for 年, 弗 for 不. 梁闇=亮闇: *Shiji* 33.1520. 梁闇=諒陰: *Liji zhuzi suoyin* 50.7/175/11, 50.7/175/14. 梁闇=涼陰: *Hanshu* 27 B3.1410

4.4
Charge to Yue

The *Documents* says, "Gaozong stayed in the beamed shack. He did not speak for three years."[1] What is "beamed shack"? The *Commentary* says, "Gaozong stayed in the mourning hut and did not speak for three years." The mourning hut is what "beamed shack" is about.

4.4.1

Zizhang asked, "What is this about?"[2] Confucius answered, "In antiquity, after the ruler passed away, it was the heir apparent who received the prime minister's reports. For three years, he did so without daring to wear his father's robes or occupy his father's seat. From the perspective of his ministers and his people, the ruler cannot be absent for even one day. That the ruler cannot be absent for even one day is just like the sky that is always there. That the filial son should observe a period of retreat means that for three years he should not assume his father's position. That is why it is said, 'So, on the one hand, there is the perspective of ministers and people, and, on the other, there is the observation of a period of retreat. Although the former is important, the latter is absolutely essential for completing the Way of the filial son.'"[3]

4.4.2

---

1. Zheng Xuan and Ma Rong had different interpretations for *liangyin* 梁闇/亮陰. Zheng Xuan glossed *liang* 梁 as *mei* 楣 (beam) and *yin* 闇 as *lu* 廬 (shack); Du Yu 杜預 (222–85) followed earlier interpretations by the old script scholars to gloss *liang* 亮 as *xin* 信 (truly) and *yin* 陰 as *mo* 默 (silent). See *SSDZSZ* 6.7b (773).
2. *Analects* 14.40; *Lunyu zhushu* 14. 130b. The answer Confucius provides in *Analects* is much more succinct and polished than the one provided here and does not invoke filial piety (*xiao* 孝); Confucius states that there is no need to bring up the example of Gaozong to describe a practice that was so common in antiquity.
3. The filial heir apparent should deal with his own sorrow first, before he takes an active role in government. In the meantime, the high ministers have a free hand.

4.4.3　**高宗**[2]有親**喪**[3],居廬三年,然未嘗言國事,而天下無背叛之心者,何也？及其為太子之時,盡已知天下人民之所好惡,是以雖不言國事也,知天下無背叛之心。

2　Cf. *Shangshu zhuzi suoyin* 43/39/11 (無逸).
3　Cf. *Shangshu zhuzi suoyin* 21/20/16 (說命上).

After his father passed away, Gaozong spent three years in the mourning hut without speaking of matters of state. Still, no one in the realm harbored rebellious intentions. Why is this? It is because, during his time as heir apparent, he already fully understood the likes and dislikes of the people in the realm. Hence, even though he did not discuss matters of state, he knew that no one in the realm harbored rebellious intentions.[4]

4.4.3

---

4   Compare 6.1.7.

4.5
Gaozong's Supplementary Sacrifice

The New Script chapter "Gaozong's Supplementary Sacrifice" narrates how Wuding, somewhere in the middle of his reign, reformed his ways after receiving an inauspicious sign in the form of a raucous pheasant that appeared as he was sacrificing to the Shang's founding ancestor. Zu Ji, his son,[1] *uses this opportunity to explain, in general terms, how and why Heaven punishes people. His lecture makes up most of "Gaozong's Supplementary Sacrifice" in the* Documents. *The content of this chapter is, almost verbatim, reproduced in* Scribe's Records.[2]

The Great Commentary *starts out with the same narration and features Zu Ji as the person who responds to the omen. However, rather than a lecture, Zu Ji engages in an outright interpretation of the omen, giving a positive spin to the sudden appearance of the wild bird. The bird symbolizes underutilized talent, which Wuding can attract if he reforms his ways. Wuding does so without fail, and the promised foreign delegations duly arrive (4.5.1). The* Great Commentary *ends with a comment by Confucius on the lessons he derived from reading the* Documents' *"Gaozong's Supplementary Sacrifice" (4.5.2).*

---

1 Pei Yin's 裴駰 commentary to *Scribe's Records* quotes Kong Anguo's opinion that Zu Ji is an advisor to the king; see *Shiji* 3.103 n. 3. Keightley identifies him as one of three sons of Wuding. He would have died before he could assume the kingship. See Keightley 2014, 180. Zu Ji also granted his father the temple name Gaozong, see note 2 in the introduction to chapter 4.4.
2 *Shangshu zhuzi suoyin* 24/22/3–8, *Shiji* 3.103.

4.5
高宗肜日

4.5.1　武丁祭成湯，**有雉**飛升鼎耳而**雊**。武丁問諸**祖己**[1]，祖己曰：「雉者、野鳥，不當升鼎。今升鼎者，欲為用也。無則遠方將有來朝者乎？」故武丁內反諸己，以思先王之道。三年，編髮重譯來朝者六國。

4.5.2　孔子曰：「吾於《**高宗肜日**》見**德**[2]之有報之疾也。」

1　Cf. *Shangshu zhuzi suoyin* 24/22/5 (高宗肜日).
2　Cf. *Shangshu zhuzi suoyin* 24/22/1, 24/22/3, 24/22/6-7 (高宗肜日)

4.5
Gaozong's Supplementary Sacrifice

When Wuding was sacrificing to the accomplished ancestor Tang, a pheasant flew up to the ear of the cauldron and shrieked. When Wuding asked Zu Ji about it, he responded, "The pheasant is a wild bird that should not mount a cauldron. That one mounted the cauldron anyhow is because it wants to be of use. Could it be that delegations from distant regions will be visiting your court?" Therefore, Wuding looked within in order to contemplate the Way of the former kings. After three years, from six countries they came for a court visit, with braided hair and multiple translators.¹ 4.5.1

Confucius said, "From 'Gaozong's Supplementary Sacrifice' I understood how swiftly virtue is rewarded."² 4.5.2

---

1   See note 9 to 4.2.6; the term used here is 重譯 rather than 八譯.
2   This comment made by Confucius is not seen in any other early text.

4.6
Admonitions to Gaozong

The composition of a document "Admonitions to Gaozong," according to Scribe's Records, *would have happened simultaneously with that of "Gaozong's Supplementary Sacrifice."*[1] *Nonetheless, there is no such chapter in the transmitted* Documents. *The chapter might have been one of the old script chapters circulating in Eastern Han.*

There appears to be no intrinsic reason as to why Wang Kaiyun places this fragment under "Admonitions to Gaozong" rather than, as Pi Xirui's edition does, under "Gaozong's Supplementary Sacrifice." Indeed, the fragment here tells a very similar story about Wuding: the arrival of a sign, its interpretation, the king's efforts at reform, and how these efforts were rewarded. The main difference lies in the nature of the sign—two mulberry trees rather than a pheasant—and in Zu Ji's more somber initial interpretation.

The story of two huge wild mulberry trees growing at court forms part of a larger story of Wuding's successful reform following the intervention of his son, Zu Ji, who correctly interprets the omen. The story occurs in several other early Chinese texts and has been ascribed to different, earlier ruler/minister pairs.[2]

---

1 *Shiji* 3.104.
2 Mr. Han's Outer Commentary to the Odes ascribes the exchange to Tang and Yi Yin; see *Hanshi waizhuan zhuzi suoyin* 3.2/15/28–3.2/16/5. *Shiji* 3.100, 13. 496, and 28.1356 ascribe it to the Shang king Tai Wu 太戊 and his minister Yi Zhi 伊陟, who was the son of Yi Yin. "Treatise on the Five Phases" in *Book of Han* does the same, but, when it adds Liu Xiang's interpretation of the omen, Liu Xiang attributes it to Gaozong, i.e., Wuding, perhaps following the *Great Commentary*; *Hanshu* 27B(C).1410. Wang Yinglin believed that the version of *Scribe's Records* is correct and that both the *Great Commentary* and Liu Xiang are mistaken; *Kunxue jiwen* 1:210.

4.6
高宗之訓

4.6.1 湯之後,武丁之前,先王道虧,刑罰犯。**桑穀俱生于朝**[1],七日而大拱。武丁召其相而問焉,其相曰:「吾雖知之,吾不能言也。」問諸**祖己**[2],祖己曰:「桑穀〔者〕、野艸也,野艸生於朝,亡乎!」武丁懼,側身修行,思昔先王之政,興滅國,繼絕世,舉逸民,明養老之禮,諸侯重譯來朝者六國。

1　Cf. *Shangshu zhuzi suoyin* 17/17/22 (咸有一德). *Shangshu zhuzi suoyin* has 祥桑穀共生于朝 for 桑穀俱生于朝.
2　Cf. *Shangshu zhuzi suoyin* 24/22/5 (高宗肜日).

4.6
Admonitions to Gaozong

Between Tang and Wuding, the Way of the former kings declined, and transgressions subject to punishments and fines were common. Two mulberry trees took root in the courtyard,[1] and after seven days they were so thick that one could barely get one's arms around them. Wuding summoned his minister and asked him about it. He said: "Even though I understand how this came about, I cannot tell you." When he asked Zu Ji the same question, the latter answered, "Mulberries are wild plants. When wild plants take root in the courtyard, the end is near." Wuding was terrified and committed himself to reforming his behavior. Yearning for the Way of governing of the former kings, he revived abolished domains, continued family lines that had been interrupted,[2] promoted people who had been left behind, and made clear the ritual importance of caring for the old.[3] From six states the regional lords came for a court visit, with multiple translators.

4.6.1

---

1   *Sang* 桑 refers to a mulberry tree, and *gu* 穀 refers to a paper mulberry tree.
2   The former kings would include Pangeng; the same expressions occur in 4.3.2 in relation to his reign.
3   On the ritual of caring for the old, see case 4 under "The *Great Commentary* on Questions of Political and Social Order" in the introduction to this book.

4.7
The Prince of the West Attacks Qi

"*The Prince of the West Attacks Li* 黎" *is one of the* Documents' *New Script chapters. The chapter is a remonstration to the last Shang king by Zu Yi* 祖伊, *an advisor who is deeply worried by the successful attack on Li by the Prince of the West (Xibo* 西伯) *and rightly fears for the life of his king and the future of his dynasty. The Prince of the West, whose personal name was Ji Chang* 姬昌, *is none less than King Wen* 文王, *the leader of the Zhou people who paved the way for the Zhou's final conquest of the Shang in 1045 by his son, Ji Fa* 姬發, *posthumously known as King Wu* 武王 *(r. 1049/45–1043 BCE).*

In the Great Commentary, *the chapter title is given as "The Prince of the West Attacks Qi." Li and Qi refer to the same place.*[1] *The* Great Commentary *chapter mentions the attack on Qi as part of an annalistic account of major events during the first six years after the Prince of the West received the mandate.*[2] *Prominent in that account is a story about the manner in which three worthies, associated with the famous military*

---

1   The Sui dynasty scholar Lu Deming 陸德明 (556–627) pointed out that Li 黎 in the *Documents* is written as Qi 耆 in the *Great Commentary*. *Shangshu yinyi* A.17a, in *Jingdian shiwen* 1:171.
2   Based on Pankenier's research on the Tsinghua manuscript "Qi ye" 耆夜, King Wen received the mandate in 1058 BCE, after he had been ruler of the Zhou people for several decades; Pankenier 2013, 202–4. The receipt of the mandate (*shouming* 受命) is referred to as year one in 5.8.2. In *Scribe's Records*, King Wen's reign stretches over a period of fifty years. *Bamboo Annals* records events relating to Xibo from the year 6 until 41 of the reign of the last king of Shang, Di Xin 帝辛 or Zhòu 紂. *Shiji* 4.116–18; *Zhushu jinian zhuzi suoyin* 1.53.6/21/17 to 1.53.23/22/17.

strategist Lü Shang 呂尚, or Taigong 太公, persuaded the Shang king to free the Prince of the West from prison (4.7.1). After he was freed, he went on to attack Qi as well as other places (4.7.2–3).

The arrangement of this chapter in Pi Xirui's edition contains parallel passages and fragments not included in Wang Kaiyun's version.

4.7
西伯戡耆

4.7.1 文王一年質虞芮，二年伐于[1]，三年伐密須，四年伐畎夷。紂乃囚之。散宜生、南宮括、閎夭三子相與學訟[2]於太公。太公見三子，知為賢人，遂酌酒切脯，除為師學之禮，約為朋友。 四子遂見**西伯**[3]于牖里[4]，散宜生遂之犬戎氏取美馬，駮身朱鬣雞目，取九六焉；之西海之

---

1 于 = 邗: *Shiji* 4.118.
2 訟 = 誦: *SSDZSZ* 3.22a (735).
3 Cf. *Shangshu zhuzi suoyin* 25/22/14 (西伯戡耆).
4 牖里 = 羑里: *Shiji* 4.116.

4.7
The Prince of the West Attacks Qi

In his first year, King Wen settled the dispute between the Yu and the Rui.[1] In his second year, he attacked Yu;[2] in his third year, Mixu; in his fourth year, the Quanyi.[3] Subsequently Zhòu put him in prison.[4] Three men, Sanyi Sheng, Nangong Kuo, and Hong Yao, went together to study litigation with Taigong.[5] When he received the three, Taigong recognized them as worthies. He then poured wine and sliced dried meat. Having thus performed the ritual between teacher and students, they formed a pact of friendship.

4.7.1

The foursome then went to visit the Prince of the West in Youli. After that, Sanyi Sheng went to the Quanrong and obtained from them nine sets of six beautiful horses with patterned coats, scarlet manes, and

---

1   According to the account in *Scribe's Records*, the leaders of Yu and Rui, on their way to the new leader to settle a dispute, were so impressed by the mores of the Zhou people that they were able to settle their dispute without his intervention; *Shiji* 4.117. The places mentioned in this chapter were all quasi-independent, strategically located entities that could easily switch their allegiance from Shang to Zhou or vice versa; for the approximate location of Yu, Li/Qi, and Chong in modern Shanxi and Henan, see Shaughnessy 1999, map 5.2.
2   This Yu 于 is different from the Yu 虞 mentioned in the previous sentence.
3   This term probably refers to a non-Zhou group rather than a place. According to Sima Zhen's 司馬貞 (8th c.) commentary to *Scribe's Records*, Quanyi 畎夷 and Quanrong 犬戎 were used interchangeably. *Shiji* 110.2881 n. 4. Quanrong is used later in 4.7.1.
4   Zhòu 紂 was the last Shang king.
5   Pi Xirui includes another parallel fragment in which there is no mention of "litigation" (song 訟); *SSDZSZ* 3.22b–23a. For Taigong (Lü Wang), see 6.2.15.

濱取白狐、青翰；之於陵氏取怪獸，大不辟虎狼、閒尾倍其身，名曰虞。之有參氏取美女。之江淮之浦取大貝如車渠。陳於紂之庭，紂出見之，還而觀之曰：「此何人也？」散宜生遂趨而進曰：「吾西蕃之臣，昌之使者。」紂大悅曰：「非子罪也，崇侯也。」遂遣西伯伐崇。

4.7.2　五年之初，得散宜生等獻寶而釋文王。文王出則克耆[5]，六年伐崇則稱王。

4.7.3　既伐于崇。

5　耆＝黎＝鬐＝阢: *Shiji* 4.118 n. 3. *Shuowen jiezi zhu* 6B.33b. Cf. *Shangshu zhuzi suoyin* 25/22/12–14.

110　　　　　　　　　　　　　　　　　　　　　　*Traditions on Yin*

rooster eyes.[6] He went to the coast of the western sea, where he obtained white foxes and albatrosses. He went to the Yuling clan and obtained from them a marvelous beast. It was so big that it was not intimidated by tigers or wolves and had a tail as long as its body. It is called a *yu*. He went to the Youcan clan and got beautiful women. He went to the banks of the Yangzi and the Huai, obtaining giant cartwheellike shells.[7] He displayed all of these at Zhòu's court. Zhòu came out to inspect the goods. Turning back, he looked him over, saying: "Who is this?" Sanyi Sheng thereupon hurried forward. "I am a subject of the western domain, an envoy of Ji Chang," he said. Zhòu was extremely pleased and said, "It is not Ji Chang who was at fault but the lord of Chong."[8] Thereupon he sent the Prince of the West to attack Chong.

At the beginning of the fifth year, because of the goods offered to him by Sanyi Sheng and the others, he released King Wen. Once King Wen left captivity, he conquered Qi. In the sixth year he attacked Chong and called himself king.[9] 4.7.2

After he attacked Chong[10] 4.7.3

---

6   Pi Xirui quotes a passage from *Six Quivers* (Liu tao 六韜) that provides a similar description of these special horses; there, however, the horse's tail is associated with a rooster, and the eyes are described as golden. SSDZSZ 3.23b (735). *The Classic of Mountains and Seas* records that this type of horse has golden eyes; *Shanhaijing zhushu suoyin* 17/73/23; Birrell 1999, 145.
7   That is, the shells of the *Tridacna* (*chequ* 硨磲).
8   It was because the lord of Chong slandered Ji Chang that the Shang king imprisoned the latter; *Shiji* 4.116.
9   King Wen (Wenwang 文王), Prince of the West (Xibo 西伯), and Ji Chang 姬昌 all refer to the same person.
10 This sentence is incomplete. Cf. 5.8.2.

卷五
周傳

5
Traditions on Zhou

5.1
Great Oath

This chapter of the Documents *is situated in the era after King Wen's death, when Ji Fa, the future King Wu, had taken over leadership of the Zhou people and was moving to overturn Shang rule.*

In the transmitted version of the Documents, *there are three "Great Oath" (Tai shi* 泰誓*) chapters relating to this series of events.*[1] *Even though these are Old Script chapters, it is clear that a "Great Oath" chapter circulated as early as the Western Han dynasty.*[2] *According to* Scribe's Records, *the* Documents *transmitted via Fu Sheng had twenty-nine chapters.*[3] *Liu Xin's letter dates the discovery of the chapter to Emperor Wu's reign and states that "when 'Great Oath' came to light, the academicians gathered to read it"* 泰誓後得，博士集而讀之.[4] *By the time* Book of Sui *compiled its account of the transmission of the* Documents, *the story was that a "woman from Henei [Commandery]"* 河內女子 *had found "Great Oath" and brought it to court.*[5] *The mid-Western Han version of the "Great*

---

1 The transmitted *Documents* gives the title of the chapter as "Tai shi" 泰誓 rather than "Da shi" 大誓. This change, according to Wang Yinglin and Chao Gongwu, was introduced in the early Tang; see *Kunxue jiwen* 1:215.
2 Wang Yinglin relates two separate stories of how an old script version of "Great Oath" reached the imperial capital: according to the first one, a copy of the chapter was found in a wall and presented to Emperor Wu (r. 141–87) toward the end of his reign; the second story relates how a woman from Henei presented a copy of the text during Xuandi's (r. 74–48 BCE) reign; *Han Yiwenzhi kaozheng* 1.19a–b.
3 *Shiji* 121.3124–25; see also the section "Master Fu's Life" of the introduction to this book.
4 *Hanshu* 36.1969, trans. Loewe 2015, 382.
5 *Suishu* 32.914–15. See also chap. 81, "Explanation Corrected" (Zheng shuo 正說), of *Weighed Discourses* (Lunheng 論衡).

Oath" chapter is not the same as the version that became part of the transmitted Documents.

The Great Commentary's "Great Oath" consists of several passages that describe events between the death of Ji Chang (King Wen) and the final attack on the Shang heartland by Ji Fa (King Wu).[6] The first two passages stand out as a pair: 5.1.1 is a quotation ascribed to the Documents (5.1.1), whereas 5.1.2 is a quotation ascribed to the Commentary that explains administrative terms used in 5.1.1. The passages that follow (5.2.3–6) provide historical lore without quotations; two of these (5.1.3 and 5.1.4) are about omens and their interpretation, with close parallels in Scribe's Records 4.120.

---

6 Scribe's Records has an account of events in this period in two chapters, a full account in "Basic Annals of Zhou" (Zhou benji 周本紀) and a condensed account in "Hereditary House of Taigong of Qi" (Qi Taigong shijia 齊太公世家). Interestingly, the act of composing "Great Oath" is in the first case placed in the eleventh year but in "Hereditary House of Taigong of Qi," in the ninth year; Shiji 4.120–21 and 32.1479–80. Bamboo Annals too provides a chronology of these events; Zhushu jinian zhuzi suoyin 1.53.29/22/29–1.54.1/23/8.

GREAT OATH

5.1
大誓

5.1.1 《書》曰:「唯四月,太子**發**[1]上祭于畢,下至于**盟津**[2]之上。乃告司徒、司馬、司空、諸節允才,「予無知,以先祖先父之有德之臣左右**小子**[3],予受先公[4],必力**賞**[5]**罰**[6],以定厥功于先祖之遺。」」

5.1.2 《傳》曰:「天子三公: 司徒公、司馬公、司空公。每壹公,三卿佐之;每一卿,三大夫佐之;每壹大夫,三元士佐之。故有三公九卿二十七大夫八十一元士。所與為天下者,若此而已。」

1　Cf. *Shangshu zhuzi suoyin* 27/23/15 (泰誓上).
2　Cf. *Shangshu zhuzi suoyin* 27/23/12 (泰誓上). *Shangshu zhuzi suoyin* has 孟津 for 盟津.
3　Cf. *Shangshu zhuzi suoyin* 27/23/15 (泰誓上).
4　公 = 功: *Shiji* 4.120.
5　Cf. *Shangshu zhuzi suoyin* 29/25/4 (泰誓下).
6　Cf. *Shangshu zhuzi suoyin* 27/23/21 (泰誓上).

5.1
Great Oath

The *Documents* says, "In the fourth month, the heir apparent Fa went up to Bi to offer sacrifices and then traveled down until he reached Meng Ford.[1] There he announced to the minister over the masses, the minister of military affairs, and the minister of works, and all other appointees endowed with ample talents, 'I am ignorant. Because of the assistance you, meritorious ministers, who served my grandfather and father, have given me, the small child, I inherited the achievements of my ancestors. I now must zealously dole out rewards and punishments so that your achievements can be established as part of the legacy of our ancestors.'"[2]

5.1.1

As the *Commentary* says, "The Son of Heaven's three excellencies are the minister over the masses, the minister of military affairs, and the minister of works.[3] Each excellency has three ministers to assist him. Each minister has three counselors to assist him. Each counselor has three chief men of service to assist him. Therefore, there are three excellencies, nine ministers, twenty-seven counselors, and eighty-one chief men of service. These, indeed, are the ones with whom he administers the realm."[4]

5.1.2

---

1 According to *Scribe's Records*, Ji Fa continued calling himself *taizi* 太子, "heir apparent," after the death of his father. This unusual appellation was meant to signal his determination to complete his father's mission in life; *Shiji* 4.120.
2 Fragment 5.1.1 can be found in nearly identical form in *Scribe's Records*; *Shiji* 4.120. In the *Great Commentary*, the fragment is ascribed to the *Documents* itself, whereas *Scribe's Records* presents it as an integral part of its own narrative.
3 See 1.1.31 and 6.1.5.
4 Pi Xirui's edition does not include this fragment in the "Great Oath" chapter but under the general heading "Commentary on the Chapters on Xia" (Xia zhuan 夏傳), *SSDZSZ* 3.10a (729). That Wang Kaiyun includes the fragment here is, presumably,

5.1.3 太子發升于舟。鼓鐘惡，[7]觀臺惡，將舟惡，**宗廟**[8]惡。中流，有白魚入于舟中，跪取出涘以燎。群公咸曰：「休哉！」

5.1.4 有火流于王屋，化為赤烏，三足。武王喜，諸大夫皆喜，周公曰：「茂哉茂哉，天之見此，以勸之也。」

5.1.5 武王伐紂，至于商郊，停止宿郊，夜，士卒皆歡樂歌舞以待旦。

5.1.6 惟丙午，**王逮師**[9]前，師乃鼓，鈘躁，師乃慆，前歌後舞，假于上下，咸曰「孜孜無怠」。

5.1.7 「正稽古立**功**[10]立事，可以永年，丕天之大律。」

---

7 惡＝亞：*SSDZSZ* 3.30b (739), Zheng Xuan's commentary.
8 Cf. *Shangshu zhuzi suoyin* 27/23/16 (泰誓上).
9 Cf. *Shangshu zhuzi suoyin* 29/24/19 (泰誓下).
10 Cf. *Shangshu zhuzi suoyin* 29/25/4 (泰誓下).

The heir apparent Fa boarded the ship. His ship was followed by one bearing bell and drum, one bearing an observatory, the admiral's ship, and one carrying the ancestral temple.[5] In midstream, a white fish jumped on board. Kneeling, he picked up the fish and brought it to the riverbank, where he grilled it [in sacrifice]. The gathered officials said in unison: "How auspicious!" 5.1.3

Flames drifted past the king's room and transformed into a scarlet crow with three feet. King Wu was delighted, as were all the counselors. The Duke of Zhou said, "How encouraging this is! If Heaven shows us such an omen, is a sign that it supports our undertaking." 5.1.4

King Wu, on his campaign against Zhòu, reached the suburbs of Shang. He stopped and spent the night there. The troops cheerfully sang and danced away the night. 5.1.5

When, on the day *bingwu*, the king moved to the front of his troops, they beat the drums and gestured elatedly; thus excited, they sang in the front and danced at the back. From high to low, they all exclaimed, "Let us spare no effort!" 5.1.6

"Precisely by examining the successes and achievements of the ancients, one can govern for a long time and abide by Heaven's great rules."[6] 5.1.7

---

because he considers it clarifies the meaning of the officials mentioned in the preceding passage.

5 Zheng Xuan interprets *miao* 廟 as *zhu* 主, "tablet." The parallel passage in *Scribe's Records* does not provide these details on the nature of Ji Fa's fleet.

6 This sentence, though not in the transmitted *Documents*, is quoted in "Treatise on Suburban Sacrifices" (Jiaosi zhi 郊祀志) of *Book of Han*, which attributes it to the "Great Oath" chapter of the *Documents*; *Hanshu* 25.1255.

5.2
Success through Battle

This chapter moves to the aftermath of the battle King Wu waged with the Shang at Muye 牧野.[1] *Like "Great Oath," "Success through Battle" is an Old Script chapter in the transmitted* Documents *for which it is clear that an earlier text under the same title circulated well before the fourth century CE. A passage in* Mencius *rejects a* Documents *text titled "Success through Battle" for its graphic descriptions of the violence of the battle.*[2] *Book of Han's "Treatise on Pitchpipes and the Calendar" (Lüli zhi* 律歷志*) too contains several passages that it ascribes to a "Success through Battle."*[3] *According to* Scribe's Records, *King Wu of Zhou authored a "Success through Battle" as part of his postconquest actions.*[4]

The "Success through Battle" chapter in the Great Commentary *acknowledges the violence of the military campaign but then immediately moves to the exemplary way in which King Wu dealt with the conquered people. It relates a conversation between King Wu and three of his advisors—Taigong, the Duke of Shao, and the Duke of Zhou—each of whom recommends a different course of action, ranging from harsh measures against the conquered to the lenient treatment proposed by the Duke of Zhou. King Wu implements the Duke of Zhou's recommendations and rapidly succeeds in earning the trust of the conquered Shang people (5.2.1).* Scribe's Records *too records the peace-promoting measures King Wu implemented in language that echoes the* Great Commentary, *but in* Scribe's Records *the*

---

1   Muye was close to the Shang capital (modern Anyang).
2   *Mengzi zhengyi* j. 28, 959–62; trans. Lau 1970, 194 (7B3).
3   *Hanshu* 21C.1015.
4   *Shiji* 4.125–27.

narrative framework about the competing advisors is missing.[5] *The second passage (5.2.2) is an enunciation by Taigong that is loosely associated with 5.2.1.*

Part of 5.2.1 is cited in the Song encyclopedia Deep Ocean of Records and Compilations *(Jizuan yuanhai* 記纂淵海*) as deriving from a chapter of the Great Commentary titled "Great War" (Da zhan* 大戰*). On that basis, Pi Xirui placed 5.2.1 as a whole under the title "Great War."*[6]

---

5   *Shiji* 4.125–27.

6   SSDZSZ 3.32a–b (740).

5.2
武成

5.2.1 武王與紂戰于**牧**之**野**[1]，紂之卒輻分，紂之車瓦裂，紂之甲魚鱗，下賀乎武王「紂死」。

武王皇皇若天下之未定，召太公而問曰：「入殷柰何？」太公曰：「臣聞之也，愛〔其〕人者、兼其屋上之烏，不愛〔其〕人者、及其胥[2]餘。何如？」武王曰：「不可。」

召公趨而進曰：「臣聞之也，有罪者殺，無罪者活。咸劉厥敵，毋使有餘烈。何如？」武王曰：「不可。」

周公趨而進曰：「臣聞之也，〔使〕各安其宅，各田其田，毋故毋**親**[3]。惟仁之親，何如？」

---

1 Cf. *Shangshu zhuzi suoyin* 31/26/16 (武成).
2 胥 = 胥.
3 Cf. *Shangshu zhuzi suoyin* 28/24/12 (泰誓中).

5.2
Success through Battle

King Wu battled with Zhòu in the fields of Mu.[1] Zhòu's troops were scattered, his chariots torn apart, his armor smashed. King Wu received congratulations from his underlings, "Zhòu has died!"

5.2.1

King Wu was apprehensive, as if the realm had not yet been settled. He summoned Taigong and asked him, "What should we do after we enter Yin?" Taigong said: "I have learned that if you care for someone, this includes taking care of the crow on his roof; but, if you do not care for someone, your dislike extends to his whole village.[2] Do you agree?" King Wu said, "No."

The Duke of Shao hurried forward and offered: "According to what I have learned, the guilty ought to be executed, the innocent spared. Completely destroy your enemies; make sure there is no valor left in them. What about that?" King Wu said: "No."

Then the Duke of Zhou hurried forward, saying, "Here is what I have learned: Make sure that everyone is at ease in his home, that everyone farms his fields; do not discriminate in favor of your friends and family; only become close to the humane. What about that?"

---

1   Zhòu 紂 is the name of the last Shang king.
2   According to Zheng Xuan, *xuyu* 胥餘 refers to the walls of a village; see *SSDZSZ* 3.32b (740).

武王曠乎若**天下**之已**定**，遂入殷，**封比干之墓**，表**商容**之閭，**發鉅橋之粟，散鹿臺之財**，[4]歸傾宮之女，而民知方。曰：「王之于**仁人**[5]也：死者封其墓，況于生者乎！王之于賢人也：亡者表其閭，況于在者乎！王之于財也：聚者散之，況于復籍乎！王之于色也：在者歸其父母，況于復徵乎。」

5.2.2　太公曰：「罵女毋歎，溼女毋乾；毋歎毋乾，是謂艱難。」

4　Cf. *Shangshu zhuzi suoyin* 31/26/18 (武成).
5　Cf. *Shangshu zhuzi suoyin* 28/24/12 (泰誓中).

King Wu, relieved, felt as if the realm was already settled. Thereafter, he entered Yin, built a tumulus at Bigan's tomb,[3] marked Shang Rong's gate,[4] opened the granary near the great bridge in Julu,[5] distributed the riches of Deer Terrace,[6] and returned all the palace women to their homes.[7] Therefore, people knew they could count on him. They said, "Here is how our king treats humane persons: he added a tumulus over the tomb for one who had died;[8] would he not do even more for a humane person who is still alive? As to worthies: he marked the village gate of a worthy one who had fled;[9] would he not do even more for a worthy person who is still around? As to wealth: the king distributed what he had confiscated; why would he ever reinstate the tax registers? As to women: the king returned the palace women to their parents; why would he ever summon other women?"

Taigong said: "'If someone scolds you, do not cringe; if someone spits at you, do not wipe it off.' Following this command is particularly difficult."

5.2.2

---

[3] Bigan was an uncle of Zhòu and was brutally killed for remonstrating with the king. It was, among other things, news of Bigan's death that motivated the Zhou forces to embark on their final campaign against Shang. *Shiji* 3.108.
[4] *Shiji* 3.108 n. 5.
[5] *Shiji* 3.105; *Shuijing zhushi* 10.954.
[6] Through levying heavy taxes on the population, Zhòu had filled the granary at Juqiao and the treasury at Deer Terrace; *Shiji* 3.105.
[7] Whereas the story about the competition between the three advisors is unique to the *Great Commentary*, the measures King Wu took toward Shang after the conquest—except for the return of the palace women—are also highlighted in *Shiji* 4.105–7.
[8] I.e., Bigan.
[9] I.e., Shang Rong.

5.3
Great Plan

"Great Plan" is one of the most celebrated chapters of the Documents. It starts out with a short narrative about how a god-given Great Plan was transmitted from Yu, the founder of Xia, through Prince Ji, a scion of the royal house of Shang, to King Wu of Zhou. The plan provides a ninefold method for successful rulership; each of the nine sections provides crucial vocabulary (most often in the form of numbered lists) and concrete advice on managing the complexities of universal government. These include

1. exploitation of material resources (the Five Material Resources, Wuxing 五行)
2. personal conduct and skills (the Five Tasks, Wushi 五事)
3. organization of one's rule through specialized departments (the Eight Tools of Government, Bazheng 八政)
4. the calendar (the Five Cycles, Wuji 五紀)
5. crucial leadership qualities of the king through which he will inspire the population (the Sovereign's Standard, Huangji 皇極)
6. government styles to be varied with external circumstances (the Three Powers, Sande 三德)
7. decision-making considering the opinions of various constituencies, including the gods, who are consulted through divination (Managing Doubt, Jiyi 稽疑)
8. meteorological phenomena that indicate areas where one's government needs improvement (the Various Verifications, Shuzheng 庶徵)

9. constituents of eudaimonia and its opposite (the Five Blessings, *Wufu* 五福, and the Six Extremes, *Liuji* 六極).¹

The "Great Plan" chapter in the Great Commentary *consists of five passages. It first dwells on the transmission narrative, seeking to reconcile Prince Ji's loyalty to Shang with the fact that the prince transmitted the Great Plan to Shang's conqueror, King Wu of Zhou (5.3.1). The following passages provide glosses and explanations for terms and phrases that occur in the* Documents' *"Great Plan." Especially noteworthy is 5.3.2, where the* Great Commentary *clearly interprets the Wuxing as Five Material Resources, pointing out their potential for human exploitation. It lists them, except for the reversal of metal and wood, in the order of the Documents' "Great Plan."*

This stands in contrast with 5.3.5, where both the order of the Wuxing and their correlation with the Five Tasks indicate proximity with the Great Commentary's *last chapter, "Tradition on the Great Plan's Five Phases" (7.1), where the five refer to phases more than to material resources.*

---

1   Nylan 1992.

5.3
鴻笵

5.3.1 武王勝殷,繼公子祿父,釋**箕子**之囚,箕子不忍為周之釋,走之朝鮮。武王聞之,因以朝鮮封之。箕子既受周之封,不得無臣禮,故于十三祀來朝,周武王因其朝而問**鴻笵**。[1]

5.3.2 **水火**者、百姓之所飲食也,**金木**者、百姓之所興作也,**土**[2]者、萬物之所資生也。是為**人用**。[3]

---

[1] 笵 = 範: Cf. *Shangshu zhuzi suoyin* 32/27/1. See also *Shangshu zhuzi suoyin* 32/27/3, 32/27/5–7 (洪範).
[2] Cf. *Shangshu zhuzi suoyin* 32/27/10–11 (洪範).
[3] Cf. *Shangshu zhuzi suoyin* 32/28/4 (洪範).

5.3
Great Plan

After King Wu defeated Yin, he continued Yin's line with Gongzi Lufu,[1] and he set Prince Ji free.[2] Prince Ji, upset that it was the Zhou that liberated him, fled to Chaoxian.[3] King Wu, informed about this, promptly enfeoffed him at Chaoxian. Having accepted a fief from the Zhou, Prince Ji was obliged to perform the rituals appropriate to a subject. Therefore, he came for a court visit in the thirteenth year. King Wu of Zhou took advantage of the court visit to ask him about the Great Plan.[4]

5.3.1

Water and fire are what people rely on to eat and drink; metal and wood are what people rely on to construct and create; earth is what allows the ten thousand things to be born. This is considered "human usage."

5.3.2

---

1   A son of Zhòu, the last Shang king.
2   Prince Ji had been imprisoned by Zhòu; *Shiji* 3.108, 38.1609.
3   Chaoxian (Chosŏn in Korean) is the name for a region straddling the northeast of modern China and northern Korea.
4   The passage seeks to reconcile Prince Ji's loyalty to his native dynasty of Shang with his transmission of the Great Plan to Shang's conqueror by explaining that he first fled to Chaoxian and was then ritually compelled to appear at the Zhou court. That Prince Ji had paid a court visit in the thirteenth year is also mentioned in the "Great Plan" in the *Documents*. *Scribe's Records* says that he transmitted the Great Plan two years after the conquest but gives only a vague date for his court visit. *Bamboo Annals* mentions a visit by Prince Ji in the sixteenth year of King Wu's reign. According to Shaughnessy, this record belongs to a set of entries that should be moved from King Wu's reign to King Cheng's reign; *Shiji* 38.1611; *Zhushu jinian zhuzi suoyin*, 1.54.5/23/16; Shaughnessy 1986, esp. 174.

5.3.3　**八政**何以先**食**[4],《傳》曰:「食者、萬物之始、人事之本也,故八政先食。」

5.3.4　聖人者、民之父母也,母能生之,能食之;父能教之,能誨之,聖王曲備之者也:能生之,能食之,能教之,能誨之也。為之城郭以居之,為之宮室以處之,為之庠序學校以教誨之,為之列地制畝以飲食之,故《書》曰:「**作民父母,以為天下王。**」[5]此之謂也。

5.3.5　**皃屬木**,言**屬金**,視**屬火**,聽**屬水**,思**屬土**[6]。火發于密,水洩于深。

5.3.6　汨[7]、亂也。

5.3.7　不叶于極,不麗于咎。毋侮鰥寡,而畏高明。[8]

4　Cf. *Shangshu zhuzi suoyin* 32/27/13-14 (洪範).
5　Cf. *Shangshu zhuzi suoyin* 32/28/1-2 (洪範).
6　Cf. *Shangshu zhuzi suoyin* 32/27/10, 32/27/12 (洪範). *Shangshu zhuzi suoyin* has 貌 for 皃 in both locations.
7　Cf. *Shangshu zhuzi suoyin* 32/27/6 (洪範).
8　叶 = 協, 麗 = 罹; 毋 = 無. Cf. *Shangshu zhuzi suoyin* 32/27/17-19 (洪範). *Shangshu zhuzi suoyin* has 協 for 叶, 罹 for 麗, and 無虐煢獨 for 毋侮鰥寡.

Why is food listed first among the Eight Tools of Government?[5] The *Commentary* says: "Food constitutes the beginning of the ten thousand things and the root of human affairs. That is why food is listed first among the Eight Tools of Government."   5.3.3

The sage is the father and mother of the people. A mother has the ability to give birth to her children and nourish them; a father has the ability to teach and instruct them. A sage king combines the abilities of both: he is able to sustain, nurture, teach, and instruct his people. He constructs cities for them to reside in, makes dwellings for them to live in, establishes schools and academies for them to receive instruction, and lays out the fields and establishes acreage to provide them with food and drink. Therefore, when the *Documents* says, "The one who acts as a father and a mother to the people is considered king of the realm," that is what it is about.   5.3.4

Demeanor is associated with wood, speech with metal, vision with fire, hearing with water, mindfulness with earth. Fire arises from the minute; water runs toward depths.   5.3.5

The character pronounced *gu* means "disorder."   5.3.6

"Even if one does not yet comply with the highest standard, one should not be implicated in blameworthy acts. Do not insult widowers and widows and revere the high and illustrious."   5.3.7

---

5   The Eight Tools of Government section of the *Documents*' "Great Plan" indeed lists food as the first of eight items, a fact to which the *Great Commentary* attaches hermeneutical significance.

5.4
Great Proclamation

The speaker in the New Script "Great Proclamation" is King Cheng.[1] His father, King Wu, had died only a few years after the conquest of Shang. King Cheng, reportedly, was very young when he inherited the rulership of Zhou, and this explains why he refers to himself as a little young man (you chong ren 幼冲人) in the Documents.*[2] In "Great Proclamation" he seeks to persuade his allies and aides to support his planned campaign to suppress a rebellion in the old territory of Shang. A son of the last Shang ruler, aided by various disgruntled scions of the Zhou royal house, was taking advantage of the weak position of King Cheng to regain power. The tortoise shells that King Cheng had consulted were auspicious, but still many of his aides counseled him to counter the oracle and abort the campaign, arguing that the Zhou royal house should first put its own internal affairs in order.*

In the Han, "Great Proclamation" was read as if the Duke of Zhou, not King Cheng, had issued it.[3] The Duke of Zhou, as the Han scholars believed, served as regent for the young King Cheng and was, via the "Great Proclamation" not only drumming up support for the campaign that he would lead, but also for his own leadership. In 7 CE Wang Mang, who had recently become the regent for the nominal Han emperor, issued

---

1   Qu Wanli 1983, 134. However, other commentators regard the Duke of Zhou as the speaker on the assumption that he had taken the title of king. The main tenets of this controversy are summarized in Liu Qiyu 2007, 582–97. Liu leans in favor of the Duke of Zhou as the speaker.
2   "Great Proclamation," in *Shangshu zhuzi suoyin* 35/31/6.
3   *Shiji* 4.132 and 33.1518.

his own "Great Proclamation" after opponents had challenged his legitimacy.[4]

"Great Proclamation" in the Great Commentary *consists of two fragments. The first assumes, in line with other Han texts, that the Duke of Zhou was the man in charge. It urges caution about oracles when making decisions of a political or military nature, recommending wide consultation and sound principles instead. Pi Xirui suggests reading this together with the "Great Plan" in the* Documents, *in which King Wu stakes out the same position regarding divination.*[5]

The second fragment is a short phrase from the Documents, *with some variation. Wang Yinglin notes how the same phrase also occurred in the "Great Proclamation" that Wang Mang issued to his generals in 7 CE to stir them, via a conscious imitation of the* Documents *speech, to suppress a dangerous rebellion against his regime.*[6] *Given that Wang Mang's "Great Proclamation" seems to mix the variants of the* Documents *and of the* Great Commentary, *Wang Yinglin thinks Wang Mang took his inspiration from the* Great Commentary.[7]

In the Documents, *the chapter "Metal Coffer" precedes "Great Proclamation." Chen Shouqi and Pi Xirui, basing themselves on the opinions of the Song scholar Ye Mengde* 葉夢得 *(1077–1148), both considered "Metal Coffer" to have been written only after the death of the Duke of Zhou and, hence, that it should follow "Great Proclamation."*[8] *Wang Kaiyun follows that opinion.*

---

4   *Hanshu* 84.3428–34.
5   King Wu proclaims that, when encountering significant issues, a ruler should consult his own heart, then his ministers and men of service, and then the common people, all before conducting divination. "Great Plan," in *Shangshu zhuzi suoyin* 32/28/7–8; *SSDZSZ* 5.1b (760).
6   Wang Mang's "Great Proclamation" uses both *xian* 獻 from the *Documents* and *yi* 儀 from the *Great Commentary* by stating "among the exemplary people there are the ninety-thousand fine men (*min xian yi jiu wan fu* 民獻儀九萬夫). *Hanshu* 84.3429.
7   *Kunxue jiwen* 1:151.
8   *SSDZJJ* 2.17b (p. 4137); *Jinwen Shangshu kaozheng* 290.

5.4
大誥

5.4.1 周公先謀于同姓。同姓從,謀于朋友;[1] 朋友從,然後謀于天下;天下從,然後加之蓍龜。[2]
　　是以君子、聖人謀義,不謀不義,故謀必成。卜義,不卜不義,故卜必吉。[3] 以義擊不義,故戰必勝。是以君子、聖人,謀則吉,戰則勝。

5.4.2 《書》曰:「民儀有十夫。」[4]

1　Cf. *Shangshu zhuzi suoyin* 35/31/11 (大誥).
2　Cf. *Shangshu zhuzi suoyin* 35/31/8 (大誥).
3　Cf. *Shangshu zhuzi suoyin* 35/31/10–11 (**大誥**).
4　Cf. *Shangshu zhuzi suoyin* 35/31/10 (大誥). *Shangshu zhuzi suoyin* has 獻 for 儀.

5.4
Great Proclamation

The Duke of Zhou first consulted within his lineage. When his lineage complied, he consulted with his allies. When his allies complied, he consulted with the realm. Only when the realm complied would he present his case to the yarrow stalks and the tortoise.[1]   5.4.1

That is why the noble man and the sage only plan what is proper, never what is improper; therefore, their plans are always crowned with success. They only divine about what is proper, never about what is improper; therefore, their divinations are always auspicious. They rely on what is proper to attack what is improper; therefore, they are always victorious in battle. Hence, when the noble man and the sage make plans, they are auspicious; when they engage in battle, they are victorious.

The *Documents* says: "Among the exemplary people there are the ten fine men."   5.4.2

---

1   In the "Great Proclamation" in the *Documents* there is only talk of divination by means of the tortoise plastron; divination by means of yarrow stalks was a later method, associated with the *Book of Changes*. There also is some resonance here with a passage in the *Documents*' "Great Plan"; see *Shangshu zhuzi suoyin* 32/28/7–8.

5.5
Metal Coffer

The chapter "Metal Coffer" seeks to dispel rumors that the Duke of Zhou intended to usurp the royal title. It does so by providing a story in which King Cheng finds, in a metal coffer, the record of a divination the Duke of Zhou had made when King Wu was lying ill: the record proved that the Duke of Zhou had offered the gods his own life to save that of King Wu and easily dispelled King Cheng's earlier suspicions about the Duke of Zhou's loyalty. "Metal Coffer" is a New Script chapter in the transmitted Documents. A version of the text has recently been attested in the form of a bamboo manuscript.[1]

The Great Commentary chapter consists of three passages. The first outlines the circumstances that led to the Duke of Zhou's punitive campaign to the east in order to put down the uprising by the old Shang clan and its Zhou allies (5.5.1). This historical narrative is also found in Scribe's Records but with variations.[2] The second passage, also with a parallel in Scribe's Records, relates the events surrounding the death and burial of the Duke of Zhou and the suburban sacrifices to King Wen in Lu (5.5.2). According to the chronology of Scribe's Records, the Duke of Zhou prayed and made his metal coffer before King Wu's death, thus before the events

---

1   The text "King Wu of Zhou was ill" (Zhou Wuwang you ji 周武王有疾) of the Tsinghua collection closely resembles Documents' "Metal Coffer." See Qinghua daxue cang Zhanguo zhujian 1:14–17, 157–62; Meyer 2014.
2   Shiji 33.1518.

described in 5.5.1, and King Cheng opened the coffer after the death of the Duke of Zhou, realizing the latter's complete loyalty to the Zhou.[3] *The third passage is a fragment. It is found in* Scribe's Records *to indicate that King Cheng was very young when his father, King Wu, died, requiring the Duke of Zhou to become his regent.*[4]

---

3   Shiji 33.1522.
4   Shiji 33.1518.

5.5
金縢

5.5.1 **武王**殺紂,立武庚,而繼公子祿父,使**管叔**、蔡叔監祿父。武王死,成王幼,**周公**[1]盛養成王,使召公奭為傅。周公身居位,聽天下為政。管叔、蔡叔疑周公,**流言于國**,曰:「**公將不利于王。**」[2] 奄君蒲姑[3]謂祿父曰:「武王既死矣,今王尚幼矣,周公見疑矣。此百世之時也,請舉事。」然

1　Cf. *Shangshu zhuzi suoyin* 34/29–30 (金縢).
2　于 = 於. Cf. *Shangshu zhuzi suoyin* 34/30/7–8 (金縢). *Shangshu zhuzi suoyin* has 武王既喪,管叔及其群弟乃流言於國,曰:「公將不利於孺子」.
3　蒲姑 = 薄姑: see *Shiji* 4.133.

5.5
Metal Coffer

King Wu killed Zhòu and established Wugeng. He continued the line with Gongzi Lufu,[1] ordering Guanshu and Caishu to keep an eye on Lufu.[2]

5.5.1

When King Wu died, King Cheng was still a child. The Duke of Zhou raised King Cheng and appointed Shi, the Duke of Shao, as his tutor. The Duke of Zhou himself assumed the highest position and administered the entire realm.[3] Guanshu and Caishu were suspicious of the Duke of Zhou and circulated rumors among the nobles' lands to the effect that "the Duke would harm the King."[4] Pugu, the ruler of Yan,[5] said to Lufu: "King Wu is already dead, whereas the current king is still young. Moreover, there are suspicions regarding the Duke of Zhou. This is an opportunity that only comes around once every one hundred generations; let

---

1 Even though Zheng Xuan claims that Wugeng and Gongzi Lufu are the same person, the grammar of the sentence here suggests that they are two different persons. Pi Xirui agrees with the *Great Commentary*. Pi associates Zheng Xuan's claim with the old script tradition and the *Great Commentary* with the Ouyang tradition and thus the new script version. *SSDZSZ* 5.1b–2a (760–61). In *Scribe's Records*, Wugeng and Lufu appear to be the same person; *Shiji* 3.108–9.
2 Guanshu and Caishu are King Wu's younger brothers. Enfeoffed in Guan and Cai respectively, they had allied themselves with the Shang rebels. *Shiji* 4.126–27.
3 The Duke of Zhou and Shi, the Duke of Shao, were also brothers of King Wu.
4 This sentence occurs with variations in the "Metal Coffer" chapter of the *Documents*. "King Wu died. Guanshu and several of his brothers circulated rumors among the states to the effect that 'the Duke would harm the young heir.'" *Shangshu zhuzi suoyin* 34/30/7–8.
5 For suppression of the rebellion, see below, 5.12.5, and the introduction to 5.15. Pugu is also written as Bogu 薄姑 in *Scribe's Records*; *Shiji* 4.133. See also Xu Zhongshu 1998, 65–68.

後祿父及三監叛也，周公以成王之命殺祿父。

5.5.2 三年之後，周公老于豐，心不敢遠成王，而欲事文武之廟。然後周公疾曰：「吾死，必葬于成周，示天下臣于成王。」成王曰：「周公生欲事宗廟，死欲聚骨于畢。」畢者、**文王**之墓也，故周公薨，成王不葬于成周而葬之于畢，示天下不敢臣也，所以明有**功**[4]、尊有德，故忠孝之道盛在成王、周公之閒。故魯郊，成王所以禮周公也。

5.5.3 成王幼在襁褓。

---

4   Cf. *Shangshu zhuzi suoyin* 34/29/27–34/30/1 (金縢).

us create a disturbance!" After that Lufu and three supervisors revolted.[6] The Duke of Zhou, using King Cheng's mandate, killed Lufu.

After three years, the Duke of Zhou retired to Feng. He did not intend to distance himself from King Cheng but wanted to serve the ancestral temples of Wen and Wu.[7] After that the Duke of Zhou became ill and said: "When I die, I, by all means, want to be buried in Chengzhou to show the realm that I am a subject to King Cheng." King Cheng objected: "Throughout his life, the Duke of Zhou has wanted to serve the ancestral temples. When he dies, I want his bones to be gathered at Bi." Bi is the site of King Wen's tomb.[8] Therefore, when the Duke of Zhou died, King Cheng did not bury him in Chengzhou but in Bi to show the realm that he did not dare to consider him a subject. This is how he made bright the one with merit and honored the one with virtue. Therefore, the way of loyalty and filial piety blossomed between King Cheng and the Duke of Zhou. Therefore, the suburban sacrifices (to King Wen) at Lu are the means by which King Cheng paid ritual homage to the Duke of Zhou.[9]

5.5.2

King Cheng was young and still in swaddling clothes.

5.5.3

---

6   In addition to Guanshu, the ruler of Wei 衛 to the east of the former Shang territory, and Caishu, the ruler of Yong 鄘 to the west, the three supervisors include another younger brother: Huoshu 霍叔, the ruler of Bei 邶 to the north. See the "Correct Meanings" (Zhengyi 正義) commentary to *Scribe's Records*; *Shiji* 3.126 (n. 1).

7   Feng was a settlement founded by the Zhou people as they migrated eastward from Mount Qi; it is slightly to the south of present-day Xi'an; *Shiji* 4.118; According to Ma Rong, Feng was also where the ancestral temple of King Wen was located; *Shiji* 33.1519 n. 1. King Cheng was governing from Chengzhou, a new city the Zhou had established farther east in the proximity of present-day Luoyang. See 5.12.

8   I.e., close to Feng. On Bi as the location of the royal household (*wangjia* 王家), see F. Li, 2008, 152 and n, 3. Sima Qian locates Bi to the southeast of Hao 鎬; *Shiji* 4. 170. An abbreviated version of this passage is found in *Scribe's Records*; *Shiji* 33.1522.

9   According to *Shiji* 4.127 and 33.1515, Lu (present-day Qufu, Shandong) is the place where the Duke of Zhou received his fief, but he had never resided there. According to *Shiji* 33.1523, to reward the virtue of the Duke of Zhou, King Cheng granted to Lu the unique privilege of making suburban sacrifices to King Wen.

5.6
Charge to Prince Wei

Prince Wei is a scion of the former Shang ruling house. When Lufu's rebellion had been put down, the Zhou rulers decided to relocate the Shang people to an area farther away from the Zhou's eastern capital of Chengzhou, to a domain later known as Song 宋. *Prince Wei was installed as leader of the Song domain, thus having to manage the conquered Shang people. That Prince Wei was chosen to lead Song presumably has to do with the fact that he had, after the conquest, shown great submissiveness to the Zhou's King Wu.*[1]

According to Scribe's Records, *"Charge to Prince Wei" is the document issued by the Duke of Zhou on the occasion of the Prince of Wei's enfeoffment in Song.*[2] *There is a New Script* Documents *chapter titled "Prince Wei" (Weizi* 微子*) that focuses on a discussion the prince had with advisors before the conquest. Among the Old Script chapters of the transmitted* Documents, *there is a "Charge to Prince Wei" that seemingly reconstructs the document mentioned in the account of* Scribe's Records.

The Great Commentary *chapter consists of only one passage. It shows Prince Wei on his way to visit the court; while passing the ruins of the old Shang capital, he gave voice to his sorrow in a song (5.6.1). Interestingly,* Scribe's Records *ascribes this same story not to Prince Wei but to Prince Ji, discussed in the "Great Plan" chapter.*[3]

---

1 *Shiji* 38.1610–21.
2 *Shiji* 4.132, 38.1621.
3 *Shiji* 38.1620–21; a speech to Liu An 劉安 (ca. 179–122 BCE), the king of Huainan 淮南, by one of his subjects that is also recorded in *Scribe's Records* ascribes the song to Prince Wei; *Shiji* 118.3087.

The Great Commentary *(in Wang Kaiyun's edition) has no "Prince Wei" but has a "Charge to Prince Wei." In Pi Xirui's edition, the reverse is true, and the chapter (following the order of the* Documents' *New Script chapters) is placed earlier in the text, between "The Prince of the West Attacks Qi" and "Great Oath."*

5.6
微子之命

5.6.1 微子將往朝周,過殷[1]之故墟,見麥秀之蘄蘄兮,禾黍之暊暊也,曰:「此父母之國,宗廟、社稷之所立也。」志動心悲,欲哭則為朝周,俯泣則近婦人,推而廣之,作雅聲,歌曰:「麥秀蘄蘄兮,禾黍暊暊;彼狡童兮,不我好兮。」[2]

---

1 Cf. *Shangshu zhuzi suoyin* 36/32/5 (微子之命).
2 蘄蘄 = 漸漸, 暊暊 = 油油: *SSDZSZ* 3.27a (737); *Shiji* 38.1621.

5.6
Charge to Prince Wei

Prince Wei was on his way to pay a court visit to Zhou. When he passed the old ruins of Yin, he saw how ripe the grain was and how lush the millet.[1] He said: "This was the land of my parents; this is where our ancestral temples and the altars of soil and grain once stood." Deeply moved and saddened, he wanted to wail because he was on his way to pay a court visit to Zhou; he wanted to lower his head and cry, but that would make him look like a woman. Instead, transforming and broadening these feelings, he composed an elegant tune.[2] The song went like this: "The grain is ripe, the millet is lush; that crafty child, he did not fancy me."[3]

5.6.1

---

1   This indicates how the former capital had been turned into farmers' fields.
2   In other words, the prince is transforming his feelings of sadness into art.
3   The crafty child refers to Zhòu, the last king of Shang, who had scorned the advice of Prince Wei and others. "Mad Boy" (Jiao tong 狡童) is also the title of one of the *Odes*, Mao no. 86; *Maoshi zhuzi suoyin* 86/39/3–9.

5.7
Praising the Millet

In the absence of a corresponding chapter in the transmitted Documents *titled "Praising the Millet," we turn to* Scribe's Records' *account of how a text called "Praising the Millet" came into being. According to* Scribe's Records, *King Cheng had offered the Duke of Zhou an auspicious growth of millet (brought to him by Ji Yu* 姬虞, *or Tangshu* 唐叔, *a younger brother of King Cheng) and accompanied his gift with a text titled "Offering the Millet." The Duke of Zhou responded by authoring "Praising the Millet."*[1] Bamboo Annals *too contains the story of the auspicious millet—albeit without mentioning the composition of an occasion piece—but situates it later in time, in the eleventh year of King Cheng, after the Duke of Zhou handed power back to King Cheng.*[2]

Wang Yinglin observed how the preface of his copy of the Great Commentary *listed a chapter titled "Praising the Millet" but that the chapter itself was missing from his edition.*[3]

In the edition of the Great Commentary *presented here, two stories are entered under the chapter heading "Praising the Millet." One is the story of the ominous growth of millet in a version that differs significantly from that of* Scribe's Records *(5.7.1). In the second story, a delegation from Yuechang in the south came bearing a white pheasant in tribute as another sign of order restored (5.7.2).*

---

1   *Shiji* 33.1518–19.
2   *Zhushu jinian zhuzi suoyin* 1.55.11/24/16.
3   *Kunxue jiwen* 1:143.

An entry in the "Annals" of Emperor Ping 平帝 (r. 1 BCE–6 CE) for 1 CE records a court visit from Yuechang,⁴ at which occasion one white and one black pheasant were offered in tribute; Wang Mang used the visit to bolster his own image as a latter-day Duke of Zhou.⁵

---

4   *Hanshu* 12.348.
5   Cheung 2006. For more on this, see case 3, "Emulating the Former Sages," in the introduction to this book.

5.7
嘉禾

5.7.1 成王之時,有三苗貫桑葉而生,同為一穗,其大盈車,長幾充箱。民得而上諸成王,王召周公而問之,公曰:「三苗為一穗,抑天下共和為一乎!」果有越常[1]氏重譯而來。

5.7.2 交阯之南有越裳國。周公居攝六年,制禮作樂,天下和平。越裳以三象、重九譯而獻白雉。曰:「道路悠遠,山川岨深,恐使之不通,故重九譯而朝。」成**王**以**歸周公**[2]。公曰:「德澤不加焉,則君子不饗其質[3];政令不施焉,則君子不臣其人。吾何以獲此賜也?」其使請曰:「吾受命吾國之黃耇,曰:『久矣,天之無別風淮雨,意者中國有聖人乎?有則

---

1 越常 = 越裳: *SSDZSZ* 5.7a (763).
2 Cf. *Shangshu zhuzi suiyin* 36/32/13 (嘉禾).
3 質 = 贄: Zheng Xuan's commentary, *SSDZSZ* 5.7b (763).

5.7
Praising the Millet

In King Cheng's time, three sprouts of grain grew so tall that they spanned the canopy of a mulberry; they joined to form one ear that was so large that it filled a cart and was almost the length of its compartment. A commoner obtained the grain and presented it to King Cheng, who summoned the Duke of Zhou and solicited his opinion. The duke said: "Three sprouts growing into one ear: this must be a sign that the realm is peaceful and united!"[1] It so happened that a group from the Yuechang came with multiple translators.

5.7.1

South of Jiaozhi is the territory of the Yuechang. The Duke of Zhou had been regent for six years,[2] had arranged the rites and composed music, and the realm was in a state of harmony and peace. The Yuechang came with three southern and nine northern translators, and offered a white pheasant.[3] They explained: "The journey is long and far, with steep mountains and deep valleys. Since we were afraid that our envoys would not be able to understand one another, we came with multiple translators to pay respect." King Cheng gave the pheasant to the Duke of Zhou. The duke said: "A noble person cannot enjoy the gifts from a place where his virtue and influence do not reach; he cannot subjugate the people of a territory where his policies and ordinances are not implemented. How

5.7.2

---

1 In *Scribe's Records* it is Tangshu, King Cheng's younger brother, who obtained the millet and was asked by the king to present it to the Duke of Zhou; *Shiji* 4.132 and 32.1518–19.
2 *Bamboo Annals* mentions the arrival at court of a group from the Yuechang for the tenth year of King Cheng, four years after the year mentioned in the *Great Commentary*. *Zhushu jinian zhuzi suoyin* 1.55.10/24/14.
3 On the basis of a passage in the "Royal Regulations" chapter in *Records of Ritual*, we take *xiang* 象 to be a southern term for "translator" and *yi* 譯 to be a northern term for the same concept. See *Liji zhuzi suoyin* 5.40/35/4–5.

盍往朝之?』」周公乃歸之于王,稱先王之神,致以薦于宗廟。周既衰,于是稍絕。

can I accept this gift?" Their envoy pleaded and said: "I received an order from my country's elders, and it says, 'For a long time there have been no windstorms or torrential rains. This must mean that there is a sage in the central domains.[4] Given that that is the case, we should go there and pay a court visit.'" The Duke of Zhou then returned the pheasant to the king. He called up the spirits of the former kings and made King Cheng present it as a sacrificial offering at the ancestral temple. After the waning of the Zhou, such visits petered out.[5]

---

[4] The "central domains" is a collective name for various Zhou allied polities, especially those situated around the lower reaches of the Yellow River.

[5] Part of this account is also in *Hou Hanshu* 86.2835. It is significant that Li Xian 李賢 (d. 684), when he annotates that account, draws on the *Great Commentary* version rather than the versions in *Mr. Han's Outer Commentary on the Odes* or *Garden of Eloquence*. This demonstrates the authority the *Great Commentary* still commanded in the seventh century. For the stories of the millet and the pheasant, see *Hanshi waizhuan zhuzi suoyin* 5.12/37/5–10 and *Shuoyuan zhuzi suoyin* 18.15/155/10–16.

5.8
Proclamation to Kang

"Proclamation to Kang" is a New Script chapter in the transmitted Documents. It starts out with a short passage on the founding of the settlement at Luo by the Duke of Zhou, but, according to many, this passage belongs to "Proclamation on Luo."[1] *The bulk of the chapter consists of several sections of speech addressed by the royal voice to Feng* 封. *Feng, or Kangshu* 康叔, *a younger brother of the Duke of Zhou, was appointed to rule the Wei* 衛 *domain. Wei was the heartland of the people of Yin or Shang before they were moved to Song. This move to Song happened after the suppression of a large rebellion that included both the son of the last Shang ruler and several elder brothers of the Duke of Zhou (see "Great Proclamation"). Kangshu's appointment to Wei was thus meant to fill up the power vacuum in the former Shang heartland.*[2] *According to Scribe's Records, not only the* Documents' *"Proclamation to Kang" but also the "Proclamation on Drink" and "Catalpa Wood" were composed for this occasion and served as the Duke of Zhou's admonishments to Kangshu.*[3]

The "Proclamation to Kang" chapter of the Great Commentary *consists of two passages. The first comments on a sentence from the disputed first passage of the* Documents' *"Proclamation to Kang." It describes the careful sampling of the mood of various constituencies that preceded the Duke of Zhou's decision to build the city at Luo (5.8.1). The second passage deals with the first royal address to Feng in the* Documents' *"Proclamation to Kang," providing a running commentary on two of its sentences (5.8.2).*

---

1 The view that the first forty-eight characters of the *Documents*' "Proclamation to Kang" belonged to "Proclamation on Luo" arose in the Song dynasty. See Qu Wanli 1983, 145-46; Gu Jiegang and Liu Qiyu 2005, 3:1298–99.
2 *Shiji* 37.1589; *Zhushu jinian zhuzi suoyin* 1.55.3/23/28.
3 *Shiji* 4.132; 37.1590.

5.8
康誥

5.8.1 周公將作禮樂,優游之三年,不能作,「君子恥其言而不見從,恥其行而不見隨,將大作,恐天下莫我知也;將小作,恐不能揚父祖功業德澤。」然後營雒以觀天下之心,于是四方諸侯率其群黨,各攻位于其庭。周公曰:「示之以力役且猶至,況導之以禮樂乎!」然後敢作禮樂,《書》曰:「**作新邑于東國雒,四方民大和會。**」[1]此之謂也。

5.8.2 《書》曰:「**惟乃丕顯考文王,克明俊德。**」[2]周人以仁接民,而天下莫不仁。故曰大矣。天之命文王,非諄諄然有聲音也。文王在位而天下大服,施政而物皆聽,令則行,禁則止,動搖而不逆天之道。故曰「**天乃大**

---

1   Cf. *Shangshu zhuzi suoyin* 37/32/21 (康誥). *Shangshu zhuzi suoyin* has 作新大邑于東國洛 for 作新邑于東國雒.
2   Cf. *Shangshu zhuzi suoyin* 37/32/23 (康誥). *Shangshu zhuzi suoyin* has 克明德 for 克明俊德.

5.8
Proclamation to Kang

The Duke of Zhou was about to compose rites and music. For three years he wavered, unable to compose: "A noble person is ashamed of his words if they are not being obeyed, ashamed of his actions if they are not being followed. If I were to compose on a grand scale, I would be afraid that none in the realm would recognize me; if I were to compose on a small scale, I am afraid I would not be able to make known the meritorious works and penetrating virtue of my father and ancestors." After that he built Luo to observe the mood of the realm.[1] Thereupon, the regional lords came from the four quarters, each leading their parties, and worked on buildings at his court. The Duke of Zhou said: "We led the way with a project requiring forced labor, and still they all arrived; what if we were to guide them with rites and music!" After that he dared to compose rites and music. When the *Documents* says, "He established a new city in the eastern domains at Luo. The people of the four quarters converged there peacefully in great numbers," that is what it is about.

5.8.1

As is said in the *Documents*: "Our greatly illustrious father King Wen was able to make bright his eminent virtue." Since the men of Zhou used humaneness to receive people, no one in the realm acted without humaneness. That is why we call it "great."[2] It is not just a verbal formula to say that Heaven gave the mandate to King Wen. When King Wen occupied his position, the realm greatly submitted to him; when he governed, all things obeyed. His ordinances were carried out, and his prohibitions were effective. He shook things up without going against Heaven's Way. Therefore, the *Documents* says: "Heaven thereupon gave the great mandate

5.8.2

---

1   Luo is the same as Luoyi.
2   In the quotation from the *Documents* that follows, "Heaven thereupon gave the great mandate to King Wen" 天乃大命文王, King Wen's mandate is qualified as "great."

命文王」[3]。文王受命一年,斷虞芮之質,二年伐于[4],三年伐密須,四年伐畎夷,五年伐耆,六年伐崇,七年而崩。

---

3   Cf. *Shangshu zhuzi suoyin* 37/32/24-25 (康誥).
4   于 = 邘: *Shiji* 4.118.

to King Wen."³ In year one of King Wen's receipt of the mandate, he settled the dispute between Yu and Rui; in year two he attacked Yu; in year three, Mixu; in year four, the Quanyi; in year five, Qi; in year six, Chong; in year seven he passed away.⁴

3   The *Great Commentary* omits the rest of the quotation from the *Documents*, which reads "Heaven thereupon gave the great charge to King Wen to carry out the task of killing the warlike Yin (*yi rong Yin* 殪戎殷)." *Shangshu zhuzi suoyin* 37/32/25.
4   The Yu 于 attacked in year two is a different character from the Yu 虞 (and Rui) mentioned in the previous sentence (see also the introduction to "The Prince of the West Attacks Qi" [4.7]).

5.9
Proclamation on Drink

"Proclamation on Drink" is a New Script chapter of the transmitted Documents. In it, the royal voice of "Proclamation to Kang" continues its speech to Kangshu, but now the theme is the danger of the overconsumption of alcohol. It lays out how rampant alcoholism on the part of the king, his ministers, and the people contributed significantly to the downfall of the Shang house. Hence, this proclamation is not just a warning to Kangshu but also helps him manage alcohol overuse among former Shang officers under his charge.

"Proclamation on Drink" in the Great Commentary *contains five sections, the first three of which explicitly deal with the problem of how to manage alcohol consumption. The* Great Commentary *posits that, from a community perspective (that of the clan), alcohol is a great tool for social cohesion but warns that individuals should limit their consumption depending on their place in the hierarchy and their age (5.9.1–3). According to the last passage, the Son of Heaven can travel outside his domain as long as he makes a ritual announcement of his departure in the ancestral temple. Regional lords are prohibited from traveling outside the boundaries of their domains (5.9.5).*

5.9
酒誥

5.9.1 天子有事,諸侯皆侍;宗[1]室有事,族人皆侍。尊卑之義也。終日,大宗已侍于賓,奠,然後燕[2]私。燕私者何也?祭已而與族人飲也。

5.9.2 宗子燕族人于堂,宗婦燕族人于房,序之以昭穆[3]。不醉而出,是不親也;醉而不出,是漢宗也;出而不止,是不忠也。親而甚敬,忠而不倦。若是,則兄弟之道備。備者、成也,成者、成于宗室也。故曰「飲而醉[4]」者,宗室之意也;「德將無醉[5]」,族人之志也。是故祀[6]禮有讓,德施有復,義之至也。

---

1 Cf. *Shangshu zhuzi suoyin* 38/34/22 (酒誥).
2 Cf. *Shangshu zhuzi suoyin* 38/34/24 (酒誥).
3 Cf. *Shangshu zhuzi suoyin*, 38/34/10 (酒誥).
4 Cf. *Shangshu zhuzi suoyin* 38/34/16 (酒誥). *Shangshu zhuzi suoyin* has 飲食醉 for 飲而醉.
5 Cf. *Shangshu zhuzi suoyin* 38/34/13 (酒誥).
6 Cf. *Shangshu zhuzi suoyin* 38/34/11 (酒誥).

5.9
Proclamation on Drink

When the Son of Heaven has matters to consider, the regional lords are all in attendance; when the clan has matters to consider, the clansmen are all in attendance. This expresses the proper duties of noble and base. As the day comes to a close, a great clan, having finished attending to its guests, makes offerings and thereafter holds a private banquet. What is holding a private banquet? Drinking with one's clanfolk after the sacrifices have ended. 5.9.1

The clan master holds a banquet for the clansmen in the hall; the clan mistress holds a banquet for the clanswomen in the inner quarters. They rank them according to their place in the family.[1] Leaving without being drunk is to fail in intimacy; not leaving when one has drunk too much is embarrassing to the clan; not trying to retain those who are leaving is to fail in attentiveness. Be close and utterly respectful; be attentive and do not relent! Thus, the brotherly way is perfected. "Perfected" means that it is complete. "Complete" means that it is complete with regard to the clan. Therefore, "drinking to the point of drunkenness" refers to the intention of the clan, whereas "Be disciplined in virtue; do not get drunk" refers to the will of individual clan members.[2] Therefore, there is a component of yielding in sacrifices and rites, and the implementation of virtue becomes rewarded. This is highly appropriate! 5.9.2

---

1   They position them as they would in an ancestral sacrifice, alternating generations between the left (*zhao* 昭) and the right (*mu* 穆).
2   The text tries to reconcile two different statements from "Proclamation on Drink" by invoking the different perspectives of, on the one hand, the clan as an entity—here metaphorically referred to as the ancestral hall (*zongshi* 宗室)—and, on the other, individual clan members.

5.9.3 古者聖帝之治天下也，五十以下，非蒸社、不敢游飲，唯六十以上游飲也。

5.9.4 王曰：「封。唯曰[7]若圭璧。。。」

5.9.5 圻者、天子之境也。諸侯曰境。天子游不出封圻，不告祖廟。諸侯非朝聘不出境。

---

7   Cf. *Shangshu zhuzi suoyin* 38/34/19 (酒誥). *Shangshu zhuzi suoyin* has 我聞惟曰 for 唯曰.

In antiquity, when sages and supreme lords ruled the realm, those fifty or under would not dare to drink at leisure; unless at the occasion of the winter sacrifice, only those above sixty dared to do so.   5.9.3

The king said: "Feng.³ It is said that just like a *gui* tablet or a *bi* disk...."⁴   5.9.4

The term *qi* refers to the domain of the Son of Heaven. The domain of a regional lord is called *jing*. If the Son of Heaven travels without leaving the boundaries of his domain, he does not announce it in the ancestral temple. The regional lords, unless they are on an assigned court visit, do not leave their domains.⁵   5.9.5

---

3   Feng is the personal name of Kangshu, the addressee of the royal speech in the *Documents* chapter.
4   Commentators regard this either as a quotation from a lost part of the *Documents* or as a variant on a phrase from the received "Proclamation on Drink," even though the latter phrase does not mention the ritual attributes. *SSDZJJ* 2.22b–23a (4139–40).
5   This passage picks up a prominent theme of the *Great Commentary*'s "Canon of Yao," that of the management of the relations between the ruler and the regional lords. *Master of Huainan* echoes this dictate that regional lords should stay put in their own domains; *Huainanzi zhuzi suoyin* 11/95/13–15 and Vankeerberghen 2014, 338–39.

5.10
Catalpa Wood

"Catalpa Wood" is a New Script chapter in the transmitted Documents. *It too is a royal address to Kangshu, that, at the end, includes Kangshu's reply. The address is about prudent management of the people: a good lord ought to go light on punishments and to take care of "widowers and widows" and of "pregnant women." The title comes from a comparison, offered in the text, between rulership and the processing of catalpa wood (a gentle ruling style is compared to the coloring of catalpa wood after it has been shaped and carved).*

The "Catalpa Wood" chapter in the Great Commentary *consists of two passages. The first stays connected with the concern for the disadvantaged of society voiced in the corresponding* Documents *chapter and emphasizes the duty of the sage and the noble person to attend to their needs (6.10.1).*[1] *The second passage is a childhood story about Kangshu and Boqin, the son of the Duke of Zhou in whose proximity Kangshu appears to have been raised. In the story, the two children visit a sage in order to learn how to approach the Duke of Zhou without inciting his ire. The* Great Commentary *appears to be the earliest source carrying this story. (6.10.2).*

---

1   This is in Wang Kaiyun's version. Chen Shouqi and Pi Xirui list the fragment at the end with other fragments they cannot place; *SSDZJJ* 3.12a and *SSDZSZ* 7.27a (793).

5.10
梓材

5.10.1 老而無妻謂之矜,[1]老而無夫謂之寡,[2]幼而無父謂之孤,老而無子謂之獨。行而無資謂之乏,居而無食謂之困。此皆天下之至悲,哀而無告者。故聖人在上,君子在位,能者任職,必先施此,使無失職。

5.10.2 伯禽與康叔見周公,三見而三笞。康叔有駭色,謂伯禽曰:「有商子者、賢人也,與子見之。」乃見商子而問焉。商子曰:「南山之陽有木焉,名曰喬。二三子往觀之。」見橋[3]實高高然而上,反以告商子。商子曰:「喬者、父道也。南山之陰有木焉,名曰杍[4]。二三子復往觀焉。」見杍實晉晉然而俯,反以告商子。商子曰:「杍者、子道也。二三子明日復見周公。」

1　矜＝敬＝鰥. Cfr. *Shangshu zhuzi suoyin* 39/35/16 (梓材); SSDZSZ 7.27a (793).
2　Cf. *Shangshu zhuzi suoyin* 39/35/16 (梓材). *Shangshu zhuzi suoyin* has 敬寡 for 矜 and 寡 from text.
3　喬＝橋: *Shangshu dazhuan shuzheng* 5.12b (766).
4　杍＝梓: Cfr. *Shangshu zhuzi suoyin* 39/35/11 (梓材).

5.10
Catalpa Wood

A "widower" is a man of advanced age who is without a wife. A "widow" is a woman of advanced age who is without a husband. An "orphan" is young in age but fatherless. A "childless person" is of advanced age but without offspring. An "indigent person" is transient but without resources; a "person in distress" has a place to live but lacks food. These are the saddest of all conditions in the world as they leave people in a desperate state with no one to call upon. Therefore, if a sage is in charge, if noble men occupy positions of importance, and if competent persons assume their duties, their first priority should be to aid these groups. Let them not fail in this duty!

5.10.1

Boqin and Kangshu went to see the Duke of Zhou.[1] Three times they went to see him, and three times they were caned. Kangshu looked frightened and said to Boqin: "There is a worthy named Master Shang; let us go together to pay him a visit." They went to see Master Shang and asked him about the situation. Master Shang replied: "There is a tree named 'Upturning' on the sunny side of the Southern Mountain; go and observe it." They saw that the fruits of "Upturning" hung high and reached upward, and returned to tell Master Shang. Master Shang said, "'Upturning' exemplifies the way of the father. On the Southern Mountain's shady side, there is a tree named 'Catalpa'; go and observe that one too." They saw that the fruits of "Catalpa" hung down and pointed toward the ground, and returned to tell Master Shang. Master Shang said: "'Catalpa' exemplifies the way of the son.[2] Tomorrow you should go and

5.10.2

---

1   Boqin received an important fief in Lu 魯; his father, the Duke of Zhou, had been enfeoffed there in absentia; *Shiji* 33.1518.
2   Both characters were produced the same way in the Han. *Shuowen jiezi zhu* 6A.3a.

入門而趨,登堂而跪。周公迎拂其首而勞之,曰:「爾安見君子乎?」二子以實對,公曰:「君子哉、商子也。」

visit the Duke of Zhou again." Upon entering the gate, they hastened forward; upon ascending the hall, they knelt. The Duke of Zhou received them with a pat on their heads to put them at ease. He said: "Can it be that you went to see a noble person?" The two children replied truthfully, and the Duke Zhou said: "A noble person indeed, this Master Shang."

5.11
Proclamation of/to Shao

"Proclamation of/to Shao" is a New Script chapter of the transmitted Documents. It first describes the founding of the new settlement at Luo, also known as Chengzhou. It also contains speeches delivered on the occasion. It is unclear whether the Duke of Zhou or the Duke of Shao, Ji Shi 姬奭, who also carried the title of grand protector (dabao 大保), delivered these speeches. Both men were heavyweights in the early Western Zhou political setting.[1]

The "Proclamation of/to Shao" in the Great Commentary consists of two fragments. The first fragment is the same as the introduction of the "Minor Xu" to the "Proclamation of/to Shao" (5.11.1).[2] The second fragment is taken from the opening sentences of the Documents' "Proclamation of/to Shao."[3]

---

1 Shaughnessy 1993a interprets these speeches as a weighty politico-philosophical debate between the Duke of Zhou and the Duke of Shao.
2 The "Minor Xu" accompanies the transmitted Documents in fifty-eight chapters; its contents are split and placed at the opening of the relevant Documents chapter.
3 For a parallel account, see Shiji 33.1519.

5.11
召誥

5.11.1　成王在豐,欲宅雒邑,使召公先相宅。[1]

5.11.2　六日乙未,王朝步自周,則至于豐,惟大保先周公相宅。[2]

---

[1] Cf. *Shangshu zhuzi suoyin* 40/36/3 (小序 to 召誥). *Shangshu zhuzi suoyin* has 洛邑 for 雒邑.
[2] Cf. *Shangshu zhuzi suoyin* 40/36/5 (召誥). *Shangshu zhuzi suoyin* has 太保 for 大保.

5.11
Proclamation of/to Shao

King Cheng was in Feng, intending to construct the settlement at Luo. He sent the Duke of Shao to first inspect the site.[1] 5.11.1

"On the sixth day, *yiwei*, the king proceeded in the morning from Zhou and subsequently arrived in Feng. The Duke of Shao, the Grand Protector, preceded the Duke of Zhou in inspecting the site." 5.11.2

---

1   The king had to make the short trip from his administrative capital at Hao 鎬 to Feng, where King Wen's ancestral temple was located, to announce his decision to establish a settlement at Luo (Luoyi 雒邑) to his ancestors. See the commentary by Ma Rong and Zheng Xuan cited in Sima Zhen's commentary to *Scribe's Records*; *Shiji* 33.1519 n. 1.

5.12
Proclamation on Luo

"Proclamation on Luo" is a New Script chapter of the transmitted Documents. In it the Duke of Zhou and King Cheng alternate addresses pertaining to the establishment of a secondary capital for the Zhou in Luo.[1] Through mutual praise, the two powerful men negotiate the particulars of how to divide power as they seek to uphold the mandate and the legacy that they inherited from King Wen and King Wu.

"Proclamation on Luo" in the Great Commentary consists of seven passages. The first uses a short sentence from the Documents, a gloss, and a long quote from the Commentary embedded in the Great Commentary to establish that, even with his long list of impressive achievements, the Duke of Zhou still remained conscious of his subservient position toward King Cheng and inspired the regional lords to follow his example (5.12.1). Next comes a very lively passage about the ancestral sacrifice perhaps in Luo in honor of King Wen and King Wu officiated by the Duke of Zhou and attended by all the regional lords (5.12.2).[2] The third passage highlights the importance of "Proclamation on Luo" among the chapters of the Documents that deal with Zhou, first, by designating the chapter as a point of culmination and then by quoting a remark of Confucius on "Proclamation on Luo." In the quotations the text provides to substantiate its claims, King Wen and King Wu still have a central place (5.12.3). The seven-year chronology of the Duke of Zhou's regency organizes the events of that period

---

[1] See also 5.11.
[2] The emphasis on King Wen and King Wu here might have to do with a sacrificial change as compared to the Yin sacrifices mentioned in "Proclamation on Luo" or, as Pi Xirui thinks, with a shift in emphasis from Hou Ji and King Wen to King Wen and King Wu as the main Zhou ancestors. *Shangshu zhuzi suoyin* 41/37/12; SSDZSZ 5.16b–5.17a (768).

year by year. It is remarkably similar to the chronology provided in Bamboo Annals (5.12.5).[3] *The three remaining passages are related to the Duke of Zhou and his son Boqin's fief in Lu. That these passages are placed in this chapter might have to do with one interpretation of a phrase in the* Documents: *ming gong hou* 命公後, *interpreted as "give the charge to the heir [Boqin] of the Duke [of Zhou]."*[4] *As in 5.10.2, the Duke of Zhou appears as a stern father (5.12.4, 5.12.6, and 5.12.7).*

---

3   *Zhushu jinian zhuzi suoyin* 23/1.54.1–24/1.55.7. *Bamboo Annals* was buried in a tomb in 299 BCE to be rediscovered in 281 BCE, but it appears that texts like it were circulating during the Han. Chavannes 1967, 5:446–79.
4   The alternative interpretation of the phrase *ming gong hou* is that the Duke of Zhou was ordered to stay behind to assist King Cheng and so did not go to his fief in Lu. Ma Nan 2012b, 360.

5.12
雒誥

5.12.1 《書》曰:「**乃女其悉自學功**。[1]」學、效也。《傳》曰:「當其效功也,於卜[2]雒邑,營成周,改正朔,立宗廟,序**祭**[3]祀,易義[4]牲,制禮作樂,一統天下,合和四海而致諸侯,皆莫不依紳端冕以奉祭祀者。其下莫不自悉以奉其上者,莫不自悉以奉其祭祀者。」此之謂也。盡其天下諸侯之志,而效天下諸侯之功也。

5.12.2 廟者、皃也,以其皃言之也。宮室中度,衣服中制,犧牲中**胖**[5],**殺**[6]者中死,割者中理。搗弁[7]者為文,爨竈者有容,椓杙者有數。大廟之中,繽乎其猶模繡也。

---

1 女 = 汝. Cf. *Shangshu zhuzi suoyin* 41/37/14 (洛誥). *Shangshu zhuzi suoyin* has 教 for 學.
2 Cf. *Shangshu zhuzi suoyin* 41/37/9 (洛誥).
3 Cf. *Shangshu zhuzi suoyin*, 41/38/4 (洛誥).
4 義 = 犧.
5 Cf. *Shangshu zhuzi suoyin* 41/37/27 (洛誥).
6 Cf. *Shangshu zhuzi suoyin* 41/38/5 (洛誥).
7 搗弁 = 拚帚: Zheng Xuan's commentary, *SSDZSZ* 5.15b (767).

5.12
Proclamation on Luo

The *Documents* says, "You must thoroughly exert yourself and learn how to be meritorious." "To learn" is to strive. The *Commentary* says, "When he strove to achieve his own merit, whether it was divining about the settlement at Luo, constructing Chengzhou, reforming the calendar, establishing an ancestral temple, arranging the sacrifices, changing the sacrificial animals, instituting rites and composing music, unifying the realm, bringing harmony to the area within the four seas, or making the regional lords arrive, he never failed to wear his girdle and adjust his cap in such a manner as to pay his respect to the one making sacrifices. Those below him did what they could to honor the one above him and did what they could to honor the one in charge of the sacrifices." That is what it is about. This is how he fulfilled the aspirations of the regional lords of the realm and made them strive to achieve merit. 5.12.1

"Ancestral temple" (*miao*, *mĭau) is demeanor (*mao*, *meau).[1] Thus one can talk about the ancestral temple from the point of view of demeanor. The palace halls were built according to the proper measurements; the clothing conformed with the regulations; the sacrificial animals were selected according to the norms; the killing was executed properly; the cutting was done according to the principles.[2] Those who cleaned formed patterns; those who cooked adopted proper postures; those who installed the sacrificial poles did so in the right numbers. Thus, within the great temple, how splendid everything is, like an exquisite piece of embroidery! 5.12.2

---

1   Note the similarity in pronunciation. Reconstruction by Li Zhenhua and Zhou Changji 1999, 287, 289.
2   Procedures for preparing the sacrificial animals are laid out in detail in the chapter "The Food Offer Ritual with One Sacrificial Animal" (Tesheng kuishi li 特牲饋食禮) in *Yili zhuzi suoyin* 15/92/7–15/97/26.

天下諸侯之悉來，進受**命**[8]于周而退見**文武**[9]之尸者，千七百七十三諸侯，皆莫不磬折玉音金聲玉色。然後周公與升歌而弦文武。諸侯在廟中者，伋然淵其志，和其情，愀然若復見文武之身。然後曰：「嗟！子乎！此蓋吾先君文武之風也夫！」及執俎抗鼎，執刀執匕者負廧而歌，憤于其情，吾先君文武之風也夫，故周人追祖**文王**而宗**武王**[10]也。

5.12.3 是故《周書》自《大誓》，就《召誥》而盛于《雒誥》。故其書曰：「**揚文武**之德**烈**，**奉對天命**，**和恆**萬邦**四方民**。」[11]是以見之也。

孔子曰：「吾于《雒誥》也，見周公之**德**。」「**光明于上下**，**勤施四方**，**旁作穆穆**。」[12]「**至于海表**，莫敢**不來服**，莫敢不來享，**以勤文王之鮮光**，**以揚武王之大訓**[13]，而天下大洽。」故曰聖之與聖也，猶規之相周、矩之相襲也。

8　Cf. *Shangshu zhuzi suoyin* 41/37/8 (洛誥).
9　Cf. *Shangshu zhuzi suoyin* 41/37/20-22 (洛誥).
10　Cf. *Shangshu zhuzi suoyin* 41/38/3 (洛誥).
11　Cf. *Shangshu zhuzi suoyin* 41/37/20-21 (洛誥). *Shangshu zhuzi suoyin* has 答 for 對.
12　Cf. *Shangshu zhuzi suoyin* 41/37/21-22 (洛誥). *Shangshu zhuzi suoyin* has 明光 for 光明, 勤施于四方 for 勤施四方. 6.1.1 also has 明光于上下，勤施于四方，旁作穆穆.
13　Cf. *Shangshu zhuzi suoyin* 47/44/14-15 (立政). *Shangshu zhuzi suoyin* has 罔有不服。以觀文王之耿光，以揚武王之大烈 for 莫敢不來服，莫敢不來享，以勤文王之鮮光，以揚武王之大訓 from text. *Han shijing jicun* 24a has 王之鮮光，以揚武王 for 以勤文王之鮮光，以揚武王之大訓 from text.

Traditions on Zhou

The regional lords of the realm all came. They stepped forward and received the charge of Zhou; they retreated to see the impersonators of King Wen and King Wu. Altogether there were 1,773 regional lords: they all bent like chime stones, emitted sounds like jades and bronzes, and were serene like jade. Subsequently, the Duke of Zhou joined them in ascending the hall in order to chant and play the strings to the glory of King Wen and King Wu. As for the regional lords who were present in the temple, instantaneously they were moved so that their aspirations deepened and their senses harmonized; astoundingly, it was as if King Wen and King Wu appeared before their eyes. The Duke of Zhou then said, "Ah! You all! This atmosphere is exactly as it was in the time of our ancestors Kings Wen and King Wu!" Even those who carried trays and cauldrons, and those holding knives and daggers stood against the wall and joined the chanting. It sprang forward from their feelings, developed internally, and then found musical expression in restrained patterns. In this manner, the men of Zhou retraced the steps of their founding ancestor, King Wen, and their succeeding ancestor, King Wu.[3]

For this reason, *Documents of Zhou* moves from "Great Oath," to "Proclamation of/to Shao," and culminates in "Proclamation on Luo." That is why the text of "Proclamation on Luo" says, "I will raise up the glorious virtue of King Wen and King Wu, uphold and respond to Heaven's charge, and bring together in harmony all the people from the myriad states and the four quarters."[4] Herewith it becomes apparent.

5.12.3

Confucius said: "In the 'Proclamation on Luo' I see the virtue of the Duke of Zhou." "Brilliantly, it shines high and low, diligently spreading its luster to the four quarters. Everywhere you are an august presence."[5] "May you reach the seas at the ends of the earth so that no one dares not to submit and no one dares not to come to make offerings, so you endeavor to achieve King Wen's bright virtue and promote King Wu's great admonitions. Thus the realm will be in a state of great harmony."[6] Therefore, it is said that two sages together are just like tracing a circle with a compass or a line with a ruler.

---

3   This relatively long fragment from the *Great Commentary* is quoted in a commentary to the *Ceremonials*, *Yili jingzhuan tongjie xu* 29.75b–76a (vol. 132, pp. 816–17). Marc Csikszentmihalyi discusses and translates part of this passage as he links the five musical tones with the five virtues. Contrary to his assumption, we believe that the passage may well have been taken from the *Great Commentary* rather than being a fabrication by Song scholars. Csikszentmihalyi 2004, 220–22 n. 37.
4   In the "Proclamation on Luo" of the *Documents*, this sentence is King Cheng's response to a speech by the Duke of Zhou.
5   In the "Proclamation on Luo" of the *Documents*, this sentence is King Cheng's praise of the virtue of the Duke of Zhou.
6   This sentence largely corresponds to one in "Establishment of the Government Officers" (Lizheng 立政) of the *Documents*, in which King Cheng is urged to become a great ruler.

5.12.4 伯禽封于魯。周公曰:「於乎!吾與女族倫,吾文王之為子,武王之為弟也,成王之為叔父也,吾於天下豈卑賤也?豈乏士也?所執質而見者十,委質而相見者三十。其來執質之士百,我欲盡智得情者千人,而吾僅得三人焉,以正吾身,以定天下。是以敬其見者,則隱者出矣。謹諸,乃以魯而驕人,可哉?尸祿之士,猶可驕也;正身之士,去貴而為賤,去富而為貧,面目黧黑而不失其所是,以文不滅而章不敗也。慎諸,乃以魯國而驕,豈可哉?」

5.12.5 周公攝政,一年救亂,二年克殷,三年踐奄,四年建**侯衛**[14],五年營成周,六年制禮作樂,七年致政。

14　Cf. *Shangshu zhuzi suoyin* 31/26/7 (武成).

After Boqin received a fief in Lu,[7] the Duke of Zhou spoke as follows: "Beware! You and I belong to the same clan. I am the son of King Wen, the younger brother of King Wu, uncle of King Cheng. I occupy a position in the realm that can hardly be called humble. I hardly have shortage of men willing to serve me. Ten men are allowed to come with their gifts and have an immediate audience; another thirty can get an audience but only after they have left their gifts for review. Of every one hundred men that come bearing gifts, of every thousand whose brains and hearts I would like to use, I can only employ three. It is in this manner that I cultivate myself and settle the realm. Thus, if one shows respect to those that one receives in audience, hermits will come out of hiding. Be careful about this! Do not become overly proud just because you have been assigned to Lu. Leave the pride to the salaried. When a properly cultivated man abandons high rank and wealth for a life of low rank and poverty, his face will darken,[8] but he will not abandon what he considers right. That is because culture and refinement do not dwindle. Carefully heed this! Do not become overly proud just because you have been assigned to Lu."[9]

5.12.4

The Duke of Zhou became regent. In the first year, he came to the rescue when rebellions broke out; in the second year, he subdued Yin;[10] in the third year, he overran Yan;[11] in the fourth year, he established lords and guards;[12] in the fifth year, he constructed Chengzhou;[13] in the sixth year, he instituted the rites and composed music; and in the seventh year he turned over his powers.

5.12.5

---

7   According to one version of events, after King Wu conquered the Shang, the Duke of Zhou was enfeoffed in Lu; the Duke of Zhou stayed in the capital to assist King Wu and later King Cheng; his son Boqin inherited the fief of Lu and ruled for forty-six years; see *Shiji* 4.127, 33.1518; *Hanshu* 21C.1016–17.
8   This is because he has to engage in manual labor.
9   This passage about Boqin also occurs in *Scribe's Records* and the "Yao Asked" (Yao wen 堯問) chapter of *Master Xun*, with significant variants. See *Shiji* 33.1518; *Xunzi zhuzi suoyin* 32/149/7–14; SSDZSZ 5.19a–b (769). A Tang commentator to *Master Xun*, Yang Liang 楊倞 (8th–9th c.), used Zheng Xuan's commentary on the *Great Commentary* to explain the *Master Xun* parallel.
10 This is the rebellion involving the son of the last Shang ruler as well as several brothers of the Duke of Zhou, discussed in "Great Proclamation."
11 Such an event is mentioned in *Scribe's Records*; *Shiji* 4.133. See also *Zhushu jinian zhuzi suoyin* 1.55.3. Several other *Great Commentary* chapters are related to the handling by the Zhou rulers of the crisis at Yan: "King Cheng's Government" (5.15), "Proclamation at Yan" (5.16), and "Many Regions" (5.17).
12 This refers to the men who were to rule and protect the colonies in the east that were being established at this time. According to Li Feng, *hou* 侯 were regional rulers located in the east, and *wei* 衛 were appointed in the polities located in the west. F. Li 2008, 44-47.
13 *Bamboo Annals* also situates the construction of Chengzhou during the fifth year of King Cheng's reign; see *Zhushu jinian zhuzi suoyin* 1.55.5/24/1–2.

5.12.6　周公封以魯,身未嘗居魯也。

5.12.7　伯禽將歸于魯,周公謂伯禽之傅曰:「汝將行,盍志而子美德乎?」對曰:「其為人寬、好自用、以慎。此三者,其美德也已。」周公曰:「嗚乎!以人惡為美德乎?君子好以道德,故其民歸道,彼其寬也,出無辨矣!是其好自用也,是以斂益之也。」

The Duke of Zhou received a fief in Lu; he never resided there personally.[14] 5.12.6

Boqin was about to return to Lu. The Duke of Zhou asked Boqin's tutor: "You are about to depart. What do you envision to be my son's virtuous points?" He answered: "As a person, he is lenient, he likes to draw on his own resources, and he is scrupulous. These three in themselves constitute virtuous points." The Duke of Zhou said: "Oh dear! How can you regard as virtuous what other people despise? A noble man likes to use morality and virtue; hence his people return to the right path. My son, instead, is 'lenient,' but it comes from his inability to distinguish![15] That he likes to draw on his own resources will only lead to his collecting all their surpluses." 5.12.7

---

14   The "Proclamation on Luo" chapter in the *Documents* mentions how the Duke of Zhou, under orders of King Cheng, had to stay in Luo to take care of matters of government. The present chapter earlier mentioned how the son of the Duke of Zhou too was enfeoffed at Lu.

15   This passage and 5.12.4 are found together in a more complete form in *Master Xun*. What *haoziyong* 好自用 (draw on his own resources) means is clear in *Master Xun*. It means someone who relies on himself but fails to acknowledge and use the strength of others. *Xunzi zhuzi suoyin* 32/149/1–7; Hutton 2014, 340–41.

5.13
Many Officers

In the New Script Documents *chapter "Many Officers," the Duke of Zhou addresses the men who formerly served the Shang dynasty and were after the conquest resettled in the Luo area by the Zhou. He urged them to give up all resistance and give the Zhou their full cooperation.*

The corresponding chapter in the Great Commentary *consists of just one fragment: it deals with an apparently unrelated matter: the rituals surrounding sexual encounters between the ruler and his queen. Whereas "Many Officers" in the* Documents *attributes the fall of Xia and Shang to their leaders' indulgence (yinyi 淫泆), 5.13.1 in contrast shows the proper way of handling desire.*[1]

Pi Xirui's edition lists more fragments with this chapter title.

---

1 *Shangshu zhuzi suoyin* 42/38/15–16; *SSDZSZ* 5.18a (825).

5.13
多士

5.13.1 古者后夫人將侍于君,前息燭,後舉燭。至于房中,釋朝服,襲燕服,然後入御于君。雞鳴,太師奏雞鳴于階下,夫人鳴佩玉于房中,告去也。然後應門擊柝,告辟也。然後少師奏質明于階下,然後夫人入庭立,君出朝。

5.13
Many Officers

In antiquity, when the royal wife attended to the ruler, she extinguished the lantern before and lit it again afterward. When she arrived in the bedchamber, she removed her court robes to put on her casual clothes. Then she initiated sexual relations with him. At cock's crow, the grand master announced that the cock had crowed beneath the stairs. The wife then sounded her jade pendants in the bedchamber and announced her departure.[1] At the main gate of the palace, the clapper was struck to announce that the gate was now open. Then the lesser master announced beneath the stairs that the day had now fully arrived. Then the royal wife entered the courtyard and stood there, while the lord left to hold court.

5.13.1

---

1 *Arrayed Traditions on Women* (Lienü zhuan 列女傳) ascribes this series of activities to Lady Jiang 姜, the wife of King Xuan 宣 of Zhou (r. 827/25–782 BCE). She entered the quarters of her husband with a lit lantern to then extinguish it to have intercourse. *Gu Lienü zhuan zhuzi suoyin* 2.1/12/28–30; Kinney 2014, 2.1/25–26.

5.14
Do Not Slack

In "Do Not Slack" in the Documents, *a New Script chapter, the Duke of Zhou has just returned the government to King Cheng and admonishes the latter to carry out his duties as king diligently.*

The corresponding chapter in the Great Commentary *consists only of a quotation from the* Documents *that is not in the received version of "Do Not Slack" or, for that matter, in the* Documents *as a whole. The sentence was first cited in* Comprehensive Discussions in White Tiger Hall *(Baihu tong* 白虎通*) as "a lost fragment" (yipian* 逸篇*) of the* Documents;[1] *it was first attributed to the* Great Commentary *in Lu Jianzeng's edition, an opinion that Wang Kaiyun endorsed.*[2] *However, as Chen Shouqi pointed out, this attribution was a mistake. The mistake was probably caused by readers confusing yi* 逸 *for "lost" and the yi* 佚*, "slack," of the chapter title.*[3]

Neither Chen Shouqi nor Pi Xirui incorporated this passage; instead, they incorporated contents from 4.4.

---

1   *Baihu tong zhuzi suoyin* 1/1/7.
2   Lu Jianzeng, *Shangshu dazhuan* 2.13b; *SSDZBZ* 5.18a.
3   Chen Shouqi, *Shangshu dazhuan,* 5.19a.

5.14
毋佚

5.14.1　《書》曰：「厥兆天子爵。」

5.14
Do Not Slack

As the *Documents* says, "Per the portent he received, 'Son of Heaven' is the title of a rank." 5.14.1

5.15
King Cheng's Government

There is no chapter titled "King Cheng's Government" in the transmitted Documents.

The Great Commentary's one fragment deals with the Duke of Zhou's invasion of Yan and the postconquest violence inflicted on it.[1] The events at Yan, as clarified in 5.12.5, took place while the Duke of Zhou was still regent.

Even though it is a gloss, the passage seems to justify the violence inflicted on Yan. The vexing problem of how to deal with conquered people is also treated in the Great Commentary's "Success through Battle" (5.2), which instead urges restraint from violence. Wang Kaiyun also remarks on the harshness of this passage, which contradicts his expectations of the contents of a Documents-affiliated text.[2]

Wang Kaiyun indicates that he found the fragment in Kong Yingda's commentary to the Odes, where it is said to belong to a "commentary" to the Documents (shuzhuan 書傳).[3] It is possible that Wang Kaiyun placed the fragment under "King Cheng's Government" because the "Minor Xu" to the Documents states how "King Cheng's Government" was composed after the events at Yan. The reconstitution of the Great Commentary made by Pi Xirui has no such chapter.

---

1   On the Duke of Zhou's invasion of Yan, see also 5.5.1 and 5.12.5.
2   SSDZBZ 5.18a–b.
3   Maoshi zhushu 15.300b. Chen Shouqi and Pi Xirui list the fragment with "Metal Coffer," which also mentions the invasion of Yan (5.5.1).

5.15
成王政

5.15.1 遂踐奄。踐之者，籍之也。籍之，謂殺其身，執其家，豬[1]其宮。

---

1 豬=赭.

5.15
King Cheng's Government

Thereupon he overran Yan.[1] To "overrun" something is to crush it. To "crush" something means to kill the person, imprison his family, and destroy his palaces.[2]   5.15.1

---

[1] That is, the Duke of Zhou.
[2] According to *Scribe's Records* and *Bamboo Annals*, Yan was not "overrun" in this manner, as its ruler, rather than being killed, was moved elsewhere. See *Shiji* 4.133 and *Zhushu jinian zhuzi suoyin* 1.55.5.

5.16
揹誥

5.16
Proclamation at Yan

There is no "Proclamation at Yan" chapter in the transmitted version of the Documents. The existence of a Great Commentary chapter titled "Proclamation at Yan" is known from Wang Yinglin. He remarked how the "Xu" to the Great Commentary, which must have contained a table of contents, lists a chapter by that title even though the copy available to him did not have the chapter itself.[1] Wang Kaiyun preserves the title but does not file a single fragment under it.

According to Kong Guanglin, who made an early reconstitution of the Great Commentary, Yan 揜 is a variant of Yan 奄.[2]

---

1   *Kunxue jiwen* :143.
2   Kong Guanglin, *Shangshu dazhuan*, 32.5a.

5.17
Many Regions

"Many Regions" *is one of the New Script chapters in the transmitted* Documents. *It is another call to regions formerly ruled by Shang to submit to the new regime. According to* Scribe's Records, *the New Script chapter was composed and delivered in Zongzhou* 宗周, *the original capital of Zhou in the West, after King Cheng returned from the campaign against Yan.*[1]

The one fragment that is listed under "Many Regions" in the Great Commentary *proposes to read a line from the* Documents *as being about appropriate levels of taxation.*[2]

---

1 *Shiji* 4.133.
2 A theme also broached in 1.1.1.

5.17
多方

5.17.1　古者十稅一，多于十稅一，謂之大桀、小桀。少于十稅一，謂之大貊[1]、小貊。王者十一而稅而頌聲作矣，故《書》曰：「**越維有胥賦小大多政。**」[2]

1　貊 = 貃: *SSDZSZ* 6.11b (775); 貊 = 貉: *Gongyang zhushu*, Xuangong 16, 208a.
2　維 = 惟. Cf. *Shangshu zhuzi suoyin* 46/43/3 (多方). *Shangshu zhuzi suoyin* has 越惟有胥伯小大多正 for 越維有胥賦小大多政.

5.17
Many Regions

In antiquity, the tax rate was one-tenth. If the rate was higher than one-tenth, it was called a great or a small evil à la Jie. If it was lower than one-tenth, it was called a small or great barbarism à la Mo.¹ A true king taxes at the rate of one-tenth, and hymns resound! As the *Documents* says, "As to your corvée and taxes, whether big or small, they contribute to your government."

5.17.1

---

1   The comparison here is with Jie, the last ruler of the Xia, and the Mo, a non-Zhou group from the north. When taxes are lower than one-tenth, the essential institutions of the state, including sacrifices, cannot be supported. A similar passage occurs in the Gongyang commentary: *Gongyangzhuan zhuzi zuoyin* 7.15.8/83/11; *Chunqiu Gongyang zhushu* 208a. Mencius also had a similar idea that one-tenth should be the appropriate tax rate. *Mengzi zhengyi* 5.91a.

5.18
Testamentary Charge
5.19
King Kang's Proclamation

In the New Script edition, the two chapters "Testamentary Charge" and "King Kang's Proclamation" appear as one under the former title. In the transmitted edition, they are separated out.[1] The chapter(s) deal with the transition of power from King Cheng to his oldest son, Ji Zhao 姬釗, *the future King Kang* 康 *(r. 1005/3–978 BCE).[2] More narrative than speech, the document tells how King Cheng, on his deathbed, provided instructions on the transition of power and how Ji Zhao, after his father's death, received the written charge. The "Testamentary Charge" provides a very detailed description of the spatial arrangement of both people and objects during the ceremony that accompanied Ji Zhao's reception of the charge.*

The two chapter titles "Testamentary Charge" and "King Kang's Proclamation" appear only in Wang Kaiyun's edition of the Great Commentary. *In other editions, 5.18.1 is included with the "Many Officers." Some editions, such as Lu Jianzeng's, also include 5.19.1 under "Many Officers," whereas other editions, such as Pi Xirui's, do not have it at all.[3]*

"Testamentary Charge" in the Great Commentary *consists of a passage containing sumptuary rules regarding buildings, specifying dimensions and the appearance of beams, walls, and pillars. Presumably Wang Kaiyun*

---

1   Liu Qiyu 1989, 68.
2   *Shiji* 4.134.
3   *Yili jingzhuan tongjie* 33.2a–b (vol. 131, p. 544) attributes this passage to the *Great Commentary*.

placed this passage here because he thought it connected with the description of the court ceremony provided in the Documents' *"Testamentary Charge" (5.18.1). The fragment collected in the* Great Commentary's *"King Kang's Proclamation" continues the theme of sumptuary rules with regard to architecture (5.19.1). There is a clear connection between 5.19.1 and the "King Kang's Proclamation" of* Documents: *they both contain the term yingmen* 應門 *(reception gate), and the term does not appear in other chapters of the* Documents *or the* Great Commentary.

5.18
顧命

5.19
康王之誥

5.18.1　天子之堂廣九雉，三分其廣，以二為內，五分內，以一為高。東房、西房、北堂各三雉。
　　　　公侯七雉，三分其廣，以二為內，五分內，以一為高。東房、西房、北堂各二雉。
　　　　伯子男五雉，三分其廣，以二為內，五分內，以一為高。東房、西房、北堂各一雉。

5.18
Testamentary Charge

5.19
King Kang's Proclamation

The hall of the Son of Heaven is nine *zhi* wide, and its depth equals two-thirds of the width.[1] The height equals one-fifth of the depth.[2] The eastern chamber, the western chamber, and the northern hall are each three *zhi*.

    The hall of a lord is seven *zhi* wide,[3] and its depth equals two-thirds of the width. The height equals one-fifth of the depth.[4] The eastern chamber, the western chamber, and the northern hall are each two *zhi*.

    The hall of a prince is five *zhi* wide,[5] and its depth equals two-thirds of the width. The height equals one-fifth of the depth.[6] The eastern chamber, the western chamber, and the northern hall are each one *zhi*.

5.18.1

---

1   We follow Pi Xirui in interpreting *nei* 內 as depth; see *SSDZSZ* 6.4a–b (772).
2   According to Zheng Xuan's commentary, one *zhi* equals three *zhang* 丈 in length; see *SSDZSZ* 6.2b (771). Since a *zhang*, in Han times, was the equivalent of about 2.3 meters, the complex here would have a width of about 62 meters, a depth of about 41 meters, and a height of about 8 meters.
3   *Gong* 公 and *hou* 侯 (lords) are the first two steps of the five-rank noble system: *gong* 公, *hou* 侯, *bo* 伯, *zi* 子, and *nan* 男. Even though there would have been a differentiation in rank, we translate both *gong* and *hou* as "lord."
4   The dimensions of a lord's building complex would be at a width of 48 meters, depth of 32 meters, height of 6.4 meters.
5   *Bo* (earls), *zi*, (princes), and *nan* (princes) are the last three steps of the five-rank noble system. Even though there would have been a differentiation in rank, we here translate *bo*, *zi*, and *nan* together as "princes"; see 2.2.1, where only *zi* and *nan* are combined.
6   The dimensions of a prince's building complex would be at a width of 35 meters, depth of 23 meters, height of 4.6 meters.

士三雉，三分其廣，以二為內，五分內，以一為高。有室無房堂。
　　其梲：天子斲其材而礱之，加密石焉。大夫達棱。士首本。庶人到加[1]。天子賁庸。諸侯疏杼。大夫有石材。庶人有石承。

5.19.1　諸侯之宮，三門三朝，其外曰皋門，次曰**應門**[2]，又次曰路門。其皋門內曰外朝，應門內曰內朝，路門內曰路寢之朝。

1　到加 = 倒茄: *SSDZSZ* 6.3b–4a (771–72).
2　Cf. *Shangshu zhuzi suoyin* 51/47/26 (康王之誥).

The hall of a man of service is three *zhi* wide, and its depth equals two-thirds of the width. The height equals one-fifth of the depth.[7] They have rooms but no chambers or halls.

As to their beams:[8] the Son of Heaven has the trunks cut and then burnished by applying the polishing stone; for ministers, the round trunks are made into square columns; for men of service, the top and bottom of the trunk are removed; common people suspend lotus from the ceiling.[9] For the Son of Heaven, an enormous wall; for regional lords, walls that are less even; for ministers, pillars resting on stone slabs; for common people, pillars that rest directly on the stone foundation.[10]

The palaces of the regional lords have three gates and three court areas. The outer gate is called "tall" gate; the next one, "reception" gate; the one thereafter, "passage" gate. Behind the tall gate, there is what is called the "outer court area"; behind the reception gate, "the inner court area"; behind the passage gate, the "court area of the main hall."

5.19.1

---

7   The dimensions of a lower noble's building complex would be at a width of 21 meters, depth of 14 meters, height of 2.8 meters.
8   We draw on the commentary of Zheng Xuan and Pi Xirui for our explanations of the sumptuary rules that follow; *SSDZSZ* 6.2b–3a (771).
9   Given the lotus's association with water, hanging lotus from the ceiling was thought to prevent fires.
10 According to Zheng Xuan, with commoners, there is no exposed base in stone that can be decorated.

5.20
Charge to Jiong 冏命

"Charge to Jiong" is one of the Old Script chapters in the transmitted Documents. According to Scribe's Records, Ji Man 姬滿, or King Mu of Zhou (r. 956–918 BCE), charged an otherwise unknown man named Jiong 冏/囧 (or Bo Jiong 伯冏) with revitalizing government affairs;[1] he then composed "Charge to Jiong" for the occasion.

In the Great Commentary, "Charge to Jiong" is just a title, with no fragments filed under it. That the title is nonetheless listed in all authoritative reconstructions is because Wang Yinglin reported that his copy of the Great Commentary contained a chapter by that name.[2] Wang Yinglin's testimony constitutes important evidence that the Great Commentary was concerned with more than just the so-called New Script chapters of the Documents.[3]

---

1   Shiji 4.134–35.
2   Han Yiwenzhi kaozheng 1.20b.
3   See the section "Master Fu, the Great Commentary, and the New Script/Old Script Controversy" of the introduction to this volume.

5.21
Oath at Xian

"Oath at Bi 費" *is a New Script chapter of the* Documents *in which the Duke of Lu—identified as Boqin, the son of the Duke of Zhou—addresses his troops and his people before battle. He urges them to fight with all available resources and threatens punishments if some dodge his command. The battle itself would have taken place early in King Cheng's reign, when various groups in the modern Shandong area rebelled against the Zhou regime.*[1]

"*Oath at Xian" in the* Great Commentary *is the corresponding chapter to "Oath at Bi" of the* Documents. *It consists of four fragments: one an idealized description of the concentric outlay of domains of various ranks (5.21.1); the second an account, parallel to that in* Scribe's Records, *of the circumstances that led to the battle and to the composition of the text (5.21.2);*[2] *and finally two fragments that are quotations from the* Documents *chapter itself (5.21.3–4).*

In 5.21.2, the place of the battle is called Xian 鮮, *whereas* Scribe's Records *designates that place as Bi* 肸.[3] *The characters* bi 肸/費 *and* xian 鮮 *are not obvious variants of one another.*[4] *The Tang commentator of* Scribe's Records, *Sima Zhen, seeking to reconcile the* Great Commentary's

---

1 *Scribe's Records* relates the circumstances of the battle and quotes some excerpts from the document; see *Shiji* 33.1524.
2 The passage is discussed in the section "An Arrangement Document" of the introduction to this volume.
3 Wang Yinglin reports that in his copy of the *Great Commentary* the title of the chapter is "Oath at Bi 肸." *Han Yiwenzhi kaozheng* 1.20b.
4 For other variants of the characters *bi* and *xian* in the context of this *Documents* chapter, see Matsumoto 1966, 584; Gu Jiegang and Liu Qiyu 2005, 4:2137.

account with that of Scribe's Records, *suggests that* xian *is not a place name but means "autumn hunt."*[5]

Pi Xirui's edition lists only one fragment under this chapter heading, a fragment that does not form part of Wang Kaiyun's "Oath at Xian."[6]

---

5   *Shiji* 33.1525 n. 2.
6   SSDZSZ 6.12b–13a (776).

5.21
鮮誓

5.21.1 古者百里之國：三十里之**遂**，二十里之**郊**，九里之城，三里之宮。
七十里之國：二十里之**遂**，九里之**郊**，三里之城，一里之宮。
五十里之國：九里之**遂**，三里之**郊**[1]，一里之城，以城為宮。
遂郊之門，執禁以譏異服，譏異言。

5.21.2 周初，**淮浦**、**徐州竝**[2]起為寇。伯禽伐之于[3]鮮[4]，作《鮮誓》。

5.21.3 敿**乃**攼，敜乃阱。[5]

5.21.4 **女**則有逸罰。[6]

---

1 Cf. *Shangshu zhuzi suoyin* 57/52/16–17 (費誓).
2 竝 = 並. Cf. *Shangshu zhuzi suoyin* 57/52/12 (費誓").
3 于 = 於.
4 鮮 = 獮/肸 = 柴 = 費: Shuowen jiezi zhu 7A.60 a–b.
5 Cf. *Shangshu zhuzi suoyin* 57/52/13–14 (費誓). *Shangshu zhuzi suoyin* has 杜 for 敿, 穽 for 阱 from text.
6 女 = 汝. Cf. *Shangshu zhuzi suoyin* 57/52/14 (費誓). *Shangshu zhuzi suoyin* has 常刑 for 逸罰.

5.21
Oath at Xian

In antiquity, in domains of 100 *li*, the outlying area stretched over thirty *li*, the suburbs over twenty *li*, the walled settlement over nine *li*, and the palace area over three *li*.[1]

In domains of 70 *li*, the outlying area stretched over twenty *li*, the suburbs over nine *li*, the walled settlement over three *li*, and the palace area over one *li*.

In domains of 50 *li*, the outlying area stretched over nine *li*, the suburbs over three *li*, and the walled settlement over one *li*. In that case, the walled settlement also served as the palace area.

At the gates of the outlying areas and the suburbs, prohibitions are enforced in order to censor unconventional clothing and deviant speech.

Early in the Zhou, in both Huaipu and Xuzhou, riots occurred. Boqin attacked them at Xian and composed "Oath at Xian."

"Block your traps, cover your pits."

"You shall receive stiff fines."

---

1 Those areas ideally were concentric circles stretching from the palace area outward.

5.22
Punishments of Fu

"*Punishments of Lü* 呂" *is a New Script chapter in the transmitted* Documents. *In Han times this chapter was also known as "Punishments of Fu." It consists of an address of King Mu of Zhou (r. 956–918 BCE) on penal law delivered to the Lord of Fu or Lü.*[1] *Even though both Fu and Lü are used in the title of the* Documents *chapter in pre-Qin texts, by Han times Fu dominated, as seen in both* Scribe's Records *and the Xiping stone inscriptions.*[2]

"*Punishments of Fu" in the* Great Commentary *also deals entirely with laws and punishments. It starts out with a list that links crimes to the Five Punishments in the* Documents *chapter. This can be construed as an attempt to show that the* Documents *too can serve as a basis for the legal organization of the state, as a possible alternative to the laws of Qin that were used in actual legal practice in early imperial times (5.22.1). Several other passages invoke the authority of Confucius. While affirming the importance of the Five Punishments (5.22.2), he also stresses*

---

1   The nature of the relationship between the Lord of Fu (Lü) and King Mu is spelled out differently in different texts. In the *Documents* chapter itself, the occasion is an unspecified charge to Lü (perhaps his appointment?). In *Scribe's Records*, the Lord of Fu reports to the king on the untoward behavior of other regional lords, which leads to the drawing up of a penal code (*xingfa* 刑法) and to the king's speech; *Shiji* 4.139. According to *Bamboo Annals*, the Lord of Fu (Fuhou 甫侯) was given an assignment in the area of the Western capital region (modern Shaanxi) in the fifty-first year of King Mu; the king's speech would have been given at this occasion. *Zhushu jinian zhuzi suoyin* 1.58.19/27/29. Zheng Xuan, quoting a text titled *Documents Explained* (Shushuo 書說), posits that the Lord of Fu became King Mu's chancellor (*xiang* 相); *Shiji* 4.138 n. 1.
2   For an overview of how various texts use either Lü or Fu, see Gu Jiegang and Liu Qiyu 2005, 4:1902–6. For the Xiping stone inscriptions, see Chen Mengjia 2005, 89; Xu Jingyuan 2007, 62; Ma Nan 2013, 9. For *Scribe's Records*, see *Shiji* 4.138–39.

the importance of applying the laws in a manner that is lenient, humane, and fair (5.22.3, 5, 7–8); he also asserts the precedence of ritual over law (5.22.9). Other passages that do not mention Confucius also stress the importance of lenience (5.22.4) or point out the dire consequences of corrupt legal practices (5.22.6).

5.22
甫刑

5.22.1 決關梁、踰城郭而略盜者,其刑臏。男女不以義交者,其**刑宮**[1]。觸易君命、革輿服制度、**姦宄**[2]盜攘傷人者,其刑劓[3]。非所事而事之、出入不以道義而誦不詳[4]之辭者,**其刑墨**[5]。降畔**寇賊**、劫略**攻攘矯虔**[6]者,其刑死。

5.22.2 子張曰:「堯舜之主,一人不刑而天下治,何則?教誠而愛深也。一夫而被此**五刑**,子龍子曰:『未可謂能為書。』」孔子曰:「不然也。**五刑**有此**教**。」[7]

---

1 Cf. *Shangshu zhuzi suoyin*, 55/51/8 (呂刑).
2 Cf. *Shangshu zhuzi suoyin*, 55/50/10 (呂刑).
3 Cf. *Shangshu zhuzi suoyin*, 55/50/11 (呂刑).
4 詳=祥.
5 Cf. *Shangshu zhuzi suoyin*, 13/15/14 (伊訓).
6 Cf. *Shangshu zhuzi suoyin*, 55/50/10 (呂刑). *Shangshu zhuzi suoyin* has 奪 for 攻.
7 Cf. *Shangshu zhuzi suoyin*, 2/3/2 (舜典).

5.22
Punishments of Fu

Those who trespass passes or bridges, transgress the city walls, or seize and steal: their punishment is to have their legs cut off at the knee. 5.22.1

Those men and women who have improper sexual relations: their punishment is castration.

Those who offend against or alter their lord's decrees, who fail to abide by the regulations concerning carriages or clothing, who engage in seditious acts, thievery, and robbery, or who injure others: their punishment is to have their nose cut off.

Those who serve those they should not serve, who enter and leave without authorization, or who utter inauspicious words: their punishment is tattooing.

Those who surrender to rebels and bandits, who plunder, rob, and embezzle: their punishment is death.

Zizhang said: "Why is it that under Yao and Shun's rule, not a single person was punished, and yet the realm was well ordered? It is because their teachings were sincere, and their concern ran deep. That a single person can be subjected to the Five Punishments prompted Zilongzi to say, 'The Five Punishments are not worthy of inclusion in the *Documents*!'" Confucius disagreed, saying: "Not so, the Five Punishments are an intrinsic part of the teaching."[1] 5.22.2

---

[1] A parallel passage in *The Kong Family Masters* (Kong congzi 孔叢子) gives a very different twist to this passage: there it is a discussion not about the appropriateness of including the Five Punishments in a canonical document but about Zilongzi's lack of mastery of the text; *Kong congzi zhuzi suoyin* 1.2/3/16–18.

5.22.3 子曰：「古之聽民者：察貧窮，哀孤獨矜寡，宥老幼不肖無告。有過必赦，小罪勿增，大罪勿纍。老弱不受刑，有過不受罪。是故老而受刑謂之悖，弱而受刑謂之剋，不赦有過謂逆，率過以小謂之枳。故與其殺不辜，寧失有罪；與其增以有罪，寧失過以有赦。」

5.22.4 君子之于人也，有其語也，無不聽者，皇于聽獄[8]乎？必盡其辭矣。聽獄者、或從其情，或從其辭。

5.22.5 聽獄之術，大略有三：治必寬；寬之術，歸於察；察之術，歸於義。是故聽而不寬，是亂也。寬而不察，是慢也。古之聽訟者，言不越情，情不越義。是故聽民之術，怒必思，思兼義，小罪勿兼。

---

8 Cf. *Shangshu zhuzi suoyin* 55/51/14 (呂刑).

The master said: "In antiquity, cases among the people were settled as follows: they took poverty into account; they were compassionate toward orphans, childless persons, widowers, and widows; they pardoned the old and the young, the unworthy, and those who had no recourse to justice. When there was a transgression, an amnesty was sure to follow. Small crimes were not combined.² Large crimes did not implicate others.³ The old and weak did not receive punishments, and those who transgressed were not considered criminals. For this reason, to subject the elderly to punishment is called 'contrary to the norms,' to subject the weak to punishment is called 'being harsh,' not to provide amnesty for transgressors is called 'going against the nature of things,' to carelessly treat mistakes as small criminal matters is called 'causing harm.' It is better to let go of criminals than to kill the innocent, and it is better to let go of transgressions and pardon than to combine them to constitute a crime."

5.22.3

Here is how the noble person treats others: when someone else speaks, he will listen to whatever he says. So why would this not be true when he hears a lawsuit? Surely, he will allow the parties to make full statements! In deciding a lawsuit, one sometimes goes by the circumstances and sometimes follows the statements.

5.22.4

Generally speaking, there are three arts for hearing a lawsuit: in deciding a case, one ought to be lenient; the art of being lenient lies in a skillful investigation; the art of skillful investigation lies in coming to the appropriate judgment. For this reason, to fail to be lenient when hearing a lawsuit brings disorder, and lenience not supported by a skillful investigation is negligence. In antiquity, those who presided over lawsuits made sure that words did not overtake circumstances, and circumstances did not overtake the appropriate judgment. Hence, as to the art of hearing people's lawsuits, holding people to account requires careful consideration; careful consideration has to be combined with an appropriate judgment, except in the case of small crimes.⁴

5.22.5

---

2   "Small crimes were not combined" (*xiao zui wu zeng* 小罪勿增) matches *xiaozui wujian* 小罪勿兼 in 5.22.3.

3   Following Zheng Xuan's gloss of *lei* 纍 as "to extend the crime to the innocent" (*yanzui wugu* 延罪無辜); see *SSDZSZ* 6.18a (779).

4   Following Wang Kaiyun's explanation, in the case of small crimes, it is fine only to carefully consider the statement of the transgressor without pronouncing judgment; see *SSDZBZ* 6.18b (779).

孔子曰：「古之刑者省之，今之刑者緐[9]之。」其教，古者有禮然後有刑，是以刑省也；今也反是，無禮而齊之以刑，是以緐也。《書》曰：『**伯夷降禮，折民以刑。**』[10]謂有禮然後有刑也。又曰：『**茲殷罰有倫**』[11]，今也反是，諸侯不同聽，每君異法，聽無有倫，是故法之難也。」

5.22.6 **獄貨非可寶**也，[12]然寶之者，未能行其法者也。貪人之寶，受人之財，未有不受命以矯其上者也。親下以矯其上者，未有能成其功者也。

5.22.7 子曰：「聽訟雖得其指，必哀矜之。死者不可復生，絕者不可復續也。《書》曰：『**哀矜哲獄。**』[13]」

5.22.8 子曰：「今之聽民者，求所以殺之；古之聽民者，求所以生之。不得其所以生之之道，乃刑殺。君與臣會焉。」

9　緐 = 繁.
10　Cf. *Shangshu zhuzi suoyin* 55/50/15 (呂刑). *Shangshu zhuzi suoyin* has 伯夷降典，折民惟刑 for 伯夷降禮，折民以刑.
11　Cf. *Shangshu zhuzi suoyin* 37/33/11 (康誥); *Shangshu zhuzi suoyin* 55/51/10 (呂刑).
12　Cf. *Shangshu zhuzi suoyin* 55/51/14 (呂刑). *Shangshu zhuzi suoyin* has 獄貨非寶 for 獄貨非可寶.
13　Cf. *Shangshu zhuzi suoyin* 55/51/11 (呂刑). *Shangshu zhuzi suoyin* has 哀敬折獄 for 哀矜哲獄.

Confucius said: "In ancient times, punishments were administered sparingly; nowadays, punishments proliferate." According to his teaching, in ancient times, rites preceded punishments, so punishments were few. Nowadays it is just the opposite: having abandoned the rites, punishments are used to govern the people, so they proliferate. As the *Documents* says, "Bo Yi sent down the rites; for regulating the people, he used punishments."[5] Also compare *Kong congzi zhuzi suoyin* 2.1/8/13–16. That means that rites preceded punishments. It also says "those penalties of Yin that embody norms." Nowadays it is just the opposite: regional lords do not hear lawsuits in a uniform fashion; every lord uses his own model, and their hearing of lawsuits fails to embody norms. No wonder that it is difficult to apply the laws!

"Ill-gotten gains from lawsuits cannot be taken as treasures." Hence, those men who treasure such ill-gotten gains failed to enact the law. Those who are covetous of the treasure of others and accept their goods will have to subject themselves to their orders so as to deceive their superiors. Those who connive with those below them so as to deceive their superiors will not be able to gain any merit. — 5.22.6

The master said: "When hearing a lawsuit, even when one has found the culprit, one should treat him mercifully. The dead cannot be brought to life, and what has been amputated cannot be reattached.[6] As the *Documents* says, 'One decides legal cases with mercy.'"[7] — 5.22.7

The master said: "Nowadays, those who hear people's lawsuits search for a pretext to kill them. In antiquity, they sought ways to preserve their lives. Only if all attempts to preserve their lives had failed would they administer the death penalty. In that case, lords and ministers met to deliberate." — 5.22.8

---

5   The corresponding sentence in the *Documents*' "Punishments of Lü" talks about rules (*dian* 典) being sent down, not rituals. See also the section "Explaining Lines of the *Documents*" of the introduction to this volume.

6   Our interpretation is based on a similar sentence in "Treatise on Penal Law" in *Book of Han*, "[the body parts that have been removed] as punishment cannot be reattached" 刑者不可復屬. See *Hanshu* 23.1098; *SSDZSZ* 19a (779). Alternatively, this sentence can also mean "[the lineage] that has been terminated cannot be continued."

7   *Kong Family Masters* explains this citation of the *Documents* with language reminiscent of 5.22.3 and 5.22.8; *Kong congzi zhuzi suoyin* 2.1/9–23.

5.22.9 子曰：「吳越之俗，男女同川而浴，其刑重而不勝，由無禮也。中國之教，內外有分，男女不同椸架、不同巾櫛，其刑不重而勝，由有禮也。語曰：『夏后不殺，不刑罰有罪，而民不輕犯。』」

5.22.10 禹[14]之君民也，罰弗及饌而天下治，一饌[15]六兩。

5.22.11 古者中刑用鑽鑿。

5.22.12 有虞氏上刑。

5.22.13 上刑挾輕，下刑挾重。[16]

5.22.14 天齊乎人，假我一日。[17]

---

14 Cf. *Shangshu zhuzi suoyin* 55/50/16 (呂刑).
15 Cf. *Shangshu zhuzi suoyin* 55/51/7 (呂刑). *Shangshu zhuzi suoyin* has 鍰 for 饌.
16 Cf. *Shangshu zhuzi suoyin* 55/51/9 (呂刑). *Shangshu zhuzi suoyin* has 上刑適輕，下服。下刑適重，上服 for 上刑挾輕，下刑挾重.
17 Cf. *Shangshu zhuzi suoyin* 55/50/23–24 (呂刑). *Shangshu zhuzi suoyin* has 天齊于民，俾我，一日非終 for 天齊乎人，假我一日.

The master said: "According to the customs of Wu and Yue, men and women can bathe together in the same stream. That their punishments, though heavy, are not effective is because they do not have the rites. According to the teachings of the central domains,[8] inner and outer should be separated, and men and women should not share a clothes stand or a towel rack. That their punishments, though not heavy, are effective is because they have the rites. As the proverb says, 'The Xia ruling house did not administer the death penalty and did not punish or fine those who had committed a crime. Nonetheless, the people did not commit offenses lightly.'" 5.22.9

When Yu ruled over the people, fines did not reach one *xuan*.[9] Nonetheless, there was order in the realm. One *xuan* equals six *liang*. 5.22.10

In antiquity, medium punishments used the drill and the chisel. 5.22.11

The harsh punishments of the House of Youyu.[10] 5.22.12

"Harsh punishments can be adjusted downward; light punishments can be adjusted upward." 5.22.13

"Heaven is in tune with its men. It gives us one single day."[11] 5.22.14

---

8   The "central domains" is a collective name for various Zhou-allied polities, especially those situated around the lower reaches of the Yellow River. The term was in use starting in the Eastern Zhou.
9   *Xuan* is the unit used in the *Documents*' "Punishments of Lü" to express the amount of the various redemptive fines.
10 I.e., Shun.
11 This sentence is also quoted in exactly the same way in "Biography of Yang Ci 楊賜" (d. 185) in *Hou Hanshu* 54.1776. We have translated this sentence according to Yang Ci's interpretation.

卷六
略說

6
Principal Teachings

6
Principal Teachings

"*Principal Teachings*" *has no equivalent in the transmitted* Documents. *Kong Yingda* 孔穎達 *(574–648), in his* Corrected Meaning of the Five Classics *(Wujing zhengyi* 五經正義*), repeatedly quotes a* Principal Teachings of the Commentary to the Documents *(Shuzhuan lüeshuo* 書傳略說*). Wang Yinglin, aware of these quotations, treats the* Shuzhuan lüeshuo *as an independent text, not as a part of the* Great Commentary.[1] *During the Qing, the compilers of the* Catalog of the Imperially Authorized Complete Library of the Four Branches *(Siku quanshu zongmu), however, took issue with Wang's point of view and put forward the claim that "Principal Teachings" is an integral part of the* Great Commentary.[2] *Almost all of the Qing editions of the* Great Commentary *put this idea in practice as they incorporate "Principal Teachings" (sometimes in one, sometimes in two juan) as part of their reconstitution of the* Great Commentary.

Wang Kaiyun, in his reconstitution of "Principal Teachings" divides the chapter in two parts. The first part, as he explains it, contains passages that "are clearly said to derive from the Principal Teachings but, in fact, explain individual sentences of the classic," whereas the second part consists of those excerpts that do not relate to any particular passages from the Documents *but are free-floating passages (fan shuo* 汎說*).*[3]

---

1 For the entry on *Shangshu dazhuan*, see *Yuhai* 37.24b–26b (708–9); for the entry on *Shuzhuan lüeshuo*, see *Yuhai* 37.28b–29a (710).
2 *Siku quanshu zongmu*, 164 (j. 12).
3 SSDZBZ 6.1.

6.1
略說上

6.1.1 古者帝王躬率有司百執事，而以正月朝迎日於東郊，以為萬物先而尊事天也。祀上帝於南郊，所以報天德。迎日之辭曰：「維某年月上日，**明光于上下，勤施于四方，旁作穆穆**，」[1]維予一人。某敬拜。」迎日東郊，《堯典》曰：「**寅賓出日**。」[2]此之謂也。

6.1.2 諸侯有德者，一命以車服弓矢，再命以虎賁三百人，三命秬鬯。諸侯三命者，皆受天子之樂，以祀其宗廟。

1　Cf. *Shangshu zhuzi suoyin* 41/37/21–22 (洛誥). See also 5.12.3.
2　Cf. *Shangshu zhuzi suoyin* 1/1/8 (堯典).

6.1
Principal Teachings, Part 1

In antiquity, the sovereign himself led the supervisors and managers to welcome the sun in the eastern suburbs at daybreak in the first month. Thus, giving a lead to the myriad things,[1] they respectfully served Heaven. By sacrificing to the Lord on High in the southern suburbs, they reciprocated Heaven's virtue. The lyrics accompanying the ceremony of receiving the sun are as follows: "This is the first day of year X, month Y. The sun brilliantly shines high and low, diligently spreading its luster to the four quarters. As an august presence, it bestows its benefits everywhere including on me, the One Man. Respectfully offered by Z." About the ceremony of receiving the sun in the eastern suburbs, "Canon of Yao" says, "Reverently, he greeted the rising sun."[2] This is what it is about. 6.1.1

Those regional lords with virtue, when they first receive their charge, are endowed with carts, clothes, bows, and arrows; the second time, they are endowed with three hundred warriors; the third time, with sacrificial wine. Regional lords who have been charged three times all receive the music of the Son of Heaven for use in sacrifices at their ancestral temples. 6.1.2

---

1   Through this ritual they initiated the season of growth before anything had sprung up.
2   For the ritual performed in autumn, see 1.1.3.

6.1.3　《傳》曰：己有三牲，必田狩者。孝子之意，以為己之所養，不如天地自然之性。逸豫肥美，禽獸多，則傷五穀。因事兵事，又不空設，故因以捕禽獸，所以共承宗廟，示不忘武備，又因以為田除害。

6.1.4　鮮者何也？秋取嘗也。秋取嘗，何以也？習鬥也者、男子之事。戰鬥不可不習，故於搜狩以閑之也。閑之者、貫之也，貫之者、習之也。凡祭、取所餘，獲陳於澤，然後卿大夫相與射。命中者，雖不中也取。命不中者，雖中者不取，何以也？所以貴揖讓之取，而賤勇力之取也。鄉之取也於囿中，勇力之取也；今之取也於澤宮，揖讓之取也。

6.1.5　天子諸侯必有公桑蠶室，就川而為之築（官）〔宮〕，有三雉。棘牆而外閉之。大昕之朝，三公之夫人浴種于川，世婦卒蠶，獻繭于夫人。繰三盆手。

The *Commentary* says, "One absolutely must obtain the three kinds of 6.1.3
sacrificial animal by hunting. In the mind of a filial son, animals raised
by oneself are not as good as those still imbued with nature's spontaneity.
Having roamed freely, the latter are fatty and tasty. Also, when there are
too many wild animals, they harm the five grains. Thus, it serves military affairs, and the hunting grounds are not set up in vain. Therefore,
on the one hand, capturing wild animals ensures that the ancestral
temple is provided for and demonstrates one's commitment to military
preparedness; on the other hand, it rids one's fields of harm."

What does "freshness" mean?[3] It means to catch them in autumn for 6.1.4
savoring. Why does one "catch them in autumn for savoring"? To practice for battle is the affair of men.[4] Thus, fighting has to be practiced, so,
by chasing and capturing, one becomes well versed in it. "To be well
versed" is to master. "To master" is to practice. Whenever there is a sacrifice, one takes the animals that remain and disperses them over the
marshlands. Then the grand ministers together go and shoot them. They
take the animals they are entitled to, even if they have failed to shoot
them, but they do not take animals they are not entitled to even if they
manage to shoot them. Why is this? In this way, one values the kind of
taking that is yielding and devalues the kind of taking that involves
bravery. To take, as used to be the case, the animals from the hunting
park is the kind of taking that involves bravery. Nowadays, one takes
the animals at the palace shooting range: this is the yielding kind of
taking.

The Son of Heaven and the regional lords must have mulberry plantations and a silkworm nursery. One should build a palace near the river for 6.1.5
this purpose, three *zhi* in size.[5] The walls of the palace should be spiked
with thorns and closed off from the outside. Early at dawn, the wives of
the three excellencies rinse the eggs in the river. Lower-ranked wives
nurse the worms to maturity and then present the cocoons to the wives of
the three excellencies. To unwind them, they rinse them thrice in a basin.

---

3   The character for freshness (*xian* 鮮) is the same character that is used in the title of "Oath at Xian." Based on this, Chen Shouqi and Pi Xirui surmise that this fragment in fact belongs there, not with "Principal Teachings"; *SSDZSZ* 6.12b–13a (776) and 7.12b (786).
4   As Wang Kaiyun also suggests, the answer to the question raised in the passage is missing, and the passage immediately settles into an explanation of what would have been the answer: "To practice for battle!" *SSDZBZ* 6.2a.
5   *Zhi* as a measurement refers to an area three *zhang* in length and one *zhang* in height. Since a *zhang*, in Han times, was the equivalent of about 2.3 meters, it means the silkworm nursery is about 6.9 meters wide and 2.3 meters high. *SSDZBZ* 6.2b (829).

6.1.6 烟氛郊社不修,山川不祝,風雨不時,霜雷不降,責於天公。臣多弒主,孽多殺宗,**五品不訓**[1],責於人公。城郭不繕,溝池不修,水泉不隆,水為民害,責於地公。

6.1.7 天子太子年十八曰**孟侯**[2]。孟侯者,于四方諸侯來朝,迎于郊者。問其所不知也,問之人民之所好惡,土地所生美珍怪異,山川之所有無。及父在時,皆知之。

6.1.8 大夫、士、七十而致仕,老於鄉里。大夫為父師,士為少師。櫌鉏已藏,祈樂已入,歲事已畢,餘子皆入學。十五始入小學,見小節,踐小義;十八入大學,見大節,踐大義。距冬至四十五日,始出學傅農事。上老平明坐于右塾,庶老坐于左塾。餘子畢出,然後皆歸,夕亦如之。餘子皆入,父之齒隨行,兄之齒鴈行,朋友不相踰。輕任并,重任分。頒白不提挈,

---

1   Cf. *Shangshu zhuzi suoyin* 2/3/10 (舜典). *Shangshu zhuzi suoyin* has 遜 for 訓.
2   Cf. *Shangshu zhuzi suoyin* 37/32/22 (康誥).

Smoke that does not rise up to make offer to Heaven and Earth,[6] failure to sacrifice to mountains and rivers, unseasonal wind and rain, and absence of frost and thunder are matters that lie within the sphere of responsibility of the Lord of Heaven. Frequent murders of lords by their ministers, or of clan heads by their heirs, as well as failure to observe the five ranks are matters that belong to the sphere of responsibility of the Lord of Humans. City walls that are not repaired, moats and ponds that are not maintained, water sources that are in short supply, and floods that harm the people are matters that belong to the sphere of responsibility of the Lord of the Earth.[7]

6.1.6

When the heir apparent to the Son of Heaven reaches the age of eighteen *sui*, he is called "preeminent lord" (*menghou*).[8] The preeminent lord was the one who met the regional lords in the suburbs when they came from the four quarters to pay homage at court. He inquired about things unbeknownst to him and asked about the likes and dislikes of the people, about treasures and extraordinary objects brought forth by the land, and about the resources of mountains and rivers. In this way, when his father was still alive, he already learned all these matters.

6.1.7

At seventy, ministers and men of service retire to spend their old age in their hometowns. Ministers then assume duty as senior masters, men of service as junior masters. After rakes and hoes have been stored, prayers and music have been offered, and the crops have been harvested, younger sons start their learning.[9] At age fifteen they enter the primary course of learning, where they are exposed to basic rules and practice simple duties. At age eighteen they enter the higher course of learning, where they are exposed to major rules and practice important duties. Forty-five days after the winter solstice, they leave their courses of learning to assist with farming. In this period, at daybreak, senior elders sit in the vestibule on the right and junior elders in the vestibule on the left. After all the younger sons have left, the elders return home as well. In the evening, it is the same. When the younger sons come in, they have to walk right behind men of their father's age and walk behind men of the same age as their elder brothers in goose formation. They cannot overtake their friends. Lighter burdens are combined and heavier burdens are divided.

6.1.8

---

6   I.e., for lack of sacrifices.
7   In 1.1.31 the minister of works is held responsible for water-related disasters.
8   Wang Yinglin believes the *Great Commentary* wrongly interprets the term "preeminent lord" 孟侯 and that, in "Proclamation to Kang" in the *Documents*, it actually refers to the leader of the regional lords. *Kunxue jiwen* 1:282.
9   According to Zheng Xuan, the eldest sons took over their fathers' positions, while the younger ones stayed in the village to engage in agricultural tasks; they were the ones to receive instruction from the senior and junior masters; *SSDZBZ* 6.3b.

出入皆如之。此之謂造士。

6.1.9 子夏曰:「昔者三王愨然欲錯刑遂罰,平心而應之,和,然後行之。然且曰:『吾意者以不平慮之乎?吾意者以不平平之乎?』如此者三,然後行之。此之謂**慎罰**。」³

6.1.10 祭之為言察也。察者、至也,至者、人事也。人事至,然後祭。祭者、薦也,薦之為言在也,在者、在其道也。

6.1.11 古之帝王者,必立大學、小學。使王太子、王子、群后之子、以至公卿大夫、元士之適子,十有三年,始入小學,見小節焉,踐小義焉;年二十,入大學,見大節焉,踐大義焉。故入小學,知父子之道、長幼之敘;入大學,知君臣之儀、上下之位。故為君則君,為臣則臣,為父則父,為子則子。小師取小學之賢者登之大學,大師取大學之賢者登之天子,天子以為左右。

---

3   慎 = 愼。Cf. *Shangshu zhuzi suoyin* 37/32/23 (康誥) and 46/42/21 (多方).

Gray-haired people should not carry things. This applies to the way there and to the way back. This is what training a man of service is about.¹⁰

6.1.9 Zixia says, "In the past, when the Three Kings wanted to tread carefully when administering punishments and fines, they calmed their hearts before responding to a case. If there was correspondence, then they would apply the punishment. Even then they asked themselves, 'Am I sure that I did not deliberate this case unfairly? Am I sure that I did not judge this case unfairly?' Only after having gone through this three times would they proceed. This is what exercising due caution with regard to punishments refers to."

6.1.10 The meaning of the word "to sacrifice" (*[ts]et-s) is to scrutinize (*[tsʰ]ˤret).¹¹ "To scrutinize" is to reach (*ti[t]-s). "To reach" applies to human affairs. After human affairs have been fully pursued, one sacrifices. "To sacrifice" is to offer (*Cə.tsˤə[r]-s). The meaning of the word "to offer" is to be present (*[dz]ˤəʔ).¹² "To be present" is to be in the same place as the Way.

6.1.11 In antiquity, the sovereigns established both a higher and a primary course of learning. It served the royal heir apparent, the princes, the sons of the other wives, down to the eldest sons of the excellencies, the ministers, and the chief men of service. At age thirteen, they entered the primary course of learning, where they were exposed to basic rules and practiced simple duties. At age twenty, they entered the higher course of learning, where they were exposed to major rules and practiced important duties. Therefore, after entering the primary course of learning, they understood the way of father and son and the hierarchy of young and old. After entering the higher course of learning, they understood the decorum of ruler and minister, and the position of superiors and inferiors. Therefore, rulers behaved as rulers, ministers as ministers, fathers as fathers, and sons as sons. The lesser masters selected worthy students of the primary course of learning to move up to the higher course of learning. The grand masters selected worthy students of the higher course of learning and recommended them to the Son of Heaven. The Son of Heaven made them his assistants.

---

10   Depending on its context, the term translated as "training a man of service," *zao shi* 造士, can refer to the process of training a scholar or to a trained scholar as in *Records of Ritual. Liji zhuzi suoyin* 5.42/35/16.
11   According to *Explaining Graphs and Analyzing Characters* (Shuowen jiezi 说文解字) and its commentators, *mian* 宀 and *ji* 祭 (to sacrifice) are semantic constituents of *cha* 察 (to scrutinize); see *Shuowen jiezi* 150b; *Shuowen jiezi zhu* 7B.9b.
12   The Guliang commentary interprets *ji* 祭 (to sacrifice) as an offering (*jian* 薦) made at the right season, with respect, and with good quality; see *Chunqiu guliang zhushu* 14.142b. Note the similarities in pronunciation. Reconstructions of the characters in this passage from Baxter and Sagart 2014, 330, 344–45, 374, 376.

6.2
略說下

6.2.1 遂[1]人為遂皇,伏羲[2]為戲皇,神農為農皇也。遂人以火紀,火、大陽也。陽尊,故託遂皇于天。伏羲以人事紀,故託戲皇于人。蓋王非人不固,人非天不成也。神農以地紀,悉地力,種穀疏[3],故託農皇于地。天地人之道備,而三五之運興矣。

6.2.2 堯八眉,舜四瞳子,禹其跳,湯扁,文王四乳。

6.2.3 八眉者、如八字者也。其跳者、踦也。扁者、枯也。言皆不善也。

6.2.4 伏羲氏沒,神農氏作;神農氏沒,黃帝、堯、舜氏作。

6.2.5 伏羲氏作八卦。

---

1 遂＝燧.
2 伏羲＝伏戲: *Xunzi zhuzi suoyin* 25/120/13.
3 疏＝蔬.

6.2
Principal Teachings, Part 2

The Fire Giver is the August One of Fire; Fuxi is the August One of Order; the Divine Farmer is the August One of Agriculture.¹ The Fire Giver regulated fire. Since fire represents great yang, and yang occupies a position of honor, the August One of Fire was entrusted with Heaven. Since Fuxi regulated human affairs, he was entrusted with humankind. Indeed, without people a king would not be able to secure his base, and without Heaven humans would not be able to be completed. The Divine Farmer regulated earth. Having understood the qualities of the soil and having planted grains and vegetables, he was entrusted with the earth. Thus the Way of Heaven, Earth, and humans became complete and the cycle of the Three August Ones and the Five Supreme Lords established.²   6.2.1

Yao had "eight"-shaped eyebrows, Shun had four pupils, Yu had a limp, Tang was paralyzed on one side, and King Wen had four nipples.   6.2.2

"Eight"-shaped eyebrows means being in the shape of the character "eight" (*ba* 八). "Having a limp" means walking lamely. "Paralyzed on one side" means withered. None of these words are compliments.   6.2.3

When the house of Fuxi declined, the house of the Divine Farmer rose. When the house of the Divine Farmer declined, the houses of the Yellow Emperor and of Yao and Shun rose.   6.2.4

Fuxi created the Eight Trigrams.   6.2.5

---

1   Ying Shao 應劭 (c. 140–before 204) quoted *Auspicious Inscriptions* (Han wen jia 含文嘉) to explain *fu* as "to distinguish (*bie* 別), to transform (*bian* 變)" and *xi* as "contribution (*xian* 獻), model (*fa* 法)." *Fengsu tongyi zhuzi suoyin* 1.1/2/18.
2   For theories about the Three August Ones and the Five Supreme Lords in the Han, see *Fengsu tongyi zhuzi suoyin* 1.1/2/19.

6.2.6 天立五帝以為相,四時施生,法度明察,春夏慶賞,秋冬刑罰。

6.2.7 多聞而齊給。

6.2.8 命五史以書五帝之蠱事[1]。

6.2.9 大庭氏王天下,五風竝異。

6.2.10 夏后逆於廟庭,殷人逆於堂,周人逆於戶。衣錦尚絅。

6.2.11 夏后氏主教以忠,周人之教以文,上教以文君子。其失也小人薄。

6.2.12 伊尹母方孕,行汲,化為枯桑。其夫尋至水濱,見桑穴中有兒,乃收養之。

6.2.13 伊尹相湯,伐桀,戰於鳴條。

1　蠱事＝故事.

Heaven established the Five Supreme Lords as its ministers. By means of the four seasons they nourished life; with rules and measures they conducted thorough investigations. In spring and summer they bestowed and rewarded; in autumn and winter they punished and fined. 6.2.6

He was knowledgeable and quick.³ 6.2.7

He ordered the five scribes to record the deeds of the Five Supreme Lords. 6.2.8

When the House of Dating ruled the world,⁴ the five winds were clearly distinguished.⁵ 6.2.9

Whereas the House of Xia received its guests in the courtyard of their ancestral temple, the men of Yin received them in their ceremonial hall and the men of Zhou in their residence. 6.2.10
 "Over their embroidered clothes, they wore a plain robe."⁶

The main teaching of the House of Xia concerned loyalty; the men of Zhou taught refinement. Their most important teaching concerned the refinement of the noble man. If it failed, they would have petty persons, shallow in behavior. 6.2.11

When Yi Yin's mother had just become pregnant, she went to fetch water and transformed into a withered mulberry tree. Her husband, looking for her, arrived at the riverbank and saw there was a baby in a hollow space in the mulberry tree. He took the baby and raised it. 6.2.12

Yi Yin became Tang's prime minister, attacked Jie, and engaged him in battle at Mingtiao.⁷ 6.2.13

---

3   According to Sima Zhen 司馬貞 (679–732), the commentator on *Scribe's Records*, this sentence refers to the Yellow Emperor. See *Shiji* 1.1.
4   Kong Yingda, in a commentary to *Zuo Tradition*, identifies the House of Dating with the lineage of Supreme Lord Yan; *Shisanjing zhushu fujiao kanji* 2:383b. The House of Dating is mentioned in the "Rifling Trunks" (Quqie 胠篋) chapter of *Zhuangzi*; *Zhuangzi zhuzi suoyin* 10/25/22.
5   Alternatively, *Imperial Readings Compiled in the Taiping Era* has "five phoenixes have different colors" (*wufeng yise* 五鳳異色); *Taiping yulan* 78.494a.
6   A quotation from *Records of Ritual*; see *Liji zhuzi suoyin* 32.30/147/16. A similar expression is also seen in the *Odes* (Mao no. 57, "Shuo ren" 碩人, and Mao no. 88, "Feng" 丰).
7   *Scribe's Records* agrees with the *Great Commentary* that the battle took place at Mingtiao but also provides two other explanations: the last ruler of the Xia dynasty, Jie, fled to Mingtiao or was exiled there by Tang, the founder of the Shang dynasty. *Shiji* 5.174, 2.88, 3.96, 130.3301.

6.2.14 狄人將攻大王亶甫,大王亶甫召耆老而問焉,曰:「狄人何欲?」耆老對曰:「欲得叔粟財貨。」大王亶甫曰:「與之。」每與而攻不免。大王亶甫贅其耆老而問之曰:「狄人又何欲乎?」耆老對曰:「欲君之土地。」大王亶甫曰:「與之。」耆老曰:「君不為社稷乎?」大王亶甫曰:「社稷、所以為民也,不可以所為民亡民也。」耆老曰:「君縱不為社稷,不為宗廟乎?」大王亶甫曰:「宗廟、吾私也,不可以吾私害民也。」遂杖策而去,過梁山,邑岐山。國人束修奔走而從之者三千乘,一止而成三千戶之邑。

6.2.15 周文王至磻谿,見呂望釣。文王拜之,尚父曰:「望釣得魚,腹中有玉璜,刻曰「周受命,呂左檢,德合于今,昌來提。」」

6.2.16 公、爵。劉、名也。

6.2.17 文王施政而物皆聽。

6.2.18 帝命周公踐阼,朱草暘生。

The Di people were about to attack Great King Danfu. Great King Danfu summoned the elders and asked them: "What is it the Di people want?" The elders replied: "They want to obtain grains and goods." Great King Danfu said: "Then give it to them." Despite making several donations, they were still under attack. Great King Danfu gathered the elders and asked: "What is it the Di people want now?" The reply was "They want your land." Great King Danfu replied: "Give it to them." The elders said: "Do you not need the land to sacrifice at the altars to soil and grain?" Great King Danfu said: "The altars to soil and grain should be used on behalf of the people. We cannot afford to lose people to maintain the altars." The elders said: "Even if you do not act on behalf of the altars, should you not do it for the sake of your ancestral temple?" Great King Danfu said: "The ancestral temple is my private affair. I cannot harm the people for something that is private." Thereupon he leaned on his staff and took off. He crossed Mount Liang and established a settlement at Mount Qi.[8] Many of the men of his domain dried their meat and hurried to follow him, filling three thousand wagons. Once they stopped, they established a settlement three thousand households strong.   6.2.14

King Wen of Zhou went to Pan stream to visit Lü Wang, who was fishing there. When King Wen bowed to him, Father Shang said: "I, Wang, caught a fish. In its belly is a jade half-disc with the following inscription: 'Zhou has received the mandate; Lü will assist. Its virtue matches the present moment. Chang will collect it.'"[9]   6.2.15

"Duke" is a noble title. "Liu" is a personal name.[10]   6.2.16

When King Wen governed, all things obeyed.[11]   6.2.17

The supreme lord commanded the Duke of Zhou to ascend the platform.[12] The vermilion grass thrived.[13]   6.2.18

---

8   A mountain near the heartland of predynastic and dynastic Zhou in Shaanxi.
9   Pan stream is in Baoji, Shaanxi, in the heartland of predynastic and dynastic Zhou. Lü Wang, also known as Lü Shang 呂尚 and Jiang Shang 姜尚, was an important military strategist in the Zhou conquest of Shang. In this passage, he is also referred to as Shangfu 尚父, Father Shang. After the conquest, he was rewarded with a fief in Qi 齊. He is also referred to as Taigong 太公. See *Shiji* 32.1477–80; see also 4.7.1. Chang is the personal name of King Wen of the Zhou, Ji Chang. For a more elaborate version of this passage in an apocryphal weft text, see *Jūshū isho shūsei*, 2:83, 3d item; Espesset 2014, 423.
10 This refers to Liu the Duke, an important figure in Zhou predynastic history. He is the subject of "Gong Liu" 公劉; see *Odes*, Mao no. 250.
11 See 5.8.2.
12 I.e., the platform from which the ruler governed.
13 See also 6.2.34.

6.2.19　周公輔幼主，不矜功，則蓂莢生。

6.2.20　成王削桐葉為珪，以封唐叔。

6.2.21　周公思兼三王之道，以施於春秋冬夏。

6.2.22　子夏讀《書》畢，見夫子。夫子問焉：「子何為於《書》？」子夏曰：「《書》之論事也昭昭如日月之代明，離離若星辰之錯行；上有堯、舜之道，下有三王之義。商所受于夫子，志之于心，弗敢忘也。雖退而巖居河沛之閒、深山之中，作壞室，編蓬戶，尚彈琴其中，以歌先王之風，則亦可以發憤忼慨，忘己貧賤。有人亦樂之，無人亦樂之，而忽不知憂患與死也。」夫子造然變色曰：「嘻！子殆可與言《書》矣。雖然，見其表，未見其裏也。」

　　顏回曰：「何謂也？」子曰：「闚其門，而不入其中，觀其奧藏之所在乎？然藏又非難也。丘嘗悉心盡志以入其閒，前有高岸，後有大谿，填填正立而已。是故《堯典》可以觀美。《禹貢》可以觀事，《咎繇》可以觀治，《鴻范》可以觀度，六誓可以觀義，五誥可以觀仁，《甫刑》可以觀誡。通斯七觀，《書》之大義舉矣。」

The Duke of Zhou assisted the young ruler but was not boastful about his achievements. As a result, the pods of the auspicious *mingjia* plant grew.[14] 6.2.19

King Cheng cut a leaf from a parasol tree and shaped it like a *gui* jade. With it, he enfeoffed Tangshu.[15] 6.2.20

The Duke of Zhou longed to unify the way of the Three Kings,[16] to implement it in all four seasons. 6.2.21

Zixia read the *Documents* to the end and went to see the master. The master questioned him, "What did you learn from the *Documents*?" Zixia replied: "In its discussion of affairs, the *Documents* is as bright as sun and the moon in their succession, as orderly as the stars in their movements. It starts with the way of Yao and Shun and ends with the righteousness of the Three Kings. What I, Shang, learned from you, master, is deeply engrained in my heart. I would not dare forget it. Even if I were to withdraw and live as a hermit on a cliff between the Yellow and Ji Rivers and build, deep in the mountains, an adobe dwelling with a straw gate, I would still strum my zither and sing the praises of the former kings. Thus, pouring forth my deep feelings, I would forget my poor and humble circumstances. Whether or not there are others to enjoy it with me, I would immediately forget sadness and death." The master's facial expression suddenly changed: "Indeed, you are almost ready to discuss the *Documents*. However, that you have seen the surface does not mean you know what is inside!" 6.2.22

Yan Hui said: "What does that mean?" The master replied: "If you peeped through the door without going inside, would you be able to see where deep-stored treasures are? Nonetheless, that they are stored should not be a difficulty. Once I, Qiu, wholeheartedly and purposefully entered the room. Before me, a high cliff arose; behind me, a great stream. Steadfast I stood there. That is how I came to see beauty through 'Canon of Yao,' affairs through 'Tribute of Yu,' good governance through 'Gaoyao,' measure through 'Great Plan,' duty through the Six Oaths, benevolence through the Five Proclamations, and admonishment through 'Punishments of Fu.' Having mastered those seven vistas, the ultimate meaning of the *Documents* issued forth."[17]

---

14 *Chongxiu Yupian* 13.1b (224.112); *Baihu tong zhuzi suoyin* 18/39/19–20.
15 As part of child's play. The Duke of Zhou later held the king to his promise; see *Shiji* 39.1635. For the ceremonial use of *gui* 圭 for regional lords, also see 1.1.15.
16 The founding kings of Xia, Shang, and Zhou.
17 For parallels in *The Kong Family Masters* and *Mr. Han's Outer Commentary to the Odes*, see *Kong congzi zhuzi suoyin* 1.2/3/25; *Hanshi waizhuan zhuzi suoyin* 2.29/14/16; and the section "Enunciations by Confucius" in the introduction to this book.

6.2.23 宣王問於子春曰:「寡人欲行孝弟之義,為之有道乎?」子春曰:「昔者衛聞之樂正子曰:『文王之治岐也,五十者杖於家,六十者杖於鄉,七十者杖於朝,見君揖杖,八十者杖於朝,見君揖杖,君曰:「趣見客,毋俟朝。」已朝,乘車輶輪,御為僕,送至於家,而孝弟[2]之義達於諸侯。九十杖而朝,見君建杖,君曰:「趣見,毋俟朝。」已朝,車送之舍。天子重鄉養:卜筮、巫醫御於前,祝饐祝梗以食;乘車輶輪,胥與就膳徹,送至於家。君如有欲問焉,明日,就其室,以珍從,而孝弟[3]之義達於四海。』此文王之治岐也。君如欲行孝弟[4]之大義。盍反文王之治岐?」

---

2 弟=悌.
3 弟=悌.
4 弟=悌.

King Xuan asked Zichun,[18] "I intend to promote filial and brotherly behavior, how should I go about it?" Zichun responded, "Once, I, Wei, heard the following from the Director of Music: 'When King Wen ruled over the area around Mount Qi,[19] those aged fifty received the staff at home,[20] and those aged sixty received it in the village. Those aged seventy received it at court, and, while having an audience with the ruler, they clasped the staff with joined palms;[21] Those aged eighty received it at court, and, while having an audience with the ruler, they clasped the staff with joined palms.[22] The ruler said, "Hurry to receive this guest, and do not make him wait for his audience." The audience completed, they mounted a small-wheeled carriage and, with the ruler's driver at their service, were escorted home. Thus, proper filial and brotherly behavior spread to the regional lords. Those aged ninety received the staff at court, and, while having an audience with the ruler, they continued to lean on their staffs. The ruler said, "Hurry to receive him, and do not make him wait for his audience." The audience completed, they were escorted by carriage to their lodgings. The Son of Heaven considered feasting the village elders important. Diviners and healers attended to them in front, chanting charms so that they would not choke. They mounted small-wheeled carriages as the musicians who performed throughout the meal escorted them home. If the ruler wished to consult them, he would go to their residence the next day, accompanied by precious gifts. Thus, the proper filial and brotherly behavior spread all the way to the Four Seas.' This is how King Wen ruled over the area around Mount Qi. If you really want to promote filial and brotherly behavior, why not change course and follow the example of King Wen's rule at Mount Qi?"[23]

6.2.23

---

18   King Xuan of Qi (r. 342–329 BCE). Zichun is probably Chun Ju 春居, who in *Mr. Lü's Annals* has a conversation about a different topic with King Xuan. *Lüshi chunqiu zhuzi suoyin* 20.7/136/22. Later in this passage, he refers to himself as Wei 衛.
19   In Shaanxi; it refers to the heartland of predynastic Zhou.
20   Examples of such staffs have been found in Han tombs.
21   Elderly people held their staffs beneath their palms while greeting because they were absolved from bowing and prostrating themselves. *SSDZSZ* 7.9b–10a (784–85).
22   The text was already corrupted by Zheng Xuan's time. Zheng Xuan speculated that, for age seventy, the text should read, "Those aged seventy received the staff at the walled city, and, while having an audience with the ruler, they had to remove their staffs 七十者杖於國，見君去杖." *SSDZSZ* 7. 8b (784). For a comparable passage, see *Liji zhuzi suoyin* 5.48/36/22–28, 12.33/76/2912, 12.33/77/1.
23   The Han histories record many instances of empirewide distributions of wine, grain, and silk to the elderly; for examples, see *Hanshu* 4.113-14 (179 BCE), 6.174 (122 BCE), 6.191 (110 BCE).

6.2.24　子曰：「君子不可以不學，見人不可以不飾。不飾無（兒）〔貌〕，無（兒）〔貌〕不敬，不敬無禮，無禮不立。夫遠而〔有〕光者、飾也；近而逾明者、學也。譬之圩邪，水潦集焉，菅蒲生焉，從上觀之，誰知非源水也。」

6.2.25　子張曰：「仁者何樂於山也？」孔子曰：「夫山者、岿然高。」「岿然高，則何樂焉？」「夫山、草木生焉，鳥獸蕃焉，財用殖焉。生財用而無私，為四方皆伐焉，每無私予焉。出雲雨以通乎天地之間，陰陽和合，雨露之澤，萬物以成，百姓以饗。此仁〔者〕之樂于山者也。」

6.2.26　子貢曰：「葉公問政於夫子。子曰：『政在附近而來遠。』魯哀公問政。子曰：『政在於論臣。』齊景公問政。子曰：『政在於節用。』三君問政，夫子應之不同，然則政有異乎？」子曰：「荊之地廣而都狹，民有離志焉，故曰在於附近而來遠。哀公有臣三人，內比周以惑其君，外障距諸侯賓客以蔽其明，故曰政在論臣。齊景公奢於臺榭，淫於苑囿，五官之樂不解[5]，一旦而賜人百乘之家者三，故曰政在節用。」

5　解＝懈.

268　　　　　　　　　　　　　　　　　　*Principal Teachings*

The master said: "For a noble man not to forgo learning is as important 6.2.24
as to dress up for formal visits. If one does not dress up, one is lacking in
demeanor. To be lacking in demeanor is disrespectful. Being disrespectful violates ritual. Having violated ritual, one will not be able to achieve
standing. That one's luster can be seen from afar is due to one's dress;
that one appears even more brilliant up close is due to learning. One can
compare this to a basin: runoff water accumulates in it, and aquatic
plants grow in it. Looking at it from above, who would know that it is not
a real spring?"

Zizhang asked: "Why does a benevolent person enjoy the mountains?"[24] 6.2.25
Confucius replied: "Mountains are majestic!" "Majestic they may be,
but why does he enjoy them?" "Well, in the mountains, grasses and
trees flourish; birds and beasts prosper, and useful resources multiply.
They generate useful resources without partiality: whenever people
from the four quarters come to exploit them, the mountains provide
for them impartially. Giving rise to clouds and rain, they connect
Heaven and Earth. Thus, yin and yang can mingle, and rain and dew
can provide moisture. Hence, the myriad things can become complete,
and the people are provided for. This is why a benevolent person enjoys
the mountains."

Zigong asked: "Lord She questioned the master about good govern- 6.2.26
ment, and you replied: 'Good government lies in bringing the close
closer and causing the distant to arrive.' When Lord Ai of Lu asked about
good government, you replied: 'Good government lies in correctly
assessing your ministers.' When Lord Jing of Qi asked about good government, you replied, 'Good government lies in saving resources.' These
three lords asked about good government, but the master's response was
different each time. This being the case, is good government not always
the same?"[25] The master responded: "Jing's hinterland is vast, and its
capital small, so people are prone to leave; hence my answer to Lord She.
Lord Ai has three ministers who form cliques at court in order to mislead
their lord and block regional lords and guests from the outside in order
to obstruct intelligence; hence my reply to Lord Ai. As to Lord Jing of Qi,
he luxuriously spends on terraces and pavilions, and revels in his pleasure gardens, indulging his senses without pause. In a single morning,
he might bestow the status of a one-hundred-chariot family on three different men; hence my reply to Lord Jing."[26]

---

24   Also see *Lunyu zhushu* 6.54b. Also see *Kong congzi zhuzi suoyin* 2.1/4/25–30.
25   According to *Commentary to the Guide to the Waterways* (Shuijing zhu 水經註),
     Lord She received his fief, named She, from Lord Hui of Chu (r. 489–432 BCE);
     Shuijing zhushi, 21.14b. Jing, later in this passage, is an alternative name for the state
     of Chu where Lord She was enfeoffed. Lord Ai of Lu reigned from 494 to 468 BCE.
26   See *Hanfeizi zhuzi suoyin* 38/122/21–26.

6.2.27　晉平公問師曠曰：「吾〔行〕年七十，欲學，恐已暮〔矣〕。」師曠曰：「臣聞〔之〕老而學者，如執燭之明，執燭之明，孰與昧行。」公曰：「善。」

6.2.28　東郭子思問於子貢曰：「夫子之門，何其雜也？」子貢曰：「夫檃括之旁多枉木，良醫之門多疾人，砥礪之旁多頑鈍。」夫子聞之曰：「修道以俟，天下來者不止，是以雜也。」

6.2.29　孔子如衛，衛人謂曰：「公甫不能聽訟。」子曰：「非公甫之不能聽訟也，公甫之聽獄也，有罪者懼，無罪者恥。民近禮矣。」

6.2.30　民擊壤而歌，鑿井而飲，耕田而食，帝力何有？

6.2.31　王者躬耕，所以共粢盛。

6.2.32　凡宗廟，有先王之主，曰都；無曰邑。

6.2.33　大夫有污豬之宮、殺君之地，雖有美菜，有義之士弗食。

Lord Ping of Jin asked Master Kuang: "I am seventy years old, and, although I would like to study, I am afraid it is too late." Master Kuang replied: "I have learned that elder students have the brightness of a handheld torch.[27] With the brightness of a hand-held torch, who would need to walk in the dark?" The lord said: "Well put!" 6.2.27

Dongguo Zisi asked Zigong: "Why are our master's disciples of such mixed caliber?"[28] Zigong replied: "Next to a bevel, one finds a lot of crooked wood; at the gate of a good doctor, there are many sick patients; next to a whetstone, there are many blunt objects." When the master heard this, he said: "I cultivated the Way and waited. There was an unending stream of visitors from all over the world. That is why the group is of such mixed caliber." 6.2.28

Confucius went to Wei. Someone in Wei told him: "Our venerable lord is not good at hearing lawsuits." The master replied: "He is good at hearing lawsuits! When he hears trials, the guilty are struck with fear, and the innocent are ashamed. This indicates that people are advancing in ritual." 6.2.29

A man played the game "striking the board" and burst out in song.[29] "I dig a well and drink; I plow the fields and eat. What does the supreme lord have to do with it?"[30] 6.2.30

A true king partakes in the plowing; hence he is able to offer millet in sacrificial vessels. 6.2.31

When in the ancestral temple there is the spirit tablet of the founding king, the place is called a "capital"; if not, it is called a "settlement." 6.2.32

If a minister comes to possess palaces that have been converted to pools of stagnant water or places where a lord has been killed, then a righteous man will not eat even the finest vegetables grown on it.[31] 6.2.33

---

27 A fuller version of this story is found in Liu Xiang's *Garden of Eloquence*. It compares the brightness of young students to that of the rising sun, of adult students to that of the sun at noon, and that of the elderly to a hand-held torch at night. See *Shuoyuan zhuzi suoyin* 3.17/22/20–24.
28 There is ample debate in early Chinese texts on how to assess the disciples of Confucius, who came from all walks of life. See Habberstad 2014. *Weighed Discourses* offers a statement about the quality of the seventy disciples of Confucius that is similar to this passage (6.2.28); *Lunheng zhuzi suoyin* 8/19/15–19.
29 For a description of the game, see *Fengsu tongyi zhuzi suoyin* 11.1/80/1.
30 *Weighed Discourses* attributes a similar story to a *Commentary* (Zhuan); in it, a man plays at striking the board, and bystanders compare him to Yao. He downplays this by singing a song that says: "At dawn, I go out to work; at dusk, I come back to rest. I dig a well and drink; I plow the fields and eat. What does Yao have to do with it?" *Lunheng zhuzi suoyin* 19/72/1–4.
31 In a memorial presented to Wang Mang in 6 CE, Zhang Song 張竦 (d. 23 CE) claims that ancient custom dictated that the palaces of rebels be turned into pools of

6.2.34　王者德及皇天，則祥風起。王者德下究地之厚，則朱草生。

6.2.35　《詩》云：「非知之艱，行之惟艱。[6]」

6.2.36　夏不數浴，非愛水也；冬不數煬，非愛火也。

6.2.37　剴切。

6.2.38　魏文侯問子夏，子夏葉拱而進。

6　Cf. *Shangshu zhuzi suoyin* 22/21/10 (説命中).

If a true king's virtue reaches to august Heaven, then auspicious winds arise. If a true king's virtue penetrates the depths of the earth below, then vermilion grass grows.[32] 6.2.34

The ode says: "Knowing is not difficult; only practice is."[33] 6.2.35

That one does not often bathe in summer does not mean that one begrudges water; that one does not often warm oneself in winter does not mean that one begrudges fire. 6.2.36

Precisely on point. 6.2.37

When Lord Wen of Wei wanted to question Zixia, Zixia clasped his hands in respect and came forward. 6.2.38

---

stagnant water; even if vegetables were to grow on the terrain, he adds, no one would eat them. See *Hanshu* 99A.4083–84.

32 See also 6.2.18.
33 This quotation is not in the transmitted version of the *Odes*.

卷七
鴻範五行傳

7
Tradition on the Great Plan's Five Phases

7
Tradition on the Great Plan's Five Phases

"Tradition on the Great Plan's Five Phases" is a unique chapter within the Great Commentary. We divide it into three parts:[1]

Part 1 (7.1.1–11) lists various inauspicious signs associated with the Five Tasks and the Royal Standard, both key concepts of the Documents' "Great Plan" (Hongfan 洪範).[2] It also contains ritual theories and prescriptions to eliminate the harms (li 沴) that will arrive if the prescriptions associated with the Five Tasks and the Royal Standard are not followed.[3] The linkage of passages 7.1.2 to 7.1.6 with the Documents' "Great Plan" chapter is even more intricate: using 7.1.2 as an example, the pattern is as follows: the first three enunciations ("demeanor," "not respectful," "deference") hark back to terminology employed in the second section of the Documents' "Great Plan" (Wushi); the punishment ("prolonged rain") and the deviance ("garments"), to the "Great Plan's" eighth section (Shuzheng); the extreme ("wickedness"), to its ninth section (Liuji); and the harm, to its first section (Wuxing).

Part 2 of "Tradition on the Great Plan's Five Phases" (7.2.1–18) is of the Monthly Ordinances (Yueling 月令) genre. It contains prescriptions for each

---

1   For the way this text was used in Western Han mantic traditions, see case 6 of the section "The *Great Commentary* on Questions of Political and Social Order" of the introduction to this volume.
2   See also table I.2 in the volume introduction.
3   "Harm" is a key term specific to this text. It is used as part of a collective (Six Harms) or as a verb to indicate that one phase harms another ("wood harms metal"). In other texts, this verbal form would be expressed with different words, for example, *ke* 克, "to conquer, overcome."

of the twelve months and for the five geographical regions (that is, the four cardinal directions and the center). It makes links with the Documents' "Great Plan" in two ways: first, it links the first month of each season with vocabulary specific to that text;[4] second, the last passage of this part (7.2.18) connects the middle month of each season as well as the central geographical region with language associated with each of the Five Material Resources of the Documents' "Great Plan." Part 2 ties each geographical area to a ritual location and provides the names of different ritual halls to be used in different seasons (the Hall of Blue-Green Yang, Qingyang 青陽, in spring; the Bright Hall, or Mingtang 明堂, in summer; the Hall of Comprehensive Luminosity, Zongzhang 總章, in autumn; and the Dark Hall, or Xuantang 玄堂, in winter). The left-hand room of each seasonal hall was to be used in the first month, the central room in the second month, and the right-hand room in the third month of each season. There is textual and archaeological evidence starting from Western Han that such ritual halls with seasonal rooms were being built.[5]

Part 3 (7.3.1–18) has much less cohesion and appears as a collection of fragments related to signs, cosmology, and geography.

This tripartite structure makes sense in terms of content but is also based on the textual history of the chapter: Part 1 (7.1) can be found in Wang Yinglin's *Ocean of Jade (Yuhai* 玉海*)* and appears in all of the earliest Qing editions (Sun Zhilu, Dong Fengyuan, Hui Dong, and Lu Jianzeng and Lu Wenchao);[6] part 2 (7.2) appears in the editions of Hui Dong and the Lus but not in the other early Qing editions; part 3 (7.3) has its basis in Sun Zhilu's edition and consists of fragments that Sun excerpted from other texts. The editions from later in the Qing (including Pi Xirui's and Wang Kaiyun's) contain all three parts. Parts 1 and 2 were inextricably linked to one another, at least from the time of Liu Xiang.[7]

---

[4] It has references to vocabulary of the second (Wushi) and eighth (Shuzheng) sections of "Great Plan"; for an overview of the sections of "Great Plan," see the introduction to 5.3. There is, however, a discrepancy between the way the months are linked to this vocabulary in the Monthly Ordinance section (7.2.1–17) and in 7.1.8.

[5] Hwang 1996; Tseng 2011, 17–88. The general term for these halls was "bright hall" (*mingtang*), but note that here Mingtang is the name of the ritual hall to be used in summer (when light is most abundant).

[6] *Yuhai* 5.30b–32a (108–9).

[7] On the textual history of "Tradition on the Great Plan's Five Phases," see the section "Textual Transmission of 'Tradition on the Great Plan's Five Phases'" of the introduction to this book.

7.1
鴻范五行傳上

7.1.1 維王后元祀[1]，**帝**令大**禹**步于上帝。維時洪祀六沴，用咎于下，是用**知不畏**而神之**怒**[2]。若六沴作見，若是共[3]禦，帝用不差，神則不怒，**五福**乃降用章于下。若六沴作見，若不共禦，六伐既侵，六極其下。禹乃共辟厥德，受命休令。爰用**五事**，建用王**極**[4]。

---

1 Cf. *Shangshu zhuzi suoyin* 32/27/5 (洪範).
2 Cf. *Shangshu zhuzi suoyin* 32/27/6–7 (洪範).
3 共 = 恭: Zheng Xuan's commentary; *SSDZSZ* 4.5a (742).
4 Cf. *Shangshu zhuzi suoyin* 32/27/9–16 (洪範).

7.1
Tradition on the Great Plan's Five Phases, Part 1

In the first year of the reign of the king, the Great Yu,[1] the supreme lord ordered him to step before the Lord on High.[2] At that time they conducted a copious sacrifice to the Six Harms. That scourges were inflicted below is because that they had not been fearful in using their knowledge and had incited the ire of the gods.[3] Once the Six Harms become active and apparent, if one wards them off with awe and if the supreme lord makes no mistakes in his performance and does not incite the ire of the gods, then the Five Blessings will descend and make glorious those below. Once the Six Harms become active and apparent, if one fails to ward them off with awe, then the Six Invaders will attack, and the Six Extremes will descend. Thus, Yu made illustrious Shun's virtue; he received his charge and brought his orders to fruition. Thereupon, he applied the Five Tasks and established the Royal Standard.[4]

7.1.1

---

1 We base our translation on Zheng Xuan's identification of *wang* 王, "king," as Yu 禹 and *hou* 后 as *jun* 君, "lord"; see *SSDZSZ* 4.4b (742).
2 Zheng Xuan identifies the lord (*di* 帝) as Shun 舜, the Lord on High (Shangdi 上帝) as Heaven (Tian 天), and *bu* 步, "step before," as *tui* 推, "extrapolate," which has divinatory connotations; see *Shangshu dazhuan shuzheng* 4.4b (742).
3 Alternatively, following Zheng Xuan's explanation of *jiu* 咎 as *ji* 極, 用咎于下 (that scourges were inflicted below) would translate as "He made an extremely abundant sacrifice." See *SSDZSZ* 4.4b–5a (742).
4 The Five Tasks and the Royal Standard (Huangji 皇極) are the first and fifth sections of the *Documents*' "Great Plan." See Nylan 1992.

7.1.2 長事，一曰皃[1]，皃之不恭[2]，是謂不肅。厥咎狂，厥罰恆雨[3]，厥極惡[4]。時則有服妖[5]，時則有龜孽[6]，時則有雞禍[7]，時則有下體生于上之痾，時則有青眚青祥。維金沴木。

7.1.3 次二事曰言，言之不從[8]，是謂不艾[9]。厥咎僭，厥罰恆陽[10]，厥極憂[11]。時則有詩妖，時則有介蟲之孽，時則有犬禍，時則有口舌之痾，時則有白眚白祥。維木沴金。

7.1.4 次三事曰視，視之不明[12]，是謂不悊[13]。厥咎荼，[14]厥罰恆燠[15]，厥極疾[16]。時則有艸[17]妖，時則有倮蟲之孽，時則有羊禍，時則有目痾，時則有赤眚赤祥。維水沴火。

---

1 皃=貌: Cf. *Shangshu zhuzi suoyin* 32/27/12 (洪範).
2 Cf. *Shangshu zhuzi suoyin* 32/27/12 (洪範).
3 Cf. *Shangshu zhuzi suoyin* 32/28/13–14 (洪範).
4 Cf. *Shangshu zhuzi suoyin* 32/29/2 (洪範).
5 妖=祅: *Hanshu* 27B(A).1353.
6 孽=孼: *Hanshu* 27B(A).1353.
7 禍=齫=禍: *Hanshu* 27B(A).1353; *SSDZSZ* 4.6b (743).
8 Cf. *Shangshu zhuzi suoyin* 32/27/12–13 (洪範).
9 艾=乂: Cf. *Shangshu zhuzi suoyin* 32/27/9, 32/27/13, 32/28/13, 32/28/16–17 (洪範).
10 陽=暘: Cf. *Shangshu zhuzi suoyin* 32/28/11, 32/28/13–14 (洪範).
11 Cf. *Shangshu zhuzi suoyin* 32/29/2 (洪範).
12 Cf. *Shangshu zhuzi suoyin* 32/27/12–13 (洪範).
13 悊=晢: cf. *Shangshu zhuzi suoyin* 32/28/13 (洪範).
14 荼=舒: Zheng Xuan's commentary, *SSDZSZ* 4.9a (744); *Zhouli zhushu* 42.662a. Cf. *Shangshu zhuzi suoyin* 32/27/10, 32/28/14 (洪範).
15 Cf. *Shangshu zhuzi suoyin* 32/28/12–15 (洪範).
16 Cf. *Shangshu zhuzi suoyin* 32/29/2 (洪範).
17 艸=草: *SSDZSZ* 4.9a (744).

The first task is demeanor. If one's demeanor is not respectful, this is 7.1.2
called lack of deference. Its scourge is insolence, its punishment is prolonged rain, and its extreme is wickedness. Sometimes there will be deviances with garments.[5] Sometimes there will be anomalies with turtles. Sometimes there will be disasters with chickens. Sometimes there will be maladies such as lower limbs growing on the upper body. Sometimes there will be ill or inauspicious omens related to the color blue. It is metal harming wood.[6]

The second task is speech. If one's speech is incoherent, this is called lack 7.1.3
of control.[7] Its scourge is usurpation, its punishment is prolonged dry spells, and its extreme is anxiety. Sometimes there will be deviances with songs. Sometimes there will be anomalies with beetles. Sometimes there will be disasters with dogs. Sometimes there will be maladies of the mouth. Sometimes there will be ill or inauspicious omens related to the color white. It is wood harming metal.

The third task is vision. If one's vision is not clear, this is called lack of 7.1.4
understanding. Its scourge is sluggishness, its punishment is prolonged heat, and its extreme is disease. Sometimes there will be deviances with grasses. Sometimes there will be anomalies with insects. Sometimes there will be disasters with sheep. Sometimes there will be maladies of the eye. Sometimes there will be ill or inauspicious omens related to the color red. It is water harming fire.

---

5   *Book of Han* cites an *Explanation* (Shuo 說) that explains the meaning of *shi ze* 時則 (sometimes), an expression that occurs repeatedly: "*Shi ze* 時則 does not mean that every disaster mentioned will necessarily occur; it might or it might not, and the order in which these disasters would occur is not determined" 言非必俱至，或有或亡，或在前或在後也. *Hanshu* 27B(A).1353.
6   Passages 7.1.2–6 differentiate various sorts of disasters associated with each task, which are difficult to distinguish in translation. We used as our guide the *Explanation* cited in *Book of Han* that distinguishes the terms used as follows: "Disasters that affect plants are called *yao* 妖 (deviance); they are in an embryonic stage and minute. Disasters that affect insects are called *nie* 孽 (anomaly); they are at the stage of budding. When the disasters affect livestock, they are called *huo* 旤 (disaster); they are in plain view. When they affect humans, they are called *e* 痾 (malady); they reveal themselves as illnesses and are insidious and severe. When even more seriously abnormal creatures appear, these disasters are called *sheng* 眚 (ill omen). Disasters from outside causes are called *xiang* 祥 (inauspicious omen); they are like signs (*zhen* 禎). When the vapors (*qi* 氣) harm one another, the disasters are called *li* 沴 (harm); they are encounters (*linli* 臨莅) out of harmony." *Hanshu* 27B(A).1353. Translations of the terms follow Espesset 2015 and 2016, 9.
7   Following Zheng Xuan's explanation of *yi* 乂 as *zhi* 治 (control); *SSDZSZ* 4.8a (744).

7.1.5　次四事曰**聽**,聽之不**聰**[18],是謂不**謀**。厥咎**急**,厥罰**恆寒**[19],厥**極貧**[20]。時則有鼓妖,時則有魚孽,時則有豕☐時則有耳痾,時則有黑眚黑祥。維火沴水。

7.1.6　次五事曰**思**[21]心,思心之不容,是謂不**聖**。厥咎霿,厥罰**恆風**[22],厥**極凶短折**[23]。時則有脂夜之妖,時則有(雩)〔夸〕[24]孽,時則有牛禍,時則有心腹之痾,時則有黃眚黃祥。維木金水火沴土。

7.1.7　**王**之不**極**[25],是謂不建,厥咎眊,厥罰恆陰,厥**極弱**[26]。時則有射妖,時則有龍蛇之孽,時則有馬禍,時則有下人伐上之痾,時則有**日月亂行,星辰**[27]逆行。

7.1.8　維五位復建。辟厥沴,曰二月三月,維兒是司。四月五月,維視是司。六月七月,維言是司。八月九月,維聽是司。十月十一月,維思心是司。十二月與正月,維王極是司。

18　Cf. *Shangshu zhuzi suoyin* 32/27/12–13 (洪範).
19　Cf. *Shangshu zhuzi suoyin* 32/28/12–15 (洪範).
20　Cf. *Shangshu zhuzi suoyin* 32/29/2 (洪範).
21　Cf. *Shangshu zhuzi suoyin* 32/27/12–13 (洪範).
22　Cf. *Shangshu zhuzi suoyin* 32/28/12, 32/28/14–15 (洪範).
23　Cf. *Shangshu zhuzi suoyin* 32/29/2 (洪範).
24　雩 = 夸: *SSDZSZ* 4.11a (745).
25　Cf. *Shangshu zhuzi suoyin* 32/27/15 (洪範). *Shangshu zhuzi suoyin* has 皇 for 王.
26　Cf. *Shangshu zhuzi suoyin* 32/29/2–3 (洪範).
27　Cf. *Shangshu zhuzi suoyin* 32/27/15, 32/28/15–32/29/1 (洪範).

The fourth task is hearing. If one's hearing is not sharp, this is called 7.1.5
failure to plan. Its scourge is crisis, its punishment is prolonged cold, and
its extreme is poverty. Sometimes there will be deviances with drums.
Sometimes there will be anomalies in fish. Sometimes there will be
disasters with pigs. Sometimes there will be maladies of the ear. Sometimes there will be ill or inauspicious omens related to the color black. It
is fire harming water.

The fifth task is mindfulness. If one is not receptive, this is called lack of 7.1.6
sagacity. Its scourge is confusion, its punishment is enduring winds, and
its extreme is early death. Sometimes there will be deviances with fatty
liver and too much sweating.[8] Sometimes there will be anomalies with
earthworms.[9] Sometimes there will be disasters with oxen. Sometimes
there will be maladies of the heart and liver. Sometimes there will be ill
or lucky omens related to the color yellow. It is wood, metal, water, and
fire harming earth.

If the king does not abide by the standard, this is called lack of determination. Its scourge is chaos, its punishment is prolonged periods without 7.1.7
sun, and its extreme is weakness. Sometimes there will be deviances with
archery. Sometimes there will be anomalies with dragons and snakes.
Sometimes there will be disasters with horses. Sometimes there will be
maladies such as those below attacking those above. Sometimes there
will be erratic movements of the sun and the moon, and stars and planets
going backward.

When these five positions are restored and their corresponding harms 7.1.8
warded off, then demeanor will preside over the second and third
months, sight will preside over the fourth and fifth months, speech will
preside over the sixth and seventh months, hearing will preside over the
eighth and ninth months, mindfulness will preside over the tenth and
eleventh months, and the Royal Standard will preside over the twelfth
and first months.

---

8   *Book of Han* provides two explanations for *zhiye zhi yao* 脂夜之妖. We draw on the first in our translation, "deviances with fatty liver and too much sweating." The other involves an excess of wind. *Hanshu* 27.B(A).1441.
9   Following Zheng Xuan's explanation of *hua* 華 as *kua* 夸, which he explains as "earthworms"; *SSDZSZ* 4.11a–b (745).

7.1.9 凡六沴之作，**歲**之朝，**月**之朝，**日**之朝，則后王受之；**歲**之中，**月**之中，**日**之中，則正卿受之。**歲**之夕，**月**之夕，**日**之夕，則庶民受之。其二**辰**以次相將，其次受之，**星辰**[28]莫[29]同。是離逢非沴，維鮮之功。

7.1.10 禦兒于喬忿，以其**月**，從其禮，祭之參[30]，乃**從**。
禦言于訖眾，以其**月**，從其禮，祭之參，乃**從**。
禦視于忽佁，以其**月**，從其禮，祭之參，乃**從**。
禦聽于怴攸，以其**月**，從其禮，祭之參，乃**從**。
禦思心于有尤，以其**月**，從其禮，祭之參，乃**從**。
禦王極于宗始，以其**月**，從其禮，祭之參，乃**從**[31]。

---

28 Cf. *Shangshu zhuzi suoyin* 32/27/15, 32/28/15–32/29/1 (洪範).
29 莫 = 暮: *SSDZSZ* 4.16b (748).
30 參 = 叄: *SSDZSZ* 4.17a (748).
31 Cf. *Shangshu zhuzi suoyin* 32/28/7-10; 32/28/15 (洪範).

Whenever the Six Harms are activated, when it happens at the beginning of the year, at the beginning of the month, or at the beginning of the day, it is the ruler who will suffer. When it happens in the middle of the year, in the middle of the month, or in the middle of the day, it is the ministers who will suffer. When it happens at the end of the year, at the end of the month, or at the end of the day, it is the common people who will suffer. As the sun and the moon succeed one another, people will be affected according to this cycle. The stars and planets in the night sky follow the same pattern. 7.1.9

If a worrisome phenomenon is encountered, it is not a harm. It is the result of diminishing.

Control demeanor so as to prevent arrogance or anger. During the months of demeanor, follow the corresponding rituals, make offerings thrice, and things will be settled. 7.1.10

Control speech so as to not to stop the masses from speaking.[10] During the months of speech, follow the corresponding rituals, make offerings thrice, and things will be settled.

Control sight so as not to be beguiled by appearances. During the months of sight, follow the corresponding rituals, make offerings thrice, and things will be settled.

Control hearing so as prevent inaccuracies. During the months of hearing, follow the corresponding rituals, make offerings thrice, and things will be settled.

Control mind so as to prevent errors. During the months of mindfulness, follow the corresponding rituals, make offerings thrice, and things will be settled.

Control the Royal Standard so as to prevent deviation from the ancestral norm. During the months of the Royal Standard, follow the corresponding rituals, make offerings thrice, and things will be settled.

---

10   Following Zheng Xuan's explanation, *SSDZSZ* 4.17a–b (748).

7.1.11 　六沴之禮，散齊七日，致齊三日。新器絜[32]以祀，用赤黍。三日之朝，于中庭祀四方，從東方始，自南至西，卒于北方。其祀禮曰《格祀》，曰：某也。方祀。曰：播[33]國率相行事。其祝也，曰：若爾神靈洪祀，六沴是合，無差無傾，無有不正。若民有不敬事，則會批之于六沴。六事之機以垂示我，我民人無敢不**敬事**[34]，上下王祀。[35]

32　絜＝潔.
33　播＝藩: *SSDZSZ* 4.19a (749).
34　Cf. *Shangshu zhuzi suoyin* 32/27/8, 32/27/12 (洪範).
35　Cf. *Shangshu zhuzi suoyin* 32/27/14 (洪範).

As to the rituals of the Six Harms: for seven days, undergo preliminary purification; for three days, undergo complete purification. Clean the new vessels for the sacrifice and use red millet. On the morning of the third day, sacrifice to the four quarters in the central courtyard. Start with the east, move from the south to the west, and end with the north. The ritual to be used is called "Regulation Sacrifice." Say: "I am X and will sacrifice to all directions."[11] Then say: "Dependent states, lead each other to carry out affairs." Then the incantation says: "In this manner, with copious sacrifices to the gods and spirits, the Six Harms will be neutralized. No mistakes, no diversions, nothing will be wrong. If it happens that the people fail to serve respectfully, I will summon the gods to determine which of the Six Harms is at stake. The Six Tasks as they operate will issue signs to warn us so that none among our people will dare not to serve respectfully. High and low participate in the royal sacrifices."

7.1.11

---

11   See Harper and Kalinowski 2017, 106, for the earliest known archaeological evidence of a generic incantation text.

7.2
鴻範五行傳中

7.2.1　東方之極,自碣石東至日出,榑木之野,帝太皥,神句芒司之。自冬日至數四十六日,迎春于東堂。距邦八里,堂高八尺,堂階八等。青稅八乘,旂旐尚青,田車載矛。號曰:「助天生。」倡之以角,舞之以羽,此迎春之樂也。

7.2.2　孟春之月,御青陽左(介)〔个〕,禱用牡,索祀于艮隅,皃必恭,厥休時雨。朔令曰:(挺)〔挺〕群禁,開閉(關)〔闔〕。通穹窒,達障塞,待優游。其禁毋伐林木。

7.2
Tradition on the Great Plan's Five Phases, Part 2

The border zone of the eastern region stretches eastward from Jieshi to where the sun rises.¹ This is the plain of the Fu trees;² it is presided over by the supreme lord Taihao and the divine being Goumang. Forty-six days after the winter solstice, welcome spring in the eastern hall. Located at eight *li* from the ruler's domain, the hall should be eight *chi* in height, with eight steps leading up to it.³ There are eight green chariots,⁴ with banners in the privileged color green and hunting carts loaded with spears. Call out: "Assist Heaven in generating life." Use *jue* as the lead tone in chanting; use the *yu* tone to dance. This is the music for welcoming spring.

7.2.1

The first month of spring. The ruler resides in the left chamber of the Hall of Green Yang. In his offerings, he uses oxen and carries out supplemental sacrifices in the *gen* corner.⁵ His demeanor must be respectful. The corresponding blessing is timely rain.⁶ These are the ordinances of the first day: relax all prohibitions, open what is closed, free what is blocked, release stoppages, have a tolerant attitude. Its prohibition: do not cut down trees.

7.2.2

---

1 This describes a mountain in Hebei very close to the Bohai Gulf. It is an important archaeological site for Qin, with remains of a palace built by the First Emperor and a stele the text of which is preserved. Tan Qixiang 1982–87, 2:9–10 (6-3).
2 Also known as Fusang 榑桑, a mythological tree associated with sunrise.
3 One *li*, in Han times, equaled 0.415 km.; one *chi* equaled 23.1 cm. This seems to be a rather low height for a ritual building.
4 A *shui* 税, according to both Pi Xirui and Wang Kaiyun, is a type of chariot for imperial use; *SSDZSZ* 4.28b–29a (754) and *SSDZBZ* 7.9b.
5 *Gen* is one of the eight trigrams of the *Changes*; its position is in the northeastern corner. *Gen* is also associated with the last month of winter; see 7.2.17.
6 Compare 7.1.2.

7.2.3 仲春之月，御青陽正室，牲先脾，設主于戶，索祀于震正。朔令曰：棄（怒）〔怨〕惡，解役罪，免（優）〔憂〕患，休罰刑，開關梁。其禁田獵不宿，飲食不享，出入不節，奪民農時，及有姦謀。

7.2.4 季春之月，御青陽右（介）〔个〕，薦用鮪，索祀于巽隅。朔令曰：宣庫財，和外怨，撫四方，行柔惠，止剛強。九門磔禳，出疫于郊，以襛春氣。

7.2.5 南方之極，自北戶南至炎風之野，帝炎帝，神祝融司之。自春分數四十六日，迎夏于南堂，距邦七里，〔堂高七尺〕，堂階七等，赤稅七乘，旂旗尚赤，田車載弓。號曰：「助天養。」倡之以徵，舞之以鼓鞉，此迎夏之樂也。

7.2.6 孟夏之月，御明堂左（介）〔个〕，嘗麥用彘，索祀于巽隅。視必明。厥休時燠。朔令曰：爵有德，賞有功，惠賢良，舉力農。其禁毋隳隄防。

The second month of spring. The ruler resides in the main chamber of 7.2.3
the Hall of Blue-Green Yang.[7] He first offers the spleen. A tablet for the
main god is established at the door, and supplemental sacrifices are
carried out at the *zhen* position.[8] These are the ordinances of the first
day: discard hatred, release corvée laborers and criminals, relieve sorrow and distress, stop penalties and punishments, open passes and
bridges. Its prohibitions: do not hunt outside of the season, do not eat
and drink without the appropriate offerings, do not enter and leave
without restraint, do not deprive the people of their farming season, do
not engage in conspiracies.

The last month of spring. The ruler resides in the right chamber of the Hall 7.2.4
of Blue-Green Yang. He uses sturgeon as an offering. Supplemental sacrifices are carried out in the *xun* corner.[9] These are the ordinances of the
first day: distribute goods from your granaries, neutralize hateful
actions from outside the borders, pacify the four quarters, practice conciliation and generosity, stop aggression. At all nine gates dismember the
sacrificial animals, exorcise pestilence from the suburbs, and drive away
evil spring airs.

The border zone of the southern region stretches south from the north- 7.2.5
facing doors to the region of the blazing winds.[10] The zone is presided over
by supreme lord Yan and the divine being Zhurong.[11] Forty-six days after
the spring equinox, welcome summer in the southern hall. Located at
seven *li* from the ruler's domain (its hall should be seven *chi* in height)
with seven steps leading up to it. There are seven red chariots, with banners in the privileged color red, and hunting carts loaded with bows. Call
out: "Assist Heaven's nurturing." Use *zhi* as the lead tone in chanting;
dance using the hand drums. This is the music for welcoming summer.

The first month of summer. The ruler resides in the left chamber of the 7.2.6
Bright Hall. He tastes the wheat and sacrifices a pig. Supplemental sacrifices are carried out in the *xun* corner. His vision must be clear, and the
corresponding blessing is timely heat.[12] These are the ordinances of the
first day: award rank to the virtuous, reward the meritorious, be generous to the worthy, promote those who dedicate themselves to farming.
Its prohibition: do not destroy dikes and banks.

---

7 A hall within the ritual complex, on its east side. *SSDZSZ* 4.29 (754).
8 Also one of the eight trigrams; its position is straight east from the center.
9 One of the eight trigrams, located in the southeast. *Xun* is also associated with the first month of summer. See 7.2.6.
10 The "north-facing doors" are named on the First Emperor's Langye stele as the southern limit of the Qin realm; see *Shiji* 6.245 and Kern 2000b, 33 n. 76.
11 On Zhurong as one of the Three Progenitors of Chu, as mentioned in the fourth century BCE Baoshan texts, see Cook and Luo 2017, 5–9 and 78–89.
12 Compare 7.1.4.

7.2.7 仲夏之月,御明堂正室,牲先肺,設主于竈,索祀于離正。朔令曰:振貧窮,惠孤寡,慮囚疾,出太祿,行大賞。其禁棄法律,逐功臣,殺太子,以妾為妻。乃令民雩。

7.2.8 季夏之月,御明堂右(介)〔个〕,牲先心,設主于中霤,索祀于坤隅,思必(睿)〔容〕,厥休時風。朔令曰:起毀宗,立無後,封廢國,立賢輔,卹喪疾。

7.2.9 中央之極,自昆侖中至大室之野,帝黃帝,神后土司之。土(玉)〔王〕之日,禱用牲,迎中氣于中室。樂用黃鍾[1]之宮,為民祈福。命世婦治服章,令民□。其禁治宮室,飾臺榭,內淫亂,犯親戚,侮父兄。

1　鍾＝鐘.

The second month of summer. The ruler resides in the main chamber of the Bright Hall. He first offers the lungs. A table for the main god is established at the stove, and supplemental sacrifices are carried out at the *li* position.¹³ These are the ordinances of the first day: bring relief to the poor, be generous to orphans and widows, be attentive to prisoners and the sick, pay generous salaries and hand out rich rewards. Its prohibitions: to abandon the laws and regulations, to exile meritorious ministers, to kill the heir apparent, to make a concubine a wife. Then order the people to pray for rain.

7.2.7

The last month of summer. The ruler resides in the right chamber of the Bright Hall. He first offers the heart. The tablet to the main god is established under the central eaves; supplemental sacrifices are carried out in the *kun* corner.¹⁴ His thinking must be mindful, and the corresponding blessing is timely wind.¹⁵ These are the ordinances of the first day: revive lineages that have been interrupted, establish heirs for those who died without, reenfeoff domains that were abolished, establish worthy aides, comfort those who have encountered death or illness.

7.2.8

The border zone of the central region stretches from mid-Kunlun to the plains of the Great Mansion.¹⁶ This zone is presided over by the Yellow Emperor and the divine being Houtu. On the day when Earth reigns, use sacrificial animals with your prayers, and welcome the central airs in the central chamber. In your music making, use the *gong* tone produced by the Huangzhong Bell to pray for blessings for the people. Order the lower-ranked wives to arrange clothing and patterns. Order the people to. . . . Its prohibitions: do not construct palaces, do not embellish terraced buildings, do not display licentious behavior, do not violate the dictates of kinship, do not offend your father or elder brothers.

7.2.9

---

13   *Li* is one of the eight trigrams; its position is due south of the center.
14   One of the eight trigrams, located in the southwest; below it is associated with the first month of autumn. See 7.2.11.
15   Compare 7.1.6.1.
16   Whereas the Kunlun Mountains are usually associated with the west, some sources, including *Master of Huainan*, associate them with the central regions. The Great Mansion is generally glossed as Mount Song 嵩 in Henan; Tan Qixiang 1982–87, 2:19–20 (2–4).

7.2.10 西方之極，自流沙西至三危[2]之野。帝少皥，神蓐收司之。自夏日至數四十六日，迎秋于西堂，距邦九里，堂高九尺，堂階九等，白稅九乘，旌旄尚白，田車載兵。號曰：「助天收。」倡之以商，舞之以干戚，此迎秋之樂也。

7.2.11 孟秋之月，御總章左（介）〔个〕，嘗穀用犬，索祀于坤隅，言必從，厥休時暘。朔令曰：審用法，備盜賊。禁姦衺，飾群牧，謹貯聚。其禁毋弛戎備。

7.2.12 仲秋之月，御總章正室，牲先肝，設主于門，索祀于兌正。朔令曰：謹功築，遏溝瀆，修囷倉，決刑獄，趣收斂。其禁好攻戰，輕百姓，飾城郭，侵邊竟。乃（今）〔令〕民畋醸，庶氓畢入于室。曰：時殺將至，毋罹其菑。

7.2.13 季秋之月，御總章右（介）〔个〕。薦用田禽，索祀于乾隅。朔令曰：除道路，守門閭，陳兵甲，戒百官，誅不法，除道成梁，以利農夫。

2　Cf. *Shangshu zhuzi suoyin*, 6/10/3–4, 6/10/17 (禹貢).

The border zone of the western region stretches from Flowing Sands 7.2.10
westward to the region of Three Dangers.[17] It is presided over by the
supreme lord Shaohao and the divine being Rushou. Forty-six days after
the summer solstice, welcome autumn in the western hall. Located at
nine *li* from the ruler's domain, the hall is nine *chi* in height and has nine
steps leading up to it. It has nine white chariots, with banners in the
privileged color white, and hunting carts loaded with weapons. Call out:
"Assist Heaven in harvesting." Use *shang* as the lead tone in your chanting, and dance using shield and axe. This is the music for welcoming
autumn.

The first month of autumn. The ruler resides in the left chamber of the 7.2.11
Hall of Comprehensive Luminosity. He tastes the grain and sacrifices a
dog. Supplemental sacrifices are carried out in the *kun* corner. His
speech must be coherent, and the corresponding blessing is timely spells
of sunshine.[18] These are the ordinances of the first day: be careful as you
apply the law, prevent robbers and thieves, prohibit evil deeds, discipline
your officials, carefully gather and store. Its prohibition: do not relax
your defensive measures.

The second month of autumn. The ruler resides in the main chamber 7.2.12
of the Hall of Comprehensive Luminosity. He first offers the liver. The
tablet of the main god is established at the gate; supplemental sacrifices
are carried out at the *dui* position.[19] These are the ordinances of the first
day: be cautious in building ostentatious projects, block the irrigation
canals, repair granaries and storehouses, preside over lawsuits, hurry to
gather the harvest. Its prohibitions: do not engage in offensive wars, do not
belittle the hundred surnames, do not embellish the city walls, do not
invade neighboring territories. Then allow people to hunt and feast;
make all commoners take shelter in their lodgings. Announce: "The
season of killing is upon us; do not trouble yourself with planting."

The third month of autumn. The ruler resides in the right chamber of the 7.2.13
Hall of Comprehensive Luminosity. For offerings, he uses birds from
the hunt. Supplemental sacrifices are carried out in the *qian* corner.[20]
These are the ordinances of the first day: open up roads, guard the ward
gates, display weapons and armor, admonish the officials, punish the
lawless, open up roads and construct bridges to benefit the farmers.

---

17 "Flowing Sands" is also mentioned in the First Emperor's stele at Langye; see Kern 2000b, 33.
18 Cf. 7.1.3.
19 One of the eight trigrams, located due west of the center.
20 One of the eight trigrams, located in the northwest; it is also associated with the first month of winter. See 7.2.15.

7.2.14 北方之極。自丁令北至積雪之野,帝顓頊,神玄冥司之。自秋分數四十六日,迎冬于北堂,距邦六里,堂高六尺,堂階六等,黑稅六乘,旌旄尚黑,田車載甲鐵。號曰:「助天誅。」倡之以羽,舞之以干戈,此迎冬之樂也。

7.2.15 孟冬之月,御玄堂左(介)〔个〕,祈年用牲,索祀于乾隅,聽必聰,厥休時寒。朔令曰:申群禁,修障塞,畢積聚,繫牛馬,收澤賦。其禁毋作淫巧。

7.2.16 仲冬之月,御玄堂正室,牲先腎,設主于井,索祀于坎正。朔令曰:搜外徒,止夜禁,誅詐偽,省醞釀,謹閉關。其禁簡宗廟,不禱祠,廢祭祀,逆天時。乃令民罷土功。

7.2.17 季冬之月,御玄堂右(介)〔个〕,薦用魚,索祀于艮隅。朔令曰:省牲牷,修農器,收秸薪,築囹圄,謹蓋藏。乃大儺以襀疾,命國為酒,以合三族,君子說[3],小人樂。

---

3 說=悅.

The border zone of the northern region stretches from Dingling northward to the region of accumulated snow. It is presided over by the supreme lord Zhuanxu and the divine being Xuanming. Forty-six days after the autumn equinox, welcome winter in the northern hall. Located at six *li* from the ruler's domain, the hall is six *chi* in height and has six steps leading up to it. There are six black chariots, with banners in the privileged color black, and hunting carts loaded with armor. Call out: "Assist Heaven in punishing." Use *yu* as the lead tone in chanting; dance using shield and spear. This is the music for welcoming winter.

7.2.14

The first month of winter. The ruler resides in the left chamber of the Dark Hall. Use sacrificial animals to pray for the new year. Supplemental sacrifices are carried out in the *qian* corner. Your hearing must be sharp, and the corresponding blessing is timely cold.[21] These are the ordinances of the first day: enforce all prohibitions, repair barricades, complete storage of the harvest, tie up cattle and horses, collect taxes on marshes. Its prohibition: do not engage in excessive craftiness.

7.2.15

The second month of winter. The ruler resides in the main chamber of the Dark Hall. He first offers the kidney. The tablet of the main god is established at the well; supplemental sacrifices are carried out in the *kan* position.[22] These are the ordinances of the first day: capture fugitives, enforce curfews, punish fraud, reduce the brewing of alcohol, cautiously close the passes. Its prohibitions: do not be frugal toward the ancestors, do not stop offerings at the altar, do not abolish sacrifices, do not go against Heaven's seasons. Allow people to stop construction.

7.2.16

The last month of winter. The ruler resides in the right chamber of the Dark Hall. He offers fish. Supplemental sacrifices are to be carried out in the *gen* corner. These are the ordinances of the first day: be frugal with sacrificial animals of pure color, repair agricultural tools, collect stalks and firewood, construct prisons, carefully preserve stored goods. Hold a great exorcism ritual in order to drive away pestilence, and order each domain to prepare the wine to unify the three clans. The noble man will take delight; the petty person will be merry.

7.2.17

---

21   Cf. 7.1.5.
22   One of the eight trigrams, located due north of the center.

7.2.18 田獵不宿,飲食不享,出入不節,奪民農時,及有姦謀,則**木**不**曲直**。
棄法律,逐功臣,殺太子,以妾為妻,則**火**不**炎上**。
治宮室,飾臺榭,內淫亂,犯親戚,侮父兄,則**稼穡**不成。
好攻戰,輕百姓,飾城郭,侵邊竟,則**金**不**從革**。
簡宗廟,不禱祠,廢祭祀,逆天時,則**水**不**潤下**[4]。

---

4   Cf. *Shangshu zhuzi suoyin* 32/27/10–11 (洪範).

If you hunt outside of the season, eat and drink without the appropriate offerings, enter and leave without restraint, deprive the people of their farming season, or condone conspiracies,[23] wood will not curve or straighten.[24]

If you abandon laws and regulations, exile meritorious ministers, kill the heir apparent, or make a concubine a wife,[25] fire will not blaze up.[26]

If you construct palaces, embellish terraced buildings, display licentious behavior, violate the dictates of kinship, or offend your father or elder brothers,[27] sowing and reaping are not successful.[28]

If you indulge in offensive wars, belittle the hundred surnames, embellish the city walls, or invade neighboring territories,[29] metal will not be malleable.[30]

If you are frugal toward the ancestors, stop offerings at the altar, abolish sacrifices, or go against Heaven's seasons,[31] water will not soak down.[32]

---

23 This repeats a set of prohibitions also found in the middle month of spring (7.2.3).
24 According to the "Great Plan" chapter of the Documents, the proper function of wood is to curve and straighten; see Shangshu zhuzi suoyin 32/27/10–11.
25 This repeats a set of prohibitions also found in the middle month of summer (7.2.7).
26 According to the "Great Plan" chapter of the Documents, the proper function of fire is to blaze and ascend; see Shangshu zhuzi suoyin 32/27/10.
27 This repeats a set of prohibitions also found in the passage on the border zone of the central region (7.2.9).
28 According to the "Great Plan" chapter of the Documents, the proper function of earth is to take seeds and give crops; see Shangshu zhuzi suoyin 32/27/11.
29 This repeats a set of prohibitions also found in the middle month of autumn (7.2.12).
30 According to the "Great Plan" chapter of the Documents, the proper function of metal is to obey and change; see Shangshu zhuzi suoyin 32/27/11.
31 This repeats a set of prohibitions also found in the middle month of winter (7.2.16).
32 According to the "Great Plan" chapter of the Documents, the proper function of water is to soak and descend; see Shangshu zhuzi suoyin 32/27/11. This entire passage (7.2.18) makes explicit the link between, on the one hand, the middle month of each season and the central geographical region and, on the other hand, the language associated with each of the Five Material Resources in the "Great Plan" chapter of the Documents. It is included in Hui Dong's and Lu Jianzeng's editions, which do not carry part 3 (7.3).

7.3
鴻范五行傳下

7.3.1　子曰：「心之精神是謂**聖**[1]。」

7.3.2　晦而月見西方，謂之朓，朓則侯王其荼。朔而月見東方，謂之朒，一謂之側匿，側匿則侯王其肅。

7.3.3　北**辰**[2]謂之燿魄。

7.3.4　地者、成萬物者也。

1　Cf. *Shangshu zhuzi suoyin* 32/27/13 (洪範).
2　Cf. *Shangshu zhuzi suoyin* 32/27/15 (洪範).

7.3
Tradition on the Great Plan's Five Phases, Part 3

The master said: "When the heart becomes quintessential and numinous, this is what is called 'sagacity.'"	7.3.1
When, on the last day of the lunar month, the moon is visible in the west, this is called "hurriedness." When there is "hurriedness," lords and kings move slowly. When, on the first day of the lunar month, the moon is visible in the east, this is called "delay." Some also call it "retardation." When there is retardation, lords and kings act hurriedly.[1]	7.3.2
The Pole Star is also called the Bright and Shining Star.	7.3.3
Earth is what completes the myriad things.	7.3.4

---

[1] When the moon—which stands for the ministers—moves faster than it should, the sun—which stands for the rulers (here "lords and kings")—appears to move too slowly. The reverse is true when the moon moves too slowly, that is, it has not disappeared on the first day of the lunar month. "Treatise on the Five Phases" in *Book of Han* ascribes this same fragment (with minor variations) to Jing Fang's 京房 *Traditions on the Changes* (*Yizhuan* 易傳) and provides an explanation by Liu Xiang 劉向; see *Hanshu* 27C.1506. Note that, according to Pi Xirui, the fragment was associated with the *Great Commentary* at least since Li Shan's commentary to *Selections of Refined Literature* and also in *Imperial Readings Compiled in the Taiping Era*; SSDZSZ 4.3b (741) and 4.4a (742). We draw on Liu Xiang's explanation in our translation.

7.3.5 天一生**水**,地二生**火**,天三生**木**,地四生**金**,地六成**水**,天七成**火**,地八成**木**,天九成**金**,天五生**土**[3]。

7.3.6 人君嫉賢疾[4]善,在下謀上,則日蝕雨雹,殺走獸。君道虧,則日蝕,人憤怨,則水涌溢;陰氣積,則下伐上。

7.3.7 正月雷微動而雉雊。雷、諸侯之象也,雉、亦人君之類也。

7.3.8 雷與[5]天地為長子,以其首長萬物,與其出入也。
　　　霜者、殺伐之表。
　　　雨雪者、陰之蓄積甚者也。
　　　雲者、起於山,彌於天,陰也。王者失中,臣下敢蔽君明,則雲陰象多蔽天光,有雲如象,謂風師,法有大兵。
　　　風屬中央,**雨**[6]屬東方。

---

[3] Cf. *Shangshu zhuzi suoyin* 32/27/10-11 (洪範). 天五生土 = 地十成土: *Liji zhushu* 283.2.
[4] 疾 = 嫉。
[5] 與 = 於: *Nan Qi shu*, 19.371.
[6] Cf. *Shangshu zhuzi suoyin* 32/28/11-15, 32/28/17-32/29/1 (洪範).

When Heaven is one, it gives birth to water. When Earth is two, it gives birth to fire. When Heaven is three, it gives birth to wood. When Earth is four, it gives birth to metal. When Earth is six, it completes water. When Heaven is seven, it completes fire. When Earth is eight, it completes wood. When Heaven is nine, it completes metal. When Heaven is five, it gives birth to Earth.[2]

7.3.5

When the ruler resents the worthy and the good, when those below plot against those above, then there will be an eclipse of the sun and hail storms that kill the legged animals.[3] When the way of the ruler is deficient, then there will be an eclipse of the sun. When people's anger spouts forward, the rivers overflow. When yin vapor accumulates, those below will attack those above.[4]

7.3.6

In the first month, there is a stirring of thunder, and the pheasant calls. Thunder signifies the regional lords; also, the pheasant is of the kind of the ruler.

7.3.7

Thunder is the eldest son of Heaven and Earth. This is because it initiates the process by which the myriad things grow and enters and exits together with them.
    Frost indicates killing and attack.
    Rain and snow are the profound accumulation of yin.
    Clouds rise up in the mountains and fill the skies; they are yin's vapor. When the king loses his central position, and the ministers below dare to obscure their lord's brightness, then clouds arise. When yin-type phenomena dominate and block the sky's light and clouds form in correspondence with these phenomena, this indicates the appearance of the wind gods, and a large-scale military conflict should arise.[5]
    Wind is associated with the center, and rain is associated with the east.

7.3.8

---

2   "Appended Phrases to the *Changes*" (Xici 繫辭) has a passage that associates the five odd numbers with Heaven and the five even numbers with earth. *Zhouyi zhuzi suoyin* 65/79/26. "Appended Phrases to the *Changes*" does not make the link between those numbers and the Five Phases. The *Great Commentary* does, and so do later commentators to "Appended Phrases to the *Changes*" such as Zheng Xuan; see *Liji zhushu* 283.2.
3   See parallel passage in *Book of Han*; *Hanshu* 27C.1480.
4   See 7.1.7.
5   *Book of Han* includes a prognostication (*zhan* 占) related to a weather pattern of 74 BCE that is very similar to these lines. It reads: "When the clouds form like an assembly of winds, this indicates the appearance of the wind gods, and a large-scale military conflict should arise" 有雲如眾風，是謂風師，法有大兵. *Hanshu* 26.1307.

7.3.9　清而明者天之體。
　　　　地不滿東南,故水潦塵埃歸焉。地者、成萬物者也。

7.3.10　日者、陽德之母。陽外發,故日以晝明,名曰曜靈。
　　　　月、群陰之宗,光內影,以宵曜,名曰夜光。
　　　　月生三日謂之霸[7]。
　　　　心之大**星**、天王也;其前**星**、太子也;後**星**[8]、庶子也。

7.3.11　**辰星**[9]者、北方水精也。

7.3.12　明王踐位,則日儷其精,重光以見吉祥。

7.3.13　季夏可以大赦罪人。

7.3.14　沙麓[10]者、山林也。

7　霸＝魄: Hanshu 21B.1015.
8　Cf. *Shangshu zhuzi suoyin* 32/27/15, 32/28/15-32/29/1 (洪範).
9　Cf. *Shangshu zhuzi suoyin* 32/27/15, 32/28/17-32/29/1 (洪範).
10　麓＝鹿: *Chunqiu zuozhuan zhuzi suoyin* A5.14.3/87/12.

What is pure and clear is Heaven's body. 7.3.9

Earth became empty in the southeast. The watery floods and mounding soils subsided in that direction.[6] Earth is that which completes the myriad things.

The sun is the mother of the yang force. Yang emits outward; therefore, the sun shines during the day. Its name is "bright spirit." 7.3.10

The moon is the ancestor of conglomerated yin; its light casts internal shadows. It is bright at night and is called "light of the night."

For three days after the moon becomes visible, it is called "dim."

The main star in Heart is the heavenly king.[7] The star that precedes it is the heir apparent; the stars that follows it are the princes.[8]

Mercury is the water essence of the northern region.[9] 7.3.11

When an enlightened king assumes his position, the sun's essence pairs itself with him. With this double source of light, there will be auspiciousness. 7.3.12

In the last month of summer, it is permissible to issue a large-scale amnesty for criminals. 7.3.13

Shalu is a forested mountain.[10] 7.3.14

---

6   This is a reference to the story of the fight between Gong Gong 共工 and Zhuanxu 顓頊 that caused the pillar linking Heaven and Earth to collapse. As a result, Heaven tilted to the northwest, and Earth sloped down toward the southeast. The story appears in *Master of Huainan* and includes the passage found here in the *Great Commentary*. We follow John S. Major's translation. *Huainanzi zhuzi suoyin* 3/18/25–26; Major et al. 2010, 115.
7   Heart is the fifth lunar lodge, containing three stars (σ, τ, α Scorpii). The Heavenly King is probably Antares (Alpha Scorpii)—the Fire Star of the Chinese tradition—leaving the two remaining stars (Sigma Scorpii and Tau Scorpii) for the heir apparent and the prince. See Pankenier 2013, 73.
8   *Scribe's Records* also uses the term "Heavenly King" in its description of Heart: "Heart corresponds to the Devotional Hall. Its large star is Heavenly King; the stars in front and behind it are the sons" 心為明堂，大星天王，前後星子屬; *Shiji* 27.1295. Sima Zhen's commentary uses the detail provided in the "Tradition on the Great Plan's Five Phases" passage to explain *Scribe's Records*. Pankenier integrates the commentary into his translation of the *Scribe's Records* passage; Pankenier 2013, 461.
9   The association of the planet Mercury with the north and with water is well attested; a similar passage occurs in *Shiji* 27.1327; trans. Pankenier 2013, 486.
10 Mount Shalu, in Han times located in Wei 魏 commandery, was written about in the *Chunqiu*, where it is said to have collapsed in the fourteenth year of Lord Xi 僖 (646 BCE). The memory of that event became important to Wang Mang: he claimed that, at the arrival of one of his ancestors (Wang He 王賀 or Wang Wengru 翁孺) in the Shalu area earlier in Western Han, a local elder referred to the collapse of Mount Shalu to predict the rise of a female sage eighty years later. This, according to Wang Mang, was his aunt, Wang Zhengjun 政君 (71 BCE–13 CE), also known as Empress Dowager Wang. See *Chunqiu zhuzi suoyin* A5.14.3/87/12; *Hanshu* 98.4013–14.

7.3.15　長狄之人，長蓋五丈餘也。

7.3.16　凡有所害謂之災，無所害而異於常，謂之異。害為已至，異為方來。

7.3.17　蓍之為言耆也。百年一本生百莖，此艸木之壽，亦知吉凶[11]者。聖人以問鬼神。

7.3.18　夫握方諸之鏡，處深澤之下，而上引太清，物類相隨，可不慎耶。

11　Cf. *Shangshu zhuzi suoyin* 32/28/8–13 (洪範).

Members of the Tall Di could be more than five *zhang* tall.[11] 7.3.15

Generally, what is harmful is called "a disaster." What is not harmful but deviates from the norm is called "an anomaly." A disaster bespeaks what has already arrived; an anomaly speaks to the future.[12] 7.3.16

Milfoil (*s-kij) means old age (*[g]rij).[13] It takes one hundred years for one root to generate one hundred stalks. Amongst grasses and trees, it is considered long-lived. It can also tell good fortune from bad fortune. The sages use it to make inquiries with the ghosts and spirits. 7.3.17

Holding a square receptacle basin and standing as low as the level of a deep body of water, one can draw great clarity from above.[14] This is because things of the same kind follow one another. One should take heed of this! 7.3.18

---

11 The Tall Di are invoked in the Gongyang and Guliang commentaries to an event reported for 616 BCE, the eleventh year of Lord Wen 文 (r. 626–609 BCE). "Treatise on the Five Phases" in *Book of Han* provides divergent late Western Han interpretations of the significance of the Tall Di, some of which are clearly in line with the interpretations provided in part 1 of "Tradition on the Great Plan's Five Phases." See *Gongyang zhuan zhuzi suoyin* 6.11.6/66/7; *Chunqiu gongyang zhushu* 11.137b; *Chunqiu Guliang zhushu* 11.108; *Hanshu* 27C(A).1471. Five *zhang* of Han times is equivalent to 11.5 meters.

12 This is an important fragment for the Chinese theory of omens; see the discussion in *Comprehensive Discussions in White Tiger Hall*. *Baihu tong shuzheng* 6:268.

13 This is a pun. The two characters are both orthographically and phonetically very close.

14 This sentence seems to conflate (1) the reference in *Master of Huainan* to a square receptacle (*fang zhu* 方諸) with which adepts collected the dew and (2) the reference in *Rituals of Zhou* to a basin (*jian* 鑒) with which water was extracted from the moon; *Huainanzi zhuzi suoyin* 3/19/9; Major 1993, 65–66; *Zhouli zhuzi suoyin* 5.35/72/12.

Appendix

Chapter Titles in the *Great Commentary* and in the *Documents*

This appendix compares chapter titles and their order in two editions of the *Great Commentary* and two editions of the *Documents*. The English translation of a chapter title is only given at first occurrence. It is not repeated in cases when there is only orthographic variation between characters in a chapter title; when the variation is phonetic, the translation is given. The numbers are either provided in the editions in question (*SSDZZZSY* and *Shangshu zhuzi suoyin*) or reflect the order of the chapters in the other two editions (*SSDZSZ* and Qu Wanli 1983).

Great Commentary in 36 chapters (Wang Kaiyun's edition, *SSDZZZSY*)	*Great Commentary* in 30 chapters (Pi Xirui's edition, *SSDZSZ*)
1.1 Canon of Yao 堯典	1 堯典
2.1 Nine Offers 九共	2 九共
2.2 Gaoyao's Counsel 咎繇謨	3 皋陶謨
3.1 Tribute of Yu 禹貢	4 禹貢
3.2 Oath at Gan 甘誓	
4.1 Proclamation of the Supreme Lord 帝告	5 帝告
4.2 Tang's Oath 湯誓	6 湯誓
4.3 Pangeng 般庚	7 般庚
4.4 Charge to Yue 說命	
4.5 Gaozong's Supplementary Sacrifice 高宗肜日	8 高宗肜日
4.6 Admonitions to Gaozong 高宗之訓	
4.7 The Prince of the West Attacks Qi 西伯戡耆	9 西伯戡耆
	10 Weizi 微子
5.1 Great Oath 大誓	11 大誓
5.2 Success through Battle 武成	12 Great War 大戰
5.3 Great Plan 鴻范	13 洪範
5.4 Great Proclamation 大誥	15 大誥
5.5 Metal Coffer 金滕	16 金滕
5.6 Charge to Prince Wei 微子之命	
5.7 Praising the Millet 嘉禾	17 嘉禾
5.8 Proclamation to Kang 康誥	18 康誥
5.9 Proclamation on Drink 酒誥	19 酒誥
5.10 Catalpa Wood 梓材	20 梓材
5.11 Proclamation of/to Shao 召誥	21 召誥

New Script *Documents* in 28 chapters (Qu Wanli's 1983 edition)	Transmitted *Documents* in 58 chapters (*Shangshu zhuzi suoyin*)
1 堯典	1 堯典
	2 Canon of Shun 舜典
2 皋陶謨	3 Great Yu's Counsel 大禹謨
	4 皋陶謨
	5 Supplementary Sacrifices 益稷
3 禹貢	6 禹貢
4 甘誓	7 甘誓
5 湯誓	10 湯誓
6 盤庚	18 盤庚上
	19 盤庚中
	20 盤庚下
	21 說命上
	22 說命中
	23 說命下
7 高宗肜日	24 高宗肜日
8 The Prince of the West Attacks Li 西伯戡黎	25 西伯戡黎
9 微子	26 微子
	27 大誓上
	28 大誓中
	29 大誓下
	31 武成
11 洪範	32 洪範
13 大誥	35 大誥
12 金縢	34 金縢
	36 微子之命
14 康誥	37 康誥
15 酒誥	38 酒誥
16 梓材	39 梓材
17 召誥	40 召誥

Great Commentary in 36 chapters (Wang Kaiyun's edition, *SSDZZZSY*)	*Great Commentary* in 30 chapters (Pi Xirui's edition, *SSDZSZ*)
5.12 Proclamation on Luo 雒誥	22 洛誥
5.13 Many Officers 多士	23 多士
5.14 Do Not Slack 毋佚	24 毋逸
5.15 King Cheng's Government 成王政	
5.16 Proclamation at Yan 揜誥	25 揜誥
5.17 Many Regions 多方	26 多方
5.18 Testamentary Charge 顧命	
5.19 King Kang's Proclamation 康王之誥	
5.20 Charge to Jiong 蔡命	27 蔡命
5.21 Oath at Xian 鮮誓	28 鮮誓
5.22 Punishments of Fu 甫刑	29 甫刑
6 Principal Teachings 略說	30 略說
7 Tradition on the Great Plan's Five Phases 鴻范五行傳	14 洪範五行傳

New Script *Documents* in 28 chapters (Qu Wanli's 1983 edition)	Transmitted *Documents* in 58 chapters (*Shangshu zhuzi suoyin*)
18 洛誥	41 洛誥
19 多士	42 多士
20 無逸	43 無逸
22 多方	46 多方
24 顧命	50 顧命
	51 康王之誥
	54 冏命
25 Oath at Bi 費誓	57 費誓
26 Punishments of Lü 呂刑	55 呂刑
10 Oath at Mu 誓	30 牧誓
21 Lord Shi 君奭	44 君奭
23 Establishment of the Administration 立政	47 立政
27 Lord Wen's Charge 文侯之命	56 文侯之命
28 Oath at Qin 秦誓	58 秦誓
	8 Song of Five Princes 五子之歌
	9 Yin's Campaign 胤征
	11 Proclamation of Zhong Hui 仲虺之誥
	12 Proclamation of Tang 湯誥
	13 Admonitions of Yi 伊訓
	14 Taijia 太甲上
	15 太甲中
	16 太甲下
	17 All-Encompassing Virtue 咸有一德
	33 Hounds of Lü 旅獒
	45 Charge to Cai Zhong 蔡仲之命
	48 Officers of Zhou 周官
	49 Jun Chen 君陳
	52 Charge to Bi 畢命
	53 Jun Ya 君牙

Bibliography

CRITICAL EDITIONS OF *SHANGSHU DAZHUAN*

SSDZBZ   *Shangshu dazhuan buzhu* 尚書大傳補注. Compiled by
            Wang Kaiyun 王闓運 (1833–1916). Preface 1885. 7 *juan*.
            In *Xuxiu Siku quanshu* 續修四庫全書, vol. 55, 797–844.
            Shanghai: Shanghai Guji, 2002.
SSDZJJ   *Shangshu dazhuan jijiao* 尚書大傳輯校. Compiled by
            Chen Shouqi 陳壽祺 (1771–1834). 3 *juan*. In *Huang Qing
            jingjie xubian* 皇清經解續編, vol. 6, *juan* 354–56, 4113–
            52. Taipei: Yiwen, 1965 [1796].
SSDZSZ   *Shangshu dazhuan shuzheng* 尚書大傳疏證. Compiled
            by Pi Xirui 皮錫瑞 (1850–1908). Prefaces by Pi Xirui in
            1895 and by Xiang Jingzhuang in 1896. 7 *juan*. In *Xuxiu
            Siku quanshu*, vol. 55, 697–794. Shanghai: Shanghai Guji,
            1995–.
SSDZZZSY   *Shangshu dazhuan zhuzi suoyin* 尚書大傳逐字索引 /*A
            Concordance to the Shangshu dazhuan*. With punctua-
            tion by D. C. Lau 劉殿爵. 7 *juan*. ICS Ancient Chinese
            Texts Concordance Series. Hong Kong: Shangwu, 1994.

OTHER EDITIONS OF *SHANGSHU DAZHUAN*

Chen Shouqi 陳壽祺 (1771–1834). *Shangshu dazhuan* 尚書大傳. Preface by
  Chen Shouqi, 1796. 5 *juan*. In *Sibu congkan chubian* 四部叢刊初編, vols.
  44–45. Shanghai: Hanfenlou, 1922 [1796].
Dong Fengyuan 董豐垣 (fl. 1738–44). *Shangshu dazhuan* 尚書大傳. Prefaces
  by Dong Cong 董熜 (1680–1747) in 1738 and 1744. 3 *juan*. National Library,
  Beijing.

Hui Dong 惠棟 (1697–1758), with corrections by Weng Fanggang 翁方綱 (1733–1818). *Shangshu dazhuan* 尚書大傳. 4 *juan*. Manuscript. 18th century. National Library, Beijing.

Kong Guanglin 孔廣林 (1745–1814). *Shangshu dazhuan* 尚書大傳. Cited in 1796. 4 *juan*. Shandong Shuju edition. 1890. National Library, Beijing.

Lu Jianzeng 盧見曾 (1690–1768), supplemented by Lu Wenchao 盧文弨 (1717–96). *Shangshu dazhuan* 尚書大傳. Prefaces by Lu Jianzeng in 1756/1757 and Lu Wenchao. 4 *juan*. National Library, Beijing.

Ren Zhaolin 任兆麟 (fl. 1780s). *Shangshu dazhuan* 尚書大傳. In *Yilin shuji* 藝林述記. Prefaces by Chu Yinliang 褚寅亮 (1715–90) in 1787, Wang Mingsheng 王鳴盛 (1722–97) in 1788, and Ren Zhaolin. 1810. National Library, Beijing.

Sun Zhilu 孫之騄 (fl. 1722–35). *Shangshu dazhuan* 尚書大傳. 3 *juan*. In *Siku quanshu*, vol. 68.

Wang Renjun 王仁俊 (1866–1913). *Shangshu dazhuan yiwen buji* 尚書大傳佚文補遺. In *Yuhan shanfang jiyishu xubian* 玉函山房輯佚書續編, 350–56. 1894. Shanghai: Shanghai Guji, 1989.

Yao Dongsheng 姚東昇 (1782–1835). *Shangshu dazhuan* 尚書大傳. In *Yishu shicun* 佚書拾存. Manuscript. National Library, Beijing.

Yuan Jun 袁鈞 (1751–1805). *Shangshu dazhuan* 尚書大傳. Preface 1795. In *Zheng shi yishu* 鄭氏佚書. Hangzhou: Zhejiang Shuju, 1888. National Library, Beijing.

PRIMARY SOURCES

Baihu tong zhuzi suoyin 白虎通逐字索引/*A Concordance to the Baihutong*. ICS Ancient Chinese Texts Concordance Series. Hong Kong: Shangwu, 1995.

Chongkan Song ben Shisanjing zhushu 重刊宋本十三經注疏. Ruan Yuan 阮元 (1764–1849). Taipei: Yiwen Yinshuguan, 1965 (1815 Nanchang Fu Xue 南昌府學 edition); incorporated in Scripta Sinica, Hanji dianzi wenxian ziliaoku 漢籍電子文獻資料庫 (hanji.sinica.edu.tw).

Chongwen zongmu 崇文總目. Comp. Wang Yaochen 王堯臣 (100–1058). In *Houzhibuzuzhai congshu* 後知不足齋叢書, comp. Bao Tingjue 鮑廷爵, book case 4. Changshu Houzhibuzuzhai edition, 1882. National Library, Beijing.

Chongxiu Yupian 重修玉篇. Gu Yewang 顧野王 (519–81), supplemented by Sun Qiang 孫強, et al.; comp. Chen Pengnian 陳彭年 (961–1017). In *Siku quanshu*, vol. 224, 1–241.

Chunqiu Gongyang zhushu 春秋公羊註疏. Xu Yan 徐彥 (7th c.). Reprinted in *Chongkan Song ben Shisanjing zhushu*.

Chunqiu Guliang zhushu 春秋穀梁註疏. Yang Shixun 楊士勳 (7th c.). Reprinted in *Chongkan Song ben Shisanjing zhushu*.

Chunqiu zhuzi suoyin 春秋逐字索引/*A Concordance to the Chunqiu*. ICS Ancient Chinese Texts Concordance Series. Hong Kong: Shangwu, 1995.

Chunqiu zuozhuan zhuzi suoyin 春秋左傳逐字索引/*A Concordance to the Chunqiu Zuozhuan*. ICS Ancient Chinese Texts Concordance Series. Hong Kong: Shangwu, 1995.

Da Dai Liji zhuzi suoyin 大戴禮記逐字索引/*A Concordance to the Dadai Liji*. ICS Ancient Chinese Texts Concordance Series. Hong Kong: Shangwu, 1992.

Fayan 法言. Yang Xiong 楊雄 (53 BCE–18 CE). Bilingual edition with English translation and notes by Michael Nylan: *Exemplary Figures*. Seattle: University of Washington Press, 2013.

Fengsu tongyi zhuzi suoyin 風俗通義逐字索引/*A Concordance to the Fengsu tongyi*. ICS Ancient Chinese Texts Concordance Series. Hong Kong: Shangwu, 1996.

Fu cheng 伏乘. Chen Feisheng 陳蜚聲 (1864–1945). 19 *juan*. Beijing: Xueyuan, 2007. Facsimile of Shihuyuan Dingshi 十笏園丁氏 edition (1925).

Gongyang zhuan zhuzi suoyin 公羊傳逐字索引/*A Concordance to the Gongyangzhuan*. ICS Ancient Chinese Texts Concordance Series. Hong Kong: Shangwu, 1995.

Gu lienü zhuan zhuzi suoyin 古列女傳逐字索引/*A Concordance to the Gu lienü zhuan*). ICS Ancient Chinese Texts Concordance Series. Hong Kong: Shangwu, 1993.

Gu wei shu 古微書. Sun Jue 孫瑴 (1585–1643). In *Siku quanshu*, vol. 194.

Hanfeizi zhuzi suoyin 韓非子逐字索引/*A Concordance to the Hanfeizi*. ICS Ancient Chinese Texts Concordance Series. Hong Kong: Shangwu, 2000.

Han shijing jicun 漢石經集存. 2 vols. Annotated and translated by Ma Heng 馬衡 (1881–1955); edited by Zhongguo Kexueyuan Kaogu Yanjiu Suo 中國科學院考古研究所. Beijing: Kexue, 1957.

Han Yiwenzhi kaozheng 漢藝文志考證. Wang Yinglin 王應麟 (1223–96). Appended to *Yuhai*, vol. 6.

Hanshi waizhuan zhuzi suoyin 韓詩外傳逐字索引/*A Concordance to the Hanshi waizhuan*. ICS Ancient Chinese Texts Concordance Series. Hong Kong: Shangwu, 1993.

Hanshu 漢書. Ban Gu 班固 (32–92). 12 vols. Beijing: Zhonghua, 1962.

Hou Hanshu 後漢書. Fan Ye 范曄 (398–446 CE) et al. 90 *juan*, 30 *zhi* (12 vols.). Beijing: Zhonghua, 1965.

Huainanzi zhuzi suoyin 淮南子逐字索引/*A Concordance to the Huainanzi*. ICS Ancient Chinese Texts Concordance Series. Hong Kong: Shangwu, 1993.

Jingdian shiwen 經典釋文. Lu Deming 陸德明 (556–627). 3 vols. Shanghai: Shanghai Guji, 1985.

Jingxue lishi 經學歷史. Pi Xirui 皮錫瑞 (1850–1908). Annot. Zhou Yutong 周予同. Beijing: Zhonghua, 1959.

Jingyi kao 經義考. Zhu Yizun 朱彝尊 (1629–1709). In *Siku quanshu*, vols. 677–80.

Jingyi shuwen 經義述聞. Wang Yinzhi 王引之 (1766–1834). In *Xuxiu Siku quanshu* 續修四庫全書, 174.247–175.369. Shanghai: Shanghai Guji, 1995–.

Jinwen Shangshu kaozheng 今文尚書考證. Pi Xirui 皮錫瑞 (1850–1908). Beijing: Zhonghua, 1989.

Jiu Tangshu 舊唐書. Liu Xu 劉昫 (887–946). Beijing: Zhonghua, 1975.

Junzhai dushu zhi jiaozheng 郡齋讀書志校証. Chao Gongwu 晁公武 (1105–80). Annot. Sun Meng 孫猛. Shanghai: Shanghai, 1990.

Jūshū isho shūsei 重修緯書集成. Vol. 2. Ed. Yasui Kozan 安居香山 and Nakamura Shohachi 中村璋八. Tokyo: Meitoku, 1975.

Kong congzi zhuzi suoyin 孔叢子逐字索引/*A Concordance to the Kong congzi*. ICS Ancient Chinese Texts Concordance Series. Hong Kong: Shangwu, 1998.

Kunxue jiwen 困學紀聞. Wang Yinglin 王應麟 (1223–96). Annot. Weng Yuanqi 翁元圻. 3 vols. Shanghai: Shanghai Guji, 2008.

Liji zhushu 禮記注疏 (a.k.a. *Liji zhengyi* 禮記正義). Annot. Kong Yingda 孔穎達 (574–648). Reprinted in *Chongkan Song ben Shisan jing zhushu*.

Liji zhuzi suoyin 禮記逐字索引/*A Concordance to the Liji*. ICS Ancient Chinese Texts Concordance Series. Hong Kong: Shangwu, 1993.

Liuyi liubie 六藝流別. Huang Zuo 黃佐 (1490–1566). Preface 1531; 1687 reprint. Harvard-Yenching Library.

Lunheng zhuzi suoyin 論衡逐字索引/*A Concordance to the Lunheng*. ICS Ancient Chinese Texts Concordance Series. Hong Kong: Shangwu, 1996.

Lunyu zhushu 論語注疏. Annot. Xing Bing 邢昺 (932–1010). Beijing: Zhonghua, 2009.

Lüshi chunqiu zhuzi suoyin 呂氏春秋逐字索引/*A Concordance to the Lüshi Chunqiu*. ICS Ancient Chinese Texts Concordance Series. Hong Kong: Shangwu, 1994.

Maoshi zhushu 毛詩注疏 (a.k.a. *Maoshi zhengyi* 毛詩正義). Annot. Kong Yingda 孔穎達 (574–648). Reprinted in *Chongkan Song ben Shisan jing zhushu*.

Maoshi zhuzi suoyin 毛詩逐字索引/*A Concordance to the Maoshi*. ICS Ancient Chinese Texts Concordance Series. Hong Kong: Shangwu, 1995.

Mengzi zhengyi 孟子正義. Comp. Jiao Xun 焦循 (1763–1820). 2 vols. Beijing: Zhonghua, 1987.

Mingtang dadao lu 明堂大道錄. Hui Dong 惠棟 (1697–1758). In *Congshu jicheng: chubian* 叢書集成：初編, 1035–36. Beijing: Shangwu, 1935.

Mozi zhuzi suoyin 墨子逐字索引/*A Concordance to the Mozi*. ICS Ancient Chinese Texts Concordance Series. Hong Kong: Shangwu, 2001.

Nan Qi shu 南齊書. Xiao Zixian 蕭子顯 (489–537). Beijing: Zhonghua, 1972.

Nan Song guangge luxulu. 南宋館閣錄續錄. Comp. Chen Kui 陳騤 (1128–1203); ed. and punctuated by Zhang Fuxiang 張富祥. Beijing: Zhonghua, 2008.

Pi Xirui quanji 皮錫瑞全集. Ed. Wu Yangxiang 吳仰湘. Beijing: Zhonghua, 2015.

Qinding siku quanshu zongmu (zhengli ben) 欽定四庫全書總目(整理本). Comp. Ji Yun 紀昀 (1724–1805). Beijing: Zhonghua, 1997.

Qinghua Daxue cang Zhanguo zhujian 清華大學藏戰國竹簡. Ed. Li Xueqin 李學勤. Shanghai: Zhongxi, 2010–.

Qing Pi Lumen xiansheng Xirui nianpu 清皮鹿門先生錫瑞年譜. Ed. Pi Mingzhen 皮名振 (1907–59). Taiwan: Taiwang Shangwu, 1981. *See also* Aque 2004.

Shangshu hegu 尚書覈詁. Yang Junru 楊筠如 (1903–46). Ed. Huang Huaixin 黃懷信. Xi'an: Shaanxi Renmin, 2005.

Shangshu jishi 尚書集釋. *See* Qu Wanli 1983.

Shangshu jizhu yinshu 尚書集注音疏. Jiang Sheng 江聲 (1721–99). Shanghai: Shanghai Guji, 1995–99.

Shangshu jinguwen zhushu 尚書今古文注疏. Sun Xingyan 孫星衍 (1753–1818). Beijing: Zhonghua, 1986.

Shangshu yinyi 尚書音義. In *Jingdian shiwen* 經典釋文, vol. 1.

Shangshu Kong zhuan canzheng 尚書孔傳參正. Wang Xianqian 王先謙 (1842–1917). In *Xuxiu Siku quanshu* 51:427–704.

Shangshu zhushu 尚書註疏. Annot. Kong Yingda 孔穎達 (574–648). Reprinted in *Chongkan Song ben Shisan jing zhushu*.

Shangshu zhuzi suoyin 尚書逐字索引/*A Concordance to the Shangshu*. ICS Ancient Chinese Texts Concordance Series. Hong Kong: Shangwu, 1995.

Shanhaijing zhuzi suoyin 山海經逐字索引/*A Concordance to the Shanhaijing*. ICS Ancient Chinese Texts Concordance Series. Hong Kong: Shangwu, 1994.

Shiji 史記. Sima Qian 司馬遷 (145?–86? BCE). 130 *juan* (12 vols.) Beijing: Zhonghua, 1959. *See also* Watson 1993; Chavannes 1967.

Shisanjing zhushu 十三經注疏. Annot. Ruan Yuan 阮元 (1764–1849). 245 *juan*. Beijing: Zhonghua, 1980.

Shisanjing zhushu fujiao kanji 十三經注疏附校勘記. 2 vols. Beijing: Zhonghua, 1996.

Shu guwen xun 書古文訓. Xue Jixuan 薛季宣 (1134–73). In *Xuxiu Siku quanshu* 42:225–378.

Shuijing zhushi 水經註釋. Li Daoyuan 酈道元 (d. 527). Annot. Zhao Yiqing 趙一清 (1709–64). In *Siku quanshu*.

Shuofu sanzhong 說郛三種. Tao Zongyi 陶宗儀 (1329–1410). Shanghai: Shanghai Guji, 1988.

Shuowen jiezi 說文解字. Xu Shen 許慎 (ca. 55–ca. 149). Beijing: Zhonghua, 1963.

Shuowen jiezi zhu 說文解字注. Duan Yucai 段玉裁 (1735–1815). Shanghai: Shanghai Guji (preface Jingyunlou 經韻樓, 1808), 1981 reprint.

Shuoyuan 說苑. Liu Xiang 劉向 (79–8 BCE). Bilingual edition with English translation and notes by Eric Henry: *Garden of Eloquence*. Seattle: University of Washington Press, 2022.

Shuoyuan zhuzi suoyin 說苑逐字索引/*A Concordance to the Shuoyuan*. ICS Ancient Chinese Texts Concordance Series. Hong Kong: Shangwu, 1998.

Shuyi ji 述異記. Ren Fang 任昉 (459–508). Ming Han Wei congshu 明漢魏叢書 edition, 1592.

Siku quanshu 四庫全書 Wenyuange 文淵閣 edition. 1773–84. Taipei: Taiwan Shangwu, 1983 reprint.

Siku tiyao bianzheng 四庫提要辨證. Yu Jiaxi 余嘉錫 (1884–1955). Beijing: Kexue, 1958.

Suishu 隋書. Wei Zheng 魏徵 (580–643), Zhangsun Wuji 長孫無忌 (d. 695), and Linghu Defen 令狐德棻 (583–666). 3 vols. Beijing: Zhonghua, 1973.

Taiping yulan 太平御覽. Comp. Li Fang 李昉 (925–96). In *Sibu congkan sanbian* 四部叢刊三編. Taipei: Shangwu, 1974.

Wenxian tongkao 文獻通攷. Ma Duanlin 馬端臨 (1254–1323). In *Siku quanshu*, vols. 610–16.

Wenxuan 文選. Comp. Xiao Tong 蕭統 (501–31); annot. Li Shan 李善 (630–89). 60 juan (6 vols.) Shanghai: Shanghai Guji, 1986.

Xin Tangshu 新唐書. Ouyang Xiu 歐陽修 (1007–72). Beijing: Zhonghua, 1975.

Xunzi zhuzi suoyin 荀子逐字索引/*A Concordance to the Xunzi*. ICS Ancient Chinese Texts Concordance Series. Hong Kong: Shangwu, 1993. See also Hutton 2014.

Xuxiu siku quanshu 續修四庫全書. Shanghai: Shanghai Guji, 2002.

Yangzhou huafang lu 揚州畫舫錄. Li Dou 李斗 (1949–1817). Annot. Wang Beiping 汪北平 and Tu Yugong 涂雨公. Beijing: Zhonghua, 1997.

Yili jingzhuan tongjie 儀禮經傳通解. Zhu Xi 朱熹 (1130–1200). In *Siku quanshu*, vol. 131.

Yili jingzhuan tongjie xu 儀禮經傳通解續. Yang Fu 楊復 (fl. 1228) and Huang Gan 黃榦 (1152–1221). In *Siku quanshu*, vol. 132.

Yili zhuzi suoyin 儀禮逐字索引/*A Concordance to the Yili*. ICS Ancient Chinese Texts Concordance Series. Hong Kong: Shangwu, 1994.

Yuhai 玉海. Wang Yinglin 王應麟 (1223–96). Vols. 1–6. 1883 Zhejiang Shuju edition. Reprint Shanghai: Jiangsu Guji and Shanghai Shudian, 1987.

Zheng Xuan 鄭玄 (127–200). "Xu" 序. In *Yuhai* 37.25b (708).

Zhizhai shulu jieti 直齋書錄解題. Chen Zhensun 陳振孫 (ca. 1183–after 1249). Shanghai: Shanghai Guji, 1987.

Zhouli zhushu 周禮注疏. Jia Gongyan 賈公彥 (7th c.). Reprinted in *Chongkan Song ben Shisan jing zhushu*.

Zhouli zhuzi suoyin 周禮逐字索引/*A Concordance to the Zhouli*. ICS Ancient Chinese Texts Concordance Series. Hong Kong: Shangwu, 1993.

Zhouyi zhuzi suoyin 周易逐字索引/*A Concordance to the Zhouyi*. ICS Ancient Chinese Texts Concordance Series. Hong Kong: Shangwu, 1995.

Zhuangzi zhuzi suoyin 莊子逐字索引/*A Concordance to the Zhuangzi*. ICS Ancient Chinese Texts Concordance Series. Hong Kong: Shangwu, 2000.

Zhushu jinian zhuzi suoyin 竹書紀年逐字索引/*A Concordance to the Zhushu jinian*. ICS Ancient Chinese Texts Concordance Series. Hong Kong: Shangwu, 1998.

Zuozhuan. Bilingual edition with English translation and notes by Stephen Durrant, Wai-yee Li, and David Schaberg: *Zuo Tradition / Zuozhuan: Commentary on the Spring and Autumn Annals*. Seattle: University of Washington Press, 2016.

SECONDARY SOURCES

Allan, Sarah. 1991. *The Shape of the Turtle: Myth, Art and Cosmos in Early China*. Albany: State University of New York Press.
———. 2012. "On *Shu* 書 (Documents) and the Origin of the *Shang shu* 尚書 (Ancient Documents) in Light of Recently Discovered Bamboo Slip Manuscripts." *Bulletin of the School of Oriental and African Studies* 75.3: 547–57.
Aque, Stuart V. 2004. "Pi Xirui and *Jingxue lishi*." Ph.D. dissertation, University of Washington.
Assmann, Jan. 2011. *Cultural Memory and Early Civilization: Writing, Remembrance, and Political Imagination*. New York: Cambridge University Press.
Bao Jiashu 鮑家樹. 2014. "*Fu Sheng* deng Guojia dajuyuan jinzhan qinggan yu wenhua de jueze"《伏生》登國家大劇院盡展情感與文化的抉擇. In *Souhu* 搜狐, April 17. http://yule.sohu.com/20140417/n398377638.shtml, last accessed May 11, 2018.
Barbieri-Low, Anthony J, and Robin D. S. Yates. 2015. *Law, State, and Society in Early Imperial China: A Study with Critical Edition and Translation of the Legal Texts from Zhangjiashan Tomb No. 247*. Leiden: Brill.
Baxter, William H., and Laurent Sagart. 2014. *Old Chinese: A New Reconstruction*. New York: Oxford University Press.
Bielenstein, Hans. 1980. *The Bureaucracy of Han Times*. Cambridge: Cambridge University Press.
Birrell, Anne. 1999. *The Classic of Mountains and Seas*. London: Penguin Books.
Bodde, Derk. 1975. *Festivals in Classical China: New Year and Other Annual Observances during the Han Dynasty 206 B.C.–A.D. 220*. Princeton: Princeton University Press.
Brashier, K. E. 2011. *Ancestral Memory in Early China*. Cambridge, MA: Harvard University Asia Center.
———. 2014. *Public Memory in Early China*. Cambridge, MA: Harvard University Asia Center.
Breuker, Remco. 2008. "Forging the Truth: Creative Deception and National Identity in Medieval Korea." *East Asian History* 35:1–73.
Cai Changlin 蔡長林. 2014. "Lun Zheng Xuan zai Pi Xirui jingshuo zhong de diwei" 論鄭玄在皮錫瑞經說中的地位. In *Lingnan Daxue jingxue guoji xueshu yantaohui lunwenji* 嶺南大學經學國際學術研討會論文集, ed. Li Xiongxi 李雄溪 et al., 941–58. Hong Kong: Wanjuanlou.
Cai, Liang. 2014. *Witchcraft and the Rise of the First Confucian Empire*. Albany, NY: State University of New York Press.
Cao Jianghong 曹江紅. 2012. "Hui Dong yu Lu Jianzeng mufu yanjiu" 惠棟與盧見曾幕府研究. *Zhongguo shi yanjiu* 中國史研究 1:177–95.
Chavannes, Édouard. 1967. *Les mémoires historiques de Se-ma Ts'ien, traduits et annotés par Édouard Chavannes*. 6 vols. Paris: A. Maisonneuve.

Chen Mengjia 陳夢家. 2005 (1957). *Shangshu tonglun* 尚書通論. Preface 1963. Beijing: Zhonghua.

Chen Tongsheng 陳桐生. 1995. *Shiji yu jin gu wen jingxue* 史記與今古文經學. In *Sima Qian yu huaxia wenhua congshu* 司馬遷與華夏文化叢書. Xi'an: Shaanxi Renmin Jiaoyu.

Chen Yang 陳揚. 2009. "Handai Fu shi yu jingxue yanjiu" 漢代伏氏與經學研究. M.A. thesis, Shandong Normal University.

Cheng Sudong 程蘇東. 2016. "*Hongfan wuxing zhuan* chengpian yu zuozhe wenti xinzheng"《洪範五行傳》成篇與作者問題新証. *Guoxue yanjiu* 國學研究 37:215–18.

———. 2022. "Liu Xiang *Hongfan* wuxing xue kaolun" 劉向〈洪範〉五行學考論. *Zhongyang Yanjiuyuan Lishi Yuyan Yanjiusuo jikan* 中央研究院歷史語言研究所集刊 93.1: 1–68.

Cheung, Martha P. Y. 2006. *An Anthology of Chinese Discourse on Translation*, vol. 1: *From Earliest Times to the Buddhist Project*. Manchester, UK: St. Jerome Publishing.

Cook, Constance, and Xinhui Luo. 2017. *Birth in Ancient China: A Study of Metaphor and Cultural Identity in Pre-Imperial China*. Albany: State University of New York Press.

Csikszentmihalyi, Mark. 2004. *Material Virtue: Ethics and the Body in Early China*. Leiden: Brill.

———. 2015. "The Social Roles of the *Annals* Classic in Late Western Han." In *Chang'an 26 BCE: An Augustan Age in China*, ed. Michael Nylan and Griet Vankeerberghen, 461–76. Seattle: University of Washington Press.

Csikszentmihalyi, Mark, and Michael Nylan. 2003. "Constructing Lineages and Inventing Traditions through Exemplary Figures in Early China." *T'oung Pao* 89.1–3: 59–99.

Cullen, Christopher. 1993. "Motivations for Scientific Change in Ancient China: Emperor Wu and the Grand Inception Astronomical Reforms of 104 B.C." *Journal for the History of Astronomy* 24.3: 185–203.

———. 1996. *Astronomy and Mathematics in Ancient China: The Zhou bi suan jing*. Cambridge, NY: Cambridge University Press.

———. 2007. "Actors, Networks, and 'Disturbing Spectacles' in Institutional Science: 2nd Century Chinese Debates on Astronomy." *Antiquorum Philosophia* 1:237–67.

Cullen, Christopher, and Anne S. L. Farrer. 1983. "On the Term Hsüan Chi and the Flanged Trilobate Jade Discs." *Bulletin of the School of Oriental and African Studies* 46.1: 52–76.

De Crespigny, Rafe. 2007. *A Biographical Dictionary of Later Han to the Three Kingdoms (23–220 AD)*. Leiden: Brill.

Di Giacinto, Licia. 2012. *The* Chenwei *Riddle: Time, Stars, and Heroes in the Apocrypha*. Gossenberg: Ostasien Verlag.

Du Jinpeng 杜金鵬 and Qian Guoxiang 錢國祥, eds. 2007. *Han Wei Luoyang cheng yizhi yanjiu* 漢魏洛陽城遺址研究. Beijing: Kexue.

Elman, Benjamin A. 1983. "Philosophy (I-Li) versus Philology (K'ao-Cheng): The Jen-Hsin Tao-Hsin Debate." *T'oung Pao* 69.4–5: 175–222.

———. 1990. *Classicism, Politics, and Kinship: The Ch'ang-chou School of New Text Confucianism in Late Imperial China*. Berkeley: University of California Press.

Eno, Robert. 2018. "The *Lunyu* as an Accretion Text." In *Confucius and the Analects Revisited: New Perspectives on Composition, Dating, and Authorship*, ed. Michael Hunter and Martin Kern, 39–66. Leiden: Brill.

Espesset, Grégoire. 2014. "Epiphanies of Sovereignty and the Rite of Jade Disc Immersion in Weft Narratives." *Early China* 37: 393–442.

———. 2015. "A Note on Chinese Portent Phenomenology and Classification in the Monographs of Han Dynasty Historiography." Invited Talk, Ruhr University, Bochum, April 29, 2015, 1–33.

———. 2016. "Sketching out Portents Classification and Logic in the Monographs of Han Official Historiography." *Bochumer Jahrbuch zur Ostasienforschung / Bochum Yearbook of East Asian Studies* 39:5–38.

Feng Haofei 馮浩菲. 1997. "*Hongfan wuxing zhuan* de xueshu tedian ji qi yingxiang: jianlun yanjiu tianren ganying shuo zhi buneng hulüe Fu Sheng" 《洪範五行傳》的學術特點及其影響—兼論研究天人感應說之不能忽略伏生. *Zhongguo wenhua yanjiu* 中國文化研究 16:37–41.

Fölster, Max Jakob. 2018. "Libraries and Archives in the Former Han Dynasty (206 BCE–9 CE): Arguing for a Distinction." In *Manuscripts and Archives: Comparative Views on Record-Keeping*, ed. Alessandro Bausi et al., 201–30. Studies in Manuscript Cultures 11. Berlin: De Gruyter.

Foster, Christopher J. 2017. "Introduction to the Peking University Han Bamboo Strips: On the Authentication and Study of Purchased Manuscripts." *Early China* 40:167–240.

Gentz, Joachim. 2001. *Das Gongyang zhuan: Auslegung und Kanonisierung der Frühlings-und Herbstannalen (Chunqiu)*. Wiesbaden: Harrassowitz.

Goldin, Paul R. 2013. "Heng Xian and the Problem of Studying Looted Artifacts." *Dao* 12:153–60.

Graham, Angus. 1989. *Disputers of the Tao: Philosophical Argument in Ancient China*. La Salle, IL: Open Court.

Grebnev, Yegor. 2016. "The Core Chapters of the *Yi Zhou shu*." Ph.D. dissertation, University of Oxford.

———. 2017. "The *Yi Zhoushu* and the *Shangshu*: The Case of Texts with Speeches." In *Origins of Chinese Political Philosophy: Studies in the Composition and Thought of the "Shangshu" (Classic of Documents)*, ed. Martin Kern and Dirk Meyer, 249–80. Leiden: Brill.

———. 2022. *Mediation of Legitimacy in Early China: A Study of the Neglected Zhou Scriptures and the Grand Duke Traditions*. New York: Columbia University Press.

Gu Guoshun 古國順. 1985. *Shiji shu Shangshu yanjiu* 史記述尚書研究. Taipei: Wenshizhe.

Gu Jiegang 顧頡剛 and Liu Qiyu 劉起釪. 2005. *Shangshu jiaoshi yilun* 尚書校釋譯論. Beijing: Zhonghua.

Gu Qian 顧遷. 2014. "Pi Xirui *Jinwen Shangshu kaozheng* shuyi" 皮錫瑞《今文尚書考證》述議. In *Di er jie "Shangshu" xue guoji xueshu yantaohui lunwen ji* 第二屆《尚書》學國際學術研討會論文集, ed. Lin Qingzhang 林慶彰 and Qian Zongwu 錢宗武, 209–22. Taipei: Wanjuan Lou.

Gu Ying 谷穎. 2005. "Fu Sheng ji *Shangshu dazhuan* yanjiu" 伏生及《尚書大傳》研究. M.A. thesis, Dongbei Normal University.

———. 2006. "Chen Shouqi shengping ji zhushu kao" 陳壽祺生平及著述攷. *Changchun Shifan xueyuan xuebao* 長春師範學院學報 25.5: 63–66.

———. 2015. "Qin boshi Fu Sheng shilüe kao" 秦博士伏生事略攷. *Dongbei Shida xuebao (zhexue shehui kexue ban)* 東北師大學報（哲学社会科学版）278.6: 135–39.

Guo Shengbo 郭聲波. 2020. "*Shiji* diming zuming cidian《史記》地名族名詞典. Beijing: Zhonghua.

Guo Weichuan 郭偉川. 2001. "Zhougong cheng wang yu Zhou chu lizhi: *Shangshu-Zhoushu* yu *Yi Zhoushu* xintan" 周公稱王與周初禮治—《尚書‧周書》與《逸周書》新探. *Huaxue* 華學 5:253–75.

Guo Xiliang 郭錫良. 2010. *Hanzi guyin shouce (zengding ben)* 漢字古音手冊（增訂本）. Beijing: Shangwu.

Guo Yi 郭沂. 2000. "Guodian zhujian yu Zhongguo zhexue (lungang)" 郭店竹簡與中國哲學（論綱）. In *Guodian chujian guoji xueshu yantaohui lunwen ji* 郭店楚簡國際學術研討會論文集, ed. Wuhan Daxue Zhongguo Wenhua Yanjiu Yuan 武漢大學中國文化研究院, 571–82. Wuhan: Wuhan Renmin.

Guojia Wenwu Ju 國家文物局, ed. 2007. *Zhongguo wenwu dituji: Shandong fence* 中國文物地圖集：山東分冊. 2 vols. Beijing: Zhongguo Ditu.

Habberstad, Luke. 2014. "The Sage and his Associates: Kongzi and Disciples across Early Texts." In *The Analects: The Simon Leys Translation, Interpretations*, trans. Simon Leys, ed. Michael Nylan, 178–92. New York and London: W. W. Norton and Company.

Han Yude 韓玉德. 1999. "Yi jingxue xing, yi guoqi wang: Han Fu Sheng jiazu xingwang shilüe" 以經學興以國戚亡：漢伏勝家族興亡史略. *Kongzi yanjiu* 孔子研究 2:114–19.

Harper, Donald John, and Marc Kalinowski, eds. 2017. *Books of Fate and Popular Culture in Early China: The Daybook Manuscripts of the Warring States, Qin, and Han*. Leiden: Brill.

He, Ruyue, and Michael Nylan. 2015. "On a Han-Era Postface (Xu 序) to the Documents." *Harvard Journal of Asiatic Studies* 75.2: 377–426.

Hou Jinman 侯金滿. 2000. "*Shangshu dazhuan* yuanliu kao"《尚書大傳》源流攷. M.A. thesis, Nanjing University.

———. 2016. "*Shangshu dazhuan* jiaodu zhaji size"《尚書大傳》校讀札記四則. *Zhongguo dianji yu wenhua* 中國典籍與文化 96.1: 128–34.

———. 2019. "Yayutang ben *Shangshu dazhuan* diben laiyuan ji chengshu kaoshi" 雅雨堂本《尚書大傳》底本來源及成書考實. *Wenshi* 文史 127.2: 27–53.

Huang Chi-shu 黃啓書. 2007. "Shi lun Liu Xiang zaiyi xueshuo zhi zhuanbian" 試論劉向災異學說之轉變. *Taida zhongwen xuebao* 臺大中文學報 2.6: 123–66.

Huang Fushan (Hung Fu-Sun) 黃復山. 1996. "Handai *Shangshu* chenwei xueshu" 漢代《尚書》讖緯學術. Ph.D. dissertation, Fu Jen Catholic University.

Huang Kaiguo 黃開國. 2000. "Jian lun Fu Sheng yu *Dazhuan*" 簡論伏生與《大傳》. *Chengdu Daxue xuebao* 成都大學學報 2:22–26.

Hunter, Michael. 2017. *Confucius beyond the Analects*. Leiden: Brill.

Hutton, Eric. 2014. *Xunzi: The Complete Text*. Princeton: Princeton University Press.

Hwang, Ming-chorng. 1996. "Ming-tang: Cosmology, Political Order and Monuments in Early China." Ph.D. dissertation, Harvard University.

Itō Michiharu 伊藤道治. 1987. *Chūgoku kodai kokka no shihai kōzō: Seishū hōken seido to kinbun* 中国古代国家の支配構造--西周封建制度と金文. Tokyo: Chūō Kōronsha.

Itō Yumi 伊藤裕水. 2020."*Shōsho daiden* to *Shōsho* kyōmon"『尚書大傳』と『尚書』經文. *Chugoku shisoshi kenkyu* 中國思想史研究 41:1–27.

Jiang Qiuhua 蔣秋華. 2013."Wang Kaiyun *Shangshu dazhuan buzhu* zhi jibu shulun" 王闓運《尚書大傳補注》之輯補述論. *Yangzhou Daxue xuebao* 揚州大學學報 17.6: 46–54.

Jiang Shanguo 蔣善國. 1988. *Shangshu zongshu* 尚書綜述. Shanghai: Shanghai Guji.

Kalinowski, Marc. 2004."Fonctionnalité calendaire dans les cosmogonies anciennes de la Chine." *Etudes chinoises* 23:87–122.

———. 2010."Divination and Astrology: Received Texts and Excavated Manuscripts." In *China's Early Empires: A Re-Appraisal*, ed. Michael Nylan and Michael Loewe, 339–66. Cambridge, UK: Cambridge University Press.

Kanaya Osamu 金谷治 (1920–2006). 1992. *Shin Kan shisōki kenkyū* 秦漢思想史研究. Tokyo: Heirakuji Shoten.

Karlgren, Bernhard. 1948."Glosses on the Book of Documents." *Bulletin of the Museum of Far Eastern Antiquities* 20:39–315.

———. 1949. "Glosses on the Book of Documents II." *Bulletin of the Museum of Far Eastern Antiquities* 21:63–206.

———. 1950. "The Book of Documents." *Bulletin of the Museum of Far Eastern Antiquities* 22:1–81.

Keightley, David N. 2014. *These Bones Shall Rise Again: Selected Writings on Early China*. Edited with an introduction by Henry Rosemont Jr. Albany: State University of New York Press.

Kern, Martin. 2000a. Review of Mark Edward Lewis, *Writing and Authority in Early China*. *China Review International* 7.2: 336–76.

———. 2000b. *The Stele Inscriptions of Ch'in Shih-huang: Text and Ritual in Early Chinese Imperial Representation*. New Haven, CT: American Oriental Society.

———. 2014. "Creating a Book and Performing It: The 'Yao Lue' Chapter of the *Huainanzi* as a Western Han Fu." In *The "Huainanzi" and Textual*

Production in Early China, ed. Sarah A. Queen and Michael Puett, 124–50. Leiden: Brill.

———. 2017. "Language and Ideology of Kingship in the 'Canon of Yao.'" In *Origins of Chinese Political Philosophy: Studies in the Composition and Thought of the "Shangshu" (Classic of Documents)*, ed. Martin Kern and Dirk Meyer, 23–61. Leiden: Brill.

Kern, Martin, and Dirk Meyer, eds. 2017. *Origins of Chinese Political Philosophy: Studies in the Composition and Thought of the "Shangshu" (Classic of Documents)*. Leiden: Brill.

Kim, Kyung-ho. 2013. "The Changing Characteristics of the *Shi* in Ancient China and Their Significance." *Sungkyun Journal of East Asian Studies* 13.2: 251–73.

Kim, Moonsil Lee. 2014. "Food Distribution during China's Qin and Han Periods: Accordance and Discordance among Ideologies, Policies, and Their Implementation." Ph.D. dissertation, University of California, Santa Barbara.

Kinney, Anne Behnke. 2014. *Exemplary Women of Early China: The "Lienü zhuan" of Liu Xiang*. New York: Columbia University Press.

Kleeman, Terry F. 1994. "Mountain Deities in China: The Domestication of the Mountain God and the Subjugation of the Mountains." *Journal of the Oriental American Society* 114.2: 226–38.

Knechtges, David. R., and Chang, Taiping, eds. 2010–14. *Ancient and Early Medieval Chinese Literature: A Reference Guide*. Leiden: Brill.

Krijgsman, Rens. 2017. "Cultural Memory and Excavated Anecdotes in 'Documentary' Narrative: Mediating Generic Tensions in the *Baoxun* Manuscript." In *Between History and Philosophy: Anecdotes in Early China*, ed. Paul van Els and Sarah A. Queen, 301–29. Albany: State University of New York Press.

Lau, D. C. 1970. *Mencius*. Harmondsworth: Penguin.

———. 1983. *Analects*. Hong Kong: Chinese University Press.

Legge, James (1815–97). 1879–1885. *The Sacred Books of the East*, vols 27–28: *The Sacred Books of China: The Texts of Confucianism*. Oxford: Clarendon Press.

———. 1939. *The Chinese Classics with a Translation, Critical and Exegetical Notes, Prolegomena, and Copious Indexes*, vol. 3: *Shu ching*. Beijing: Wen Tien Ko.

Lewis, Mark. 1999. *Writing and Authority in Early China*. Albany: State University of New York Press.

———. 2006. *The Construction of Space in Early China*. Albany: State University of New York Press.

Leys, Simon. 1997. *The Analects of Confucius*. Translation and notes by Simon Leys. New York: Norton.

Li, Feng. 2008. *Bureaucracy and the State in Early China: Governing the Western Zhou*. Cambridge, UK: Cambridge University Press.

———. 2013. *Early China: A Social and Cultural History*. Cambridge, UK: Cambridge University Press.
Li Huiling 李慧玲. 2008. "Kong Yingda *Maoshi zhengyi* zhong *Shangshu dazhuan* de yiming bianxi" 孔穎達《毛詩正義》中《尚書大傳》的異名辨析. *Shanghai Daxue xuebao* 上海大學學報 15.2: 76–80.
Li Min 李民. 1995. "*Shangshu*, 'Jinteng' de zhizuo shidai ji qi shiliao jiazhi"《尚書·金縢》的製作時代及其史料價值. *Zhongguo shi yanjiu* 中國史研究 no. 3, 109–16.
Li, Wai-yee. 2007. *The Readability of the Past in Early Chinese Historiography*. Cambridge, MA: Harvard University Asia Center.
Li Xiaoyu 李曉宇. 2008. "Wang Kaiyun shoupin Zunjing shuyuan shishi kao" 王闓運受聘尊經書院史事考. *Sichuan Daxue xuebao (zhexue shehui kexue ban)* 四川大學學報（哲學社會科學版）2: 23–27.
Li Xueqin 李學勤. 1999a. "Dui gushu de fansi" 對古書的反思. In *Dangdai xuezhe zixuan wenji: Li Xueqin* 當代學者自選文集：李學勤, 19–20. Hefei: Anhui Jiaoyu.
———. 1999b. "Guodian chujian he Ru jia jingji" 郭店楚簡和儒家經籍. *Zhongguo zhexue* 中國哲學 20:19–20.
———. 1999c. "Lun Wei Jin shiqi guwen Shangshu de chuanliu" 論魏晉時期古文尚書的傳流. In *Dangdai xuezhe zixuan wenji: Li Xueqin* 當代學者自選文集：李學勤, 633–46. Hefei: Anhui Jiaoyu.
Li Xueqin 李學勤 and Lü Wenyu 呂文郁, eds. 1996. *Siku da cidian* 四庫大辭典. Changchun: Jilin Daxue.
Li Zhenhua 李珍華 and Zhou Changji 周長楫. 1999. *Hanzi gujin yinbiao (xiuding ben)* 漢字古今音表（修訂本）. Beijing: Zhonghua.
Liao Mingchun 廖名春. 1999. "Jingmen Guodian chujian yu xian Qin Ru xue" 荊門郭店楚簡與先秦儒學. *Zhongguo zhexue* 中國哲學 20:35–74.
———. 2000. "Guodian chujian yin Shu lun Shu kao" 郭店楚簡引書論書考. In *Guodian chujian guoji xueshu yantaohui lunwenji* 郭店楚簡國際學術研討會論文集, ed. Wuhan Daxue Zhongguo Wenhua Yanjiu Yuan 武漢大學中國文化研究院, 111–27. Wuhan: Wuhan Renmin.
Liu Guangsheng 劉光勝. 2012. "Qinghua jian yu xian Qin *Shu* jing zhuan liu" 清華簡與先秦《書》經轉流. *Shixue jikan* 史學集刊 1:76–85.
Liu, Guozhong. 2016. *Introduction to the Tsinghua Bamboo-Strip Manuscripts*. Translated by Christopher Foster and William French. Leiden: Brill.
Liu, Li, and Hong Xu. 2007. "Rethinking Erlitou: Legend, History and Chinese Archaeology." *Antiquity* 81.314: 886–901.
Liu Qiyu 劉起釪. 1989. *Shangshu xueshi* 尚書學史. Beijing: Zhonghua.
———. 2002. "Shangshu shuo lüe" 尚書說略. In *Jing shi shuo lüe: Shisan jing shuo lüe* 經史說略：十三經說略, 27–64. Beijing: Beijing Yanshan.
———. 2007. *Shangshu yanjiu yaolun* 尚書研究要論. Jinan: Qi Lu Shushe.
Loewe, Michael. 1986. "The Former Han Dynasty." In *Cambridge History of China*, vol 1: *The Ch'in and Han Empires 221 B.C.–A.D. 220*, ed. Denis

Twitchett and Michael Loewe, 103–222. Cambridge, UK: Cambridge University Press.

———. 2000. *A Biographical Dictionary of the Qin, Han and Xin Periods, 221 BC–AD 24*. Leiden: Brill.

———. 2006. *The Government of the Qin and Han Empires: 221 BCE–220 CE*. Indianapolis: Hackett Publishing.

———. 2011. *Dong Zhongshu, a "Confucian" Heritage and the "Chunqiu Fanlu."* Leiden: Brill.

———. 2015. "Liu Xiang and Liu Xin." In *Chang'an 26 BCE: An Augustan Age in China*, ed. Michael Nylan and Griet Vankeerberghen, 369–90. Seattle: University of Washington Press.

Ma Nan 馬楠. 2012a. "*Hongfan wuxing zhuan* zuozhe buzheng"《洪範五行傳》作者補證. *Zhongguo shi yanjiu* 中國史研究 1:144.

———. 2012b. "*Zhou Qin liang Han Shujing kao*" 周秦兩漢書經攷. Ph.D. dissertation, Peking University.

———. 2013. "Xiping shijing *Shangshu* hangshu tuiding ji fuyuan" 熹平石經《尚書》行數推定及復原. *Zhongguo dianji yu wenhua* 中國典籍與文化 1:4–18.

———. 2016. "Ma Rong Zheng Xuan Wang Su ben *Shangshu* xingzhi taolun" 馬融鄭玄王肅本《尚書》性質討論. *Wen shi* 2:95–106.

Ma Shiyuan 馬士遠. 2014. *Liang Han "Shangshu" xue yanjiu* 兩漢《尚書》學研究. Beijing: Zhongguo Shehui Kexue.

Major, John S. 1993. *Heaven and Earth in Early Han Thought: Chapters Three, Four, and Five of the "Huainanzi."* Albany: State University of New York Press.

Major, John S., et al. 2010. *The Huainanzi: A Guide to the Theory and Practice of Government in Early Han China*. New York: Columbia University Press.

Mashima Junichi 間嶋潤一. 2002. "Jō Gen *Shōsho chū* to *Shōsho daiden*" 鄭玄『尚書注』と『尚書大伝』. *Tōyō shi kenkyū* 東洋史研究 60.4: 700–732.

Matsumoto Masaaki 松本雅明. 1966. *Shunjū Sengoku ni okeru shōjo no tenkai* 春秋戰國における尚書の展開. Tokyo: Kazama Shobō.

Meyer, Dirk. 2012. *Philosophy on Bamboo: Text and the Production of Meaning in Early China*. Leiden: Brill.

———. 2014. "The Art of Narrative and the Rhetoric of Persuasion in the 'Jin Teng' (Metal Bound Casket) from the Tsinghua Collection of Manuscripts." *Asia* 68.4: 937–68.

———. 2021. *Documentation and Argument in Early China: The Shàngshū (Venerated Documents) and the Shū Traditions*. Berlin: Walter de Gruyter.

Morgan, Daniel Patrick. 2013. "Knowing Heaven: Astronomy, the Calendar, and the Sagecraft of Science in Early Imperial China." Ph.D. dissertation, University of Chicago.

———. 2017. *Astral Sciences in Early Imperial China: Observation, Sagehood and the Individual*. Cambridge, UK: Cambridge University Press.

Nienhauser, William H. Jr., ed. 1994–. *The Grand Scribe's Records*. 9 vols. Bloomington and Indianapolis: Indiana University Press.

Nylan, Michael. 1992. *The Shifting Center: The Original "Great Plan" and Later Readings*. Monumenta Serica Monograph Series 24. Nettetal: Steyler Verlag.
———. 1994. "The Chin Wen/Ku Wen Controversy in Han Times." *T'oung Pao* 80.1–3: 83–145.
———. 1995. "The Ku Wen Documents in Han Times." *T'oung Pao* 81.1–3: 25–50.
———. 2000. "Textual Authority in Pre-Han and Han." *Early China* 25:205–58.
———. 2001. *The Five "Confucian" Classics*. New Haven: Yale University Press.
———. 2009. "Classics without Canonization: Learning and Authority in Qin and Han." In *Early Chinese Religion, part 1: Shang through Han (1250 BCE–220 AD)*, ed. John Lagerwey and Marc Kalinowski, 721–76. Leiden: Brill.
———. 2011. *Yang Xiong and the Pleasures of Reading and Classical Learning in China*. New Haven: American Oriental Society.
———. 2018. "Han Views of the Qin Legacy and the Late Western Han 'Classical Turn.'" *Bulletin of the Museum of Far Eastern Antiquities* 79–80:73–121.
———. 2021. "On *Hanshu* 'Wuxing zhi' 五行志 and Ban Gu's Project." In *Technical Arts in the Han Histories: Tables and Treatises in the "Shiji" and "Hanshu,"* ed. Mark Csikszentmihalyi and Michael Nylan, 213–80. Albany: State University of New York Press.
Nylan, Michael, and Griet Vankeerberghen, eds. 2015. *Chang'an 26 BCE: An Augustan Age in China*. Seattle: University of Washington Press.
Nylan, Michael, and Thomas A. Wilson. 2010. *Lives of Confucius: Civilization's Greatest Sage Through the Ages*. New York: Doubleday.
Pankenier, David. 2013. *Astrology and Cosmology in Early China: Conforming Earth to Heaven*. Cambridge, UK: Cambridge University Press.
Petersen, Jens Østergård. 1995. "Which Books Did the First Emperor of Ch'in Burn? On the Meaning of *Pai Chia* in Early Chinese Sources." *Monumenta Serica* 43:1–52.
Pines, Yuri, Gideon Shelach-Lavi, Lothar von Falkenhausen, and Robin D. S. Yates. 2014. *Birth of an Empire: The State of Qin Revisited*. Berkeley: University of California Press.
Qian Mu 錢穆 (1895–1990). 2001. *Xian Qin zhuzi xinian* 先秦諸子繫年. Beijing: Shangwu.
———. 2012. *Qin Han shi* 秦漢史. Beijing: Shenghuo, Dushu, Xinzhi Sanlian Shudian.
———. 2015. *Liang Han jingxue jinguwen pingyi* 兩漢經學今古文平議. Beijing: Shangwu.
Qiu Xigui 裘錫圭. 2000. *Chinese Writing*. Translated by Gilbert Louis Mattos and Jerry Norman. Berkeley: University of California Press.
Qu Wanli 屈萬里. 1983. *Shangshu jishi* 尚書集釋. Taipei: Lianjing Chuban Shiye.

Qu Yanqing 曲延慶. 2000. "Fu Sheng ji qi jiguan zhi bianzheng" 伏生及其籍貫之辯證. *Chunqiu* 春秋 6:55–58.

Queen, Sarah A. 1996. *From Chronicle to Canon: The Hermeneutics of the "Spring and Autumn," according to Tung Chung-shu*. New York: Cambridge University Press.

Robinson, Rebecca. 2021. "Employing Knowledge: A Case Study in Calendar Reforms in the Early Han and Roman Empires." In *Rulers and Ruled in Early Greece, Rome and China*, ed. Hans Beck and Griet Vankeerberghen, 369–96. Cambridge, UK: Cambridge University Press.

Sanderovitch, Sharon. 1997. "Presence and Praise: Writing the Imperial Body in Han China." Ph.D. dissertation, University of California, Berkeley.

Sanft, Charles. 2005. "Six of One, Two Dozen of the Other: The Abatement of Mutilating Punishments under Han Emperor Wen." *Asia Major*, third series 18.1: 79–100.

———. 2008–9. "Edict of Monthly Ordinances for the Four Seasons in Fifty Articles from 5 C.E.: Introduction to the Wall Inscription Discovered at Xuanquanzhi, with Annotated Translation." *Early China* 32:125–208.

———. 2014. *Communication and Cooperation in Early Imperial China Publicizing the Qin Dynasty*. Albany: State University of New York Press.

———. 2017. "Concepts of Law in the *Shangshu*." In *Origins of Chinese Political Philosophy: Studies in the Composition and Thought of the "Shangshu" (Classic of Documents)*, 446–74. Edited by Martin Kern and Dirk Meyer. Leiden: Brill.

Schafer, Edward. 1977. *Pacing the Void: T'ang Approaches to the Stars*. Berkeley: University of California Press.

Schuessler, Axel. 2007. *ABC Etymological Dictionary of Old Chinese*. Honolulu: University of Hawaii Press.

Shandong Sheng Zouping Xian Difangzhi Bianzuan Weiyuanhui 山東省鄒平縣地方志編纂委員會. 1992. *Zouping xianzhi* 鄒平縣志. Beijing: Zhonghua.

Shaughnessy, Edward L. 1981–82. "'New' Evidence on the Zhou Conquest of Shang." *Early China* 6:57–79.

———. 1985–87. "The 'Current' *Bamboo Annals* and the Date of the Zhou Conquest of Shang." *Early China* 11/12:33–60.

———. 1986. "On the Authenticity of the *Bamboo Annals*." *Harvard Journal of Asiatic Studies* 46.1: 149–80.

———. 1993a. "The Duke of Zhou's Retirement in the East and the Beginnings of the Minister-Monarch Debate in Chinese Political Philosophy." *Early China* 18:41–72.

———. 1993b. "*I Chou shu* (*Chou shu*) 逸周書." In *Early Chinese Texts: A Bibliographical Guide*, ed. Michael Loewe, 229–33. Berkeley: Society for the Study of Ancient China and Institute of East Asian Studies, University of California.

———. 1993c. "*Shang shu* 尚書 (*Shu ching* 書經)." In *Early Chinese Texts: A Bibliographical Guide*, ed. Michael Loewe, 376–89. Berkeley: Society for the

Study of Ancient China and Institute of East Asian Studies, University of California.

———. 1997. *I Ching: The Classic of Changes*. New York: Ballantine Books.

———. 1999. "Western Zhou History." In *The Cambridge History of Ancient China*, ed. Michael Loewe and E. Shaughnessy, 292–351. Cambridge, UK: Cambridge University Press.

———. 2006. "The Editing and Editions of the *Bamboo Annals*." In *Rewriting Early Chinese Texts*, 185–263. Albany: State University of New York Press.

Silk, Jonathan. 2013-14. "Establishing/Interpreting/Translating: Is It Just That Easy?" *Journal of the International Association of Buddhist Studies* 36/37:205–25.

Soffel, Christian. 2004. *Ein Universalgelehrter verarbeitet das Ende seiner Dynastie—eine Analyse des Kunxue jiwen von Wang Yinglin*. Wiesbaden: Harrasowitz.

Sommer, Matthew Harvey. 2000. *Sex, Law, and Society in Late Imperial China*. Stanford: Stanford University Press.

Su Dechang 蘇德昌. 2013. *"Hanshu" wuxingzhi yanjiu*《漢書·五行志》研究. Taipei: Guoli Taiwan Daxue.

Sukhu, Gopal. 2005. "Yao, Shun, and Prefiguration: The Origins and Ideology of Han Imperial Genealogy." *Early China* 30:91–153.

Sun Ji 孫機. 2008. *Handai wuzhi wenhua ziliao tushuo* 漢代物質文化資料圖説. Shanghai: Shanghai Guji.

Sun Wenbo. 2018. "Bureaus and Offices in Qin County-Level Administration— in Light of an Excerpt from the Lost *Hongfan wuxing zhuan* (Great Plan Five Phases Commentary)." *Bamboo and Silk* 1:71–120.

Tan Qixiang 譚其驤. 1982–87. *Zhongguo lishi dituji* 中國歷史地圖集. Shanghai: Ditu.

Tang Jigen 唐際根, Yue Hongbin 岳洪彬, He Yuling 何毓靈, Niu Shishan 牛世山, Yue Zhanwei 岳占偉, and Jing Zhichun 荊志淳. 2016. "Huanbei Shangcheng yu Yinxu de luwang shuiwang" 洹北商城與殷墟的路網水網. *Kaogu xuebao* 考古學報 3:319–25.

Tian, Tian. 2015. "The Suburban Sacrifice Reforms and the Evolution of the Imperial Sacrifices." In *Chang'an 26 BCE: An Augustan Age in China*, ed. Michael Nylan and Griet Vankeerberghen, 263–92. Seattle: University of Washington Press.

Tjan, Tjoe Som. 1949. *Po Hu T'ung: The Comprehensive Discussions in the White Tiger Hall*. Leiden: Brill.

Tseng, Lillian Lan-ying. 2011. *Picturing Heaven in Early China*. Cambridge, MA: Harvard University Asia Center and Harvard University Press.

Van Auken, Newell Ann. 2016. *The Commentarial Transformation of the "Spring and Autumn."* Albany: State University of New York Press.

van Els, Paul, and Sarah Queen, eds. 2017. *Between History and Philosophy: Anecdotes in Early China*. Albany: State University of New York Press.

van Ess, Hans. 1993. *Politik und Gelehrsamkeit in der Zeit der Han (202 v. Chr.– 220 n. Chr.): Die Alttext/Neutext-Kontroverse*. Wiesbaden: Harrasowitz.

———. 1994. "The Old Text/New Text Controversy: Has the Twentieth Century Got It Wrong?" *T'oung Pao* 80.1–3: 146–70.

———. 1999. "The Apocryphal Texts of the Han Dynasty and the Old Text/New Text Controversy." *T'oung Pao* 85.1–3: 29–64.

———. 2014. "Emperor Wu of the Han and the First August Emperor of Qin in Sima Qian's *Shiji*." In *Birth of an Empire*, ed. Yuri Pines, Gideon Shelach-Lavi, Lothar von Falkenhausen, and Robin D. S. Yates, 239–57. Berkeley: University of California Press.

Vankeerberghen, Griet. 2007. "Rulership and Kinship: The *Shangshu dazhuan*'s Discourse on Lords." *Oriens Extremus* 46:84–100.

———. 2010. "Texts and Authors in the *Shiji*." In *China's Early Empires: A Re-appraisal*, ed. Michael Nylan and Michael Loewe, 461–79. University of Cambridge Oriental Publications 67. Cambridge, UK: Cambridge University Press.

———. 2014. "The Discourse about Lords (*zhuhou*) in the *Huainanzi*." In *The Huainanzi and Textual Production in Early China*, ed. Sarah A. Queen and Michael Puett, 326–50. Leiden: Brill.

———. 2015. Pining for the West: Chang'an in the Life of Kings and Their Families during Chengdi's Reign." In *Chang'an 26 BCE: An Augustan Age in China*, ed. Michael Nylan and Griet Vankeerberghen, 347–66. Seattle: University of Washington Press.

Wang, Aihe. 2000. *Cosmology and Political Culture in Early China*. Cambridge, UK: Cambridge University Press.

Watson, Burton. 1993. *Records of the Grand Historian: Han Dynasty II*. New York: Columbia University Press.

Wilson, Thomas A. 1995. *Genealogy of the Way: The Construction and Uses of the Confucian Tradition in Late Imperial China*. Stanford: Stanford University Press.

Wu Zhixiong 吳智雄. 2008. "Lun *Shangshu dazhuan* jiben zhi sixiang yaoyi" 論《尚書大傳》輯本之思想要義. *Hanxue yanjiu* 漢學研究 26.4: 1–32.

Xia Dazhao 夏大兆 and Huang Dekuan 黃德寬. 2014. "Guanyu Qinghua jian 'Yin zhi,' 'Yin gao' de xingcheng he xingzhi—Cong Yi Yin chuanshuo zai xian Qin chuanshi he chutu wenxian zhong de liubian kaocha" 關於清華簡《尹至》《尹誥》的形成和性質——從伊尹傳說在先秦傳世和出土文獻中的流變考察. *Wenshi* 108.3: 213–19.

Xin Deyong 辛德勇. 2016. *Haihun hou Liu He* 海昏侯劉賀. Beijing: Shenghuo Dushu Xinzhi Sanlian Shudian.

Xu Jingyuan 許景元. 1981. "Xinchu Xiping shijing Shangshu canshi kaolüe" 新出熹平石經尚書殘石考略. *Kaogu xuebao* 2:185–97.

———. 2007. "Xinchu Xiping shijing Shangshu canshi kaolüe" 新出熹平石經《尚書》殘石考略. In *Han Wei Luoyang cheng yizhi yanjiu* 漢魏洛陽城遺址研究, ed. Du Jinpeng 杜金鵬 and Qian Guoxiang 錢國祥, 57–69. Beijing: Kexue.

Xu Xingwu 徐興無. 2012. "Jingdian chanfa yu zhengzhi shushu: *Hongfan wuxingzhuan* kaolun" 經典闡發與政治術數——《洪範五行傳》考論. *Gudian wenxian yanjiu* 古典文獻研究 15:8–62.

Xu Zhongshu 徐中舒. 1998. "Pugu, Xuyan, Huaiyi, Qunshu kao" 蒲姑、徐奄、淮夷、群舒攷. *Sichuan Daxue xuebao (Zhexue shehui kexue ban)* 四川大學學報（哲學社會科學版）3:65–76.

Yakobson, Alexander. 2021. "Augustus, the Roman Plebs and the Dictatorship, 22 BCE and Beyond." In *Rulers and Ruled in Ancient Greece, Rome, and China*, ed. Hans Beck and Griet Vankeerberghen, 269–99. Cambridge, UK: Cambridge University Press.

Yang Guoyi 楊國宜. 2007. "Juyou zhongyao shiliao jiazhi de 'Mingchao zaiyi biannianshi': Sun Zhilu ji qi *Er shen yelu*" 具有重要史料價值的"明朝災異編年史"—孫之騄及其《二申野錄》. *Anhui Shifan Daxue xuebao (renwen shehui kexue ban)* 安徽師範大學學報（人文社會科學版）35.4: 420–28.

Yang Jiagang 楊家剛. 2013. "'Yaodian' yu Qindai zhidu ji Qin guan cang zhi *Shu* zai kaocha"《堯典》與秦代制度及秦官藏之《書》再考察. *Lantai shijie* 蘭臺世界 10:125.

Yang Jie 楊傑. 2014. "*Shangshu dazhuan* chengming kao" 尚書大傳稱名考. *Guji zhengli yanjiu xuekan* 古籍整理研究學刊 1:106–8.

Yang Kuan 楊寬. 1980. "Lun Qin Han de fenfengzhi" 論秦漢的分封制. *Zhonghua wenshi luncong* 中華文史論叢 13.1: 23–37.

Yang, Shao-yun. 2015. "The Politics of Omenology in Chengdi's Reign." In *Chang'an 26 BCE: An Augustan Age in China*, ed. Michael Nylan and Griet Vankeerberghen, 323–46. Seattle: University of Washington Press.

Yang Tianyu 楊天宇. 2008. *Zheng Xuan Sanlizhu yanjiu* 鄭玄三禮注研究. Beijing: Zhongguo Shehui Kexue.

Yasui Kōzan 安井香山 and Nakamura Shōhachi 中村璋八. 1975. *Chōshū isho shūsei: Tsuketari kōkan sakuin* 緯書集成：附校勘索引, 2: *Sho: Chuko* 書：中候. Tokyo: Meitoku Shuppansha.

Yoshikawa, Tadao. 1991. "Scholarship in Ching-chou at the End of the Later Han Dynasty." *Acta Asiatica* 60:1–24.

Zhang Bing 張兵. 2004. "Fu Sheng Hongfan wuxingzhuan dui wuxing xueshuo de xishou yu yingyong" 伏生《洪範五行傳》對五行學說的吸收與應用. *Kongzi yanjiu* 孔子研究 5:37–42.

———. 2005. "'Hongfan' quanshi yanjiu"《洪範》詮釋研究. Ph.D. dissertation, Shandong University.

Zhang Huanjun 張煥君 and Diao Xiaolong 刁小龍. 2009. *Wuwei Han jian "Yili" zhengli yu yanjiu* 武威漢簡「儀禮」整理與研究. Wuhan: Wuhan Daxue.

Zhao, Lu. 2019. *In Pursuit of the Great Peace: Han Dynasty Classicism and the Making of Early Medieval Literati Culture*. Albany: State University of New York Press.

Zheng Yuji 鄭裕基. 2003. "Chen Li zhengli Chen Shouqi *Shangshu dazhuan dingben* pingshu" 陳澧整理陳壽祺尚書大傳定本評述. *Zhonghua jishu xueyuan xuebao* 中華技術學院學報 26:232–47.

———. 2009. "Guojia tushuguan suo cang Hui Dong jiben *Shangshu dazhuan* ewu juli" 國家圖書館所藏惠棟輯本《尚書大傳》訛誤舉例. *Zhonghua jishu xueyuan xuebao* 中華技術學院學報 41.11: 287–314.

Zhong Zhaopeng 鍾肇鵬. 1991. "Jinwen Shangshu, Qi Shi yu chenwei" 今文尚書, 齊詩與讖緯. In *Chenwei lunlüe* 讖緯論略, 135–40. Liaoyang: Liaoning Jiaoyu.

Zhou Zhenhe 周振鶴. 2017. *Xi Han zhengqu dili* 西漢政區地理. Beijing: Shangwu.

———. 2021. *Hanshu dilizhi huishi (zengding ben)* 漢書地理志匯釋 (增訂本). 3 vols. Nanjing: Fenghuang.

Zito, Angela. 1997. *Of Body and Brush: Grand Sacrifice as Text/Performance in Eighteenth-Century China*. Chicago: University of Chicago Press.

Zong Jinghang 宗靜航. 2006. "Du Chen Shouqi jijiao *Shangshu dazhuan* ouji" 讀陳壽祺輯校《尚書大傳》偶記. *Zhonghua wenshi luncong* 中華文史論叢 82:267–80.

Place Name Index

The *Great Commentary* refers to places associated with different periods of antiquity. Our identification aims to clarify how their locations were understood in the Han, when the *Great Commentary* was written.

Most of the information below is based on (1) *Scribe's Records* and its three main commentaries, (2) Guo Shengbo 郭聲波 2020, and (3) Zhou Zhenhe 周振鶴 2021. We use Tan Qixiang 譚其驤 1982–87, vols. 1–3, to determine corresponding modern locations.

Entries include the significance of the place in the *Great Commentary* (association with a specific occasion, event, or person), its modern location (county, city, and province), alternate versions of the name, and the numbered passages in the *Great Commentary* where the place name appears.

Romanization is *pinyin* throughout, except for a few commonly accepted names, such as Yangzi for Jiang 江 and Yellow River for He 河. The entries are in natural order: for example, Mount Tai rather than Taishan, thus listing all the mountains together. Cross-references are provided to alternate names of the places included.

Bi 畢. Burial site of early Zhou kings and Duke of Zhou 周公. To the southeast of the Zhou capital Hao 鎬. In Xianyang 咸陽, Shaanxi. 5.1.1, 5.5.2.

Bo 薄/亳. An early Shang capital established by King Tang 汤. Possible locations: Jingbo 景亳 located near Shangqiu 商丘 city, Henan; Bo 薄/亳 located near Yanshi 偃師, Luoyang 洛陽 city, Henan. 薄: 4.2.1, 4.2.3; 景亳: 4.2.8.

Buqi 不齊. Place unknown. 4.2.2.

Chaoxian 朝鮮. Place where Prince Ji 箕子 took refuge. Understood in the Han to be in the area around present-day Pyongyang, North Korea. 5.3.1.

Chengzhou 成周. Literally "Accomplished Zhou." Possibly an epithet for Luo/Luoyi 雒邑. 5.5.2, 5.12.1, 5.12.5. *See also* Luo.

Chong 崇. A settlement first under Shang control and later conquered by the Zhou. Hu 戶 county, Xi'an 西安 city, Shaanxi. 4.7.1–3, 5.8.2.

Dai 代. A.k.a. 岱. The area where Mount Tai is located. 1.1.16. *See also* Mount Tai.

Daishan 岱山. *See* Mount Tai.

Dajiao 大交. A legendary place to the south where Mount Huo is located. 1.1.16.

Dark City 幽都. A legendary place to the north where Mount Hong is located. 1.1.16.

Deer Terrace 鹿臺. The terrace built by the last Shang king in his capital, Chaoge 朝歌. In Qi 淇 county, Henan. 5.2.1.

Dunqiu 頓丘. The place where Shun 舜 sold goods. Qingfeng 青豐 county, Puyang 濮陽 city, Henan. 1.1.9.

Feng 豐. An early settlement founded by the Zhou people. In Hu 戶 county, Xi'an 西安 city, Shaanxi. 5.5.2, 5.11.1–2.

Flowing Sands 流沙. Desert area in Zhangye 張掖 city and Jiuquan 酒泉 city in Gansu, Ningxia, and Erjin Banner 額濟納旗 in Inner Mongolia. 7.2.10.

Fuxia 負夏. The place where Shun 舜 engaged in seasonal trade. Located in the Wei 衛 domain. 1.1.9.

Great Mansion 大室. A.k.a. Taishi 太室. A mountain in the Mount Song range, Henan. 7.2.9. *See also* Mount Song.

He 河. *See* Yellow River.

Hengshan 恆山. *See* Mount Heng.

Hongshan 宏山. *See* Mount Hong.

Huai 淮. One of the "Four Rivers" 四瀆; modern Huai River 淮河. 3.1.3, 4.7.1.

Huaipu 淮浦. Area along the Huai River. 5.21.2.

Huashan 華山. *See* Mount Hua.

Huoshan 霍山. *See* Mount Huo.

Ji 濟. A.k.a. 沇. One of the "Four Rivers" 四瀆; modern Ji River 濟水. 濟: 3.1.1, 3.1.3; 沇: 6.2.22.

Jiang 江. *See* Yangzi River.

Jianggu 降谷. A.k.a. Hangu Pass 函谷關. Mount Xiguan 西關 in Lingbao 靈寶 city, Henan. 3.1.1.

Jiaozhi 交阯. Located in the deep south. Western Han commandery covering northern Vietnam and the southern parts of Guangdong and Guangxi. 1.1.34, 5.7.2.

Jieshi 碣石. Possibly a mountain in Qinhuangdao 秦皇島, Hebei, and close to sea. 7.2.1.

Jingbo 景亳. *See* Bo.

Ju Bridge 鉅橋. A bridge in Julu 鉅鹿 with adjacent granary. In Julu 巨鹿 county, Xingtai 邢臺 city, Hebei. 5.2.1.

Juding 鉅定. A lake in the southeast of Guangrao 廣饒 county, Dongying 東營 city, Shandong. 3.1.1.

Juqiao 鉅橋. *See* Ju Bridge.

Juye 鉅野. In Juye 巨野 county, Heze 菏澤 city, Shandong. 3.1.1.

Kunlun 昆侖. A mountain in legend. Possibly 40 km. south of Jiuquan city 酒泉, Gansu, or north Qinghai 青海. Not to be confused with the modern Kunlun mountains. 7.2.9.

Lei Marsh 靁澤. The marsh where Shun 舜 fished. Ju 莒 county, Shandong. 1.1.8.

Liangshan 梁山. *See* Mount Liang.

Lishan 歷山. *See* Mount Li.

Liugu 柳穀. A legendary place to the west where Mount Hua 華山 is located. 1.1.16.

Liusha 流沙. *See* Flowing Sands.

Lu 魯. Domain, capital at Qufu 曲阜 after the enfeoffment of Boqin; southwestern Shandong. 4.2.2, 5.5.2, 5.12.4, 5.12.6–7, 6.2.26.

Luo 雒. A.k.a. **Luoyi** 雒邑. A settlement established during King Cheng's 成王 reign. By Han times understood to be located near Luoyang. 5.8.1, 5.11.1, 5.12.1, 5.12.3. *See also* Chengzhou.

Lutai 鹿臺. *See* Deer Terrace.

Meng Ford 盟津. A.k.a. Mengjin 孟津. A ford on the Yellow River 黃河, where Ji Fa 姬發 crossed the river to attack the last Shang king. In Mengjin 孟津 county, Luoyang 洛陽 city, Henan. 5.1.1.

Meng Reservoir 孟諸. A.k.a. Mengzhu 孟豬, Mingdu 明都. In Shangqiu 商丘 city, Henan. 3.1.1. 明都: 3.1.13.

Mengjin 盟津. *See* Meng Ford.

Mengzhu 孟諸. *See* Meng reservoir.

Mingdu 明都. *See* Meng reservoir.

Mingtiao 鳴條. The site of the war between King Jie 桀 of the Xia and King Tang 湯 of the Shang. Possible locations: western Xia 夏 county, Yuncheng 運城 city, Shanxi, or in Fengqiu 封丘 county, Xinxiang 新鄉 city, Henan. 6.2.13.

Mixu 密須. Western Lingtai 靈臺 county, Gansu. 4.7.1, 5.8.2.

Mount Dai 岱山. *See* Mount Tai 泰山.

Mount Heng 恆山. One of the Five Marchmounts. Modern Heng Mountain 恆山, Shanxi. 恆山: 3.1.3; 宏山: 1.1.16.

Mount Hong 宏山. *See* Mount Heng.

Mount Hua 華山. One of the Five Marchmounts. Modern Hua Mountain 華山, Shaanxi. 1.1.1, 3.1.3.

Mount Huo 霍山. One of the Five Marchmounts. Located in the southeast of modern Huoshan 霍山 county, Anhui. 1.1.16, 3.1.3.

Mount Li 歷山. Located in Yongji city, Shanxi. 1.1.10.

Mount Liang 梁山. A mountain near Qian 乾 county, Xianyang 咸陽 city, Shaanxi. 6.2.14.

Mount Qi 岐山. An early settlement of the Zhou. Modern Mount Qi 岐山, in Qishan 岐山 county, Baoji 寶鷄 city, Shaanxi. 6.2.14; 岐: 6.2.23.

Mount Song 嵩山. One of the Five Marchmounts. Modern Song Mountain 嵩山, Henan. 3.1.3.

Mount Tai 泰山. A.k.a. Daishan 岱山. One of the Five Marchmounts. Modern Tai Mountain 泰山, Shandong. 1.1.16; 岱山: 3.1.3.

Mount Tu 塗山. Southeast of Huaiyuan 懷遠 county, Anhui. 2.2.14.

Muye 牧(之)野. Fields of Mu near late Yin capital; near modern Anyang, Henan. 5.2.1.

Pan Stream 磻谿. The stream on which Lü Wang 呂望 fished and King Wen of Zhou 周文王 came to visit him. In Qishan 岐山 county, Baoji 寶雞 city, Shaanxi. 6.2.15.

Panxi 磻谿. *See* Pan Stream.

Qi 耆. A.k.a. 黎. In Changzhi 長治 county, Shanxi. 4.7.2.

Qishan 岐山. *See* Mount Qi.

Rui 芮. South of Yuncheng 運城 city, Shanxi. 4.7.1, 5.8.2.

Sanwei 三危. *See* Three Dangers.

Shalu 沙麓. A mountain in eastern Daming 大名 county, Hebei. 7.3.14.

Songshan 嵩山. *See* Mount Song.

Taishan 泰山. *See* Mount Tai.

Taishi 大室. *See* Great Mansion.

Three Dangers 三危. Possibly the mountain in the southeast of Dunhuang 敦煌 city, Gansu. 7.2.10.

Tushan 塗山. See Mount Tu.

Wei 衛. Domain, capital at Diqiu 帝丘 after 629 BCE; in southwestern Puyang 濮陽 county, Henan. 6.2.29.

Xian 鮮. A.k.a. Xi 肸, Bi 箅/費. In Fei 費 county, Shandong. 5.21 (title), 5.21.2.

Xuzhou 徐州. One of the nine provinces that Yu 禹 divided. A large area covering modern Shandong, Jiangsu, and Anhui. 5.21.2.

Yan 奄. First a domain in the Shang land in Henan; moved to Lu after the failure of its rebellion in early Zhou. Possible locations: (1) Wen 溫 county, Henan; (2) Qufu 曲阜, Jining 濟寧 city, Shandong. 5.5.1, 5.12.5, 5.15.1.

Yangzi River 江. One of the "Four Rivers" 四瀆; modern Yangzi River 長江. 3.1.1, 3.1.3, 4.1.7.

Yellow River 河. One of the "Four Rivers" 四瀆; modern Yellow River 黃河. 1.1.9, 3.1.1, 3.1.3, 6.2.22.

Yin 殷. The settlement where Pan Geng moved his capital; also used as a name for the Shang dynasty. 3.2.1, 5.2.1, 5.3.1, 5.6.1, 5.12.5, 5.22.5, 6.2.10.

Yingbo 滎播. The marshlands in Xingyang 滎陽 county, Zhengzhou 鄭州 city, Henan. 3.1.12.

Youdu 幽都. *See* Dark City.

Youli 牖里. A.k.a. Youli 羑里. The place where the last Shang king held the Prince of the West 西伯 captive. In Tangyin 湯陰 county, Henan. 4.7.1.

Yu 虞. In Pinglu 平陸 county, Yuncheng 運城 city, Shanxi. 4.7.1, 5.8.2.

Yu 于. A.k.a. 邘. In Qinyang 沁陽 county, Henan. 4.7.1, 5.8.2.

Yuyi 禺鐵. A.k.a. 嵎夷. The area to the west of the Liao 遼 River. 3.1.11.

Personal Name Index

The personal and group name entries below are given in natural order (e.g., Duke of Zhou rather than Zhou, Duke of). Cross-references are provided when a person (or group) has multiple names, such as King Wen / Chang / Prince of the West. For such people, our translation always follows the designation of the original text. Most of the information below is based on *Shangshu dazhuan shuzheng* and *Scribe's Records* and its three main commentaries.

Entries include alternative names of a person, relationship to other significant people (e.g., Boqin was the son of the Duke of Zhou), and other important aspects (e.g., Taihao was associated with the east, spring, and wood), followed by number designations for passages in the *Great Commentary* where the name appears. Subentries distinguish alternative names used in the text.

August One of Agriculture 農皇. *See* Divine Farmer.
August One of Order 戲皇. *See* Fuxi.
Bigan 比干. The uncle of the last Shang king; brutally killed for remonstrating with the king. 5.2.1.
Bo Jiong 伯冏. *See* Jiong.
Bo Yi 伯夷. Minister of the legendary sage ruler Yao. 5.22.5.
Boqin 伯禽. Son of the Duke of Zhou; enfeoffed in Lu 魯. 5.10.2, 5.12.4, 5.12.7, 5.21.2.
Caishu 蔡叔. Son of King Wen of Zhou. Younger brother of King Wu and the Duke of Zhou. Revolted against the Zhou. 5.5.1.
Chang 昌. *See* King Wen.
Chengwang 成王. *See* King Cheng.
Confucius 孔子 (**551–479 BCE**). Personal name Kong Qiu 孔丘. A.k.a. Master 子, 夫子. 孔子: 1.1.5, 4.4.2, 4.5.2, 5.12.3, 5.22.2, 5.22.5, 6.2.25, 6.2.29; 丘: 6.2.22–24; 子: 2.1, 5.22.3, 5.22.7–9, 6.2.22, 6.2.24, 6.2.26, 6.2.29, 7.3.1; 夫子: 6.2.22, 6.2.26, 6.2.28.
Da Yu 大禹. *See* Yu 禹.

Danzhu 丹朱. Son of Yao; unfit to succeed the throne of his father. 1.1.7, 2.2.7.

Dating shi 大庭氏. **House of Dating**. A lineage of antiquity. 6.2.9.

Dawang Danfu 大王亶甫. *See* Great King Danfu.

Divine Farmer 神農. A.k.a. August One of Agriculture 農皇; Shennong 神農. A legendary sage ruler; skilled in agriculture. 神農: 6.2.1, 6.2.4; 農皇: 6.2.1.

Dongguo Zisi 東郭子思. A contemporary of Confucius and his disciple Zigong. 6.2.28.

Duke of Shao 召公. Brother of the Duke of Zhou and King Wu of Zhou. Personal name Ji Shi 姬奭. 召公: 5.2.1, 5.5.1, 5.11.1; 奭: 5.5.1.

Duke of Zhou 周公. Son of King Wen of Zhou; younger brother of King Wu of Zhou; uncle of King Cheng. Personal name: Ji Dan 姬旦. 2.1.4, 2.2.5, 5.1.4, 5.2.1, 5.4.1, 5.5.1–2, 5.7.1–2, 5.8.1, 5.10.2, 5.11.2, 5.12.2–6, 6.2.18–19, 6.2.21.

Earl He 和伯. A legendary figure of antiquity; associated with autumn sacrifice at Mount Hua 華山. 1.1.16.

Earl Xi 羲伯. A legendary figure of antiquity; associated with summer sacrifice at Mount Huo 霍山. 1.1.16.

Earl Yi 儀伯. A legendary figure of antiquity; associated with spring sacrifice at Mount Tai 泰山. 1.1.16.

Fa 發. *See* King Wu.

Father Shang 尚父. *See* Lü Wang.

Fei Chang 費昌. Originally a subject of the Xia dynasty, later Tang's 湯 charioteer when Tang defeated Jie. 4.2.8.

Feng 封. *See* Kangshu.

Fire Giver 遂人, a.k.a. Suihuang 遂皇. Legendary figure who introduced fire to humans. 遂人: 6.2.1; 遂皇: 6.2.1.

Fuxi 伏羲. A.k.a. August One of Order 戲皇. Legendary progenitor of humankind and the Eight Trigrams. 伏羲: 6.2.1, 6.2.4–5; 戲皇: 6.2.1.

Fuzi 夫子. *See* Confucius.

Gaoyao 皋陶/咎繇. A legendary figure who assisted in the governance of Shun and Yu. 皋陶: 2.1.6; 咎繇: 2.2, 6.2.22.

Gaozong 高宗. Shang King. Posthumous name of King Wuding 武丁 (d. ca. 1189 BCE). 高宗: 4.4.1, 4.4.3, 4.5.2, 4.6; 武丁: 4.5.1, 4.6.1.

Gong Liu 公劉. *See* Liu the Duke.

Gongzi Lufu 公子祿父. *See* **Lufu**.

Goumang 句芒. A divine figure of antiquity associated with the east, spring, and wood. 7.2.1.

Great King Danfu 大王亶甫. Legendary figure of antiquity. Ancestor of Zhou. 6.2.14.

Great Yu 大禹. *See* Yu 禹.

Guanshu 管叔. Younger brother of King Wu of Zhou. 5.5.1.

Hebo 和伯. *See* Earl He.

Hong Yao 閎夭. One of the three worthies who learned from Taigong 太公 (Lü Wang) and assisted in the release of King Wen of Zhou. 4.7.1, 4.7.2.

House of Youyu 有虞氏. *See* Shun.

Houtu 后土. A divine figure of antiquity associated with the center and earth. 7.2.9. *See also* Yellow Emperor.

Huangdi 黃帝. *See* Yellow Emperor.

Ji Chang 姬昌. *See* King Wen of Zhou.

Ji Fa 姬發. *See* King Wu.

Ji Yu 姬虞. *See* Tangshu.

Jie 桀. Last king of the Xia dynasty. 4.2.2–4, 4.2.6–7, 5.17.1, 6.2.13.

Jin Pinggong 晉平公. *See* Lord Ping of Jin.

Jiong 臩/冏. A.k.a. Bo Jiong 伯臩. A man assigned by Ji Man 姬滿, or King Mu of Zhou (r. 956–918 BCE), to revitalize government affairs. 5.20.

Jizi 箕子. *See* **Prince Ji**.

Kangshu 康叔. Younger brother of King Wu of Zhou and the Duke of Zhou; enfeoffed in Wei 衛. Personal name Feng 封. 康叔: 5.10.2; 封: 5.9.4.

King Cheng 成王 **of Zhou** (r. 1042/35–1006 BCE). Early Zhou king; Son of King Wu of Zhou. Personal name Ji Song 姬誦. 2.1.4, 5.5.1–3, 5.7.1–2, 5.11.1, 5.12.4, 5.15, 6.2.20.

King Kang 康王 **of Zhou** (r. 1005/3–978 BCE). Personal name Ji Zhao 姬釗. 5.19.

King Wen 文王 **of Zhou**. A.k.a. Prince of the West 西伯. Personal name Ji Chang 姬昌. 文王: 2.2.5, 4.7.1–2, 5.5.2, 5.8.2, 5.12.2–4, 6.2.2, 6.2.15, 6.2.17, 6.2.23; 昌: 4.7.1, 6.2.15; 西伯: 4.7.1; 周文王: 6.2.15.

King Wu 武王 (r. 1049/45–1043 BCE). King Wu of the Zhou, who defeated the Shang; son of King Wen, brother of the Duke of Zhou, father of King Cheng; personal name Ji Fa 姬發. 武王: 5.1.4–6, 5.2.1, 5.3.1, 5.5.1, 5.12.2–3, 5.12.4; 發:5.1.1, 5.1.3.

King Wuding 武丁. *See* Gaozong.

King Xuan 宣王 (r. 342–29 BCE). King of Qi 齊. 6.2.23.

Kongzi 孔子. *See* Confucius.

Liu the Duke 公劉. As described in the *Odes*, Liu the Duke led the migration of the Zhou people to Bin 豳. 6.2.16.

Lord Ai of Lu 魯哀公 (r. 494–68 BCE). A contemporary of Confucius. 6.2.26.

Lord Jing of Qi 齊景公 (r. 547–490 BCE). A contemporary of Confucius. 6.2.26.

Lord Ping of Jin 晉平公 (r. 557–32 BCE). A contemporary of Master Kuang. 6.2.27.

Lord She 葉公. Enfeoffed in She 葉 by Lord Hui of Chu 楚惠王 (r. 489–32 BCE). A contemporary of Confucius. 6.2.26.

Lord Wen of Wei 魏文侯 (r. 445–396 BCE). 6.2.38.

Lu Aigong 魯哀公. *See* Lord Ai of Lu.

Lü Wang 呂望. A.k.a. Lü Shang 呂尚, Jiang Shang 姜尚, Taigong 太公, and Father Shang 尚父. An important military strategist in the Zhou conquest of Shang; enfeoffed in Qi 齊. 太公: 4.7.1, 5.2.1–2; 呂望: 6.2.15; 尚父: 6.2.15.

Lufu 祿父. A.k.a. Gongzi Lufu 公子祿父. Descendant of last Shang king. Killed after revolt against the Zhou. 5.3.1, 5.5.1.

Master 子/夫子. *See* Confucius.

PERSONAL NAME INDEX

Master Kuang 師曠. An expert in music who served at the court of Lord Ping of Jin. 6.2.27.
Master Shang 商子. A legendary, worthy figure of Zhou. 5.10.2.
Nonghuang 農皇. *See* Divine Farmer.
Nangong Kuo 南宮括. One of the three worthies who learned from Taigong 太公 (Lü Wang) and assisted in the release of King Wen of Zhou. 4.7.1, 4.7.2.
Pangeng 盤庚. The ruler of Shang who moved his capital to a new settlement called Yin 殷. 4.3 (title).
Prince Ji 箕子. Kin of the last Shang king. 5.3.1.
Prince Wei 微子. Brother of the last Shang king; enfeoffed in Song 宋. 5.6.1.
Prince of the West 西伯. *See* King Wen of Zhou.
Pugu 蒲姑. Ruler of Yan 奄. A contemporary of King Wu of Zhou. Possibly a place name in *Shiji*; a.k.a. Bogu 薄姑. 5.5.1.
Qi 啟. Son of the legendary sage ruler Yu. First ruler of the Xia dynasty. 2.2.14.
Qi Jinggong 齊景公. *See* Lord Jing of Qi.
Qiu 丘. *See* Confucius.
Quanrong clan 犬戎氏. A.k.a. Quanyi 畎夷. A legendary non-Zhou population group of antiquity. 犬戎氏: 4.7.1; 畎夷: 4.7.1, 5.8.2.
Queen Mother of the West 西王母. A divine female figure. 1.1.12.
Rushou 蓐收. A divine figure of antiquity associated with the west, autumn, and metal. 7.2.10.
Sanyi Sheng 散宜生. One of the three worthies who learned from Taigong 太公 (Lü Wang) and assisted in the release of King Wen of Zhou. 4.7.1, 4.7.2.
Shaogong 召公. *See* Duke of Shao.
Shaohao 少皞. A legendary figure of antiquity associated with the west, autumn, and metal. 7.2.10.
Shang 商. *See* Zixia.
Shang Rong 商容. A worthy in the service of the Shang who was not listened to. 5.2.1.
Shangfu 尚父. *See* Lü Wang.
Shangzi 商子. *See* Master Shang.
Shegong 葉公. *See* Lord She.
Shen 參. A.k.a. Master Zeng 曾子. A disciple of Confucius. Personal name Zeng Shen 曾參. 2.1.6.
Shennong 神農. *See* Divine Farmer.
Shi 奭. *See* Duke of Shao.
Shi Kuang 師曠. *See* Master Kuang.
Suihuang 遂皇. *See* Fire Giver.
Suiren 遂人. *See* Fire Giver.
Shou 受. *See* Shun.
Shun 舜. A.k.a. Shou 受, Yu 虞, House of Youyu 有虞氏. Legendary sage ruler of antiquity who succeeded Yao and abdicated his seat to Yu 禹. 舜: 1.1.5, 1.1.7–13, 1.1.32, 2.1.2–6, 2.2.6, 5.22.2, 6.2.2, 6.2.4, 6.2.22; 受: 1.1.13; 虞: 1.1.5, 1.1.26–27, 2.2.6; 有虞氏: 5.22.12.

Supreme Lord Yan 炎帝. A legendary figure of antiquity associated with the south, summer, and fire. 7.2.5.

Taigong 太公. *See* Lü Wang.

Taihao 太皞. A legendary figure of antiquity associated with the east, spring, and wood.. 7.2.1.

Tang 湯. Legendary founder of the Shang dynasty. 4.2.1–3, 4.2.6–7, 4.3.1, 4.5.1, 4.6.1, 6.2.2, 6.2.13.

Tang 唐. *See* Yao.

Tangshu 唐叔. A younger brother of King Cheng who was enfeoffed in Tang 唐. Personal name Ji Yu 姬虞. 6.2.20.

Wei 衛. *See* Zichun.

Wei Wenhou 魏文侯. *See* Lord Wen of Wei.

Weizi 微子. *See* Prince Wei.

Wenwang 文王. *See* King Wen of Zhou.

Wuding 武丁. *See* Gaozong.

Wugeng 武庚. Descendant of last Shang king. 5.5.1.

Wuwang 武王. *See* King Wu.

Xia 夏. *See* Yu 禹.

Xibo 西伯. *See* King Wen of Zhou.

Xie 契. A legendary figure of antiquity; minister of Shun 舜. 1.1.36.

Xihuang 戲皇. *See* Fuxi.

Xiwangmu 西王母. *See* Queen Mother of the West.

Xuanming 玄冥. A divine figure of antiquity associated with the north, winter, and water. 7.2.14.

Xuanwang 宣王. *See* King Xuan.

Yan Hui 顏回. Disciple of Confucius. 6.2.22.

Yandi 炎帝. *See* Supreme Lord Yan.

Yao 堯. A.k.a. Tang 唐. Legendary sage ruler of antiquity who abdicated his seat to Shun. 堯: 1.1.7, 1.1.12, 1.1.26–27, 1.1.34–36, 2.1.3, 5.22.2, 6.1.1, 6.2.2, 6.2.4, 6.2.22; 唐: 1.1.26–27, 2.2.6, 2.2.7.

Yellow Emperor 黃帝. A legendary figure of antiquity associated with the center and earth. 6.2.4, 7.2.9.

Yi Yin 伊尹. Originally minister of the last Xia ruler, Jie 桀, and then minister of the founder of the Shang dynasty, Tang 湯. 4.2.1, 6.2.12–13.

Yibo 儀伯. *See* Earl Yi.

Yu 禹. A.k.a. the Great Yu 大禹 and Xia 夏. Legendary sage ruler of antiquity who tamed the great flood. Successor of Shun. 禹: 2.1.6, 2.2.6, 3.1.3, 5.22.10, 6.2.2, 6.2.22, 7.1.1; 大禹: 7.1.1; 夏: 2.2.6.

Yu 虞. *See* Shun.

Yu Shun 虞舜. *See* Shun.

Yuling clan 於陵氏. A legendary non-Zhou population group of antiquity. 4.7.1.

Youcan clan 有參氏. A legendary non-Zhou population group of antiquity. 4.7.1.

Youyu clan 有虞氏. *See* Shun.

PERSONAL NAME INDEX

Yuechang 越常/裳. Name of population group of antiquity from the deep south. 越常: 5.7.1; 越裳: 5.7.2.
Zhòu 紂. Di Xin 帝辛, the last king of the Shang dynasty, which was conquered by King Wu of Zhou. 4.7.1, 5.1.5, 5.2.1, 5.5.1.
Zhou Wenwang 周文王. *See* King Wen of Zhou.
Zhougong 周公. *See* Duke of Zhou.
Zhuanxu 顓頊. A legendary figure of antiquity associated with the north, winter, and water. 7.2.14.
Zhurong 祝融. A divine figure of antiquity associated with the south, summer, and fire. 7.2.5.
Zi 子. *See* Confucius.
Zichun 子春. A contemporary of King Xuan of Qi. Personal name Wei 衛. 子春: 6.2.23; 衛: 6.2.23.
Zigong 子貢. Disciple of Confucius. Personal name Duanmu Ci 端木賜. 6.2.26, 6.2.28.
Zilongzi 子龍子. A contemporary of Zizhang and Confucius. 5.22.2.
Zixia 子夏. Disciple of Confucius. Personal name Bu Shang 卜商. 子夏: 6.1.9, 6.2.22, 6.2.38; 商: 6.2.22.
Zizhang 子張. Disciple of Confucius. Personal name Zhuansun Shi 顓孫師. 1.1.5, 4.4.2, 5.22.2, 6.2.25.
Zu Ji 祖己. Son of Gaozong of the Shang dynasty. 4.5.1, 4.6.1.

General Index

For place names and personal names in the translated text, see the separate Place Name Index and Personal Name Index. References to figures and tables appear in italics.

academicians, xx, xxvii–xxx, liii, lxxiv, lxxxviin20, lxxxviiin32, lxxxviiin37, lxxxviiin38, xcivn150, 115; *Documents* specialists, xxxvi–xxxvii, lxxxixn55, lxxxixn65; Liu Xin's letter to, xxx, lxxi–lxxii, 115. *See also* classicists; Fu, Master; Ni Kuan; Xiahou Sheng
Academy of Revering the Classics (Zunjing Shuyuan), lxxx
administrative terms, 117; vocabulary for divisions, 39, 45n6
"Admonitions to Gaozong," 101
agriculture, 57, 255n9; linked with seasons, xlviii–xlix, 11
Ai, Han Emperor, xxix
Ai, Lord of Lu, 35n3, 269n25
alcoholism, 173. *See also* "Proclamation on Drink"
Analects, lxxii, xciin122, 33, 71n5, 93n2, 265n17
ancestral temples, 13, 21, 51, 53, 151, 151n7, 157, 173, 177, 253, 261, 263; and demeanor, 193; of King Wen, 187n1; "Pure, the Ancestral Temple," 39, 45, 45n7, 45n9; sacrifices, lx, 19, xcvn167, 165, 175n1, 189,

189n2, 193n2, 251; tablets, 21n25, 121n5, 271
Ancient Chinese Texts Concordance Series, lxxx
Annals (Chunqiu), xvii, xxx, lviii, lxiv, lxxxiv, 307n10; Gongyang commentary, lxx, xcin107, 61n8, 217n1, 309n11; Guliang commentary, xcin107, 257n12, 309n11
anti-Qin rebellions, xx–xxi
apocrypha, lxxxvi, xcixn284, xcixn286
"Appended Phrases to the *Changes*" (Xici), 305n2
architecture: building dimensions by rank, 223n2, 232n4, 232n5, 232n7; stone pillars, 225n10; sumptuary laws regulating, 219–21
armillary sphere (*huntian yi*), 15n17
arrangement document (*xu*), xxxviii, xlii–xliv, xci–xciin112. *See also* "*Xu*" *under* Documents; Great Commentary
Arrayed Traditions on Women (Lienü zhuan), 203n1
"as morning turns into morning" (*dan fu dan xi*), li, 49n23

347

asterisms, xlix. *See also* constellations; stars
"Auspicious Clouds," li, 49

baixing (Hundred Families/people), 27n35
Bamboo Annals (Zhushu jinian), li, xciiin132, 83nn9–10, 105n2, 191n3; chronologies of events, 105n2, 117n6, 135n4, 191, 197n13; on crisis at Yan, 211n2; on Lord of Fu, 235n1; story of auspicious millet, 159; on transfer of power to Yu, 51n25; on tribute from Yuechang, 163n2
bamboo strips. *See* Tsinghua University bamboo-strip manuscripts
banquets, 175
Barbieri-Low, Anthony, lxiii
"battle" (*zhan* or *dan*), 71n5
bayi (eight translators), 83n8, 99n1
bayin (Eight Timbres), 19, 19n22
"beamed shack" (*liangyin*), xxxix–xl, 93, 93n1. *See also* mourning hut
bells, 39, 43, 47, 53
Bi (place), 151, 151n8
bibliocaust of 213 BCE, xx–xxii, xxvi, xxvii, xxxi, liii; lifting of ban, lxxxviiin30, lxxxviiin34
Bigan, 129n3, 129n8
Biyong (Circular Moat), lxi, lxii, xcvn170, 49, 49n18
Bo (site), 75, 81nn2–3
Bo Yi, xlvii
Book of Han (Hanshu): account of Master Fu, lxxxviin15; "Annals" of Emperor Wu, 25n28; "Annals" of Emperor Ping," lx, 161; "Bibliographical Treatise," lxxxii; "Biographies of the Classical Scholars," xxxvi, xxxvii; on calendar reform, lvi, lvii, xcivn158; description of teacher-disciple networks, xxxvii; *Documents* narrative, xxxi; on the office of the Commissioner of Ceremonial, lxxxviiin38; omens and divine texts, lxxxiv; on plot to depose Liu He, lxvi; reading of *lu* in *Documents*, 13n11; on regional lords, liv–lv; and "Tradition on the Great Plan's Five Phases," lxiv, lxxxi–lxxxii, xcixn271, 283nn5–6, 285n8, 305n3, 305n5; "Treatise on Penal Law," 243n6; "Treatise on Pitchpipes and the Calendar," 123; "Treatise on the Five Phases," lxxxii–lxxxiv, xcivn159, xcixn271, 101n2, 303n1, 309n11; "Treatise on the Suburban Sacrifices," 121n6
Book of Later Han (Hou Hanshu), xix, lxxxviin15, 165n5; "Biography of Yang Ci," 245n11
Book of Submitted Doubtful Cases (Zouyanshu), lxiii
Book of Sui (Suishu): bibliographical treatise, lxxvi, xcviiin261; on "Commentary of the Five Phases," lxxxvi; on transmission of *Documents*, 115
Boqin, xliii, 179, 191, 229; fief at Lu, 181n1, 191, 197n7, 197n9, 199n14
Bright Hall (Mingtang), 279, 279n5, 293, 295
burial alive of scholars, xxii

Caishu, 149n2, 151n6
calendar, 65–67, 69nn1–3; in ninefold method for successful rulership, 131; predictions, xcivn149; reform, xxxvi, lv–lix, xcivn153, xcivn159, 193
"Canon of Shun," lxviii, xcvin192, 5, 5n5, 7. *See also* "Canon of Yao"
"Canon of Yao," xcin108, xcvn176; as apocryphal text, xcixn284; and "Canon of Shun," lxviii, 5, 5n5, 7; on ceremony of receiving the sun, 251; compared with "Proclamation of the Supreme Lord," 75; dating of, 5; in *Documents*, xliv, xlvi–xlvii, xlix, 1, lxxxixn55, 5, 13n7,

15n14, 19n21, 29n37, 45n10, 265; Eight Earls, lxxiv, 51n24; "foothills," 47n16; on forms of rulership, 5–7; glosses of words, xlv; in *Great Commentary*, lii–liii, liv, xlvi–xlvii, xlviii–xlix, xcixn284, 5, 7, 177n5; on *gui* jades assigned to regional lords, xlvi–xlvii; on law, xcvn176; manipulation of stars, lxxiv–lxxv, 9n1; "Nay" means "No," 13, 13n10; on penal system, 5, 7; reference to *Explanation*, xli; on relations between regional lords and ruler, lii–liii, liv, xciiin137, 177n5; sections on Shun, 5, 7, lxxxviiin23, xciiin140; term *qishi*, xcvin194. *See also* Shun; Yao
Cao Cao, xxxii
Cao Pi, xxxii
castration, li, lxii, 239
Catalog of the Imperially Authorized Complete Library of the Four Branches (Qinding Siku quanshu zongmu), xlviii, lxxvii–lxxviii, lxxix, lxxxvi, 249
"Catalpa Wood," xlv, li, xcn70, 179, 181n2
central domains, lx, 61, 61n6, 165, 165n4, 245, 245n8
Ceremonials (Yili), 195n3. *See also* Wuwei *Ceremonials*
Ceremony to Nourish the Elders, lxi–lxii, xcvn169
Chang'an, xv, xix, xxii, xxiii, xxviii, xxix, xxxvi, lxxxviin16
Changes, xxx, lxiv, lxxxixn60, xciin123, 143n1; eight trigrams, lxxxiv, 291n5, 293nn8–9, 295nn13–14, 297nn19–20, 299n22
Changyi, King of, lxxxi
Chao Cuo, xxiii, xxx, *xxxiv*, xxxvi, lxxi, lxxxviiin39; home commandery, *xxv*
Chao Gongwu, lxxvii
Chaoxian, 135nn3–4

"Charge to Jiong," lxviii, lxix, xcvin196, 227
"Charge to Prince Wei," 153–55, 157n3
"Charge to Yue," xcin108, xciin120, 89, 91; *liangyin* in, xxxix–xl, 89
chariots, 75, 83n11; *shui*, 291n4
Chen Feisheng, lxxxviin18
Chen Mengjia, lxxxixn55, xcvin198
Chen Qiaozong (Puyuan), lxxiv, xcviin220
Chen She, rebellion of, xx
Chen Shouqi, xvi, lxx; and "Do Not Slack," 91, 205; edition of, lxxx, 7, 33, 49n22; on "King Cheng's Government" and "Metal Coffer," 209n3; on "Nay" means "No" in "Canon of Yao," 13n10; on "Oath at Xian" and "Principal Teachings," 253n3; on order of "Metal Coffer" and "Great Proclamation," 141
Chen Zhensun, lxxvii
Cheng, Han Emperor, xxxi, lxxxii, 87n3
Cheng, King: brothers of, 159, 163n1; and campaign against Yan, 215; and Chengzhou, 151n7, 197n13; and Duke of Zhou, lix–lx, 151n9, 191n4; Duke of Zhou as regent for, lix, 139–41, 147, 205; in "Establishment of the Government Officers," 195n6; and "Great Plan," 135n4; in "Metal Coffer," 145; and "Praising the Millet," 159; in "Proclamation of/ to Shao," 187n1; in "Proclamation on Luo," 189, 195nn4–5; as speaker in New Script "Great Proclamation," 139; transition of power to Ji Zhao, 219
Chengzhou, 151n7, 153, 185, 197n13. *See also* Luo/Luoyi
chenwei corpus (apocrypha), lxxxvi, xcixn284, xcixn286
Chinese Ancient Texts Database (CHANT), lxxx

GENERAL INDEX 349

Chong, lord of, 111n8
Chongwen Imperial Library catalog
  (*Chongwen zongmu*), lxxvii
Chu (state), 269n25
Chun Ju, 267n18
Chunyu Yue, liii–liv
Circular Moat (Biyong), lxi, lxii,
  49n18, xcvn170
clans, 175, 175n2, 197
Classic of the Mountains and Seas
  (Shanhaijing), 111n6
Classic of the Way and the Power
  (Daodejing), xcin107
"classical turn," xxix
classicists, xx, xxii, xxv, xxxvii, xlv,
  lix, lxiv, lxxiii–lxxiv, xcvn163. See
  also academicians; Zheng Xuan
clothing: color for official garments,
  lv–lvi, lviii, xcivn161; Five Robes
  with five insignia, 41, 41n2; laws
  regulating, lxii, 39, 75; patterns,
  lxix; of the supreme lord, lxxiv
commentarial forms, xxxviii, xcin107
Commentary (Zhuan), within *Great
  Commentary*, xxxviii, xxxix, 39n1,
  89, 189
*Commentary to the Guide to the
  Waterways* (Shuijing zhu), 269n25
Commissioner for Ceremonial, xxii,
  xxix, lxxxviiinn37–38, xcivn150
*Comprehensive Discussions in White
  Tiger Hall* (Baihu tong), 205
Confucian temples, xxv
Confucius: conversation on travel
  by the ruler, 21n25; dialogue with
  Lord Ai of Lu, 35n3; disciples of,
  271n28; as editor of superior *Documents*
  version, xxx–xxxi, lxxi,
  lxxii; enunciations by, xliv–xlv,
  xciin123; and the Five Punishments,
  lxiii, 235–37; on "Gaozong's
  Supplementary Sacrifice," 97,
  99n2; on meaning of mourning
  hut passage, xxxix–xl, 89, 93n2; on
  "Proclamation on Luo," 189; as

textual layer of *Great Commentary*, xxxix, xliv. See also *Analects*
constellations, 9n1, 15n17. See also
  stars
corulership, liii, liv
Csikszentmihalyi, Mark, 195n3
Cullen, Christopher, 15n17

dances, 17n20. See also music
Danzhu, 51n26
Dark Hall (Xuantang), 279, 299
de (virtue), 77n2
Deep Ocean of Records and Compilations
  (Jizuan yuanhai), 125
Deer Terrace, 129n6
Di Xin (Zhòu), 105n2, 109n4, 127n1,
  129n3, 135n2, 157n3
Ding Baozhen, lxxx
disasters associated with the Five
  Tasks, lxiv, lxxiv, 283–85, 283n6
divination: caution against, 141,
  141n5; by Duke of Zhou in "Metal
  Coffer," 145; in "Great Proclamation,"
  143n1; by King Cheng, 139;
  in rulership, 131. See also *Changes*;
  omens
"Do Not Slack," 91, 205
documents (category of texts),
  xxvi–xxvii
Documents (Shangshu): and bibliocaust
  of 213 BCE, xx–xxii, xxxi;
  "Canon of Yao," xliv, xlvi–xlvii,
  xlix, l, lxxxixn55, 5, 13n7, 15n14,
  19n21, 29n37, 45n10, 265; "Catalpa
  Wood," 167, 179; chapter titles,
  lxviii, *311–15*; "Charge to Jiong,"
  227; "Charge to Prince Wei" and
  "Prince Wei," 153, 155; "Charge to
  Yue," 89, 91; converted from seal
  script, xxix–xxx, lxx, lxxxviin12;
  "Do Not Slack," 91, 205; edited by
  Confucius, xxx–xxxi, lxxi, lxxii;
  "Establishment of the Government
  Officers," 195n6; forged
  chapters, xxvi, xxxi, lxx, lxxi,

lxxvi, lxxxixn48, xcvin192, xcviin215; "Gaoyao's Counsel," lxviii, 39, 47n16, 53n28, 265; "Gaozong's Supplementary Sacrifice," 97; "Great Oath," 115–17, 115n1, 119n2, 121n6; "Great Plan," li, lxiv–lxv, lxxx–lxxxi, lxxxiv, lxxxv, xcvin185, 131, 133, 135n4, 137n5, 141, 143n1, 265, 277–79, 279n4, 281n4, 301n24, 301n26, 301n28, 301n30, 301n32; "Great Proclamation," 139, 141, 141n6, 143n1; "Great Yu's Counsel," 45n10; as guide to rulership, xl, xlii, lii; hidden and retrieved by Master Fu, xx–xxii, xxiv–xxv; historical narrative and anecdotes, xviii, xciiin130; interpretation and explanation, xv, xvi; on King Wen's mandate, 169n2, 171n3; "lost fragments," 205; lost Old Script chapters, lxix, xcvin197; "Many Officers," 201; "Many Regions," 215; "Metal Coffer," 141, 145, 145n1, 149n4; "Minor Xu," xliii–xliv, 33, 89, 185, 185n1, 209n3; New Script and Old Script chapters, xvi, lxvii–lxxv, lxxxixn47–49, 91, 227; "Nine Offers," 35n1; "Notes on Collation," xcn70; number of chapters, xxii, xxix, xxx, xxxi, xcn70; "Oath at Bi," 229; "Oath at Gan," 65, 67; "Pangeng," 85, 87n1; "The Prince of the West Attacks Li," 105; "Proclamation of the Supreme Lord," 75; "Proclamation of/to Shao," 185; "Proclamation on Drink," 167, 173, 177nn3–4; "Proclamation on Luo," 189, 191, 195nn4–5, 199n14; "Proclamation to Kang," 167, 173, 255n8; "Punishments of Fu/Lü," xlvii–xlviii, lxii, xcvn179, 25n29, 235, 235n1, 243n5, 243n7, 245n9, 265; Qing scholarship, xvi–xix; "Success through Battle," 123; "Supplementary Sacrifices," lxviii, 39, 41–43n2, 57, 57n1; "Tang's Oath," 79, 81n1; on taxation, 215; term *lu*, 13n11; "Testamentary Charge" and "King Kang's Proclamation," 219, 221; texts not transcribed into clerical script, xix–xxx; three scholarly lineages of Western Han, xxxvi, xcin97; title of, lxxxixn60; "Tribute of Yu," 61n8, 265; use of term *liangyin*, 91; versions of, xxii, xxvi, xxxi–xxxii; Western Han authorized version, xvi, xxvi–xxvii, xxxi, lxxxixn55, xcin97; Xiahou and Ouyang versions, xxxvi, xxxvii, lxxii, lxxxixn65, xcn70, xcin97, 13n11; of Xiping Stone Classics, *xxviii*, xxix, xcn70; "Xu," xxix, xlii–xliv, lxxvi, xcn70. *See also* Fu, Master; New Script chapters; Ni Kuan; Old Script (Guwen) chapters; Xiahou Sheng; *and names of individual chapters*
Documents: Accurate Observations (Shangshu zhonghou), lxxxvi
Dong Cong, xcviiin244
Dong Fengyuan, lxxviii, lxxxv, 279
Dong Zhongshu, lviii, lxiv, lxxxiv, xciiin143, xcvn162, xcixn271, xcixn275
Du Jin, *Fu Sheng Transmitting the Classics*, xxiv
Du Lin, xxx
Du Yu, 93n1

Eight Earls, lxxiv, 17, 21, 51, 51n24
Eight Timbres (Bayin), 19, 19n22
Eight Tools of Government (Bazheng), 131, 137, 137n5
elderly, lx, 103n3, 267n23, 271n27; Ceremony to Nourish the Elders, lxi–lxii, xcvn169; staffs for, 267nn20–21
Eliot, T. S., "still point of the turning world," 15n17

GENERAL INDEX 351

Elman, Benjamin, xcvin204
Eno, Robert, lxxxviiin34
even and odd numbers, 305n2
evidential scholarship, lxix–lxx, lxxii
exegetical traditions, xvii, xxxviii, lxxx
Explaining Graphs and Analyzing Characters (Shuowen jiezi), 257n11
Explanation (Xun), xxxviii, xli–xlii, xcin110

fangshi, xxxvii, xcivn149
Farrer, Anne, 15n17
Fei Chang, 83n11
Feng (Kangshu), 167, 173, 177n3, 179
Feng (settlement), 151, 151nn7–8, 187n1
filial behavior, xxxix, xl, 13, 21, 25n28, 93, 93nn2–3, 47, 47n14, 151, 253, 267; of Shun, 35n2, 47n15
Fire Star, xlviii, xlix, 9, 9n1, 307n7
First Emperor (Qin shi huangdi): imperial project, xxvii; imperial tours, xx, lxxxviiin23, xciiin140; Langye stele, 293n10, 297n17; palace of, 291n1; sons and heir, lii, liii
fish, 51, 59–61, 59n1, 59nn4–5, 121, 263, 299; anomalies in, *lxvii*, 285; products from, 59nn1–2
Five Blessings (Wufu), 133, 281
Five Classics (Wujing), xxviii, lxvii, lxxiii, 249
Five Cycles (Wuji), 131
Five Dependencies (*fu*), 57, 57n1, 59
Five Lakes, 59, 59n5
Five Marchmounts, 17n19, 21, 21n23, 57, 61, 61nn7–8
Five Material Resources/Phases (Wuxing), lxiv, xcvin185, 65, 131, 133, 279, 301n24, 301n26, 301n28, 301n30, 301n32. See also Five Phases
five musical tones, 195n3
Five Phases, lxxx, lxxxii–lxxxiii, *lxxxiii*, 71n7, xciiin135, xcivn154, xcivn161, 305n2; correlated with twelve months and five directions, lxxxv; as translation for *wuxing*, lxxxv, xcixn280. See also *Book of Han*: "Treatise on the Five Phases"; Five Material Resources/Phases; "Tradition on the Great Plan's Five Phases"
Five Proclamations, xliv, 265
Five Punishments, lxii–lxiii, 235–37, 239, 239n1
five-rank noble system, 41n1, 61n7, 223n3, 223n5
Five Supreme Lords, 259–61, 259n2
Five Tasks (Wushi), lxiv, lxxxii, *lxxxiii*, 131, 133, 281–85, 281n4; disasters associated with, *lxiv–lxvi*, lxxxv, 277, 283–85, 283n6
Five Tones, 19, 19n22, 21
five virtues, 195n3
Florilegium of Minor Literature (Shuofu), lxxvii
Flowing Sands, 297n17
Forest of Stelae (Xi'an), xxxi
Four Associates, 39, 43, 45, 45n4
Four Marchmounts, 17n19, 21n23. See also Five Marchmounts
Four Rivers, 57, 61
Four Seas, xlix, 17, 57, 49, 59, 193, 267
Four Seasons correlative thinking, lvi, xlix, xciin128, xciiin135
Fu, Lord of, 235, 235n1
Fu, Master (Fu Sheng): as academician at the Qin court, xix, lxxxviin19; annotation of "Thorough Explanations of the *Documents*," xcin110, 27n32; associated with New Script *Documents*, lxx, lxxiv, lxxvi; authorship of *Great Commentary*, xv, xxxvii–xxxviii, lxx, lxix, lxxii; committed *Documents* to memory, xvii, xxi, lxxxviiin33; conversion of *Documents* from seal script into clerical script, lxxxviin12; descendants of, xxxii, xxiii, *xxxiii*; disciples and

intellectual heirs, xxxii–xxxvi, *xxxiv–xxxv*; flight from capital, xx–xxi; as Former Teacher, xxv; hiding of *Documents* text, xx–xxii, xxiv–xxv; hometown, xix, xxv, *xxv*, lxxxviin16; life of, xix–xxiii; and lost old script chapters, xxxi, lxxi, lxxvi; name of, xix, lxxxviin15; in name of Pi Xirui's studio, lxxi; portrayed in art and theater, *xxiii*, *xxiv*, xxv; Qing attention to, lxx–lxxi; reading of *lu* in *Documents*, 13n11; shrine to, in Zouping County, xxv; standard narrative, xxiv–xxv; tomb of, *xxv*; and transmission of *Documents*, lxxi, lxxxviin18, 115; visit by Han envoy, xxii–xxiii, xxviii, xxxvi, lxxxviiin38; Zheng Xuan on, xviii. *See also* Fu family genealogy

Fu family genealogy, xxxii, *xxxiii*, xcn90

Fu Ru, *xxxiii*

Fu Sheng. *See* Fu, Master

Fu Xi, xcn90

Fu Xi'e, *xxxiii*

Fu Zhan, xix, xxxii, xcn87; in Fu family genealogy, *xxxiii*

Fudan University, li

Fusang (Fu tree), 291n2

Fuxi, 259; name of, 259n1

Gan, battle at, 65. *See also* "Oath at Gan"

Gaoyao, 39, 47n16. *See also* "Gaoyao's Counsel"

"Gaoyao's Counsel," xliv, xcin108; as apocryphal text, xcixn284; in *Documents*, lxviii, 39, 47n16, 53n28, 265; in *Great Commentary*, lxviii, 39; hymn "Auspicious Clouds," li; on regional lords, xciiin137; of Xiping Stone Classics, *xxviii*

Gaozong. *See* Wuding (Gaozong of Shang)

"Gaozong's Supplementary Sacrifice," xciin119, 97, 99, 99n2, 101

Gen (trigram), 291n5

geographical terms, 57

Gong Gong, 307n6

Gongsun Hong, xxxvi

Gongsun Qing, xcivn149

Gongyang commentary, lxx, xcin107, 61n8, 217n1, 309n11

governors (*tong*), 21, 21n24. *See also* Three Governors theory

Grand Inception (Taichu) calendar reform, lv, lviii. *See also under* calendar

Great Commentary (Dazhuan): authorship, xv, xxxvii–xxxviii, lxx, lxix, lxxii; chapter titles, xvi, lxviii, 311, *312–15*; circulation of, from Han to Tang, xv, 165n5; commentarial techniques, xxxviii, xlv; *Commentary* within, xxxviii, xxxix, 39n1, 89, 189; complexity of, xviii; *Documents* chapters included, lxviii–lxix; editions and versions, xvi, xlviii, lxxix, xcvin194, xcviiin247; explanation of lines of *Documents*, xlvii–xlviii; "Gaoyao's Counsel" combined with "Supplementary Sacrifices," lxviii; glosses of words, xlv–xlvi; grounding of court practice in classics, lxi–lxii; historical lore, li; intertextuality with contemporary texts, xlviii–l, li; New Script affiliation, lxviii, lxxvi, 7; Old Script chapters, lxxiii–lxxiv, lxxvi–lxxvii; overlap with *Scribe's Records*, li; as part of *chenwei* (apocrypha) corpus, lxxxvi, xcixn286; on political and social order, lii, xciiin135; "Punishments of Fu" used for "Punishments of Lü," lxviii; Qing editions, lxxi–lxxii, lxxvii–lxxx, lxxxiv–lxxxv, lxxxvi, xcviin239; and Qing *kaozheng* scholarship, lxix–lxxi;

Great Commentary (Dazhuan) (*continued*)
  reading of *lu* in *Documents*, 13n11; references to *Commentary* and *Explanation*, xxxviii–xlii; on regional lords, lii–lv, xciiin140; Song editions, lxxvi–lxxvii, lxxviii, lxxix; as teachings of several *Documents* specialists, xxxvii–xxxviii; textual layers, xxxviii–xxxix, xliv; on theoretical passages in the *Documents*, l–li; on three advisors to King Wu, 129n7; title of, lxxxvin2; "Traditions on Yin" part, lxix; "Traditions on Yu" part, lxix; transmission of, lxxvi–lxxvii; as Western Han text, lxxvi, lxviii; "Xu," xliii, xliv, xxxviii, lxxvi, 213. *See also* Chen Shouqi; Fu, Master; Hui Dong; Lu Jianzeng; Lu Wenchao; Pi Xirui; Sun Zhilu; "Tradition on the Great Plan's Five Phases"; Wang Kaiyun; *and names of specific chapters*
Great Dipper, 15n17
"Great Oath," xxx, lxviii, xcin108; as apocryphal text, xcixn284; in *Documents*, 115–17, 115n1, 119n2, 121n6; fragment 5.1.1 in *Scribe's Records*, 119n2; in *Great Commentary*, 117, 119n2, 119n4; old-script version, 115n2; transmission of, 115–17
"Great Plan," xliv, lxxxii, lxxxv, xcin108; in *Documents*, li, lxiv–lxv, lxxx–lxxxi, lxxxiv, xcvin185, 131, 135n4, 137n5, 141, 143n1, 265, 277–79, 279n4, 281n4, 301n24, 301n26, 301n28, 301n30, 301n32; on ninefold method for successful rulership, 131–33. *See also* "Tradition on the Great Plan's Five Phases"

"Great Proclamation," 167, 197n10; in *Documents*, 139, 141, 141n6, 143n1; in *Great Commentary*, 141, 141n6; speaker in, 139n1; of Wang Mang, 139–41
"Great War," lxviii, 125
"Great Xia" melody, 49n21
gu (orphan), xlv
Guanshu, 149n2, 149n4, 151n6
gui jades, xlvi, 265n15
Guliang commentary, 257n12, 309n11
guyue ("That is why the text says"), 11n4, 195

Hall of Blue-Green Yang, 279, 293
Hall of Comprehensive Luminosity, 279, 297
Han learning (Hanxue), lxx
Hanshi waizhuan (*Mr. Han's Outer Commentary on the Odes*), xliv, xlviii, xcin107, xciin122, xcvn167, 101n2, 165n5, 265n17
Hanshu. See *Book of Han*
haoziyong (draw on his own resources), 199n15
harms (*li*), lxiv–lxv, *lxvii*, 277, 277n1, 283n6; Six Harms, lxv, *lxvi*, lxxxv, 277n1, 281, 285, 287–89
He and Xi, 9n1, 19n21; Earl He and Earl Xi, 19n21
Heart (lunar lodge), 307nn7–8
Heaven and Earth, pillar linking, 307n6
Heavenly King (star), 307n8
heir apparent, xxxix, 93n3, 95n4, 255, 257, 301; Emperor Jing as, xxiii; Gaozong as, xl, 93–95; Ji Fa as, 119–21, 119n1; stars for, 307, 307n7; of Yao, 13
hou (lords) and *wei* (guards), 197n12
Hou Ji, 189n2
House of Dating, 261n4
House of Ying (Qin dynastic house), liii

354 GENERAL INDEX

Hu, lord of, 65
Huainanzi. See Master of Huainan
Huan Rong, xcvn174
Huanbei, 85n1
Huang Shi, xvi
Hui, Emperor of Han, lxxxviiin30, lxxxviiin34
Hui, Lord of Chu, 269n25
Hui Dong: as book collector of Wuzhong, lxxix; edition of, 279, 301n32; role in reconstitution of *Great Commentary* text, xvi, lxxvii, lxxviii, lxxix, lxxxv, xcviin239; "Supplementary Material" chapter, lxxviii; version of "Tradition on the Great Plan's Five Phases," lxxix; viewed Old Script chapters as inauthentic, lxx
Hundred Days' Reform, lxxv
Hundred Families (*baixing*), 27n35
Huo Guang, lix, lxvi, lxxxi, xcviin189
Huoshu, 151n6

Imperial Readings Compiled in the Taiping Era (Taiping yulan), lxxxiv, 261n5, 303n1

jade transverse (*yuheng*), 15, 15nn16–17
Ji, Prince of Shang: and the Great Plan, 131, 133, 135n4; imprisoned by Zhòu, 135n2; song of, 153; visit to Zhou court, 135n4
Ji Chang. *See* Wen, King of Zhou
Ji Fa. *See* Wu, King of Zhou
Ji Man (King Mu of Zhou), 227, 235, 235n1
Ji Shi (Duke of Shao), 123, 149n3, 185, 185n1
Ji Yu (Tangshu), 159, 163n1, 265
Ji Yun, lxxviii
Ji Zhao (King Kang of Zhou), 219. *See also* "King Kang's Proclamation"
Jia Kui, lxxiii, lxxiv

Jia Yi, xciiin143
Jian Qing, xxxvii, *xxxiv*
Jiang, Lady, 203n1
Jiaozhi, 29n37
Jie of Xia, 75, 79, 81n4, 217n1, 261n7
Jing (state of Chu), 269n25
Jing, Han Emperor, xxiii, lxxxviiin39
Jing Fang, lxiv; *Traditions on the "Changes,"* 303n1
Jiong (Bo Jiong), 227. *See also* "Charge to Jiong"
Juqiao, granary at, 129n6

Kang, King of Zhou (Ji Zhao), 219. *See also* "King Kang's Proclamation"
Kang Youwei, xcviin215
Kangshu (Feng), 167, 173, 177n3, 179
kaozheng movement, lxix–lxx, lxxii
Karlgren, Bernhard, translations of, 45n4, 47n11
Keightley, David, 97n1
Kern, Martin, xx, lxxxixn48, xcin112; on the bibliocaust, xxvii, lxxxviiin32; on Shun, xciiin140
"King Cheng's Government," 197n11, 209, 209n3
"King Kang's Proclamation," 219, 219n3, 221
Kong Anguo, xxix, xxxvi, xcn90, xcn93, 97n1
Kong Family Masters (Kong congzi), li, 239n1
Kong Guanglin, 213
Kong Yingda, lxxxvin2, 19n22, 209, 249, 261n4
Kunlun Mountains, 295n16

Langye stele, 293n10, 297n17
law, lxii–lxiv; and lenience, 237. *See also* penal system
Legge, James, 61n7
li. *See* harms
Li (Qi), 105

GENERAL INDEX 355

Li (trigram), 295n13
Li Feng, 197n12
Li Gong, xcvn174
Li Ke, lxxxviin18
Li Shan, 13n10, 303n1
Li Si, xxv, liii
Li Xian, 165n5
Liang Qichao, lxxv
liangyin (beamed shack), xxxix–xl, 89–91, 93, 93n1
life cycle, xcivn156, 69nn2–3
Ling, Eastern Han Emperor, xxix
Liu An (king of Huainan), 153n3
Liu Bang, xxi, liii, liv, xcvn176
Liu Fenglu, xcvin204
Liu He, lxv, lxvi–lxvii, lxxxi, lxxxvi, xcvin189; tomb in Jiangxi, xcvin187
Liu kings, lxxxviiin39
Liu Qiyu, xxi, lxxxixn55, 139n1
Liu the Duke, 263n10
Liu Xiang: as cataloger in imperial archives, xv, xxx, xxxi, lxxvi; explanations in *Book of Han*, 303n1; *Garden of Eloquence* (Shuoyuan), li, xcvn167, 165n5, 271n27; interpretations cited in "Treatise on the Five Phases," xcixn271, 101n2; and "Tradition on the Great Plan's Five Phases," lxxxi–lxxxiv, lxxxvi, xcviiin261, 279. *See also* Liu Xin
Liu Xin, *xxxv*, lxx; accusations against academicians, xxix, xxx, lxxi, lxxii, 115; accusations by Kang Youwei, xcviin215; advocated inclusion of additional chapters, xxix; influence on Eastern Han scholars, lxxiii; interpretations cited in "Treatise on the Five Phases," xcixn271; narrative of *Documents*, xxx–xxxi; narrative of Master Fu, xxiv; promotion of old script chapters, xxix–xxx, lxxi–lxxii, lxxiii; Qing criticism of, lxxi–lxxii; and "Tradition on

the Great Plan's Five Phases," lxxxi, xcviiin261
Liu Zhao, xcviiin261
liuzong (six honored ones), 15, 15n18
Loewe, Michael, xcvn162
lords, 223n3; halls of, 223, 223n2, 223n4. *See also* regional lords
lotus stems, 225, 225n9
lu (inhospitable land/administrative acts), readings of, 13n11
Lu (place): documents-related materials from, xxix, xcn93; fief of Duke of Zhou, 151n9, 191, 197n7, 199n14; scholars at Qin court, xx, lxxxviiin26
Lu, Duke of, 229. *See also* Boqin
Lü, Lord of, 235, 235n1
Lu Deming, 105n1
Lu Jianzeng: *Collection from Elegant Rain Studio*, lxxix; *Great Commentary* edition, 205, 219, 279, 301n32; role in reconstitution of *Great Commentary* text, xvi, lxxvii, lxxviii–lxxix, xcviiin247; and "Tradition on the Great Plan's Five Phases," lxxxi, lxxxv, lxxxvi
Lü Wang (Lü Shang, Jiang Shang, Shangfu, Taigong), 107, 123, 125, 263n9
Lu Wenchao, xvi, lxx, lxxvii, lxxviii–lxxix; *Great Commentary* edition, lxxix–lxxx, lxxxv, 279
Lufu, Gongzi, 135n1, 149n1, 153
lunar lodges, 9n1, 307nn7–8
Luo/Luoyi (settlement), 169n1, 185, 187n1, 189, 199n14, 201; "Proclamation at Luo, 167, 167n1. *See also* Chengzhou
Lüshi chunqiu. See *Mr. Lü's Annals*
Luxuriant Gems of the Spring and Autumn (Chunqiu fanlu), xcvn162

Ma Duanlin: *Comprehensive Study of Government Institutions Based on Authoritative Sources and Later*

Interpretations (Wenxian tongkao), lxxvii, 91
Ma Rong, lxxiii, 33, 65–67, 93n1, 151n7, 187n1
Managing Doubt (Jiyi), 131
"Many Officers," 201, 219
"Many Regions," 197n11, 215
Master Han Fei (Han Fei zi), xlviii, xcin107, 29n37
Master Mo (Mozi), 29n37
Master of Huainan (Huainanzi), xlviii, 295n16; Monthly Ordinances, li; "Overview of the Essentials," xcin112; on pillar linking Heaven and Earth, 307n6; reference to square receptacle, 309n14; on regional lords, 177n5; "Responses of the Way," xcin107; "The Ruler's Techniques," xlix–1; "Xu," xlii
Master Xun (Xunzi), xlviii, 25n30, 199n15; dialogue of Lord Ai of Lu and Confucius, 35n3; "Yao Asked," 197n9
melodies (*yao*), 17n20, 49n21
memorial cultures, xvi–xvii, xxi
"men of service" (*shi*), 23n26; clothing and chariots for, 75; recommendation for office, 25n28; training of, 257n10
Mencius, 123, 217n1
menghou (preeminent lord), 255n8
Mercury (planet), 307n9
merit system of promotion, 7, 27
"Metal Coffer": bamboo manuscript, 145; in *Documents*, 141, 145, 145n1, 149n4; following "Great Proclamation," 141; in *Great Commentary*, 145, 149n1; on invasion of Yan, 209n3
Meyer, Dirk, xvii, lxxxixn48
mi (careful), 29n36
Ming, Han Emperor, lxi–lxii
ming gong hou (give the charge to the heir of the Duke), 191, 191n4

Mingtang (Bright Hall), 279, 279n5, 293, 295
Mingtiao, battle at, 261n7
Mo (group from the north), 217, 217n1
monthly ordinances: and seasonal sacrifices, lxiv, lxv; Yueling genre, li, 9n12, xciin128, 277
"Monthly Ordinances of the Four Seasons" (Sishi yueling), xciin128
moon, movement of, *lxvii*, 285, 303n1
mourning hut, xxxix–xl, 89–91, 93, 93n1
Mr. Han's Outer Commentary on the Odes (Hanshi waizhuan), xliv, xlviii, xcin107, xciin122, xcvn167, 101n2, 165n5, 265n17
Mr. Lü's Annals (Lüshi chunqiu), 65n1, 267n18; Monthly Ordinances, li; "Xu," xlii, xcin112
Mu, King of Zhou (Ji Man), 227, 235, 235n1
Mulberry Forest, 83, 83n9
mulberry trees, 103, 103n1, 163, 253, 253n5
music, 17, 49n21, 291; song of Prince Wei, 153
Muye, 123, 123n1

National Center for the Performing Arts (Beijing), xxv
New Book of Tang (Xin Tangshu), bibliographical treatise, lxxvi
New Script chapters: "Canon of Yao," 5, 7; "Catalpa Wood," 167, 179; chapter titles, lxviii, 313, 315; "Do Not Slack," 91, 205; "Gaoyao's Counsel," 39; "Gaozong's Supplementary Sacrifice," 97; "Great Proclamation," 139; "Many Officers," 201; "Many Regions," 215; "Metal Coffer," 145; "Oath at Bi," 229; "Oath at Gan," 65; "Pangeng," 85; "Prince Wei," 153, 155; "The Prince of the West Attacks Li," 105; "Proclamation of/to Shao,"

New Script chapters (*continued*) 185; "Proclamation on Drink," 173; "Proclamation on Luo," 189; "Proclamation to Kang," 167, 173; "Punishments of Lü," 235; "Tang's Oath," 79; "Testamentary Charge," 219; "Tribute of Yu," 57. *See also* New Script/Old Script controversy; *and titles of individual chapters*

New Script/Old Script controversy, xvi, lxvii–lxxv, xcviin199, 227

New Script studies, lxx, xcvi–xcviin204

Ni Kuan, xxxvi–xxxvii; and calendar reform, lv–lix, xcivn149

"Nine Offers," lxviii, lxix, 33, 35n1, 75

nine provinces, 57

North Star, 15, 15n17

Notes on the Tradition on the Five Phases (Wuxing zhuan ji), lxxxii

Nylan, Michael, lxxxixn55

"Oath at Bi," xliii

"Oath at Gan," 65; on calendar and life cycle, lviii, xcivnn156–57; gloss for "to battle" (*zhan*), xlv; Six Ministers, lxxiv; on succession of three eras, lvi–lviii, xcivn158

"Oath at Qin," xcn70

"Oath at Xian": composed by Boqin, xliii; and fragment from "Principal Teachings," 253n3; in *Great Commentary*, 229–31; title of, 229–31, 229n3, 253n3

Obscure Records from the Cavern (Dong ming ji), lxxxviin18

Odes: annotated by Zheng Xuan, lxxiv; commentary of Kong Yingda, 209; Fu family and, xxxii; "Gong Liu," 263n10; "Jiao tong," 157n3; quotations from, 261n6, 273n33; "Sacrificial Odes of Zhou," 45n7; targeted in Qin bibliocaust, xx–xxi. See also *Mr. Han's Outer Commentary on the Odes*

"Offering the Millet," 159

offerings to ancestors, 21, 21n25. *See also* ancestral temples

official garments, color for, lv–lvi, lviii, xcivn161

Old Book of Tang (Jiu Tangshu), bibliographical treatise, 27n32, xcin110

Old Books on Subtle Matters (Gu wei shu), lxxxiv

Old Master (Laozi). *See Classic of the Way and the Power*

Old Script (Guwen) chapters: "Canon of Yao" and "Canon of Shun," lxviii, 5, 7; "Charge to Jiong," 227; "Charge to Prince Wei," 153; "Charge to Yue," 89, 91; as forgeries, xvi, xxvi, lxx, lxxi, lxxvi, lxxxixn48, xcviin192, xcviin215; "Gaoyao's Counsel" and "Supplementary Sacrifices," lxviii, 39, 41–43n2; "Great Oath," 115, 115n2; Liu Xin's promotion of, xxix–xxx, lxxi–lxxii, lxxiii; lost, xxix–xxx, xxxi, lxix, lxxi, lxxvi, xcviin197; "Pangeng" chapters, 85; Pi Xirui's view of, lxxi, lxxii, lxxiv, lxxv; "Success through Battle" and "Great War," lxviii, 123–25; recovered from wall, xxx. xcn93. *See also* New Script/Old Script controversy; *and under titles of individual chapters*

omens, 97, 101, 117, 283–85, 283n6, 305, 305n5; and Great Plan's Five Phases, lxiv–lxvii, *lxvii*, lxxiii–lxxiv, lxxxvi, 101n2; Liu Xiang's catalog of, lxxxii, lxxxiii; theory of, 309n12

open philology, xvii, lxxxviin10

oracle bones, 89

Ouyang family: disciples of Master Fu, xv, *xxxv*; Master Ouyang, xviii, xxxvi, lxxiv; Ouyang Gao, *xxxv*, xxxvi, xxxvii, xcin97

Ouyang version of *Documents*, xxxvi, xxxvii, lxxii, lxxxixn65, xcin97, 13n11, 149n1

Pan stream, 263n9
"Pangeng" (chapter), xcn70, xciiin137, 85, 85n2
Pangeng (king of Shang), 85, 103n2; capital of, 85, 85n1
Pankenier, David, 105n2, 307n8
Pei Yin, commentary to *Scribe's Records*, 97n1
penal system, 235, 235n1, 241nn2–4, 243, 243n6; corporeal punishments, 25n31; Five Punishments, lxii–lxiii, 235, 239, 239n1; symbolic punishments, 25nn30–31; of Yao and Shun, 5–7
pheasants, 41, 97, 99, 101, 305; offered as tribute, lix–lx, xcvn167, 159–61, 163–65
philological methods, xvi, xvii, lxix–lxx, lxxxviin10
phoenix, 35, 35n3
Pi Xirui, 13n11, 15n17, 33n1, 59n4, 223n1; *Annotations to the Great Commentary*, lxxi; association with Xia Jingzhuang, lxxii, xcviin209; challenges to Zheng Xuan's interpretations, lxxiv–lxxv, 149n1; chapter titles, 312, 314; and "Do Not Slack," 91, 205; edition of *Great Commentary*, xvi, lxviii, lxxvii, lxxx, lxxxv, 49n22, 101, 219, 291n15, 303n1; emphasis on New Script interpretations, lxxi, lxxx; "Gaozong's Supplementary Sacrifice" chapter, 101; on "Great Proclamation," 141; *History of Classical Thought*, lxxi, lxxiv; literary productions of, xcviin207; on "Metal Coffer," 141, 149n1, 209n3; *Notes and Corrections to The Great Commentary*, xvi, lxxi, lxxiv, lxxv, xcviin208; "Oath at Xian" chapter, 231, 253n3; on "Oath at Xian" and "Principal Teachings," 253n3; on "Pangeng," 87n1; and "Prince of the West Attacks Qi," 107, 109n5, 111n6; "Prince Wei" chapter, 155; on "Proclamation on Luo," 189n2; as social reformer, lxxv; studio of, lxxi; on "Testamentary Charge," 223n1, 225n8; treatment of "Catalpa Wood," 179n1; treatment of "Great Oath," 119n4; treatment of "King Cheng's Government," 209, 209n3; treatment of "Many Officers," 201; treatment of "Oath at Gan" and "Principal Teachings," 67; treatment of "Success through Battle" and "Great War," 125; treatment of "Tradition on the Great Plan's Five Phases," lxxx, lxxxv, 279; view of Zheng Xuan, lxxiii, lxxiv, lxxx; and Wang Kaiyun, lxxv–lxxvi

"Piety Achieved," 49, 49n21
Ping, Han emperor, lx, 161
pitch pipes, 19, 19, 43, 43n3, 47, 47n13
"Praising the Millet," lix–lx, lxviii, lxix, 159, 165n5
pregnant women, 179, 261
Prince of the West. *See* "Prince of the West Attacks Qi/Li, The"; Wen, King of Zhou
"Prince of the West Attacks Qi/Li, The," 105–7, 109n5, 111n6
"Principal Teachings," lxi, xcin108, xciin120–21, xcvin195, 249, 253nn3–4; dialogue between Confucius and Zixia, xliv, 265; glosses of words, xlv–xlvi; passage on Three Regulators, 67; on regional lords, xciiin137, 251
"Principal Teachings of the Commentary to the *Documents*" (Shuzhuan lüeshuo), 249
"Proclamation at Yan," lxviii, lxix, 197n11, 213

"Proclamation of the Supreme Lord," lxviii, lxix, 75
"Proclamation of/to Shao," 185, 185n1, 187n1
"Proclamation on Drink," xlviii, xcn70, xciiin137, 167, 173, 175n2, 177nn3–4
"Proclamation on Luo," xcin108, xciin119, xciiin137, 167, 167n1; in *Documents*, 189, 191, 195nn4–5, 199n14; in *Great Commentary*, 189, 195n3
"Proclamation to Kang," xcn70, 167, 171n3, 173, 225n8
Pugu (Bogu), 149n5
"Punishments of Fu/Lü": in *Documents*, xlvii–xlviii, lxii, xcvn179, 25n29, 235, 235n1, enunciations by Confucius, xliv, xciin121, 243n5, 243n7, 245n9, 265; in *Great Commentary*, xlvii, lxii–lxiii, lxviii, 235; on penal law, li, lxii–lxiii; on regional lords, xciiin137; title of, lxviii, xcvin193, 235
"Pure, the Ancestral Temple," 39, 45n7, 45n9

Qi (Li), 105–7
Qi (son of Yu), 53n28, 65
Qi (state), xix, xx, lxxxviiin16, lxxxviiin18, lxxxviiin26
Qi, Mount, 263n8, 267n19
Qian Mu, xxi
qilin (unicorn), 29n38, 35n3
Qin dynasty, liii; academicians, xix–xx, xxvii–xxviii; political achievements, xxii; and regional lords, 11. *See also* academicians; bibliocaust of 213 BCE
Qing scholarship: *Documents*, xviii–xix; memorial culture, xvi–xvii; philological methods, xvi, xvii, lxix–lxx; political agenda, lxxii; promotion of Western Han scholarship, lxx–lxxii; treatment of "Tradition on the Great Plan's Five Phases," lxxxvi. *See also* Pi Xirui; Wang Kaiyun
Qin–Han transition, xxi–xxii, liii
qishi (Seven Beginnings), lxviii, xcvin194, 19, 19n22; as seven pitches, 19n22
Qu Wanli, lxxxixn47, xciin125, xcvin192, 313, 315
Quanrong/Quanyi, 109, 109n3

ranks, liv; five-rank noble system, 41n1, 61n7, 223n3, 223n5
rebellion of 154 BCE, lii, lxxxviiin39
Records of Ritual (Liji): Monthly Ordinances, li; quoted in "Principal Teachings," 261n6; "Royal Regulations" chapter, 61n7, 163n3; Shun playing "Southern Wind," 35n2; on *zao shi* (trained scholar), 257n10
regional kings (*zhuhouwang*), lii, liv. *See also* regional lords
regional lords, lii–lv, xciiin140, 235n1, 251; estates of, 85, 87n2; leader of, 255, 255n8; relations with ruler, xlvi–xlvii, lii–liii, 7, 79, 177n5, 189, 305; travel of, 173, 177n5. *See also* lords
"Regulation Sacrifice," 289
Ren Zhaolin, *Compiled Records from the Forest of Arts* (Yilin shuji), lxxx
ritual and law, xlvii, 237, 243n5
ritual halls, 279, 279n5
rituals: incantation texts, 289n11; seasonal, 11nn5–6, 251n2; of sex between ruler and queen, 201, 201n1; of Shun at Mount Tai, 15n14; to welcome the sun, 251n1; Zheng Xuan's interpretations, lxxx
Rituals of Zhou (Zhouli), lxxiii, xcviin215, 309n14
rivers and mountains, 57. *See also* Five Marchmounts

Royal Standard (Wangji), lxiv, lxxxii–lxxxiii, *lxxxiii*, xcvin184, 281, 281n4, 285, 287; inauspicious signs associated with, lxiv, lxv–lxvi, *lxvi*, lxxxv, 277
Ru underground, xxix, xcn71
rui (insignia), xlvii
rulership: in "Catalpa Wood," 179; co-, liii, liv; *Documents* as guide to, xl, xlii, lii; meteorological phenomena and, 131, 305; ninefold method, 131–33; nonpurposeful, 33; styles of governing, 5–7, 5n1, 65; of Yao and Shun, 7, 33

sacred peaks, 17n19
sacrifices, lv, 11n6, 83n9, 97, 255n6; ancestral, lx, xcvn167, 19, 165, 175n1, 189, 189n2, 193n2, 251; to founders of noble lines, 85, 87n3; meaning of term *ji* for, 257nn11–12; suburban, 121n6, 145, 151, 151n9. *See also* ancestral temples; "Gaozong's Supplementary Sacrifice"; rituals; "Supplementary Sacrifices"
Sanft, Charles, lxii, xcvn179
Schafer, Edward, 17n19
Schuessler, Axel, 71n5
Scribe's Records (Shiji): on "Admonitions to Gaozong" and "Gaozong's Supplementary Sacrifice," 101; and the authentic *Documents*, lxxii, 115; "Basic Annals of Zhou," 117n6; on battle at Bi, 229, 229n1; on battle at Mingtiao, 261n7; on bibliocaust, xx–xxi; "Biographies of the Classical Scholars," xx–xxi, xxxvi, lxxxviin17; biography of Dong Zhongshu, xcixn275; on Boqin, 197n8; "Canon of Yao," 15n12; character Jiong, xcvin196; on "Charge to Prince Wei," 153; on Commissioner of Ceremonial, lxxxviiin38; on Confucius as source of *Documents* traditions, xxxi; on crisis at Yan, 197n11, 211n2; description of Heart, 307n8; "Gaozong's Supplementary Sacrifice," 97; "Great Oath," 117n6, 119nn1–2, 121n5; "Hereditary House of Taigong of Qi," 117n6; on King Wen of Zhou, 105n2; "Many Regions," 215; on Master Fu, xix, xxii, xxvii; "Metal Coffer," 145–47, 149n1, 149n5, 151n8; "Oath at Bi," xliii; on "Pangeng," 85n2; Pei Yin's commentary, 97n1; and "Praising the Millet," 159, 163n1; on "Proclamation of the Supreme Lord," 75; "Punishments of Fu/Lü," lxviii, 235, 235n1; reading of *lu* in *Documents*, 13n11; on "Shao music with flute," 47n16; Shun playing "Southern Wind," 35n2; Sima Zhen's commentary, 109n3, 229–31, 261n3, 307n8; song of Prince Wei, 153n3; on "Success through Battle," 123–25, 129n7; on transmission of Great Plan, 135n4; "Treatise on Pitch Pipes," 43n3; "Treatise on the Feng and Shan Sacrifices," 61n7; on Wuding's dream, 89; "Xu," xlii, xliv, xciin112; "Xu" fragments for *Documents*, xlii–xliii; "Zhengyi" commentary, 151n6
seal script and clerical script, xxix–xxx, lxx, lxxxviin12
seasons, xlviii–l; Four Seasons correlative thinking, lvi, xlix, xciin128, xciiin135; and monthly ordinances, lxiv, lxv, xciin128; rituals for, 11nn5–6, 251n2, 279; stars used to fix, 9n1
Second Emperor, xciiin139
Selections of Refined Literature (Wenxuan), 13n10
Seven Beginnings (*qishi*), lxviii, xcvin194, 19, 19n22
Seven Kingdoms Rebellion of 154 BCE, lii, lxxxviiin39

GENERAL INDEX   361

Seven Pitches, 19n22
sexual encounters, of ruler and queen, 201, 203n1
Shalu, Mount, 307n10
Shang (Yin) dynasty: call to submit to Zhou in "Many Regions," 215; capital of, 85n1; conquered by Zhou, 105, 115–17, 123, 129n3, 197n7, 215, 263n9; downfall attributed to alcoholism, 173; fall of, 201; last ruler of, 105n2; officers who served, 201; people moved to Song, 153, 167; and "Proclamation of the Supreme Lord," 75; sacrifices, 97; transition from Xia, 79, 81, 81n3; uprising against Zhou, 145, 149n2, 149n5, 153, 167, 197n10; under Wuding, 89. See also Tang (Shang founder); Zhòu
Shang Rong, 129, 129n9
Shangshu, as title, lxxxixn60. See also *Documents*
Shao, Duke of (Ji Shi), 123, 149n3, 185, 185n1
"Shao" melody, 47n16, 49n21
Shaughnessy, Edward, 135n4, 185n1
She, Lord, 269n25
shi. See "men of service"
shi ze (sometimes), 283n5
Shiji. See *Scribe's Records*
Shiqu Pavilion (Weiyang Palace), xxix
Shun: appointment of Yu as successor, 47n16, 49n22; "Canon of Shun," lxviii, xciiin140, 5, 5n5, 7; in "Canon of Yao," xlvi–xlvii, lxxiv–lxxv, lxxxviiin23, xciiin140, 47n16; filiality of, 47n15; in "Gaoyao's Counsel," 39, 47n16; headgear, 35n3; as legendary figure, xciiin131; marriage of, 13n9; Minister of the Masses of, 29n39; in "Nine Offers," 33; penal system of, 5, 245n10; reign of, 47, 47n12;

ritual and musical performances of, 35n2, 39; rulership of, 7, 33; sent into wilds by Yao, 13n11; style of government, 332; succeeded by Yu, 51n25; as successor to Yao, 5, 15n15, 39, 49n17, 51n26; tours of inspection, lxxxviiin23, xciiin140, 5, 7, 15n14, 19–21; in "Tradition on the Great Plan's Five Phases," 281n2
shuo (incipient), xlv
Shuofu (*Florilegium of Minor Literature*), lxxvii
Shuowen jiezi (Explaining graphs and analyzing characters), 257n11
Shusun Tong, lxxxviiin23
Shuzhuan lüeshuo (*Principal Teachings of the Commentary to the Documents*), 249
Si Yue, xlvii
signs. See omens
Siku editors. See *Catalog of the Imperially Authorized Complete Library of the Four Branches*
Silk, Jonathan, "open philology," lxxxviin10
silkworms, 253, 253n5
Sima family, lxxii. See also *Scribe's Records*; Sima Qian; Sima Zhen
Sima Qian, lv; narrative of Master Fu, xxiv, lxvii. See also *Scribe's Records*
Sima Zhen, 109n3, 229–31, 261n3, 307n8
simplicity and refinement, 71, 71n5
Six Arts in Genres and Subgenres (Liuyi liubie), lxxxiv
Six Extremes (Liuji), 133
Six Harms, lxv, *lxvi*, lxxxv, 277n1, 281, 285, 287–89
"six honored ones" (*liuzong*), 15, 15n18
Six Oaths, xliv, 265

Six Pitch Pipes, 19, 19, 43, 43n3, 47, 47n13
Six Quivers (Liu tao), 111n6
Six Tasks, 289
Song (domain), 153, 167
Song, Mount, 295n16
"Southern Wind," 35n2
Sovereign's Standard (Huangji), 131
Spring and Autumn Annals (Chunqiu). See *Annals*
staffs for elderly, lxi, 267nn20–21
stars, xlix, lxxiv–lxxv, 9n1, 15n17, 307nn7–8; Fire Star, xlviii, xlix, 9, 9n1, 307n7; North Star, 15, 15n17
"Statutes on Enrollment" (Fu lü), lx–lxi
Stele Inscriptions (Qin), xx
"striking the board" (game), 271nn29–30
students, 271, 271n27
"Success through Battle," lxviii, 123, 129n7, 209
sumptuary laws, 39, 219–21, 225n8
Sun Jue, lxxxvi
Sun Xingyan, xciin125
Sun Zhilu, xvi, lxxvii, lxxviii, lxxix, lxxxv, 279
"Supplementary Sacrifices" (Yi ji), lxviii, 39, 41–43n2, 51n26, 57, 57n1, xcvin192, xcvin194
symbolic punishments, 25nn30–31

Tai, Mount, 15n14
Tai Wu, 101n2
Taigong (Lü Wang/Lü Shang), 107, 123, 125, 263n9
Tall Di, 309n11
Tang (Shang founder), 75, 79, 81n3, 261n7; advised by Yi Yin, xxvii, 79, 81n5, 101n2; charioteer of, 83n11; sacrifice at Mulberry Forest, 83n9. See also "Tang's Oath"

"Tang's Oath," xcvn176, 79, 81n1
Tangshu (Ji Yu), 159, 163n1, 265
taxation, xlix, xciin127, 129n6, 215; one-tenth rate, 217n1
teacher-disciple networks, *xxxiv–xxxv*, xxxvii, lxxxi
Teaching the Classics (Jiangjing tu), xli
ten heavenly branches, 53n28
ten methods, 47, 47n14
"Testamentary Charge," xciiin137, 219–21, 223nn1–2, 225n8, 225n10
"that is what it is about," xlviii–xlix, 9, 15, 45, 47, 87, 137, 169, 193
"that is why the text says" (*guyue*), 11n3, 195
thinking in fives, 21n23
"Thorough Explanations of the *Documents*" (Shangshu changxun), xcin110, 27n32
Three August Ones, 259, 259n2
Three Excellencies (San Gong), 7, 11, 13, 27, 27n34, 35, 61, 253
Three Governors (Santong) theory, lvi–lix, *lviii*, 65, xcivn158, xcvn162
Three Kings, 71, 257, 265, 265n16
Three Powers (Sande), 131
Three Progenitors of Chu, 293n11
Three Regulators (Sanzheng), lvi–lviii, xcivn157, 65–67, 69, 69n1, 71, 71n4
Tjan, Tjoe Som, xcvin199
"Tradition on the Five Phases" (Wuxing zhuan), lxxix, lxxxi, lxxxv, xcviiin262. See also "Tradition on the Great Plan's Five Phases"
"Tradition on the Great Plan's Five Phases" (Hongfan Wuxing zhuan; in *Great Commentary*): as apocryphal text, lxxxvi, xcixn286; as "argumentative," lxxxvin9; in *Book of Han*, lxiv, lxxxi–lxxxii, xcixn271, 283nn5–6, 285n8, 305n3,

"Tradition on the Great Plan's Five Phases" (*continued*) 305n5; cited in Song and Ming, lxxxiv; eleven-part structure, lxxxii–lxxxiv; integrated as chapter of *Great Commentary*, lxxxiv–lxxxv; Monthly Ordinances section, 277–79, 279n4; on regional lords, xciiin137; relation with *Book of Han*'s "Treatise on the Five Phases," lxxxii–lxxxiv, *lxxxiii*, xcivn159, xcixn271, 303n1, 309n11; signs of harm, lxiv–lxvi, *lxvi*; in Sun Zhilu's edition, lxxx, lxxxv; textual transmission, lxxxi–lxxxii; three-part division in *Great Commentary*, lxxxv, 277–79; use of term *wuxing*, lxxxv–lxxxvi, xcixn280, 133; versions of Hui Dong and Lu Jianzeng, lxxix, lxxxvi; in Wang Kaiyuan's and Pi Xirui's editions, lxxx, lxxxv; as Western Han omenological guide, li, lxiv, lxxxvi, xciiin134, 277n1. See also *Documents*: "Great Plan"; *Tradition on the Great Plan's Five Phases* (independent text)

Tradition on the Great Plan's Five Phases (Hongfan Wuxing zhuan; independent text), lxvi–lxvii, lxxxi–lxxxii, lxxxv, xcviiinn261–62, xcviin264

translators, 83n8, 99n1, 103, 163n3

"Tribute of Yu," xliv, xciiin137, 57, 57n1, 61n8, 265; as apocryphal text, xcixn284; on Xiping Stone Classics fragment, *xxviii*

Tsinghua University bamboo-strip manuscripts, xxvii, 89–91; "Qi ye," 105n2; "Zhou Wuwang you ji," 145n1

Tui (magistrate), lxiii

Van Ess, Hans, xcvin199
Various Verifications (Shuzheng), 131

Wang Chong, 83n9
Wang consort family, lxxxii
Wang He, 307n10
Wang Kaiyun: base text, lxxix; chapter titles, 312, 314; "Charge to Prince Wei," 155; on "Do Not Slack," 205; edition of *Great Commentary*, xvi, lxviii, lxxv, lxxvii, lxxx, 75, 291n15; on "Nay" means "No" in "Canon of Yao," 13n10; "Nine Offers," 33; and Pi Xirui, lxxv–lxxvi; preface of, lxxvi; "The Prince of the West Attacks Qi," 107; on "Punishments of Fu," 241n4; reconstitution of "Principal Teachings," 249, 253n4; treatment of "Admonitions to Gaozong," 101; treatment of "Charge to Yue," 91; treatment of "Great Oath," 119–21n4; treatment of "King Cheng's Government," 209; treatment of "Metal Coffer" and "Great Proclamation," 141; treatment of "Oath at Gan," 67; treatment of "Oath at Xian," 231; treatment of "Proclamation at Yan," 213; treatment of "Testamentary Charge" and "King Kang's Proclamation," 219–21; treatment of "Tradition on the Great Plan's Five Phases," lxxx, lxxxv, 279

Wang Mang, xxx, lxxiii, lxxxiv, xcivn160; ancestry of, 307n10; "Great Proclamation" of, 139–41, 141n6; as latter-day Duke of Zhou, lx, 161; memorial presented by Zhang Song, 271–73n31

Wang Mingsheng (Xizhuang), *Latest Opinions on the Documents*, lxxiv

Wang Mo, lxxix–lxxx
Wang Niansun, 29n36
Wang Renjun, lxxx
Wang Wei, *Fu Sheng Transmitting the Classics* (attrib.), *xxiii*

Wang Wengru, 307n10
Wang Yinglin: on "Admonitions to Gaozong," 101n2; called attention to lost old-script chapters, xxx, lxix, lxxvi; on "Charge to Jiong," 227; on edition of *Great Commentary* from Song, lxxvii; on "Great Oath," 115nn1–2; on "Great Proclamation," 141; on "Nine Offers," 33, 35n1; on "Oath at Xian" and "Oath at Bi," 229n3; and "Pangeng" passage, 85; on "Praising the Millet," 159; on "Principal Teachings," 249; on "Proclamation at Yan," 213; on "Proclamation of the Supreme Lord," 75; *Yuhai*, xcixn279, 279
Wang Zhengjun (Empress Dowager Wang), 307n10
Watson, Burton, 61n7
Wei (domain), 167
Wei, Prince, 153, 153n3, 157n3; "Charge to Prince Wei," 153–55
Wei Hong, xxiii, *xxxiii*, lxxiii, lxxiv
Weighed Discourses (Lunheng), xcn84, 115n5, 271nn28, 30
Wen, Han Emperor, xxii, xxviii, xxx, xcivn159
Wen, King of Zhou (Ji Chang/Prince of the West), 105, 111, 111n8, 171n4; ancestral temple at Feng, 151n7, 187n1; mandate of, 105n2, 169–71, 169n2, 171n3; names of, 111n9, 263n9; rulership of, lxi, 263; sacrifices to, 145, 151, 151n9, 189, 189n2. See also "Prince of the West Attacks Qi/Li, The"
Western Han court: academicians, xxviii–xxix, xxxi, lxx, lxxi, lxxxixn65; interpretation of signs, lxiv, lxv; men of service, liv; rescinding of ban on private ownership of texts, xxviii; scholarly lineages, xxxvi, xcin97
widows and widowers, 179

Writing of the Luo River (Luo shu), lxxxiv
Wu, Han Emperor, xxxvi, liv, lxxxi; "Annals" of, 25n28; calendar reform of 105–4 BCE, lv–lvi, lviii–lix; and "Great Oath," 115n2; reign of, xxviii, xxx, xxxvii, lix, lxxxixn65, 115
Wu, King of Zhou (Ji Fa), 189, 189n2; ancestral sacrifices to, 189; brothers of, 149nn2–3; conquest of Shang, 105, 115–17, 123, 197n7; death of, 139; on divination, 141, 141n5; as heir apparent, 119n1, 121n5; in "Metal Coffer," 145; received "Great Plan" from Prince Ji, 131–33, 135, 135n4; submissiveness of Prince Wei toward, 153; three advisors, 129n7
Wu Hu, lxxxviin16
Wu Zhixiong, xciiin135
Wuding (Gaozong of Shang), xxxix, xl, 89–91, 93n2, 97; in "Admonitions to Gaozong," 101; sons of, 97n1; temple in honor of, 89n2. See also "Gaozong's Supplementary Sacrifice"
Wugeng, 149, 149n1
wusheng (five tones), 19–21, 19n22
Wuwei Ceremonials, lxix, xcviin198; "Mourning Clothes" chapter, lxix
wuxing, use of term, lxxxv, xcixn280, 133. See also Five Material Resources/Phases; Five Phases

Xi and He, 9n1, 19n21; Earl Xi and Earl He, 19
Xia calendar, 69n3
Xia dynasty, li, lvi–lviii, xciiin131, 75, 201; transition to Shang, 79, 81, 81n3. See also Jie of Xia
Xia Jingzhuang: preface to Pi Xirui's *Notes and Corrections*, lxxi, lxxii, xcviin209; view of Zheng Xuan, lxxiii–lxxiv

GENERAL INDEX 365

Xiahou family, *xxxiv*; interpretations of *Documents*, xv, xxxvii, 13n11, lxxxixn65, xcn70; tradition on "Great Plan," lxvii, lxxxi–lxxxii; Xiahou the elder and Xiahou the younger, lxxxixn65, xcin97. *See also* Xiahou Sheng; Xiaohou Shichang

Xiahou Jian, *xxxiv*, xxxvii, xcin97

Xiahou Sheng, *xxxiv*, xxxvii, lxxxvi, xcin97, xcvin189; disciples of, xxxvii; use of text *Tradition on the Great Plan's Five Phases*, lxv–lxvii, lxxxi, xcviiin262

Xiahou Shichang, *xxxiv*, lxxxi, xcviiin264

Xian, Han Emperor, empress of, xxxii

Xiang, King of Wei, xciiin132

Xianyang, xix, xxi–xxii

Xianyang Palace symposium, liii

Xibo (Prince of the West). *See* Wen, King of Zhou

Xie (Minister of the Masses), 29n37

Xiping Stone Classics, *xxviii*, xxix, xlii, xcvin193, 235; term *qishi*, lxviii

xu (arrangement documents), xxxviii, xlii–xliv, xci–xciin112. See also under *Documents*; *Great Commentary*

Xu Shang, lxxxi–lxxxii

Xu Shen, *Divergent Interpretations of the Five Classics*, lxxiii; *Explaining Graphs and Analyzing Characters*, 257n11

Xuan, Han Emperor, xxxvii, lxvi–lxvii, lxxxixn65

Xuan, King of Qi, 267n18

Xuan, King of Zhou, 203n1

xuanji, interpretation of, lxxv, 15, 15n17

Xuanquanzhi, edict from, 9n12

Xue Jixuan, lxxxviiin33, 33

Yan, campaign against, 197, 197n11, 209, 211, 211n2, 215; character for Yan, 213; use of term "overrun," 197, 211, 211n2

Yan Hui, xliv

Yan Ruoqu, lxx

Yan Shigu, xcivn159

Yan Yanzhao, lxxix

Yang Ci, 245n11

Yang Liang, commentary on *Master Xun*, 197n9

Yang Xiong, *Exemplary Figures* (Fayan), xxxi

Yao: abdication of, 15n15, 49n17; choice of successor, 5, 51n26; as legendary figure, xciiin131; pacification of Jiaozhi, 29n37; reign of, 47n12; rulership of, 5n1, 7, xciiin140; Shun as successor to, 39, 49n17; testing of Shun, 13n11; "Yao Asked," 197n9. *See also* "Canon of Yao"

Yao Dongsheng, lxxx

Yates, Robin, lxiii

Ye Mengde, 141

Yellow Emperor, 261n3

Yi Yin, xxvii, 79, 81n5, 101n2

Yi Zhi, 101n2

Yi Zhoushu, xxxi

Yin sacrifices, 189n2

Ying Shao, lxxxviiin38, 259n1

yingmen (reception gate), 221

Yinxu, 85n1

yinyi (indulgence), 201

"Yong" melody, 49n21

Youdu, 29n37

Yu: advice on government to Shun, 39, 47n16; dynastic transition from Shun, 39, 47n16, 49n22, 51n25; marriage of, 53n28; musical pieces in praise of, 53n27; in "Oath at Gan," 65, 65n1; texts transmitted by, lxxxiv, 131; travels of, 57

Yu and Rui, 109n1, 171n4

Yu Jiaxi, xcviiin250
Yue. *See* "Charge to Yue"
Yuechang, 163n2; offer of pheasant in tribute, lix–lx, 159–61, 163–65
Yueling. *See* monthly ordinances
yuheng (jade transverse), 15nn16–17

zaiwei (participants in the ritual), 45n10
Zengzi, 21n25
zhan (to battle), xlv, 71n5
Zhang, Master, xviii, *xxxiv*, xxxvi, lxxxi
Zhang Anshi, lxvi
Zhang Ba, xxxi, xcn84
Zhang family, xv. *See also* Zhang, Master
Zhang Song, 271–73n31
Zhang Yan, lxxxviin15
Zhangjiashan, lx–lxi; *Zouyanshu*, lxiii
Zhao, Han Emperor, lxv, lxvii
zheng (regulators), lvi–lvii, 69n1, xcivn155
Zheng Xuan: annotations of classics, xv, lxxx, 187n1, 304n44; on authorship of *Great Commentary*, xxxvii, xxxviii; commentary on "Testamentary Charge" and "King Kang's Proclamation," 223n2, 225n8, 225n10 ; commentary on "Tradition of the Great Plan's Five Phases," lxxxiv, 281nn1–3, 283n7, 285n9, 287n10; commentary to *Great Commentary*, xv, xviii, lxxvi, lxxx, 13n10, 19n22, 47n14, 255n9; on complexity of *Great Commentary*, xviii; criticism of, lxxi, lxxiii–lxxv, lxxvi; glosses of, 17n20, 93n1, 121n5, 127n2, 241n3; on Lord of Fu, 235n1; on "Metal Coffer," 149n1; and "Nine Offers," 33n1; on "Principal Teachings," 267n22; on "Proclamation on Luo," 197n9; reading of *lu*, 13n11; *Sanlizhu*, xcvin198; and transmission of *Great Commentary*, lxxiii, lxxvi–lxxvii, lxxviii; on Three Regulators, 65; "Xu" to *Great Commentary*, xxxviii, lxxvi
zhengyue, xcivn155, 69n1
Zhòu (last Shang king), 105n2, 109n4, 127n1, 129n3, 135n2, 157n3
Zhou, Duke of: address to men who served Shang, 201; admonishments to Kangshu, 167; as advisor to King Wu, 123; brothers of, 167, 197n10; in "Catalpa Wood" story of Kangshu and Boqin, 179; and "Charge to Prince Wei," 153; death and burial, 145; in "Do Not Slack," 205; fief at Lu, 151n9, 181n1, 191, 191n4, 197n7; founding of Luo, 167; invasion of Yan, 145, 197n11, 209, 211n1; loyalty to Zhou, 145; in "Metal Coffer," 145; officiated ancestral sacrifice, 189; painting of, lix; and "Praising the Millet," 159, 163n1; in "Proclamation of/to Shao," 185n1; in "Proclamation on Luo," 189, 195nn4–5, 199n14; as regent for King Cheng, 139–41, 147, 189–91, 209, 265n15; relations with King Cheng, 189; reputation for virtue, lix–lx, 151n9, 195n5; sons of, 179, 191; as speaker in "Great Proclamation," 139, 139n1; and Wang Mang, lx, 161. *See also* Boqin
Zhou, King Kang of (Ji Zhao), 219
Zhou dynasty: ancestral sacrifices, 189n2; central domains, 245n8, 165n4; conquest of Shang, 105, 115–17, 123, 129n3, 197n7, 215, 263n9; rebellions against, xliii, xciin118, 145, 149n2, 149n5, 153, 167, 197n10, 229. *See also* Cheng, King; Chengzhou; Kang, King of Zhou; Mu,

GENERAL INDEX 367

Zhou dynasty (*continued*)
    King of Zhou; Wen, King of
    Zhou; Wu, King of Zhou
Zhuang Cunyu, xcvin204
Zhuangzi, 65n1; "Rifling Trunks"
    (Quqie) chapter, 261n4
Zhuanxu, 307n6
Zhurong, 293n11
Zichun, 267n18

Zilongzi, 239n1
Zixia, xliv, lxxxviin18
Zizhang, xxxix–xl, 89, 93n2
Zongzhou, 215
Zu Ji, 89n2, 97, 97n1
Zu Yi, 105
Zuo Tradition (Zuozhuan), xcn84, xcin107, xcviin215; Kong Yingda's commentary, 261n4